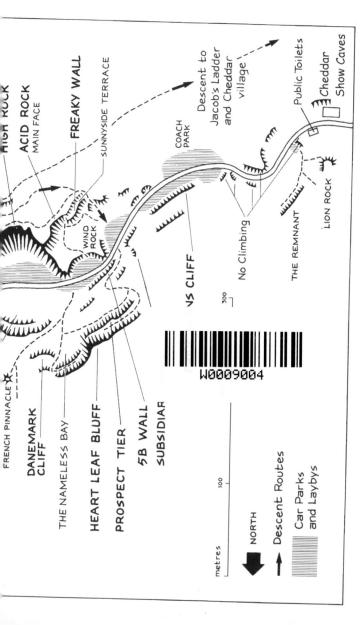

Climbers' Club Guides
Edited by Nigel Coe

Avon and Cheddar

by

Martin Crocker

Fairy Cave Quarry by **Mike Raine**
The Holcombe Quarries by **Gordon Jenkin**

Artwork
by
Don Sargeant

Volume 2: Cheddar

 Published by The Climbers' Club

Full bibliographical information will be found in Volume 1.

© The Climbers' Club 2004

Crocker, Martin   Avon and Cheddar
(Climbers' Club Guides)

British Library Cataloguing in Publication Data

A catalogue record for this book is available from the British Library

796.552

ISBN 0-901601-76-5

Volume 1 also contains:

Climbers' Club information

Author's Acknowledgements

A General Introduction, including access information, conservation and geology notes, and details of the area's drilled gear policy.

A complete Historical

Typeset and prepared for printing by John Willson
Slide scanning by Redheads Digital, Sheffield
Printed through Colorcraft Ltd, HK
Produced by The Ernest Press, Glasgow G46 6AQ
Distributed by Cordee, 3a de Montfort Street, Leicester LE1 7HD

Contents

Maps and Diagrams

6 Contents

Photos: [1]Carl Ryan, [2]Don Sargeant,
[3]Nigel Coe, [5]Dick Broomhead

All maps and diagrams by Don Sargeant
([6]from originals by Martin Crocker; [7]from original by Dick Broomhead)

Guidebook Disclaimer

This guide attempts to provide a definitive record of all existing climbs and is compiled from information from a variety of sources. The inclusion of any route does not imply that it remains in the condition described. Climbs can change unpredictably: rock can deteriorate and the existence and condition of *in-situ* protection can alter. All climbers must rely on their own ability and experience to gauge the difficulty and seriousness of any climb. Climbing is an inherently dangerous activity.

Neither The Climbers' Club nor the authors and editor of this guidebook accept any liability whatsoever for any injury or damage caused to climbers, third parties, or property arising from the use of it. Whilst the content of the guide is believed to be accurate, no responsibility is accepted for any error, omission, or mis-statement. Users must rely on their own judgement and are recommended to insure against injury to person and property and third party risks.

The inclusion in this guidebook of a crag or routes upon it does not mean that any member of the public has a right of access to the crag or the right to climb upon it. Before climbing on any crag in this guidebook, please read the access and conservation notes in the General Introduction (from page 14 in Volume 1).

Cheddar Gorge Restrictions

Most of the climbs in Cheddar Gorge are subject to one seasonal restriction or another. The restrictions have been imposed for a variety of ecological and public-safety reasons: they *must* be adhered to. A single breach could result in the total and permanent closure of the whole Gorge to climbing. The restrictions have been agreed by the BMC.

Since most climbs are affected, the customary [R] has **not** been printed by each climb in the Cheddar Gorge route descriptions. The small number of climbs that are subject to a permanent, all-year-round restriction are marked by [PR]. It should be noted that climbing is disallowed throughout most of the Gorge *except* during the winter months. Further advice and warnings will be found in the various crag introductions.

Stars

Because of the rapid changes that can occur to routes due to revegetation or, conversely, loose rock and ivy clearance, and because of the relatively low traffic on the climbs, stars have not been used for Cheddar Gorge.

Cheddar Gorge

Vegetation is abundant, but far from detracting, it rather enhances the natural beauty of the gorge and of individual climbs.
(W K Marples & R Bates, 1931)

Cheddar is an equal force to any limestone crag in England…
(Ed Hart & Mick Haffner, 1973)

The biggest, the shortest; the loosest, the soundest; the grimmest, the brightest. You name it, and Cheddar's probably got it.
(Arnis Strapcans, 1976)

If you're lucky like we were earlier this year, you can find yourself climbing in shorts in spring, but remember I said only if you're lucky!
(Gareth Parry, 1997)

Introduction

Cheddar Gorge is perhaps the most breathtaking natural feature in the south of Britain. This 150-metre deep canyon, with its massive and sheer limestone walls and its show caves, not only attracts thousands of tourists during the summertime but also offers a unique opportunity for competent climbers to experience some of the best and most atmospheric outcrop climbs in the country.

Against a background of both increasing environmentalism and concern for the local economy, the pressures on the Gorge have heightened enormously in recent years. Strong, often competing, land-use interests have rendered climbing environmentally sensitive and legally onerous in terms of public safety. Consequently, a policy of seasonal and crag-specific restrictions operates, which has been agreed between Cheddar Caves, which owns the south side, the National Trust, which owns the north side, and the British Mountaineering Council. Following major cliff-restoration and safeguarding work during the 90s, there is now a great opportunity for new arrangements to be agreed that will help reinstate the true potential for sustainable climbing in the Gorge, without unduly compromising other interests. It is the responsibility of climbers to avail themselves of the details of any new or revised agreement by seeking advice from the BMC and its publications – and to comply with them.

The village of Cheddar is situated 25 kilometres south-west of Bristol and is easily accessible and well signposted from the A38 or from the M5, junctions 21 or 22. From the village, the B3135 runs north-eastwards through the

Gorge, enabling cars to be driven up almost to belaying distance of some of the crags. During the climbing season there is ample parking space in the car-parks provided. Only the car-parks nearest the village are pay and display. A word of caution: don't leave anything of any value on display in your car; break-ins are not uncommon.

Cheddar can cater for all the usual culinary needs. More to the point, the Cheddar Caves' vicinity provides sufficient distractions to justify not going climbing at all: tearooms, cafés, clothing and craft shops, pubs, takeaways, and (if any excuse is needed) plenty of opportunity for a right old legbending on the local scrumpy! There are telephones and toilets next to Gough's Cave, and, of course, it would be remiss not to make a 'good public relations' trip into the landowner's delightful show caves and 'Cheddar Man and the Cannibals' museum, or to go 'adventure caving' (see www.cheddarcaves.co.uk for details). Support the local economy and it will value you.

If not day-tripping, accommodation for short breaks and weekends is in good supply: local pubs, the Cox's Mill in the Gorge, self-catering cottages, plenty of bed and breakfast establishments, a youth hostel, and camping and caravan sites (summer). Contact www.cheddarcaves.co.uk for details.

Access

South Slope: (right-hand side looking up the Gorge). The access position is currently being renegotiated with the landowner. The existing arrangements derive from previous consents, which are as follows.

The owner of the South Slope of the Gorge, Longleat Enterprises Ltd, had been asked to agree to permit climbing on his land during the periods shown below, subject to the following conditions:
1. Climbing must not commence in any part where vehicles are parked beneath the cliff face.
2. Every care must be taken to ensure the safety of other visitors and to cause no nuisance of any nature.
3. Every care must be taken to protect the vegetation in the Gorge, which is an SSSI, since its rare plant species are of great national importance.
4. The foot of the climbing site should be left clean and tidy on completion of the climb.
5. The owner of the land disclaims any liability for injury or damage caused through the granting of this consent.
6. This consent applies only to climbers who are properly insured to cover third party risk.

The above applies to individual cliffs as follows.

Top End Quarries, Top End Cliffs, The Reservoir Walls, Shoot Gully Walls: Climbing is allowed throughout the year except from 15 July until 31 August inclusive and on Easter and the two May bank holiday weekends.

Pinnacle Bay: Climbing is allowed from 1 October until 15 March inclusive.

Castle Rocks: Climbing is allowed from 1 October until 15 March inclusive. However, the routes *It Must be the Russians* and *Doomwatch* (first two pitches only), together with all routes on Madrugada Wall from *Madrugada* to *Palo Alto* (Sunset Buttress) inclusive, remain banned. This is because there is no rock-catch fence beneath them, and rocks could fall directly into the road.

Horseshoe Bend Buttress, Sunset Buttress, The Zawn, Great Rock, Priest Rock, The Amphitheatre, High Rock, Wind Rock, Acid Rock: Climbing is allowed from 1 October until 15 March inclusive.

North Slope: (left-hand side looking up the Gorge). The owner of the North Slope, The National Trust, had been asked to agree that small numbers of climbers will be permitted to climb on its land during the periods shown below, subject to the following conditions:
1. Compliance with the conditions appertaining to the South Slope.
2. No further new routes or gardening without authority from the Warden or the National Trust Regional Headquarters.
3. Descent to be made from climbs as specified in the text.
4. Access to and from cliffs to be made as specified.

The above applies to the individual cliffs as follows.

Lion Rock: Climbing is banned.

The Remnant, Pride Evans Cliff, Subsidiary Walls, The Tiers, Nameless Bay, French Pinnacle: Climbing is allowed from 1 October until 15 March inclusive.

The Quarry: Climbing is permitted here throughout the year except from 1 July until 31 August inclusive, and on Easter and the two May bank holiday weekends.

Hounds Bluff: Climbing is allowed from 1 October until 15 March inclusive.

Arch Rock, Stepped Wall, Overshoot Wall: Climbing is allowed all year round.

Blackrock Quarry: Group use is not permitted but use by individual climbers is not restricted.

Why the restrictions? First and foremost, there is loose rock in the Gorge, some of which may still remain on climbs in spite of cleaning, and this can constitute a risk to the safety of pedestrians and motorists. **The extreme caution with which loose or suspect rock should be treated and the importance of minimizing the risk of stonefall into the road or other public areas cannot be over emphasized.**

Secondly, the Gorge has been designated a Site of Special Scientific Interest and it is desired to minimize the number of persons (not only climbers!)

having access to those parts where extremely rare plants, including the famous Cheddar Pink, grow, or where protected species of bird such as the Raven may nest. It is a criminal offence to interfere with certain protected species of plant or animal.

Climbing in Cheddar Gorge: What to Expect!

'I've given up on-sighting at Cheddar due to loose rock, vegetation, and missing gear.'

(A local climber, 1999)

Few of us, even seasoned traditionalists, who climb in Cheddar have an easy time in the prevailing conditions. Modern tastes can't hack it, full stop. Most tolerable winter weekends these days witness a climber-free Gorge, save perhaps the few that drive up to take a look and then drive away again. Cheddar Gorge is still out of fashion. But does it matter? To climb at Cheddar has always required a belief in the maxim that 'the more effort you make, the more you get out '. And if you cruise a clean classic on a crisp winter's day; well, that's a bonus. The previous guidebook posed the question: 'Is it all numb fingers, ivy, and loose rock?' The informed answer is: 'yes, of course it is'. But it doesn't have to be – if climbers choose to participate. Strategically, there has never been more to play for than there is now, with vast potential to open up, re-clean, and re-equip major cliffs for sustainable use all-year round, bar the peak holiday periods. The landowners are sympathetic and now understand the status of the unique climbs in the Gorge, some of which are 'world class'. In the meantime, climbers make their own choice in the knowledge that their actions will determine our say in a vision for the Gorge. For those who choose to climb here, read on.

The Battle with Vegetation and Loose Rock: The Landowners Act

'We are taking advantage of having climbers in close contact with the rock faces and bringing down, under controlled conditions, any loose or potentially dangerous rock they find.'

(National Trust Warden, 1988/89)

Climbers have been fighting a losing battle with ivy growth and vegetation for decades. It is almost inconceivable that, in 1931, Marples and Bates had no such problems when pioneering *Knight's Climb* in a cleaner and tranquil Cheddar Gorge. In those days, the Gorge was less vegetated, as evidenced by early photographs. With time, however, an invasive strain of ivy took root and by the late 60s had spread remorselessly across the Gorge's pristine white sheets of limestone, fracturing the rock's surface, levering away previously stable formations, and precluding the growth of rare wild flowers and other more valuable plants. Then along came the climber. Systematically the ivy frontier was pushed back to reveal magnificent new lines of great acclaim. But with fears for public safety, climbing was soon outlawed – and the ivy came back. Despite flushes of climbing activity during the 70s and 80s the cycle of revegetation was at best a tentative equilibrium; one bad winter, or one piece of bad press that turned climbers away, could make all the difference. Great sheets of ivy that had been cleared would often rematerialize two or three years later covering up climbs as if they had never existed.

At long last during the late 80s, prompted by public and employer liability concerns because of the risk of loose rock falling into the road or car parks, the landowners, Cheddar Caves and The National Trust, embarked on a massive and costly loose rock, scrub, and ivy clearance programme that was to last right across the 90s. It is still continuing. At the turn of the Millennium we have a completely different-looking Gorge. Last of all the Pinnacle Bay has been cleaned and its fantastic serrated arc is now unmasked of foliage. Throughout, most large loose blocks and unstable rock formations have been jettisoned to the base of the Gorge and carted away, and there are unobtrusive runs of rock-catch fences below many cliffs. Behind the fences and roaming the most inaccessible parts of the Gorge is the landowner's secret weapon: the Soay sheep. Tactically introduced as the key to the conservation masterplan (but with added value to the tourism plan), these goat-like beasts spend their days not only posing for photographs but munching religiously away at ivy and scrub that otherwise infects the Gorge's splendid calcareous upland botany.

The Effects of Loose Rock and Scrub Clearance upon Climbing

The crags have not been cleaned with climbers in mind. While large-scale material that threatened public safety will have been taken off, it must not be assumed that all loose rock has been removed from climbs. Inherently, the very hard limestone here is prone in places to looseness because of friability and weathering of joint systems. Not all cliffs in the Gorge have been cleared: the largest uncleared stretch comprises Sunset Buttress and Great Rock (left half), i.e. from *Irradiation* to *The Prow* inclusive. Some climbs have been substantially altered by rock removal; where this appears significant the double dagger †† is allocated. This does not mean that the route is unclimbable; it means that caution, at least, be exercised. Elsewhere, expect many routes to have lost (or gained) holds.

Cleaning operations have necessarily required the dislodging of enormous quantities of debris: rock, foliage, and earth. Hundreds of climbs have been detrimentally affected. In particular, mud has rained down onto the less steep climbs causing cracks to clog up, holds to be covered, and nut placements to be obscured. In turn these pockets of earth have been exploited by an infestation of grass and tenacious plant life, especially Pellitory of the Wall, a nettle-relation which looks nothing like a nettle but which can be recognised by its red-coloured stems, and red Valerian, an alien invader which has got completely out of control. These have replaced ivy as climbers' No. 1 enemy: they are extremely widespread, quick-growing, and incredibly hard to remove on-sight on a steep climb. Where a climb appears from below to be materially vegetated, a ❀ symbol is allocated. Most of these (but not all) will require safety-conscious and eco-friendly re-cleaning prior to an ascent. The judgement is yours to make on site.

Treat fixed gear, particularly abseil stations, on crags that have been cleared with special care. Assume fixtures will have been hit by dislodged rock, and pre-check and/or back up all fixed gear as a matter of course. It's your life.

Many trees on cleared crags have been felled. Some climbs relied on trees for belays and, to a lesser extent, protection. The guidebook has attempted to identify those climbing-significant trees still in place. Otherwise, tree stumps have been left; but it is wise to assume that these have rotted and are not reliable: find alternatives.

The removal of foliage and the banking-up of debris and rocks on terraces and in gullies has compromised some access routes; especially in the Pinnacle Bay area. Check the text for any changes. Great care will be needed not to dislodge any loose material when moving around.

One major, yet incidental, benefit to climbers (and to their peace of mind in an already high-stress climbing environment) is the erection of extensive rock-catch fences underneath many cliffs. Their purpose is to minimize the risk of rocks falling into the road or the car-parks. They are not an excuse for recklessness, however. Some popular cliffs like The Tiers on the north slope are not protected by rock-catch fences, and the usual strong warning regarding the ever-present risk of dislodging rocks into the road or car-parks applies.

Remember to treat the fences with respect; all can be passed or bypassed without damage to them.

Protection

Essentially, Cheddar Gorge is a traditional climbing environment. Most routes are protectable by leader-placed protection. Away from the larger crack-lines, the rock typically lends itself to small-wire protection; three, or even four, sets may be required on some of the longer, hard pitches. The leader should carry a nut-tool to clean nut slots that may have clogged – or cobwebbed – up. Fixed gear, including pegs, *in-situ* threads, and the odd bolt will be encountered; the usual warning about its use applies.

The Gorge also has a quota of (what can be loosely described as) sport routes. They range from those derived from the free-climbing of (part-bolted) aid routes of the 60s to customized 90s stainless-steel-bolted routes. The guidebook describes on a route-by-route basis the bolt system deployed (although this will generally be evident before climbers commit themselves).

Some routes are furnished with 'abseil stations'. Most will have been fixed for the purposes of the first ascent and so may not be as trustworthy now as required. Some were fixed in the late 80s as a temporary measure to ameliorate access concerns (possible disturbance of loose rock and Cheddar Pink at the cliff-edge). Many awaited renewal under agreed sponsorship which was withdrawn before the work could start. There should be no climbs where a climber will have no other option but to use the abseil station; topping-out is nearly always a possibility (and probably occurred on the first ascents), or – if the worst comes to the worst – back-up gear can always be left permanently or recovered after the descent. Do not trust fixed gear that could be unreliable. Some abseil stations, mainly on the more recent sport climbs, are of a modern specification and, with correct use, should not be unsatisfactory.

Loose Rock

Despite cleaning operations, climbers will still regularly encounter loose rock on climbs (and disturbable rocks and other objects on some approaches). **Climbers must exercise extreme caution** in dealing with loose or suspect rock and must behave in a manner at all times that minimizes the risk of rock or other objects (e.g. dropped gear) from landing in the road, car-parks, or any other area where **people or property could be at risk**. It is the enhanced risk to public safety that is the foundation of the restricted-access agreement.

Climatic Conditions: Cold Is Best

'Mild, windy, and wet' just about sums up the average southern winter. But if you have chosen to climb in the Gorge then you will already have decided to grit your teeth and make the best of it, or have the ability to respond quickly when the weather conditions are favourable. It is rare to find a day when you can't climb anything. The Gorge has a vast variety of differently orientated and angled crags that can be matched to prevailing weather conditions. Check out the introductions to the crags for help, check the weather forecast the night before, and bear in mind the following:

Conditions Conducive to Climbing:
• 'cold highs' (anticyclones with north or north-westerly airstreams)
• brisk and bright south-west to northerly airstreams
• cooler (and drier) airstreams generally, especially after a cold front has passed over – which can convert a soaking wet Gorge to a fairly dry one in a few hours
• sub-zero easterlies that freeze up any seepage… perfect!!

Conditions Not Conducive to Climbing:
Warm *and* moist airstreams behind warm fronts and associated with 'warm highs' (anticyclones with mild southerly or south-easterly airstreams). Mild and humid conditions simply do not agree with Cheddar Gorge, and when introduced by a warm front can lead in a matter of minutes to 100% of the rock surface literally running with condensation. This can prove a fairly traumatic experience if caught out! Generally the crags higher up the Gorge and greater in altitude are slowest to clear themselves of condensation.

Some crags are affected by seepage after prolonged rain; but, perversely, they all start and stop dripping at different intervals and according to wind speed and relative humidity. Best just to see what the deal is on site, and be prepared for a wet hold here or there.

Operating across the winter months with limited daylight can add an extra edge to local outcrop climbing. On the longer climbs, leisurely climbing parties take on the very real risk of benightment. A head torch is a must on late-start multi-pitch routes (and it reassures the rescue team to know where you are when you get stuck 100 metres up a cliff with no chance of escape).

If winter climbing doesn't appeal, remember that a reasonable selection of crags is open all or most of the year: make use of them!

Ethics

If you've read this far, you know you are going to be up against it; some concessions in style and ethics are going to have to be made. Some routes will require public-safety-conscious re-cleaning, some routes will need their gear pre-checking, and many routes are downright bold and will merit prior top-rope practice at the best of times. It's cold, it's damp, you can't warm up; be realistic: E5 is going to feel like E7, pre-practised or not. Award yourselves bonus E-points just for trying!

On-Site Judgement

'…people shouldn't do the routes if they are not up to them, and if they try them, it's totally their responsibility.'
            (Extract from petition of ten young Bristol signatories, 7.11.88)

In the domain of climbing, where individuals decide to entertain risks to their own lives, there can be no substitute for a climber's own judgement. This Guidebook can only offer a broad guide as to what to expect. Conditions of climbs in Cheddar Gorge have a notorious habit of changing like the wind and rain. Given the constraints, no climbs have been specifically re-climbed for the purpose of this guidebook. The most reliable way to assess what a climber is likely to encounter on the day is by a careful study of the intended climb there and then. A short walk up the hillside opposite can be very helpful, and binoculars will give you a more informed view. Given the inherent quality of some of the climbs, making the effort to re-clean the route in an eco-friendly fashion would be a more philanthropic and satisfying alternative to whingeing. Routes re-cleaned and re-opened should be reported to the author or to The Climbers' Club co-ordinator for new-route information so that others can benefit from your work. Don't be reluctant to do your bit for safe and sustainable climbing in Cheddar Gorge.

Approach and Descent Routes

South Slope

For high-level crags whose climbs are reached from the cliff-top, the most direct means of approach is Shoot Gully. For The Amphitheatre it is marginally quicker (but a lot more complicated on first acquaintance) to use The Descent Couloir right of Acid Rock. There are two usual means of descent when the top of the South Slope is reached during normal daylight hours: Shoot Gully and The Descent Couloir. The only safe descent after dark is Jacob's Ladder. Consult the maps and diagrams on pages 19, 46, and 99.

1 Shoot Gully For climbs completed on Pinnacle Bay, Castle Rocks, and Sunset Buttress, the quickest means of descent is by Shoot Gully. This is the deepest gully on the South Slope, situated towards the top (east) of the Gorge and immediately on the Cheddar (west) side of the covered reservoir area. Sections of the gully involve very steep and muddy scrambles and require special care in wet or icy conditions. The upper third can be bypassed by a path on the left (east), the top of which is located in a grassy gully 60 metres beyond Shoot Gully.

2 The Descent Couloir For climbs completed on High Rock and Acid Rock, locate a faint track that starts within a small wood above the top of High Rock. This track (as does a similar one running along the cliff edge at a lower level) leads rightwards, facing in, through scrub, initially in the direction of Cheddar, to a couloir with a thin scree-strip that runs straight down the slope. The couloir is steep initially and leads with two steep scrambles on sloping holds to a short chimney. The rock-catch fence across the gully (that runs east underneath Sunnyside Terrace) soon follows, and below it an easy scramble left (facing out) of a short chimney finally leads to the car-park immediately west of Wind Rock. The section between the top of the couloir and the top of the upper chimney can be avoided by sliding less steeply under yew trees 40 metres to the west.

3 Jacob's Ladder A preferred descent, and the only safe descent after dark, is to follow the well-worn path that runs and descends westwards along the cliff-top to a look-out tower next to the path. The tower marks the top of Jacob's Ladder, a long series of steps leading down to the road. A fee may be levied but not outside normal working hours, when the gate is left open to enable stragglers to exit.

North Slope.

Descent from routes on the north slope is by reversing the approaches; consult the text and diagrams. Care needs to be taken since it is all too easy to dislodge rocks and scree and start them rolling in the direction of traffic, or people walking up the hillside.

Top End Quarries

These two small quarries are situated next to each other, a little above the road, near the northern end of the Gorge, and about a kilometre upstream of the covered reservoir. There is an unsurfaced car-park just to the left of the quarries, on the east side of the road. The climbs here have generally only been soloed, and the grades reflect solo style. Although the rock is solid, the exits are high and steep, and some will merit a quick peek on an abseil rope.

Access: Climbing is allowed throughout the year except from 15 July until 31 August inclusive and on Easter and the two May bank holiday weekends.

The Left-Hand Wall

Bombay Duck   8 metres   Very Severe 4b   (14.4.88)
Towards the left end of the wall, climb a slabby face above a hawthorn tree.

Crashed Matt   8 metres   Very Severe 5b †   (24.5.99)
Make a hard move into a groove and move left to exit.

Terminate a Tourist Today   9 metres   E1 5a   (14.4.88)
A very nice pitch. Climb intricately up the slabby face to the left of a wide chockstone-filled crack.

Will It? Won't It?   8 metres   Hard Very Severe 4c †   (24.5.99)
Thug up the crack, wondering how hard to pull on the chockstones.

Mattus Mattus   8 metres   E5 5c †   (24.5.99)
Starting immediately left of a ledge, climb straight up the wall to a pocketed crack. Make a long move around the left end of the roof, and exit on good holds through a notch. The crux is at 7 metres, but protection looks reasonable for a lead (probably E3 5c).

Magnus Pyke   8 metres   E3 5b   (14.4.88)
From the left end of a ledge, climb slightly rightwards and up to the right end of the roof. Stretch round for a good hold and exit with a mantel. Protectable if led (E1/2).

Think (Cheddar) Pink   8 metres   E1 5a   (14.4.88)
Follow the steep water-worn crack rightwards to a trying finish. HVS if led.

The Right-Hand Wall

At the left end of the wall is a cave at ground level, normally replete with empty lager cans, and maybe one or two wild-camping revellers sleeping it off.

Lager-spiker   7 metres   E2 6a/b †   (12.5.99)
Pull over the cave roof and extend for a two-finger-pocket below a tiny roof at 5 metres. Finish up the arête, taking full account of the ferocious hawthorn below your backside.

Larger-biker   7 metres   E4 6a †   (12.5.99)
A high crux. From jugs to the right of the cave, climb the leaning wall, with
a very hard move to a difficult-to-use finger-slot. Haul over using the tree.

Rough Roader   7 metres   E1 5a †   (12.5.99)
Take the rightward-rising flake to a steep finish.

Rough Sleeper   7 metres   E1 5b †   (12.5.99)
A metre left of *Camp Fire's Burning*, climb direct up the steep wall on
improving holds.

Camp Fire's Burning   8 metres   Very Difficult
The obvious corner 8 metres right of the cave.

Phantom Bolts   7 metres   E2 6b   (?/12.5.99)
Start below a short impending face near the right end of the wall. Make
dynamic moves direct past the ghost of a bolt to good holds above a
bulge. Finish more easily. A mystery bolt is in place on the easy ground
above the crux. The landing is fairly comfortable.

Top End Cliffs

One kilometre up the Gorge from the Cheddar Showcaves complex, on the
right, is a stone-walled enclosure delimiting a covered reservoir. Beyond the
reservoir the road curves around a rocky shoulder; the buttresses that become
visible on the right mark the right-hand extremity of the Top End Cliffs, which
extend up-road as a series of isolated crags for half a kilometre. The Far Bay is
the most remote and easterly of the developed cliffs, and is identified by a
25-metre slabby wall at its back. The Swine Cliff, which commences about
300 metres beyond the covered reservoir, is the series of roadside walls
undercut left of centre by a large cave, the Pigs' Hole. Between Swine Cliff and
the Reservoir Walls is the Near Bay. Here, two prominent buttresses project
from 30 metres up the hillside, the right-hand of which, Pepys Rock, extends
westwards in the form of a high, slabby wall: Quaking Wall.

Access: These cliffs, whilst lacking the grandeur of other areas in the Gorge,
have yielded an interesting selection of mainly single-pitch climbs that are
unfettered by the usual restrictions. Climbing is permitted here throughout
the year, except from 15 July to 31 August inclusive and on Easter and the
two May bank holiday weekends. **Great care** should, of course, be
exercised at all times when climbing on crags that rise directly from the road.

The character of the rock and style of climbing here is quite distinctive.
Slabby walls are commonplace and, though these tend to remain dank and
lichenous in mild and humid conditions, the climbing is rather better than
appearances suggest, and always technical. Outside winter, vegetation can
get the upper hand, but some of the best routes stay clean.

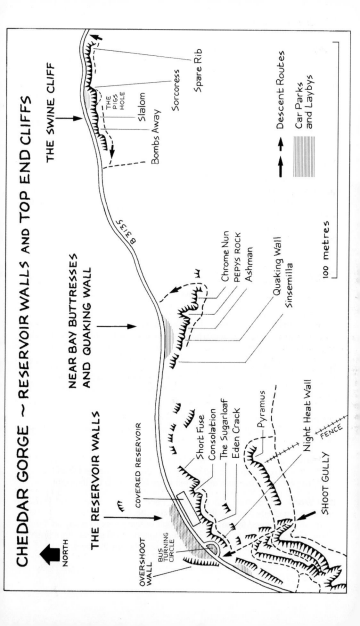

The Far Bay
In the back of the bay is a slabby, grey wall giving three worthwhile pitches.

All the Juicy Bits   15 metres   E3 5c   (18.9.88)
The thin crack in the left-hand side of the wall is climbed past a peg to an abseil retreat from the tree-stump above.

Vanity   15 metres   E1 5a   (18.9.88)
The central, stepped groove, starting from a tree stump. Follow the groove without an abundance of protection. Abseil from a small tree.

Eaten Alive   25 metres   E2 5b/c   (18.9.88)
The continuous seam in the right-hand side of the wall. Start 2 metres before the right arête.
Climb up past a ledge (peg) to a small pod just left of the arête. Swing left and follow the wider crackline to a rightward exit. Abseil from trees.

Swine Cliff
At the left-hand end of the cliff is a broad wooded gully (which provides a way down).

Spare Rib   18 metres   Very Severe 4b   (15.4.80)
The slabby left-facing corner that overlooks the wooded gully; a good-looking and clean line. Exit left around the small roof at the top.

Porker's Pride   20 metres   Very Severe 4b † ❀   (16.4.80)
50% overgrown. Right of *Spare Rib* is a narrow corner. This route takes the wall to the right again.

Trotter   24 metres   Severe 4a ❀   (15.4.80)
75% overgrown. The short right-facing corner below two prominent square-cut roofs in the centre of the buttress. Continue up the flake crack and slab above, and a short final corner.

The next four routes start in an overhung niche 10 metres left of the cave. Ivy growth at the foot of the climbs is normally easily stripped, but a bigger cleaning effort is required for *The Sow*.

The Sow   25 metres   Hard Very Severe ❀   (15.4.80)
100% overgrown. A line based on the tall corner 12 metres left of the cave, but with an excursion up the left edge of the slab on the right.

Bolt Wars   10 metres   E5 6b F7b   (1.7.94)
Forces a direct line through the overhung niche.
From an ivy-covered ledge, climb through bulging rock to a jug on the lip. Climb the face above to a stainless-steel-bolted abseil station (that hasn't been put in yet!). Two stainless-steel bolts protect (which have).

Progressive Rock   25 metres   E4 6b   (25.5.80)
Climb strenuously rightwards along the obvious crack, head-banging under the roofs (peg), to gain welcome jugs on vertical ground. Climb the crack above and finish via a short groove.

Pump Up the Volume   25 metres   E4 6b/c F7b   (30.3.95)
Step right from the ivy-covered ledge and climb up to a finger-rail beneath the roofs (good wires). Climb up through the roof stack with great difficulty (8mm bolt). Join and finish up *Progressive Rock*.

Cream Tease   25 metres   E5 6b   (9.6.87)
A fine and really pumpy pitch, but currently spoiled by the prospect of big falls on a manky old bolt. Start below the undercut arête 8 metres left of the cave.
Climb steeply to the roofs (peg). Power straight through (8mm bolt) to gain a good hold in a tiny niche (poor peg). Move up onto the easier arête and the top.

Newton's Wal...!   25 metres   E2 5b   (9.4.81)
Good when clean. Start 6 metres left of the cave.
Climb leftwards up to and over small block roofs to gain cracks in the steep wall right of the arête. Follow the cracks to a groove and the exit of *Cream Tease* on the left.

Chic   25 metres   Hard Very Severe 5a ✿   (28.4.75)
An ironic name for a route that has been overgrown for virtually all of its life. The corner 6 metres left of the cave, with an exit left around the roof near the top.

Sorceress   25 metres   E6 6b   (26.6.85)
A regional psych-piece that sees regular successes. Above the left-hand side of the cave is a slim, open groove in a compact wall. This provides a stylish route of protracted technicality and great boldness. Start just outside the cave entrance, by two slopers.
Climb slightly leftwards via the slopers to the roof (peg). Move left to a resting-place at the base of the groove (small cam). Bridge thinly up the groove, and bear rightwards (crucial small wire in an invisible pocket) to good holds above a small roof. Step left and continue direct to the upper groove, which is followed, barely easing, past a lousy peg to the capping roof. Step left to an easy exit.

Follow the Slick Red Road   25 metres   E6 6b   (14.8.87)
A great pitch, often chalked-up, that battles along the clearly geared-up line through the roofs left of the cave. Hard F7b+ for the redpoint. Start as for *Sorceress*.
Move up onto the slopers but pull fiercely rightwards to the first roof (peg and *in-situ* thread). Now climb straight through the roofs with powerful undercut moves (two *in-situ* threads) until the holds run out. Hard moves lead over the lip (peg) and rightwards to the foot of a shallow groove. Climb the groove (peg) to a sapling on the right and good tree above.

Variation
Gdansk   E6 6b   (12.5.88)
From the foot of the shallow groove, swing left and climb a thin crack past a featherweight projecting hold to an old abseil station just below the top.

Jazz Defector   12 metres   E6 6c   (4.8.87)
An off-beat roof problem that improvises a subtle line over the roof of the Pigs' Hole. A long reach is an asset. Start just inside the cave entrance. Boulder diagonally leftwards up a short rib to a good hold under the roof. Move left (peg on ...*Slick Red Road*) and make a horrendous stretch for a poor jam in a slot above the roof (*Eco-bolt*). Traverse wildly right along the lip to gain a bottomless groove and better holds. *Eco-bolt* and *in-situ* thread belay.
Variation
Licking Tarmac   15 metres   E7 6c F8a+ †   (4.02)
Follow *Jazz Defector* to the jam in the slot over the roof. From here, take the desperate eco-bolted line to an abseil station. Three bolts.

The next set of climbs is situated on the grey, slabby wall right of the cave. A prominent feature is a roof in the centre of the wall that forms an overhanging shield.

Sidewinder   20 metres   E2 6a   (28.6.94)
This wends through the strip roofs immediately right of the cave.
Make a strenuous pull over the first roof (10mm bolt and sling), and trend diagonally rightwards onto the wall above. Climb the wall on good holds (two pegs) to a roof. Surmount the roof to reach another roof (peg and *in-situ* thread) and finish up the groove on the right.

Another Winner   20 metres   E2 5b   (5.6.80/18.7.85)
A fairly direct line up the left-hand side of the wall. Start beneath the overhanging shield.
Climb a mossy groove to a ledge at 3 metres. Hard climbing leads to the roof forming the shield, which is taken on undercuts. Step left above the roof to a short corner and then move up and leftwards again to a small, strip roof (peg). Traverse right below the roof and finish up the obvious groove.

Loser's Choice   20 metres   E2 5c †   (18.3.95)
Start at a tree stump, 2 metres right of *Another Winner*.
Step up and bear left to get established on a small projecting foothold on a rib: bold. Climb to undercuts in the roofs, and overcome them at their widest point. Now take a direct line (peg), and exit via a groove on the left as for *Another Winner*.

Slalom   20 metres   E5 6a   (18.1.87)
Hard and fairly serious. Start as for *Loser's Choice*.
Climb incipient cracks to the small roof at 8 metres. Make a very tricky sequence of moves through the bulge (poor peg) and then move up and leftwards to good footholds in the centre of the wall. Climb up slightly rightwards to undercuts in a small roof and proceed boldly over the bulge above. A short groove leads through the final roof to the top.

Trail of the Snail   25 metres   E2 5c   (29.7.87)

An unusual pitch that deposits a natural right-to-left line across the wall.
Start below the right end of the roof forming the shield.
Climb easily to bulges. Make steep moves over the bulges (peg) to a
leftward-slanting groove (*in-situ* thread). Follow the groove (peg on *Slalom*)
to good holds in the centre of the wall. Now move diagonally leftwards to
the undercut block of *Another Winner* (peg), and finish as for that route.

Grand National   25 metres   E1 5b ❀   (4.4.81)

A dynamic little climb, worth a quick abseil to reclean.
Follow *Trail of the Snail* and reach a diagonal undercut slot on the right.
Climb up past the slot and continue directly up the wall above with
difficulty to good holds and an easier finishing groove.

One for the Road   25 metres   Very Severe 4c ❀   (4.4.81)

A very vegetated line of weakness left of the orange-coloured buttress.

An orange-coloured buttress now dominates the scene; at its base is a
rectangular roadside recess, the starting place for the following four routes.

Mental Revenge   25 metres   E3 5b/c †   (24.7.85)

From the left end of the recess, climb steeply past loose blocks to an
overhang at 7 metres. Pull over into a small groove and step right. Climb
directly up the wall at first, but then trend slightly rightwards to a sapling
and an easy finish.

Heartbleed   25 metres   E4 6b   (4.10.86)

A good pitch; dynamic and then delicate. Start in the centre of the recess.
Climb through the bulges (peg, *in-situ* thread, and 8mm bolts) to a larger
roof at 7 metres. Undercut over the roof to get established on the headwall
(peg). Climb the wall very slightly leftwards (to join *Mental Revenge*), and
trend back slightly rightwards to a sapling and the top.

Bombs Away   25 metres   E5 6a   (4.10.86)

A varied route of character that climbs the groove, orange wall, and roof
in the centre of the buttress. Start in the right-hand side of the recess.
Climb a shallow groove with long, hard reaches between jugs to the
break. Move up into the obvious V-groove – resident weed permitting –
and step right onto a rib below the smooth orange wall. Balance boldly up
the wall (*in-situ* micro-thread) to the roof. Pull around to superb holds (peg)
and climb straight to the top.

Towser   25 metres   E5 6a/b   (5.9.93)

Climb an easy rib right of the recess to a large ledge. Step left and ascend
a steep slab diagonally rightwards to crozzly holds below the roof. Reach
over to good underclings (*Friend* 1½ and peg); then make some hard
moves leftwards along the lip of a small roof (poor peg). Climb the
obvious crack to finish. Heart-racing stuff.

Another Roadside Attraction   25 metres   E5 6a   (7.6.94)
Takes the slab and exciting bulging rib left of the right arête of the buttress.
Climb easily to the base of the slab. Follow a prominent, thin crack in the
slab to good holds below the roof (peg). Make extending moves over the
roof, swing left, and make a committing finish slightly leftwards over
bulging rock (two stainless-steel bolts).

Don't Cry on My Hard-shoulder   20 metres   E2 5a ✿   (10.6.94)
The sparsely protected right-hand arête of the buttress.
Climb a groove in the arête to a ledge on the left under a roof. Haul over
the roof on dubious holds until just below a grassy ledge with loose blocks.
Avoiding the ledge, traverse right to an easy finishing groove.

To the right of the arête is a bulging, west-facing wall, which attracts the
powdery white lichen that you thought could only be found in Cheedale.
Routes will require rebrushing from time to time. All the routes have tree
belays at the top.

Don't Let Me Down   20 metres   E5 6b †   (23.3.86)
The smooth, pocketed wall immediately right of the arête. A desperate
pitch that shoots well above the pain barrier.
Climb a shallow groove just right of the arête to the left end of a pedestal
ledge at 6 metres. Make a very committing step up onto the smooth wall
above. Now with gritted teeth (and taped fingers), climb straight up the
smooth wall on sharp finger-pockets to an easier groove that leads to the
top.

'Hold, Hold, Hold!'   20 metres   E5 6b/c F7b+   (16.5.94)
A gnarly face route; one of the best hard climbs this side of Shoot Gully.
Plough straight through the initial overhangs on big holds to the pedestal
ledge (and a lie-down if desired). A tenuous crux move over a bulge is
followed by a step left. Now put your thinking-cap on and climb the rib
above to easier ground and the top. Three bolts (one *Eco*) and an *in-situ*
thread.

Hold Me Tight   20 metres   E5 6b †   (2.3.86)
The long dusty grey groove that forms the right edge of the west-facing
wall. A very hard crux, and serious to boot.
Climb a vague groove to gain the lower right-hand end of the
pedestal-ledge. Step right to undercuts and make difficult moves over the
bulge to good holds in the base of the shallow groove. Follow the groove
more comfortably to the top. One peg (removed).

The remaining climbs on Swine Cliff are to be found in the bay to the right.
All are set a safe distance back from the road.

Motherless Child   18 metres   Hard Severe 4b   (5.9.93)
The obvious curving corner-crack at the left end of the bay. Follow the
corner, move left onto the wall, and then climb up and right to a ledge and
a tree. Finish up the slab behind the tree.

Life's Too Short for Plucking Mushrooms
18 metres   Hard Very Severe 5a (5.91)
Starting 2 metres right of *Motherless Child*, climb a slab and the good but spaced holds above to the tree on *Motherless Child*. One peg (removed).

Victims of Circumstance   18 metres   Very Severe 4c   (5.91)
To the right of *Motherless Child* is a right-facing corner; climb the corner to the tree on *Motherless Child* and exit as for that route.

Teenage Riot   18 metres   E3 6b F7a+   (22.6.94)
A three-move wonder, with the motivating presence of a pruned-sharp tree beneath. Start 2 metres right of the right-facing corner.
Climb easy rock to the tree beneath a blank wall. Three (or less?) moves up the wall lead to easy ground and the top. Two stainless-steel bolts.

Arachnophilia   14 metres   Hard Very Severe 5a ✿   (10.93)
Start at a shattered undercut crack 3 metres right of the right-facing corner. Gain the crack and follow it to a hand-ledge where it ends (good wires). Stand on the ledge and move right, then up carefully (peg – removed) through a tiny overlap. Finish leftwards.

It's in the Trees   15 metres   Severe ✿   (5.9.93)
Follow steep parallel cracks to a tree stump before continuing leftwards up the obvious ramp.

Groovy Baby!   14 metres   Very Severe 4c   (11.6.94)
Climb the left-hand of two corners at the right end of the bay to a tree on the right. Abseil off.

Groovy Man!   14 metres   Hard Severe 4b   (11.6.94)
The right-hand corner at the right end of the bay. Climb the lower corner, move left, and finish up the continuation corner.

The Near Bay Buttresses and Quaking Wall
Chrome Nun Buttress
The left-hand of the two larger buttresses that project from the (currently wooded) hillside can be identified by a long roof at two-thirds height. Scramble up a very mobile scree slope to the routes (trying not to dislodge any rocks).

We're Civilized   25 metres   E5 6a   (9.7.87)
Good, steep, but sparsely-protected wall climbing on the left-hand side of the buttress. Start by scrambling up to trees below the left arête of the buttress.
Climb a short, easy groove to an undercut bulge. Pull up a tiny groove piercing the bulge (good *RPs*) and move up and right onto the wall (8mm bolt). Make a hard move to an obvious jug on the right; then reach back left and follow more jugs to the roofs (peg). Pull through the roofs on superb holds and finish up the short groove.

The Moon Is Made of Green Cheese   27 metres   E5   6b   F7b   (21.7.87)
Cruel moves on unusual rock. The *in-situ* gear has seen better days (but little action). Start at a smooth grey slab in the centre of the buttress. Climb straight up the centre of the slab to the left-hand end of a ledge. The shallow overhanging groove above is taken on weak undercuts (two 8mm bolts and an *in-situ* thread) until better holds lead over the bulge (peg) to the main roof (peg). Pull through the roof with difficulty (peg and *in-situ* wire) to finish at a small tree.

Chrome Nun   30 metres   E5   (18.11.73/8.9.84)
A ferocious and insecure pitch. Start at the slab as for the last route.
1   12m.   5b.   Climb the centre of the slab to a ledge and small tree belay on the right.
2   18m.   6b.   Climb the thin crack rising from the right-hand end of the ledge to an overlap (peg). Some baffling and strenuous moves lead leftwards over the bulge to easier climbing and the roof above (peg). Pull over the roof into a short groove (two pegs), and exit right.

Pepys Rock

The tall and slender right-hand buttress with substantial east and west faces is Pepys Rock. Its east face forms the right wall of a semi-circular bay at the top of the scree slope, and is the gloomy home for the first two nondescript routes.

One of These Days   18 metres   E2   5b   (16.6.87)
Follow a small groove in the left-hand side of the face to a depression (peg). Move up and right (8mm bolt), step right, and run it out to easier ground and the top.

Theatre of Hate   18 metres   E2   5b   (19.5.87)
Fringe theatricals up the centre of the grey wall.
Trend easily rightwards to a slim right-facing groove. Climb the steep wall to the right of the groove (jammed nut) to good handholds (8mm bolt). Move slightly right and continue intricately (peg) to the top.

The nose of Pepys Rock is climbed by **Germaline** (30 metres Severe ❀ 6.4.74), starting up the obvious crack on the left to gain the top of a pinnacle; and on its right-hand side by **Resolution** (35 metres Very Severe 4b ❀ 5.1.73). Both routes came with warnings when first climbed; they are still loose and now overgrown.

The west face of the buttress may be climbable by the following two pitches. Both retreat from an **(old) abseil station**, somewhere beneath the unruly hanging ivy (which needs a cut).

Cut Glass   20 metres   E2   5c   (16.6.87)
The system of thin grooves in the centre of the face. Start below a groove, 4 metres along a vegetated ledge that runs leftwards around the buttress. Start up the initial scoop and move right (peg) to a narrow groove. Climb the groove (peg) and pull up and leftwards over a bulge (peg) to the base

of a narrowing groove and ramp. Follow the ramp easily at first and then more delicately up its right-hand rib to the abseil station.

Igor 18 metres E5 6b †   (19.5.87)
Another esoteric, and hard, pitch that could only have been produced in the 80s. Start 3 metres left of the vegetated gully bounding Pepys Rock. Climb directly up the steep wall, passing a small roof (and 8mm bolt) with difficulty. From better holds above, clip the peg on the right and climb decisively up the left-hand rib to a thin crack (good wires). Pull directly up to the ramp of *Cut Glass* and follow it to the abseil station.

Quaking Wall

Right of Pepys Rock (and separated from it by a vegetated gully) is a broad, slabby wall some 30 metres in height. Resplendent in plant-life, this wall extends rightwards to a broad rocky shoulder, beyond which commence the Reservoir Walls. Currently most of the routes need a reclean to reveal their true selves.

Late Entry 30 metres E3 5c ❀   (31.8.81)
A sustained and absorbing route which takes the tall, left-facing groove that runs up the left-hand end of the wall. Start 4 metres right of the base of the gully.
Climb steeply up a pocketed crack for 5 metres and move right from a hanging block into the base of the groove. Climb the groove over a bulge to a ledge. Continue up the groove over a second bulge and move up slightly rightwards to a narrowing in the roof. Pull over and trend rightwards across the short wall above to a tree at the cliff edge.

Claire's Complexity 30 metres E4 5c ❀   (31.8.81)
An excellent wall climb with good but spaced protection. Start at a cave just above head-height, 8 metres right of the gully.
Climb the wall immediately left of the cave to a narrow groove on the left (which contains a sapling). Follow the groove until it fades; then make bold moves up and slightly rightwards on improving holds to a break. Move diagonally leftwards to a narrowing in the roof and a junction with *Late Entry*. Pull over and trend rightwards across the short wall above to a tree at the cliff edge.
Variation
Africa Corps 27 metres E4 5c ❀   (18.3.95)
A direct start and finish to *Claire's Complexity*. Climb the shaky arête 4 metres left of *Claire's Complexity* to a ledge at 10 metres. Follow the groove and bold face of *Claire's Complexity* to a break. Step right, move up to a better break, and then pull over a roof on superb holds to an exit groove.

Ashman 30 metres E2 5c † ❀   (22.4.80)
Start at the cave, as for *Claire's Complexity*.
Climb over the right-hand side of the cave roof with difficulty (peg) and bear rightwards to a flake. Follow the long groove above past a bulge to a final overhang. Pass this with care and finish easily.

Bloody Tourists   33 metres   E3 5c   (11.5.80)
A good line, and at one time a popular route, which climbs the prominent
V-groove and thin crack in the centre of the wall. Start at the right end of a
vegetated terrace (approached from the left) at a tree.
Step off the tree and enter the groove with difficulty (peg). Climb the
groove to a ledge out to the left. Step back right and climb the crack to a
roof. Make a short hand-traverse to a prow on the right and finish up the
short wall above.

The Deceiver   33 metres   E1 5b   (5.5.80)
An elegant pitch that climbs the groove set in the arête right of *Bloody
Tourists*. Start below the V-groove, as for *Bloody Tourists*.
Move right and climb up into the groove in the arête. Follow the groove
and take the bulge above directly to a ledge on the left. Climb the crack
and wall above to the prow on *Bloody Tourists* and finish up the short wall
above.

New Friends   45 metres   Hard Very Severe 5a ✿   (5.5.80)
Completely obscured by greenery, it's anyone's guess where the bones of
the route are. Reportedly it started up a crack at the lowest point of the
wall.

The final route is situated on rock, more-or-less, to the right of a swathe of
vegetated rock/rocky vegetation.

Sinsemilla   27 metres   E1 5b   (25.6.81)
An interesting climb which takes the groove and crack in the slabby
right-hand section of the wall. Start near the right end of the wall, below a
corner.
Pull over the bulge (thread) and climb the corner (peg) to a good ledge.
Move diagonally leftwards to a niche, and climb the thin crack in the
slabby wall to a yew tree belay.
Direct Start E3 5c (14.8.87). Climb the awkward groove and crack 3
metres left of the ordinary start (*in-situ* thread) to a small sapling and peg.
Pull up into the niche of the parent route.

The Reservoir Walls

The Reservoir Walls is the series of walls just above road-level that extend
from behind the stone-walled enclosure of the covered reservoir to the base
of Shoot Gully. Despite some brittle rock and widespread mediocrity, a small
selection of good-quality solid routes, including a couple of popular easier
climbs, is on offer.

Access: Climbing here is permitted throughout the year, except from 15 June
to 31 August inclusive, and on Easter and the two May bank holiday

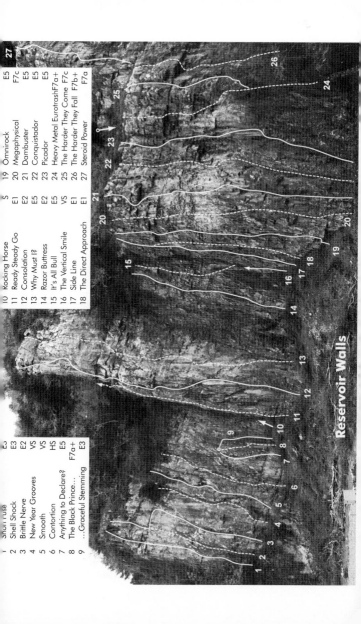

27

1	Short Fuse	E3
2	Shell Shock	E3
3	Brittle Nerve	E2
4	New Year Grooves	VS
5	Smooth	VS
6	Contortion	HS
7	Anything to Declare?	E5
8	The Black Prince...	F7a+
9	...Graceful Stemming	E3

10	Rocking Horse	S
11	Ready Steady Go	E1
12	Consolation	E2
13	Why Must I?	E5
14	Razor Buttress	E2
15	It's All Bull	E5
16	The Vertical Smile	VS
17	Side Line	E1
18	The Direct Approach	E1

19	Omnirock	E5
20	Megaphysical	F7c
21	Dambuster	E5
22	Conquistador	E5
23	Picador	E5
24	Heavy Metal Eurotrash	F7a+
25	The Harder They Come	F7c
26	The Harder They Fall	F7b+
27	Steroid Power	F7a

Reservoir Walls

weekends. It would be prudent, however, to avoid any rock directly above the road during any other busy times. For the Night Heat Wall: the owners have indicated that there may be a conflict between climbing and the use of the bus turning-circle beneath. Access may become restricted to when the open-topped bus is not running. **Please keep yourself informed.**

Descend, unless otherwise stated, by taking a slight path westwards along the cliff-top and following the lower section of Shoot Gully.

Short Fuse Wall

Above the left end of the reservoir, the crags start with a 30-metre wall characterized by a series of parallel grooves. The routes on the wall finish on a narrow, wooded terrace, **descended** by a 20-metre abseil down the corner (*Rocking Horse*) at its right end.

At the base of the wall, in its centre, is the tiny, gated entrance of a cave (Reservoir Hole). A narrow ledge leads leftwards from the cave; its left end is the starting platform for the following climbs (tree belays).

Shrapnel   33 metres   E1 5b ❀   (14.2.76)
An obscure pitch that climbs the groove on the extreme left-hand side of the wall.
Climb the shallow groove in the rounded nose of the wall past a small tree to a small roof on the left. Pull over to its right and follow the blank groove above, until it is possible to finish up the wide crack on the left.

Effendi   30 metres   E2 5b   (18.4.82)
A sustained eliminate that clings to the overhung rib near the left end of the wall. Start below a scoop at 3 metres.
Gain the scoop and move left to an obvious flat hold. Climb up and rightwards into a groove and follow this and a thin crack over the bulge to a small roof. Pull over on good holds and move right to a deep crack leading to the terrace.

Short Fuse   30 metres   E3 5c   (25.10.75)
The narrow V-groove in the left-hand side of the wall. A compelling line with absorbing, technical climbing throughout. The best route on the wall. Start as for *Effendi*.
Climb up into the scoop on the right of the nose and bear steeply rightwards to a small ledge below a smooth wall. Climb up to the V-groove and follow it with sustained interest (peg) to a horizontal break and small ledge. Continue up the groove above to the top.

Shell Shock   25 metres   E3 5b   (7.6.76/11.4.95)
The shock comes with trying to tiptoe over shattered 'crockery'.
Take the thin, broken crack right of *Short Fuse* to better holds below the shattered wall. Climb precariously up to gain a jug in a short white groove and, using a suspect jug on the right (sound enough in 95), reach the break above. Climb a groove to the terrace, as for *Brittle Nerve*.

Time to Hang up Your Boots   25 metres   E5 6a †   (11.4.9.)
Worth considering before setting off. A serious lead, this is the blunt rib left of *Brittle Nerve*.
A short layback crack points the way; climb it. Now, using layaways on either side of the rib, flow up to small ledges. Inject the crag with wires, step left, and make worrying moves up the line of weakness in the shattered white wall to reach a break. Finish up a groove, as for *Brittle Nerve*.

Brittle Nerve   33 metres   E2 5c   (25.7.81)
A normally fine pitch that has the nerve not to be too brittle. It climbs the thin groove bounding the left-hand side of the holdless 10-metre face in the centre of the wall. Start half-way along the narrow, vegetated ledge, below the groove.
Climb the groove with some difficulty to reach ledges on the left (holds to the right help somewhat). Make a rising traverse rightwards above the very smooth face (peg) to the horizontal break above. Traverse left along the break (peg) to an easy groove, which leads to the terrace.

In the right-hand side of the wall are three parallel grooves, the first of which contains a yew tree at its top.

New Year Grooves   25 metres   Very Severe 4c   (6.1.73)
The leftmost and strongest of the groove-lines. Start 4 metres left of the cave.
Climb a short groove (sometimes ivied) to a block roof. Move up and leftwards into the main groove-line and climb it with good protection to the yew tree near the top. Abseil descent.

Smooth   27 metres   Very Severe 4c ❀   (25.10.75)
The central groove of the trio, which currently features a huge detached flake (threatening an interruption to local water supplies). Start 2 metres left of the cave.
Climb a steep, thin crack and groove to a tree below the flake. Climb the flake crack and continue up the groove above to the terrace.

Contortion   25 metres   Hard Severe 4b ❀   (2.12.73)
The rightmost of the three grooves is unfortunately under ivy attack. Start at the cave. The groove is tricky to start but soon eases and leads up to the terrace.

Anything to Declare?   14 metres   E5 6a   (12.4.95)
The fear will give you away. Furtive climbing up the scarred groove right of the small cave; come practised in placing twisted wires while pumped-up. Start 4 metres right of the cave.
Inch up the groove to an overlap on the left. With continuing commitment, bear rightwards past another overlap to a ledge on the right. Continue easily up the groove to a stainless-steel bolted abseil station.

The Black Prince of the South-West   12 metres   E5 6b F7a+   (12.4.95)
Powerful climbing left of *The Art of Graceful Stemming*. Some wires required.

te and wall to arrive thankfully on a ledge. Continue up the
right to a stainless-steel-bolted abseil station. Three
el bolts.

The Art of Graceful Stemming   27 metres   E3 6a   (13.8.83)

A sometimes frustrating, but always entertaining problem. Start below the
orange corner with a very narrow right wall, 7 metres right of the cave.
Stem, gracefully or otherwise, up the narrow corner to good holds at 8
metres. Traverse left to a large sloping ledge, and climb the corner above
until a final move left gains the top of *Contortion*. Alternatively, use the
abseil station of the previous route.

Between Short Fuse Wall and the large, columnar pinnacle is a small bay, at
the back of which are two corner-cracks.

Wall End   25 metres   Severe 4a ❀   (8.4.76)

Climb the left-hand corner-crack past a roof to the terrace; normally
overgrown.

Rocking Horse   20 metres   Severe 4a   (1950)

Step off a rocking block and climb the right-hand corner-crack to a tree at
the right end of the terrace. An off-width chimney is normally avoided, but
provides good sport for the masochist.

Behind the reservoir is a 45-metre columnar pinnacle, the setting for the
following clutch of routes.

The Wayward Eliminate   45 metres   E4 ❀   (1.2.87)

A very direct line up the pinnacle. Two contrasting pitches, the second of
which climbs perilously up the true arête of the pinnacle. Start as for
Rocking Horse.
1 27m. 6a. Climb the easy groove to the right of *Rocking Horse* for 6
metres. Step right and climb very steeply up the thin crackline in the centre
of the smooth wall, passing a prehistoric peg/patch of rust. From more
broken rock above (old peg), step right to a big flake on the arête and
climb the arête easily to a good ledge and peg belays on the right.
2 18m. 6a. Move back left and climb a steepening, narrow slab in the
arête of the pinnacle (two pegs) to a good hand-ledge where it begins to
lean uncomfortably. Reach straight up to good holds and scamper
rightwards to a resting-place on the tip of the arête. Exit easily.

Ready Steady Go   45 metres   E1 ❀   (1.65/2.2.74)

Sounds of the 60s. Relegated to the history books. The climb follows the
narrow front face of the pinnacle. Start beneath the left arête of the pinnacle.
1 27m. 5b. Climb diagonally rightwards quite steeply (peg) to ledges on
the edge of the right arête (or reach this point via the short corner right of
the arête at 5c: peg). Move up and leftwards to a short, steep wall (peg),
which is climbed with difficulty to easier ground leading to a good ledge
and peg belays.

Return of the Gunfighter (F7c), Spacehunter Wall
Climber: Ian Vickers   Photo: Paul Twomey

Fornicator Simulator (F8b, first free ascent)
Spacehunter Wall
Climber: Ian Vickers   Photo: Paul Twomey

2 18m. 5a. Step left and climb leftwards to the start of a roof-capped groove (peg). Climb up the groove and through the overhang to the top.

Consolation   45 metres   E2   (2.8.66/27.5.75)
The Reservoir classic! One of Cheddar's most popular and invigorating climbs, it takes the elegant groove and arête in the front of the pinnacle, and reserves its crux for the top. Start below the dominating groove right of the arête of the pinnacle.
1 27m. 5a. Climb the sustained and twisting smooth groove to a bulge. Swing left onto a ledge and continue steeply up the crack in the centre of the pinnacle to a good ledge and peg belays.
2 18m. 5c. Above the stance is a hanging groove above roofs. Gain the groove from the left with difficulty (peg), and climb it (peg) before stepping up, heart-in-mouth, onto a massive, perched flake (if it's still there!). Stretch out left to a thin crack, which leads sensationally through the roofs in the final arête to the top.
Variation
B.A.D.   E4 †   (31.8.86)
1a 6a. From the top of the initial smooth groove, pull over a bulge and climb directly to the stance. Serious.

Why Must I?   45 metres   E5 †   (18.7.81/5.10.85)
The smooth, orange-coloured wall forming the west-facing side of the pinnacle. Scant small-wire and RP protection and very sustained and pumpy climbing make this an uncompromising proposition, high in the grade. Start at the base of an obvious crack that bounds the wall on its right, 6 metres right of Consolation.
1 27m. 6b. Climb the crack for 3 metres and move left onto the face. Work up slightly rightwards and then step back left to a thin flake-line. Climb the flake and make unobvious, hard moves up and rightwards to enter a short bottomless groove that soon leads to better holds in a horizontal break. Continue straight up the wall to a niche, and break out leftwards to bush and cam belays.
2 18m. 5b. Climb the crack behind the belay, hard to start, and move left behind a large, cracked block to finish.

Can't Help Myself   42 metres   E6 6b †   (19.7.95)
Escalade fatale. One hell of a lead.
Follow *Why Must I?* for 12 metres; then take a slight ramp that leads rightwards onto a small hanging slab (*in-situ* thread). Make very hard moves up a steep wall to an undercut flake. From a break above (peg), climb diagonally right to improving holds and easier ground. Trend left to a small tree (possible belay). Climb straight up the right side of the arête, with spaced gear and strenuous climbing, to a tree just below the top of the pinnacle.

Cirrus   45 metres   Hard Very Severe ❀   (24.10.73)
The crack that bounds the pinnacle on the right. Start as for Why Must I?.

1 27m. 5a. Climb the crack to a tree. Continue up the ivied groove above to a roof on the left, which is taken on its left to ledges and tree belays.
2 18m. 4b. Follow the groove on the right until a move right gains a rib leading to the top.

The cliff-line now falls back into a rather dank bay.

Toss of a Coin   27 metres   Very Severe 4c ❀   (1.6.69)
In the left wall of the bay is an overgrown, smooth-walled corner. Climb the corner, using good holds on the right wall (peg). Move left above the corner (peg), and climb the rib to a yew tree. Abseil off.

Razor Buttress   27 metres   E2 5c   (29.6.81)
The groove and wall left of the deep chimney provide a worthwhile pitch (and a close shave with fragile rock).
Climb the grassy groove fairly easily at first. Gain the steeper, blank section above from the left (peg) and climb the crack above to a niche. Step left around the rib and finish up the wall above. Abseil from trees.

It's All Bull   20 metres   E5 6a †   (9.5.94)
A curious climb up the shallow, overhanging groove left of the chimney. Follow *The Vertical Smile* for 8 metres; then step left into a scoop. Proceed up the groove above (two wire-clip bolts) and reach a break. Pull into the continuation groove, and continue direct on good holds to the big tree at the top.

The Vertical Smile   27 metres   Very Severe 4c   (20.12.72)
There's not a laugh to be had in the brooding chimney in the back of the bay. Climb the chimney directly, and exit slightly leftwards out of the cave near the top. Abseil from trees.

To the right of the chimney is a rounded, groove-seamed buttress capped by bulges and roofs. There is lots of low-grade rock here, but, typically, the climbing is much better than it looks. All the routes between *Side Line* and *Big Softy* end on a vegetated ledge with a yew tree. *In-situ* slings on the yew tree offer a possible anchor for an abseil descent, but watch out for loose rock on the way down.

Side Line   27 metres   E1 5b ❀   (17.4.81)
Climb the shallow groove 4 metres right of the chimney to a bulge. Pull over into a continuation crack and climb it until it disappears into loose bulges. Step right and follow the thin crack on the right past a roof and sapling to the top.

The Direct Approach   27 metres   E1 5b   (27.6.81)
Scruffily honest climbing. Start 5 metres down and to the right of the chimney.
Climb rightwards to saplings above a leftward-facing groove. Get established on a hanging slab from the left. Climb the thin corner above, to finish past a roof and sapling as for *Side Line*.

Omnirock   27 metres   E5 6a   (23.4.94)

Thoughtful climbing on quite a good line, which starts up the obvious groove (above a spindly sapling 5 metres up). Start behind a large tree stump.

A line of jugs leads slightly rightwards over roofs to the sapling at the base of the groove. Climb the groove to a bulge beneath a black wall. Climb direct (stainless-steel bolt) before bearing minimally rightwards to an inset jug (stainless-steel bolt). Trend leftwards to a niche and pull over the centre of the roof above. Either abseil with caution from the small tree on the right, or bear left to the exit of *The Direct Approach*.

The next four routes on the buttress start up remarkably similar grooves, and are described in relation to the stone wall abutting the cliff on the right.

Megaphysical   30 metres   E6 6b F7c   (15.5.95)

Undercutting galore on an energy-depleting line through the centre of the bulging buttress. Start below an ill-defined groove, 12 metres left of the wall.

Follow the technical groove to a rest below bulges. Powerfully force a line on hard-to-read rock to better holds and the top. Seven stainless-steel bolts.

Dambuster   30 metres   E5 6a †   (23.6.85)

A pernicious undertaking that aims for the largest overhang in the buttress, near the top. The bombs have long been dropped but the dam's still holding. Start below a shallow groove (containing a vertical flake crack at 7 metres) 10 metres left of the wall.

Climb the groove to a ledge on the right. Continue delicately up the groove until it is possible to step left, and then climb rightwards onto a rib. Move up to a thin crack (*in-situ* thread) and cross the bulging wall leftwards to a peg 2 metres below the capping overhang. Move up, and swing left and then back right across the lip of the overhang to the top.

Conquistador   30 metres   E5 5c †   (8.9.82)

An evil pitch. Start at the lowest point of the buttress, at the foot of the most prominent groove, 8 metres left of the stone wall.

Climb the groove to small ledges. Move up and left (8mm bolt); then quiver up onto a pinnacle of flakes and certain catalepsy. Continue directly until good holds appear on the right, and then bear leftwards to finish.

Picador   30 metres   E5 6a   (16.9.72/17.6.82)

A very respectable route which combats the most obvious line of weakness in the right-hand side of the buttress. Start below a rightward-slanting groove, 6 metres left of the wall.

Follow the groove easily rightwards for 7 metres to a ledge below steeper pink rock. Bridge up with difficulty (poor pegs) until hard moves up to the left gain easier ground. Climb up to the yew tree.

Heavy Metal Eurotrash   25 metres   E5 6b F7a+   (5.94)

Swift-moving thrills with one very hard move. Start where the stone boundary wall abuts the cliff.

From the top of the wall, climb easily slightly rightwards at first and then direct past an 8mm bolt to a shaky ledge on the left beneath a bulge. Traverse left for 2 metres before improvising up the steep, shattered wall to a massive side-hold. Plough through the roofs above with some great moves on bucket holds. Five stainless-steel bolts.

The Harder They Come   20 metres   E6 6b/c F7c   (5.94)
Power-endurance climbing, and quite sequency. Start where the boundary wall abuts the cliff.
Follow *Heavy Metal Eurotrash* past the 8mm bolt (which has saved at least one life) to the ledge beneath the bulge. Now follow an intricate bulging line up a thin groove in the buttress to exit up the obvious hanging corner. Four stainless-steel bolts and one *in-situ* wire (at the top).

The Harder They Fall   18 metres   E6 6b F7b+   (6.9.85)
A dramatic pitch with a whole host of difficulties compressed into a short distance. Of test-piece status since its rebolt in 1993. Start 3 metres up to the right of the stone wall.
Climb a narrow, rightward-slanting ramp and swing left across a steep wall to the base of a shallow groove in the roof-capped leaning wall (good spike runners – thin tapes required). Move up to layaways (*Eco-bolt*), and work desperately up the groove (*Eco-bolt*) to the roof and a welcome rest on a jug over its lip. Pull over (small wire) and scramble to belays.

Big Softy   18 metres   E5 6b F7b   (6.5.88)
'Way hard!' Desperate climbing up the wall to the right of *The Harder They Fall*, which cries out for a rebolt.
Follow *The Harder They Fall* for 8 metres to the spike runners. Pull up and right over the overlap and work up a faint groove (two 8mm bolts) to a small roof. Make some 'too-hard-for-6b' stretches up and left to the base of a short groove (peg), and climb this to ledges.

Steroid Power   18 metres   E4 6b F7a   (2.6.94)
An unsatisfying bolt-route up the grooved arête and wall above the previous three routes (but not so bad as a second pitch); start from the belay ledge.
Climb to the base of a roof-capped groove. Tackle the strenuous groove, and (ignoring a leftward escape onto the arête) pull right around the roof onto the face above. Climb the face to the top. Five stainless-steel bolts.

Right of the stone wall, rising rightwards above White Spot Cave, is the major crack-system climbed by *Eden Crack*. The next route aims for the smooth grey wall left of a right-angled corner (*Temptation*) high on the cliff.

Beyond the Hydra Centaurus Supercluster   33 metres   E5 †   (9.5.88)
…lies the answer to the origin of the Universe – apparently. The answer to this problematic route is scarcely any easier to find. Start at the base of the diagonal crack taken by *Eden Crack*.
1 15m. 6b. Climb easily to the base of an open groove. Climb the groove (8mm bolt) and pull rightwards onto a rounded rib. A frustrating

sequence up a thin crack (good wires) leads to better holds (peg) and a good ledge above. Peg and nut belays.
2 18m. 6b. Step left and follow an easy groove to flat ledges below the grey headwall. From the left end of the highest ledge, climb straight up the steep wall on technical holds (peg) to reach a good break (*in-situ* chockstone: fallen out!) and the top a little higher.

Eden Crack   33 metres   Moderate   (1931)
An elementary climb, but with charm and a good view. Start at the base of the crack, 6 metres up and to the right of the stone wall abutting the cliff.
1 18m. Climb the right-hand of two parallel cracks to a large ledge, tree, and optional belay. Continue up a step to a second ledge and tree belays above an ivy mass (The Garden of Eden).
2 15m. Continue up the obvious corner-crack to the top.

Temptation   25 metres   Hard Severe 4b   (5.65)
One of the few really attractive climbs of this grade in the Gorge: good-natured and protectable. Start from the tree on the first large ledge, 10 metres up *Eden Crack*.
From the tree, traverse delicately leftwards across a steep wall, and then climb up into the base of the corner. Follow the corner past a tree to the top.

Mars   25 metres   Very Severe 4c   (16.4.78)
An enjoyable eliminate that climbs the thin crack in the right wall of the *Temptation* corner. Start from the large ledge as for *Temptation*, 10 metres up *Eden Crack*.
From the back of the ledge, climb a flake to a roof above the ledge. Traverse left beneath the roof to the base of a corner and left again to a sapling below a crack. Climb the thin crack past a tree near the top.

Milky Whey   25 metres   E2 5c   (22.3.75/23.4.78)
Fine and precise climbing in the smooth corner above *Eden Crack*. Start from the same ledge as *Temptation*, 10 metres up *Eden Crack*.
From the back of the ledge, climb a flake to the roof above the ledge. Traverse left beneath the roof to the base of the smooth corner. Climb thinly up the corner (peg) until the rib on the right can be gained. Climb carefully up more broken ground to finish up a small groove.

Bolt Action   9 metres   E5 6b F7b   (8.6.94)
Tough sport action over the roof above the first large ledge up *Eden Crack*. Start from the same ledge as *Temptation*, 10 metres up *Eden Crack*.
Climb easily up to the roof via a large flake; then make gutsy moves to get established on the wall above. Press on up the wall to a stainless-steel-bolted abseil station. Three stainless-steel bolts.

Small Is Big   12 metres   E4 6b †   (28.9.86)
A paradoxical route! To the left of the finish of *Eden Crack* is a smooth, leaning wall of perfect rock; this is unlikely to succumb without a fair

amount of effort. Start from the second large ledge, 18 metres up *Eden Crack*. Tree belays.
Climb strenuously up the wall on finger edges (8mm bolt) to an incipient break (difficult-to-on-sight gear). Pull over the bulge to jugs and continue directly to the top.

Night Heat Wall

Immediately left of the base of Shoot Gully is a west-facing, black-streaked wall which has a small, deep cave (White Spot Cave) below its left-hand end. Many tourists peer into this cave, so don't drop anything on their heads.

One Foot in the Grave   12 metres   E4 6a   (22.12.86)
Short but serious. Start 4 metres left of White Spot Cave. Climb the wall using holds in grooves (peg) and so gain an old abseil station.

Sidekick   13 metres   E4 6a/b   (5.7.94)
Single rope users will have trouble with this quasi-sport route. Start 2 metres left of the cave.
Climb up to an overlap and surmount it with difficulty (8mm bolt) to small but positive holds (8mm bolt). Make a hard move up right (peg) to a slot (cam); then continue up left and back right to a welcome rest (8mm bolt). Traverse left to the old abseil station atop *One Foot in the Grave*.

Dig for Victory   36 metres   E3 † ❀   (8.4.73/1976)
A good first pitch, though the route is deflected into some serious territory by vegetation on the second. Start at White Spot Cave.
1 12m. 5a. Climb out over the cave roof and follow the groove and wall above to ledges.
2 24m. 5c. Climb the narrow groove above to ivy. Move across the shattered wall on the right to a crack which leads to the top.
Variation
2a The Sting 24m. E1 5a † †† (11.9.78). Nondescript and probably too scary for 'new man'. Climb the corner just to the right of pitch 2 for 8 metres. Move right and then climb the more broken wall, trending diagonally rightwards to a short finishing crack.

Plaque   15 metres   E4 6a †   (10.2.03)
Good moves up the right-hand side of the rib right of the cave. Technically easy for the grade, though care needs to be taken to fit the best protection on the bulge. Start 3 metres right of the cave.
Climb to a bulge (wire on right, and micro-cam above). Undercut the slightly wobbly 'teeth' and reach a hand-ledge above. Swing immediately left on the ledge (peg), and then climb the rib on its right-hand side to ledges. Scramble right to the left-hand end of the terrace.

Hung Jury   15 metres   E2 5b   (28.7.94)
An amenable and well-protected pitch up the slabby groove right of White Spot Cave. 'The use of a mysterious line of bat-hook holes provides a deranged alternative!' Start 5 metres right of White Spot Cave.

Night Heat Wall

Eden Crack

White Spot Cave

Shoot Gully

Climb up to a small overlap (wires and 8mm bolt above). Pull up rightwards to good holds and then move up and back left to a thin break (peg). (Alternatively, from the overlap, climb straight up the slab at 6a.) Continue straight up to a ledge and walk rightwards to belay on the terrace.

Return of the Upsetters 15 metres E3 6a † (10.2.03)
A nice upper wall. Place the good wire runner 5 metres up *Hung Jury* at the base of its groove, and climb back down. Take a direct line up bulging rock to the right, with a very difficult move on layaways to gain a jug above the obvious projecting nose. Climb the centre of the compact grey wall above to ledges. Walk right to the left-hand end of the terrace.

Django 36 metres E3 (10.65/8.76/10.5.94)
A lively adventure of some antiquity. It side-steps excitedly across the white wall above and right of White Spot Cave. Start at the large corner-crack right of the cave.
1 12m. 4b. Climb the corner-crack to a bolt and cam belay on the terrace.
2 24m. 5c. Climb the short and most obvious corner above the belay to a break (peg). Traverse right along the descending break for 5 metres (peg) and move up onto a white scar (a reminder of the route's notorious perched flake). Enter a shallow groove with difficulty and finish up a steep crack.
Variation
Stargazer E3 (31.10.93)
A direct start to the second pitch. Start just left of a short flake crack in the wall, 6 metres right of the corner.
2a 24m. 5c. Climb the wall (cam and good wire placements on the right) to reach some flat jugs (8mm bolt). Pull up to join *Django* at the white scar (8mm bolt). Finish as for *Django*.

Witch's Brew 15 metres E5 6a † (10.2.03)
The arête of the pillar right of the first, corner-crack pitch of *Django*. Steady, but needing the usual degree of care. Climb the arête past a small ledge on the right (essential medium cam) to a bulge (peg). Swing out right to get stood up on a triple-pointed overhang ('the witch'), and then step back left to finish up a short crack left of the arête.

Far Away Thoughts 18 metres E3 5c † (12.4.95)
A scrappy route with a committing start that sets about the toughest-looking rock right of White Spot Cave. Start below a blunt arête right of the *Django* corner.
Trend up and rightwards (peg) to better holds and a horizontal break. Exit via a slabby corner above.

The following five pitches start from the narrowing rock terrace that runs beneath the leaning, black-streaked wall from Shoot Gully.

Chartbuster   25 metres   E4 6a   (4.12.93)
Yet to become a smash-hit; more B-side material really. Nonetheless it offers exciting climbing on a good line. Start on the terrace, at the belay of *Stargazer*.
Move left and make a thin starting move over the first bulge (immediately left of a black streak). Climb boldly up on good holds to the descending break of *Django* (*Friend 2*). Push on up the white wall above (peg), making use of some good sideholds (and a reassuring *Rock 3* placement on the left), and enter a thin, angular groove. Climb the groove to jugs and small ledges, and then proceed direct up a wall past a good break to a tree belay on the right.
Variation
New Entry   18 metres   E4 6a †   (7.94)
Start on the terrace, at the bolt and cam belay of *Django*.
Climb the groove and arrange essential cam protection. Surmount the bulge via the obvious undercut to gain better holds, step up right onto a loose pedestal, and finish as for *Chartbuster*.

Catalogues of Fear   20 metres   E5 6a ††   (3.4.81)
A serious lead that tackles the centre of the wall. Some of the loose blocks that used to be hung on may have been pulled off! Start from the terrace at a short flake crack 8 metres right of *Django*'s belay.
Climb very boldly up the solid white wall on finger-ledges past a weak hidden peg to the obvious niche (peg). Move up, and exit carefully from the left-hand side of the niche (peg) over a bulge to easier ground leading rightwards to the top.

The remaining routes on the wall occupy the right-hand black-streaked section. They start from a narrower rock ledge a few metres above the terrace.

Spy in St Pauls   18 metres   E5 6b   (1.10.86)
Fine, pumpy climbing on good rock. Start above and just to the right of a short flake crack, at the left end of the rock-ledge.
Climb up on good finger-edges in the white rock; then crank fervently up left (8mm bolt) to jugs in the right-hand side of the obvious niche (peg). Bridge up rightwards into a groove and climb it to a small roof. Pull over (*in-situ* thread) to finish.

All Guns Blazing   20 metres   E6 6c F7c   (16.8.94)
A power-mad pitch that takes on the steepest rock on the wall; hard at F7c. Start from the rock ledge, 5 metres from the chimney at the right end of the wall.
Climb up 2 metres, and swing left on jugs to initiate a snatch-sequence up the wall. A high rock-over into a shallow scoop ends the shoot-out, and leads to the exit of *Macabre*. Six stainless-steel bolts.

Macabre   25 metres   E5 6b   (11.10.85/1.10.86)
A superb route which may still be the best on the wall. Very strenuous and sustained. Start from the rock-ledge, 5 metres from the chimney at the right end of the wall.

...hite wall on finger-ledges to a short crack (vital wire). Extend
...r a narrow ledge and move right to a slight groove (peg). From
...ve, move left (8mm bolt) to reach good undercuts. Finish straight
up the wall above (*in-situ* thread).

Heat's On   15 metres   E5 6b F7b   (5.7.94)
Exemplary climbing on a bolt-protected eliminate line. 'This will popularize
the wall!' (Like hell it did.)
From a small flake and some pockets, climb direct past a narrow, sloping
shelf before reaching up left to the shake-out jug and peg on *Macabre*.
Move up, as for *Macabre*, but then reach right to good sideholds,
enabling the wide break above to be reached. Finish absolutely direct.
Three stainless-steel bolts, a peg, and an *in-situ* thread.

The Night Heat   15 metres   E5 6b †   (25.9.85)
A highly exacting pitch (i.e. don't fall off) that takes a system of incipient
grooves in the right-hand side of the wall. Very difficult and strenuous to
protect adequately. Start just left of the chimney at the right end of the wall.
Climb a narrow, square-cut groove and then finger traverse leftwards (small
wires on the right) to reach good holds in the base of a shallow groove.
Continue over a series of exhausting bulges to the top. Cams useful.

Wait until the Darkness Comes   15 metres   E2 5b   (25.10.87)
Steep climbing up the shallow corner above the chimney formed by the
large flake at the right end of the wall.
From the top of the flake, climb the corner (two pegs) to reach good holds
on a tiny ledge. Continue past a deep break (large cam) to the top.
Variation
Get Into the Groove   15 metres   E4 5c   (1.6.94)
Climb up to the first peg. Follow the leftward-curving undercut groove to its
close. Pull over on the right to finish past twin horizontal breaks.

Shoot Gully Walls

High above the Reservoir Walls and just east of Shoot Gully are two levels of
isolated buttresses, walls, and pinnacles nestling amongst trees. Though not
in Shoot Gully itself, the climbs may be approached by scrambling up the
gully and branching off along the appropriate well-worn track. There is a
rock-catch fence 25 metres up the gully which can be passed to its right.

The climbing on these esoteric crags is quite unlike anything else in the
Gorge. Short and secluded but pleasantly divorced from the road, the small
selection of low-grade climbs on offer are especially conducive to a relaxed
afternoon's or evening's adventure. There's also potential for more.

Access: Climbing is allowed throughout the year except from 15 July until 31 August inclusive and on Easter and the two May bank holiday weekends. (A different arrangement exists for the last three routes in this section: see below.)

The Sugarloaf   12 metres   Difficult ❀   (1931)
Immediately up the slope above *Eden Crack* is a dainty, flat-topped pinnacle, unfortunately molested by ivy. It can be reached from Shoot Gully by branching left 10 metres above the rock-catch fence, or it can be combined with *Eden Crack*. The pinnacle is climbed direct.

There are several equally antique climbs left of *The Sugarloaf*: **East Climb** (8 metres Moderate 1931), and **Green Wall** (9 metres Very Difficult 1931).

Twenty metres above the rock-catch fence in Shoot Gully a narrow rock ledge leads leftwards beneath a cliff that has been consumed by ivy; **Spitting Dust** (25 metres Hard Very Severe 5a † 19.7.85) used to go up there via a groove and leftward hand-traverse.

Near the top of the wooded slope above the Reservoir Walls is a large, fairly broken tier of rock some 35 metres high. At the left-hand end of the tier is a flying buttress, behind which the opposite sides of a chimney provide *Pyramus* and *Thisbe Chimney*. A descending wooded terrace leads rightwards from the foot of the buttress past a wooded bay containing a cave (Whitebeam Slitter Cave) to join Shoot Gully two-thirds of the way up. When approaching from the gully, turn left at the second major crossroads, immediately above a steep scrambling section of the gully. (The right-hand branch leads out below the Warlord Wall.) The climbs can be combined with *Sugarloaf* and *Eden Crack* by a direct ascent of the hillside: as close to a mountaineering excursion as you'll get in these parts.

Pyramus   15 metres   Moderate   (1931)
The chimney in the left-hand face of the flying buttress leads to a window. Squirm through this to the top.

Pyramus Arête   25 metres   Very Severe 4b   (10.5.00)
Climb a wide crack below the left arête of the flying buttress, and step right over loose blocks onto the edge (safer to reach this point from the next climb). Follow the steep arête above on positive holds to the top of the buttress.

Snout's Wall   25 metres   E1 5b   (10.5.00)
Step left from the foot of *Thisbe Chimney*, and climb easily to the foot of a narrow overhanging groove in the right arête of the flying buttress. Move up the groove, strenuous but well-protected, to easier ground and the top.

Thisbe Chimney   15 metres   Very Difficult   (1931)
Climb the narrow chimney in the right-hand face of the flying buttress, past the window, to the top.

Thisbe Crack   20 metres   Severe 4a   (1946)
The fine flake crack and groove immediately to the right of the flying
buttress is climbed to a huge jammed block, where a step left or right
leads to easier rock and the top.
Variation
Thisbe Slab   20 metres   Severe 4a   (1946)
From a pothole, climb the groove in the right-hand edge of the slab (or the
slab itself) right of the flying buttress to an overhang. Traverse left into
Thisbe Crack.

Thisbe Rib   20 metres   Hard Very Severe 5a †   (10.5.00)
An excellent pitch. From the pothole, climb the groove on the right-hand
edge of the slab to an overhang. Pull straight over the overhang to jugs,
and follow the fine rib above to finish right of the jutting overhang.

The Sixth Thisbe   20 metres   E3 5c †   (10.5.00)
Follow *Thisbe Rib* to the overhang. Swing right, and move up to better
holds in an incipient crack. Take pockets in the grey face above and exit
via a short crack. Good climbing, but be patient with the yew tree.

The remaining routes here are located in the wooded bowl, at the back of
which is a cave smelling of badgers (which no self-respecting speleologist
would dream of entering).

Narrow Buttress   36 metres   Severe   (1946)
1 12m. Climb the clean narrow slab that forms the left-hand rib of the
wooded bowl to a grassy ledge.
2 24m. Climb the wall above by the easiest line, but take care with the rock.

Narrow Crack   36 metres   Severe   (1946)
A worthwhile climb. Near the right-hand edge of the bay, 8 metres right of
the cave, is a steep crack.
1 12m. 4a. Climb the crack to a good ledge.
2 24m. Follow the rib above to the top.

Groove and Rib   36 metres   Severe ❀   (1946)
1 12m. Climb the chimney to the right of *Narrow Crack* to a good ledge.
2 24m. Follow the rib above to the top.

In an obscure location, at the very top of Shoot Gully, is a smooth, white wall
on the right. The wall is composed of compact and near-flawless rock in its
upper half and provides three routes, all of which start 6 metres along a
narrow, grassy ledge beneath the wall.

Access: For the next three routes, climbing is allowed from 1 October until
15 March inclusive.

Mud in Your Eye   15 metres   Hard Very Severe 5b † ❀   (22.2.86)
From the base of a ramp, climb up and leftwards to sloping ledges below
the steeper, compact wall. A hard reach leads to good holds (*in-situ*
thread), and easier climbing gains the top.

Crackshot   15 metres   E3 6a † ❀   (22.2.86)
A neat pitch, climbing the central line of the wall via some piquant moments.
Climb the wall to the right of trees to a small sapling at 6 metres. Continue
up the flake above to a jug below the smoother upper section. A difficult
incipient crack is now taken to good finishing holds and the top.

Up against the Wall!   15 metres   E5 6a † ❀   (22.2.86)
A micro-traumatic experience. The blunt white rib to the right of *Crackshot*
is marginally protected by *RPs*.
From the small sapling 6 metres up *Crackshot*, move right and climb a
groove to the smoother upper face. Place a good wire in a slot to the left
of a rib and layback bravely around right into a slight groove. Long,
committing reaches lead up the rib, maybe to the top.

Pinnacle Bay

To the west of Shoot Gully, the South Slope rises very steeply to some 150
metres above road level in the form of four tiers. These extend from the great
stepped ridge of *Genesis*, which forms the right edge of Shoot Gully, across
to the first of the three deep gullies of Castle Rocks, Terrace Gully.

The first, roadside tier is displaced from the upper three by a broad grassy
shoulder, and is divided into two fairly distinct walls, Ginsberg Wall to the left
and Yew Tree Wall to the right. The second tier, the Long Wall, is the strip of
cliff, about 25 metres high, which extends from the *Genesis* ridge to merge
with the base of a buttress where tiers two, three, and four coalesce.
Immediately right of the upper half of Shoot Gully, the third and fourth tiers
combine to create the showpiece of this cliff: the Warlord Wall, a dome-
shaped face, clean and overhanging for most of its 55-metre height.

Take your shades and enjoy the full afternoon sun if climbing on Long Wall
or the Warlord Wall, early or late in the season. Exposure to the other
elements here can only enhance that all-essential weather-beaten look!

In February 2003 the ten-year complete ban on climbing on Pinnacle Bay's
Long Wall and Upper Tiers (and Castle Rocks) was replaced by a seasonal
restriction. Fortunately there were a few weeks left in the 2002/03 season to
take stock of the crags' condition, restore a few of the routes, and establish
some new climbs on the upper tier especially. Gone are most of the loose
rock and vegetation that had hampered development prior to the clearance
work which the landowner carried out in 1998/99. A safer and open
climbing environment where protected by the rock-catch fence beneath
Long Wall is now available to climbers.

Access: Climbing is allowed from 1 October until 15 March inclusive.

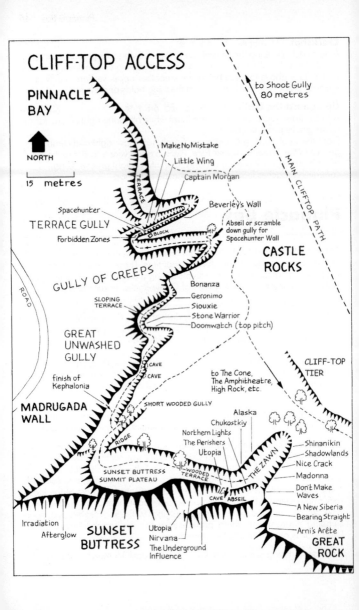

Ginsberg Wall

To the right of the base of Shoot Gully, at road level, is a clean white wall, which is rather featureless apart from its series of slim grooves, and a rectangular blind cave towards the right-hand side. A narrow, vegetated ledge slants up leftwards from the cave and is the start for routes left of *Get That Man*.

The cliff features a tightly packed group of hard pitches, which couldn't be easier to get to. The rock is reasonable, dries very quickly, and is normally free of seepage. Also, the cliff stays drier than most in the rain. Unfortunately, whilst most of the rock is clean, the exits have been altered by descaling operations, and may be worth checking out beforehand by abseil.

Descent: Either abseil from trees, or walk to the left (facing in) and descend the bottom section of Shoot Gully, past the rock-catch fence.

At the left end of the cliff, accessible from the base of Shoot Gully, is a crack above a yew tree, which gives the following climb.

Eight-Line Poem   20 metres   Hard Very Severe 5a ❀   (23.4.78)
Climb directly up the crack to finish in trees.

Mooney's Route   27 metres   E3 6a   (15.3.95)
An excellent, if poorly-protected, climb. Start as for *Eight-Line Poem*.
Climb the crack for 3 metres. Traverse right below an overlap and follow a groove (*in-situ* thread) to easier ground. Continue to a tree and the top.

Mir   27 metres   E5 6a †   (6.1.01)
Consistently good climbing; bold to start. Start 3 metres left of a narrowing in the slanting ledge, at a tree stump.
Climb a difficult steep wall to good fingerholds and wire placement above a small overlap. Take a slight groove above, which leads to bigger holds on the wall. Climb direct past a short crack and swing right onto a ledge. Step back left above a roof, and continue easily to the top.

2001   27 metres   E4 6a †   (6.1.01)
An enjoyably swift and well-protected start leads to scrappy climbing. Start 2 metres left of the narrowing in the slanting ledge.
Climb a steep wall into a narrow groove rising from a gap between two roofs. Good fingerholds on the left of the groove enable dynamic progress to be made to the ledge above. Follow the obvious line above, and pull up into a rather vegetated groove. Take the groove to a muddy ledge; then move left to top out.

The next two climbs start from a tree just below the narrowing in the slanting ledge.

Canary in a Coalmine   27 metres   E2 5b † ❀   (18.10.80)
A line up a groove and wall above the narrowing in the slanting ledge.

Ginsberg Wall

1	Mir	E5
2	2001	E4
3	Canary in a Coalmine	E2
4	Blitz	E3
5	Ripe Old Age	E5
6	Heaven-Sent Direct	E7
7	Hell-Bent	E6
8	Just Plain Bent	E5
9	Draggin' Along	F7c+
10	Barbarian	E6
11	Get That Man!	E4
12	Ginsberg	E4
13	Ginseng	E5
14	Rat, Tat, Tat	E5
15	Engineers	E2
16	Putnam's Folly	HVS
17	Condensation Street	E3
18	Quarante Pourcent...	E3

Yew Tree Wall

19	April Fools	S
20	Gobbledegook	E2
21	Another Dick on the Wall	E5
22	Pilferer	E2
23	Turkey Trot	E5
24	Croaking in Woking	E4
25	The Knack	E3
26	Tell It Like It Is	E5
27	A Simple Tale	E5
28	Mr X	E2
29	Yew Tree Groove	VS
30	No Bolts Please...	S

Move up onto a pedestal. Climb the groove to ledges. Continue up the scoop in the wall above to a small roof. Pull over (peg) and climb a vegetated groove to the top.

Blitz   30 metres   E3 6a   (4.10.80)
A wandering line of considerable interest. Start as for *Canary in a Coalmine*. Move up onto the pedestal. Climb the groove to ledges at 9 metres. Traverse rightwards and climb a committing shallow groove to better holds (peg on the left). Make awkward moves up into a niche, swing right into the more distinct groove, and climb it to easier ground. Traverse rightwards along the horizontal break above to a tree.

Donner und Blitzen   20 metres   E4 6b †   (27.9.86)
Highly charged. Start at the hawthorn tree right of the narrowing in the ledge.
From a small, triangular foot-ledge, climb directly to the foot of a smooth wall (8mm bolt). A frenetic sequence on opposing layaways leads up the wall to a good crack and resting-place on *Blitz*. Climb the groove and niche as for *Blitz*, but pull straight over the roof on good holds, before moving leftwards to a tree.

To the left of the low central overhangs are three shallow rightward-tending grooves.

Ripe Old Age   25 metres   E5 6b   (27.9.86)
The leftmost groove. Start at the hawthorn tree, as for *Donner und Blitzen*. Climb up to a small block overhang and, using the obvious downward-pointing spike, move up past an 8mm bolt to a thin crack. Bridge out rightwards into the groove, and climb it and the bulge above on good holds to a small ledge. Climb a small rib, and continue up the wall to the groove of *Blitz*. Traverse rightwards along the break to a tree, as for that route.

Heaven-Sent   27 metres   E6 6b †   (5.10.85)
A delivery from God. A bold solution to the central and deepest of the rightward-tending grooves. The climbing is intricate, sustained – and superb. Start just to the right of the hawthorn tree.
Climb to a peg in a bulge at 6 metres. Move right, keeping low, and pull over the bulge with a decisive long reach for a slanting edge which enables a resting-place in the groove to be reached (good wire). Climb straight up the groove on small but positive holds (*in-situ* thread out left) to twin pegs where it blanks out. Traverse diagonally rightwards across the bulge (jammed nut on the right) and pull through the roofs into the scoop above using the obvious undercut. Traverse leftwards above the roof to a groove that leads easily to the belay tree of *Blitz*.
Variation
Heaven-Sent Direct   25 metres   E7 6b   (15.3.95)
An extraordinarily beautiful climb with an all-out climax.

Climb the parent route to the twin pegs before the traverse right. Climb straight through the roof above, to the final groove: very intense indeed.

Hell-Bent   27 metres   E6 6c   (27.10.85)
The undercut third groove mixes super-hard moves with super-serious situations. It never did become popular. Start 5 metres right of the hawthorn tree, below a short, angular groove.
'Pedal' precariously up into the groove and clip the 8mm bolt on the right. Move right to undercuts and dyno blindly up into the groove. Continue seriously up the groove (*in-situ* thread) and then more easily up the rib above to a junction with *Heaven-Sent* (jammed nut). Follow that route through the roofs to the tree belay.
Variation
Just Plain Bent!   E5 6c   (14.10.89)
A slightly harder but safer entry into the groove of *Hell-Bent*. Starting 3 metres to its right, climb through the bulges via an obvious undercut and two 8mm bolts. If brave, jump off from the resting-place; if braver, continue as for *Hell-Bent*.

Draggin' Along   12 metres   E6 6c F7c+ †   (5.10.91)
Too powerful for words – well, almost. Start from the ledge below tiered roofs. Climb straight through them via four mainly homemade bolts and a 'ballistic throw' for the obvious undercut. Retreat from an old bolt belay.

Barbarian   25 metres   E6 6b   (29.9.84/22.12.86)
Pure aggression. A line through the roofs in the centre of the wall. The crack above is no pushover either. Start below the roofs, at the right end of the vegetated ledge.
Climb steeply to the double roof and a 10mm bolt. Thuggish moves, with useful hidden holds out right, lead over the roofs (10mm bolt) to a resting-place on the steep slab (8mm bolt). Move boldly up and leftwards to the base of the thin crack and climb it with good wire protection past two horizontal breaks to better holds above a small roof. Climb more easily rightwards to a tree belay.

Get That Man!   30 metres   E4 6b   (20.12.86)
Has seen more ascents than many. A very direct line of good quality up the overhung corner and wall to the left of the crack of *Ginsberg*. Start at road-level, 3 metres left of the cave.
Trend easily up leftwards past horizontal breaks to a ledge below the short corner. Pull up into the corner (*in-situ* thread) and climb over the bulge past an *in-situ* thread and 10mm bolt onto the steep wall. Move up the wall (peg) and then power over the overhang above (peg and jammed nut) to the tree of *Barbarian*.

Ginsberg   30 metres   E4 6b   (1966/16.4.80)
The classic of the wall. The steep crackline rising from the rectangular blind cave provides a magnificent pitch. The main difficulties are reasonably protected.

Climb steeply through the left-hand side of the cave roof on good holds to the base of the crack and a ledge at 9 metres. Continue directly (peg) but overcome the bulge where the crack fades by stepping right and then back left with a trying move (peg). Gain a provident resting-place at a horizontal break and a chance to ponder the difficulties looming overhead. Surmount the roof with difficulty (poor peg, but good wires) and climb more easily to a tree on the right.

Ginseng   27 metres   E5 6c ††   (11.11.85)
A devastating route with some finger-wrecking moves over the upper roofs and the intrinsic deterrent of a long runout. The route has not been reclimbed since a significant lump of rock was removed from the crux. Start up *Ginsberg* but veer right above the cave to a ledge (good cams in the horizontal break). Trend up slightly leftwards to another break and make a hard move to a pocket below a thin, right-facing corner. Move up slightly leftwards and then continue on jugs to a good rest and 8mm bolt below the roofs. Climb straight up through the (dismantled) roofs with great difficulty (8mm bolt) and pull over into a short groove. Exit rightwards to a tree belay.

Rat, Tat, Tat   27 metres   E5 6b   (12.5.87)
An entertaining eliminate that takes a surprisingly independent line up the right-hand side of the blank wall above the cave. Start at the right-hand side of the cave.
Climb easily up and leftwards to a small sapling above the lip (*in-situ* thread). Now take the steep wall directly past a 10mm bolt until hard moves can be made slightly leftwards over a small roof (jammed nut) to gain the obvious resting-place. Move right (10mm bolt) into a slim groove and climb directly, keeping to the left of the shattered rock, to a niche (*in-situ* thread). Continue up past an *in-situ* wire and pull over the roof on good holds to reach the top.

Engineers   27 metres   E2 5b ††   (15.10.80)
A testing pitch that follows the shallow groove above the right-hand side of the cave. Just adequate protection can be arranged, but the route feels bold. Start on the right-hand side of the cave.
Gain the groove easily and follow it to its close at a small roof. Avoid the roof by climbing on the right, and then move back left to regain the line (good cam). Climb the crack and the bulge above to tree belays. The direct version is E4.

Putnam's Folly   30 metres   Hard Very Severe 5b   (5.5.77)
Around the arête from *Engineers* is a prominent corner. Start 4 metres right of the cave.
Move up into the corner and climb it to a ledge (peg). Take the bulge direct and finish more easily leftwards to tree belays.

Condensation Street   30 metres   E3   5c †   (16.12.00)
An interesting route with reasonable protection. Care is required with the
rock. Start 8 metres right of the cave.
Climb a steep wall past a break (cams) to a left-facing layback edge.
Follow the edge, which forms a flake; then trend right to small resting
ledges. Move up the white wall on good holds, and then enter the obvious
corner. From the top of the corner, step left and climb a scoop to a loose
rubbly exit and trees.

Quarante Pourcent Matière Grasse   30 metres   E3   6a ❀(15.12.94)
A worthwhile route which is not overprotected. Start 9 metres right of the
cave, below a prominent, short, left-facing V-groove which begins 5 metres
above the ground.
Gain the V-groove and climb it to ledges on the right. Continue up the wall
with difficulty (peg) to gain better holds and protection in a shallow
right-facing corner. Climb the corner, and continue more easily to ledges
below the roofs. Pull boldly over, slightly leftwards, to easier ground; then
trend rightwards to tree belays.

The next two routes lay under ivy for two decades before being shown the
light. Tread carefully.

The Core   30 metres   E2   5b † ††   (18.10.80)
Start as for *Quarante…* below the short groove. Climb the groove to
ledges on the right. Trend right and then left to easier ground. Climb the
short wall and groove above to the top.

Gruesome Groove   30 metres   E2   5b † †† ❀   (12.10.80)
Not nice. Check you've got life insurance beforehand. Start below a
prominent pedestal 12 metres up, 3 metres left of a chimney (*April Fools*).
Gain the pedestal via the obvious line. From its top, traverse right to a slim
corner in the headwall and climb it to the top.

Yew Tree Wall

This buttress is the continuation of the Ginsberg Wall at road level, and is
opposite Stepped Wall. **Descent** is made to the right.

April Fools   27 metres   Severe   4a ††   (3.4.70)
A dirty joke. The obvious chimney, which effectively separates Yew Tree
Wall from Ginsberg Wall.

A pre-placed rope is best used to descend from the next three routes. All pull
up onto a ledge 6 metres below the top which used to contain a good tree.
Now there is only a scrawny bush and the exit groove is vegetated.

Prince Andrew   20 metres   E3   5b   (19.11.95)
The thin orange groove right of the chimney. A very serious lead with
dubious rock and poor protection. Start at the foot of the chimney of *April
Fools*.

Trend rightwards into the groove. Follow the groove past a highly-suspect block and pull over a fragile bulge with difficulty. Climb up over a small overhang; then continue on good holds to a ledge containing a bush. Descend as described above.

William in Chile   20 metres   E2 5c   (10.12.00)
Very enjoyable climbing on small positive holds up the blunt arête right of the chimney. Start 2 metres right of the chimney.
Climb direct onto the rib and follow it (sustained) to a step left into *Prince Andrew* at the small overhang. Continue on good holds to a ledge containing a bush. Descend as described above.

Gobbledegook   20 metres   E2 5b 🌣 ☀   (12.10.80)
The orange wall and open groove 5 metres right of the chimney provides an interesting pitch when clean.
A holdless wall guards entry to the open groove; climb the rib of *William in Chile* for 4 metres and then move right into the groove. Follow the groove to a peg and move left and up to a ledge containing a bush on the left. Descend as described above, or finish up a groove in the headwall.
Direct Start E3 6b † (10.12.00). From the left end of the obvious pedestal, make a long thin move up the 'holdless wall' to gain jugs in the base of the groove. A reasonable *RP* protects.

Another Dick on the Wall   27 metres   E5 6b   (4.12.94)
The same old dreary story: poor gear, suspect rock, and hard moves. Start 2 metres left of the crack of *Pilferer*.
Pull up onto a shattered pedestal. Step right and reach up right to an out-of-sight (as opposed to out-a-sight) bucket in a small groove (vital *Rock 3*). Take the groove direct with difficulty to reach a ledge (traversed by *Pilferer*). Step right to climb a thin crack in the rib and finish up the little groove of *Pilferer*.

Pilferer   27 metres   E2 5c   (10.1.76)
Well worth doing – if clear of ivy. Start at the crack in the left arête of the smooth corner.
Climb strenuously up the crack and move up into a scoop. Make hard moves to gain better holds and climb the ramp on the left before a swing left at a small roof leads to a tree stump. Finish as for *Gobbledegook*.

Turkey Trot   25 metres   E5 6a   (4.10.80)
The smooth corner left of centre of the buttress. A nigh-on impeccable climb, with seriously deficient protection, that would be a classic if it were on Chee Tor. The loss of holds at 9 metres has bumped the grade up one notch.
Climb directly up the corner (past 'wobble potential' at 9 metres) to reach a good ledge at half height. Continue up the slender and only slightly safer corner (peg) to tree belays just below the top.

Croaking in Woking   25 metres   E4 6a   (17.11.85/6.12.86)
A direct line up the buttress and headwall between the grooves of *Turkey Trot* and *The Knack*.
Climb, with a peculiar move over a small roof, to gain a good block hold. Pull up and right onto a small ledge and continue more easily to the horizontal break. Pull over the roof onto the headwall, and finish either straight up or diagonally rightwards.

The Knack   27 metres   E3 6a   (29.3.84)
A convoluted pitch which attempts to find the easiest way over the roof above the shorter, right-hand corner. Bold for the grade.
Climb the corner for 5 metres and trend leftwards below the roofs to their left end. Place a good runner in the small corner on the left (on *Croaking in Woking*) and make blind moves rightwards along the lip of the roof to good holds. Pull round to finish up the more amiable groove on the right.

Tell It like It Is   20 metres   E5 6b   (17.11.85)
But the truth can hurt. Start below the crack in the right wall of *The Knack*. Climb the thin crack (*in-situ* thread), and continue more delicately to a 10mm bolt below the roofs. Extend for a smooth flat hold on the lip, or make a concoction of awkward moves leftwards below the roof and reach over to the same hold (peg with sling). Lunge for a jug on *The Knack* (*in-situ* wire) and finish up its short groove.
Variation
A Simple Tale   20 metres   E5 6b   (19.12.86)
Desperate. From the bolt below the roof, stretch around right into the groove and climb it past a further 10mm bolt (with sling) to the top.

Mr X   20 metres   E3 5c   (4.10.80)
Climb the arête between *The Knack* and *Yew Tree Groove*, starting up its left-hand side and finishing on the right. Fairly nasty.

Yew Tree Groove   15 metres   Very Severe 4c   (21.12.72)
Climb the short, deep groove at the right-hand end of the buttress to the yew tree (kindly left intact by the demolitionists).

No Bolts Please, We're British!   12 metres   Severe 4a   (16.2.94)
Climb the wall to the right of *Yew Tree Groove*.

Long Wall

The second tier of Pinnacle Bay rises from the head of a grassy slope above the first tier. From the stepped arête of *Genesis*, the wall slants downwards for 120 metres to a short gully, which separates it from the buttress where the three higher tiers merge. A path, the second path branching rightwards from Shoot Gully (20 metres above the rock-catch fence), runs beneath the entire length of the cliff and is currently the only permitted means of access.

The crag had a lot going for it in the 80s when extensive development left a veritable gold mine of middle-grade routes. Cleaning operations in the late

Pinnacle Bay

11	Exiled!	E3
12	Warlord	E3
13	Every Step of the Way	E6
14	Brainbiter	E2

15	Winter Chimney	HS
16	Cool Hand Luke	E2
17	The Perfect Game	E3
18	Seventy-foot Chimney	VS

1	Exodus	HVS
2	Blurred Vision	HVS

3	Brusque	E5
4	Black Night	S
5	Sloe Gin	HS
6	Phantom Gardener	HVS
7	The Demon Trundler	HVS
8	Pure Joy	E3
9	Megalomania	HVS
10	Tremorgans	E2

Genesis

LONG WALL

Access from Shoot Gully

SPACEHUNTER WALL

Gully of Creeps

Terrace Gully

19

Castle Rocks

Approach to Spacehunter Wall ←

19 Spacehunter	E6	
20 Abdominal Cave-in	E4	
21 Geronimo	S	
22 Stone Warrior	E4	

23 It Must Be the Russians	E2	
24 Doomwatch	E1	
25 Kephalonia	E5	
26 Rape of the Sabine Women	E3	

NB Dashed sections of 23 and 24 are banned.

SUNSET BUTTRESS

BURMESE WALL

MADRUGADA WALL

Great Unwashed Gully

Gully of Creeps

90s changed all of that, removing considerable quantities of loose rock (including some dodgy blocks on the routes), as well as the tree belays at the top of the cliff. By 2003 some of the trees had grown back enough to provide substantial belays. An alternative is nut belays in the rock wall at the back of the large terrace above the cliff. Many of the routes will require recleaning before an ascent.

Descent: Either abseil from trees or walk up an easy and solid goat track to the terrace beneath the *Warlord* wall, from which Shoot Gully is gained.

Mea Culpa   18 metres   E2 5b   (18.10.92)
This tackles the sharp arête at the left end of the wall. Start easily, surmount the first bulge on its left-hand side, and then take the second bulge direct.

Exodus   20 metres   Hard Very Severe 5a   (16.2.80)
Climb the groove and crack 5 metres right of the arête to the top. Abseil from trees on the left of the ridge.

Genesis   101 metres   Hard Very Severe   (15.1.61/1973)
A long and disjointed climb of some antiquity which follows the great stepped arête overlooking Shoot Gully. A number of variations are possible. A determined party should be able to handle the grassier parts.
1 20m. 5a. Climb the initial groove of *Exodus* for a few metres but trend diagonally rightwards up a scoop to a bulge (peg). A long reach up to the right gains a huge hold and a grassy crack. Follow the crack and the corner above to large ledges on the ridge.
2 33m. Scramble up the crest of the ridge to block belays on the large terrace above.
3 24m. 4b. Climb the arête above via a broken groove in its right-hand side; move right after 8 metres into another groove which leads to a notch in the arête.
4 24m. The ridge above leads easily to the top.

The next three routes all finish at a decapitated tree that has been reborn; it provides a solid abseil point.

Needs of the Many   20 metres   E2 5c †   (6.3.2003)
Start 10 metres right of the arête, at the front of the protruding section of this wall.
Climb a line of weakness above a low flake-crack, and move up left onto a ledge at 7 metres. Work up right into a rightward-slanting crack and follow it to its close (good wires, though the crack feels hollow). Make steep moves slightly left into a recess, and take the flake above to ledges. Trend right to the tree.

Spock Philosophy   20 metres   E5 6a †   (9.3.2003)
Serious stuff: fingery climbing with specific gear placements on rock that likes to be treated tenderly. Start a metre right of the previous route.
Climb to a good break at 5 metres. Continue straight up through bulging rock (twisted wire in pocket) with committing moves to gain a tiny vertical

crack – wire placement! Technical moves above, without recourse to the crack on the left, lead up to some long moves past the right end of a small overhang. Climb easily to the tree.

The following four routes start next to a small, partially dismantled pedestal block 15 metres right of the arête.

The Burner   20 metres   Hard Very Severe 5b   (12.7.83)
Climb the steep wall just to the left of the pedestal and right of a crumbled peg to the obvious layback crack. Follow the crack briskly before moving leftwards at its top to finish at the tree.

Blurred Vision   20 metres   Hard Very Severe 5a   (14.9.85)
The right-facing groove above the small pedestal block; clearly a fine line. Climb up above the pedestal to the corner. Follow the corner to a roof, which is avoided on the left.

Floaters   20 metres   E4 5c †   (8.3.86)
The smooth wall to the right of the corner of *Blurred Vision*. Scant protection but good rock. Start 2 metres right of the pedestal.
Climb the wall to a superb jug in a scoop. Levitate up the wall (peg) to a short groove. Pull over the bulge above (*in-situ* thread) and trend leftwards to the exit of *Blurred Vision*.

Creeping Weakness   20 metres   E3 5c ††   (14.10.85)
A case of mounting fear. Start as for *Floaters*.
Climb the wall for 3 metres, as for *Floaters*, but then make bold moves up and rightwards to the base of a groove. Progress up the groove and the bulge above on excellent holds, and finish up the wall to the right of a small overhang.

Show Some Restraint   20 metres   E1 5a/b †   (14.9.85)
Twenty metres from the left-hand arête of the wall, a shrub-filled groove leads to a big scar below a tree stump (where a gigantic flake used to be). This route climbs flake cracks to the left.
Climb the flake crack just left of the groove and move right to gain a short corner. Break out leftwards along a line of undercut flakes to finish.

The gigantic flake of **Fellatio** (12.10.85) is lying on the terrace behind you: not too harsh a blow for climbers.

Further right the path drops down below an impressive section with stepped overhangs at two-thirds height.

'Any Moment Now'   15 metres   E2 5c   (8.3.86)
A line up the steep orange wall left of the stepped overhangs.
From down to the left of the overhangs, climb straight up the centre of the wall with mounting difficulties to gain a small ledge and an old abseil station.

Tusk   25 metres   E3 6a †   (13.3.2003)
One awkward section only. Start below the left end of the stepped roofs.

Climb straight up to an angular flake in a slight groove. Gain a vertical slot above. Traverse left 2 metres beneath the left-hand roofs using parallel flake cracks to their left. Climb the left-hand crack and then climb diagonally rightwards right fairly easily to the top. (It is also possible to continue leftwards to the single 8mm bolt 'lower-off' of *Any Moment Now*.)

The Ides   25 metres   E4 6a †   (15.3.2002)
Some really good climbing through the stepped roofs. Follow *Tusk* to the angular flake and slot. Reach a series of slopers right of the first roof, and problematically gain an undercut beneath the second (peg). A few energetic moves over the roof on big holds and easier ground is reached.

Brusque   20 metres   E5 6b   (8.3.86)
An uncompromising pitch, the hardest on Long Wall, which heads for the open groove in the stepped overhangs. Start below a thin crack leading up to the roofs.
Move up the wall and follow the thin crack to the first roof. Layback up to a good hold, step awkwardly left, and (with protection from precariously placed small wires in a vertical crack) surmount the second roof. Pull over the limb-tangling third roof, and climb more easily up the open groove to an exit on the right.

One of the crag's most distinct landmarks is the dirty groove and crack in the centre of the wall.

Ice Cool   20 metres   E1 5b † ✿   (24.11.85)
To the left of the groove and crack in the centre of the cliff is a short corner commencing at 10 metres.
From the base of the groove, climb up and leftwards to a crack, which is followed to the short corner. Move up until a leftward traverse leads to the finish of *Brusque*.

Black Night   20 metres   Severe 4a ✿   (27.10.85)
The groove and crack in the centre of the cliff.

Black Magic Woman   25 metres   Hard Very Severe 5a † †† (27.11.85)
To the right of *Black Night* the path drops down below a narrow rounded buttress characterized by a flake-line in its upper half.
Pick a line up the buttress and then make difficult moves to gain the flake. Climb the flake and continue more easily on the left to the top.

White Lady   25 metres   E1 5c   (14.10.85)
The hanging corner 6 metres right of *Black Night* is a captivating line. Start below a short, rightward-curving corner-crack.
Follow the crack rightwards to a ledge below the undercut corner. Pull over the roof and climb the corner (peg), before stepping left to finish on the arête.

Sloe Gin   25 metres   Hard Severe 4a   (12.10.85)
The impressive right-facing corner. Climb an initial flake crack to an overhang below the corner. Pull strenuously round and climb the corner to the top.

Heirloom   25 metres   E3 5c † 🏵 (18.1.90)
Climb the wall, roof, and slab immediately to the right of the corner of *Sloe Gin*.

Live Dust   25 metres   Severe † 🏵 (27.10.85)
Climb the vegetated wide flake crack 6 metres to the right of *Sloe Gin*, and move leftwards to flakes in the wall. Trend right to the top.

Right of the corner of *Sloe Gin* are two excellent roof-capped corners; both come equipped with a full quota of plant-life, however.

Phantom Gardener   25 metres   Hard Very Severe 5a 🏵 (15.2.81)
The left-hand corner can't wait for the phantom. A sustained pitch. Climb the corner, move leftwards at 10 metres, and continue directly, passing the roof on its left, to the top.

Ecocritical   25 metres   E5 6a † (24.1.87)
You've got to be green to get on this one. The ominously blank wall between the pair of roof-capped corners: serious and satisfying.
Climb directly onto a projecting ledge 5 metres up (*in-situ* thread). Step up, and make committing moves, with a useful sidehold out left, to a thin grey flake-line endowed with better holds (peg). Climb straight up the flake to an overhang (*in-situ* thread). Traverse leftwards to a small groove, and climb it and the wall on the right to finish.

The Demon Trundler   25 metres   Hard Very Severe 5a 🏵 (8.9.68)
Behind trees and under vegetation, this was once a 'hard and gloomy' climb. It could become a climb of character and interest again.
Climb the right-hand corner via an awkward constriction to a niche below an overhang. Pull over on good holds and climb the corner to the top.

Demonic Arête   25 metres   E1 5b (17.10.85)
A very fine pitch with a poorly protected start and an exciting finish. The route takes the right arête of *The Demon Trundler*'s corner.
From the foot of the corner, climb diagonally rightwards to a narrow groove in the arête. Climb the groove (peg) and continuation flake to an overhang, which gives a few sensational moves before an exit can be made, as for *The Demon Trundler*, on the left.

Candy 'O'   25 metres   E2 5b (18.10.85)
The rock is better than it looks. Start 2 metres right of *The Demon Trundler*. Climb up to a short groove. Move up towards the arête and then right to gain the obvious undercut flake. Pull up right to good holds above the bulge (peg) and continue up the flake crack and corner above to the top.

The final section of the wall, before it terminates in the gully at its right-hand end, comprises a very steep buttress with overhangs at half height, vanquished by the next route.

Pure Joy   27 metres   E3 6a   (27.11.85)
A challenging and strenuous route that climbs the rightward-stepped
overhanging groove in the left-hand side of the buttress.
Climb a vague groove to the roofs (peg). Pull leftwards into a short
bottomless groove (peg) and battle up and then right under the overhangs
to their end. Follow the groove above carefully to the top.

Big Deal   25 metres   Very Severe 4b ❀   (15.10.85)
An imposing lead for the grade; 12 metres left of the gully at the right end
of the wall is a groove with a roof-capped niche at 8 metres.
Climb steeply up the groove and take the bulge on its left to the niche.
Continue up the crack out to the left, but move right to finish.

Kaput Four Fingers   20 metres   E3 6a/b   (27.3.88)
Highly technical climbing up the smooth pillar to the right of *Big Deal*
makes this an enjoyable route.
Climb straight up the face of the pillar without deviation to reach better
holds where the angle eases. Continue to exit slightly leftwards. Two pegs
and an 8mm bolt.

Misty Morning   27 metres   E2 5c   (18.10.85)
Delightful climbing and situations, but far from inescapable. Six metres left
of the gully is a short, steep flake crack.
Climb the crack to an overhang and pull up with difficulty to a sloping
ledge beneath a second roof (peg). Move up to good holds and, ignoring
the easy groove above, follow a line of thin flakes out leftwards onto the
wall. At their end, finish up the wall above.

Beyond the gully at the end of Long Wall is the base of a buttress that rises
fairly consistently for 90 metres to the top of the Gorge. The buttress is divided
horizontally into a series of steep walls by narrow vegetated terraces at half
and three-quarters height, giving escape walk-offs if needed. Unfortunately,
despite being stripped of their cloaks of ivy, the following four routes don't
quite live up to expected standards of hygiene. Short of major abseil cleaning
sessions, some ground-up pioneering spirit 'big wall style' may be in order to
re-open the routes. It could even catch on.

Approach from the path leading to the right-hand end of Long Wall.
(Neighbouring climbs on the upper part of the buttress that commence from
either of the two higher terraces are described under the Upper Tiers
section.)

Nagging Doubts   40 metres   E1 5b †† ❀   (12.4.81)
The left arête of the lower wall which overlooks the gully. Start below an
obvious crack, just right of the gully.
1 20m. 5b. Gain the crack and climb it with difficulty to a tree stump on
the left which overlooks the gully.
2 20m. 4c. Move right to a groove, and climb it to the arête. Follow the
arête to the lower terrace below the upper tiers. Walk off left below the
Warlord Wall, or continue up one of a selection of equally vegetated routes.

Megalomania   98 metres   Hard Very Severe   †† ✿(21.11.70/11.1.75)
Potentially a really good route with varied climbing, and a big sense of
scale for the grade. The top two pitches are not too vegetated. Start 12
metres right of the gully, at an obvious grassy flake crack.
1 18m. 4b. Climb the crack and groove to a large tree stump.
2 25m. 4c. Climb the crack behind the belay to a bulge and ledge
above. Continue up the crack until it is possible to traverse leftwards to pull
up to the lower terrace and belays in a shallow cave.
3 25m. 5a. Climb the overhanging crack and groove rising out of the
right-hand side of the cave. Traverse delicately rightwards just above the
level of a peg to gain a shallow groove in the wall. Follow this to belays on
the upper terrace.
4 30m. 5b. To the right of the steep arête above (*Babylon*) is a fine
groove. Climb a technical wall slightly rightwards to enter the groove (peg)
which is followed at a sustained and exhilarating standard to the top.

Tremorgans   98 metres   E2 †† ✿   (13.3.71/29.9.83)
An interesting route, harder and much more sustained than its neighbours.
1 18m. 4b. Climb the flake crack and groove of *Megalomania*, but bear
rightwards to a stance on a grassy pedestal.
2 25m. 5b. Move right to a shallow groove and climb it past a ledge and
shrub. Continue up the crack above to the lower terrace.
3 25m. 5c. Above the belay is a narrow tower with a thin crack in its
centre. Climb up to the crack and follow it steeply until a dynamic layback
gains big holds. Climb straight up to the upper terrace for stump and nut
belays. (The crack on the right of the small tower provides an easier
alternative at 4c.)
4 30m. 5b. In the centre of the wall above is a thin, broken crack and
groove. Climb the crack and groove until a tricky mantelshelf gains a wide
crack above. Finish up the crack.

Immunity Syndrome   95 metres   E1 †† ✿   (5.6.71/20.4.75)
Another route in the expedition class, with potential to offer a variety of fine
climbing on a good line. Some rock has been removed in the vicinity of
pitch 2. Start towards the right end of the wall, below a groove leading to
a large yew stump 6 metres up.
1 20m. 4a. Climb the groove towards the tree stump until a rising
traverse rightwards leads to belays in the left-hand side of a broad gully
(Terrace Gully).
2 20m. 4c. Make an awkward step up to the left above a bulge to a
ledge beneath two steep cracks. Start up the left-hand crack and follow it
to a small roof. Now step right and follow the right-hand crack to the lower
terrace.
3 25m. 5a. In the right end of the wall above nestles a handsome
groove. Climb the groove with interest (peg) and move left to a ledge. Step
back right and climb the crack to the upper terrace. Belay beneath a deep
6-metre-high crack.

4 30m. 5b. High in the upper wall is a narrow chimney. Climb the crack to a bulge. Work rightwards with difficulty for 2 metres and make steep moves up the wall to enter the chimney. Struggle up this to the top.

A short distance to the right of the starts of the preceding routes is quite a large cave at the base of Terrace Gully. The cave contains a large tell-tale mound of earth, behind which some goats will normally be digesting the day's ivy.

Bamboleo   9 metres   E3 6a † ✿   (28.10.90)
Climb out of the left-hand side of the cave into a triangular niche. Cut right and follow a crack to an old abseil station.

Abdominal Cave-in   12 metres   E4 6b † ✿   (28.10.90)
Gain a crack in the right-hand side of the cave roof directly. Undergut around the roof (8mm bolt) to reach better holds over the lip. Continue easily to an old abseil station. Strenuous for the tall!

The Upper Tiers

'On the upper ledges nailed boots are useful and an ice axe might be comforting.'   (W K Marples & R Bates, 1931)

Right of the *Genesis* ridge, the upper tiers combine to form a magnificent, overhanging wall, the Warlord Wall. To its right, the bay is divided by the upper terrace into two walls. The lower, which is often grassy and less steep, is the least worthy of the two. The upper is where the quality climbing is to be found and runs to a series of cracks, chimneys and arêtes – now more striking with the ivy curtains down. A shallow cave 80 metres along the lower terrace is visited by *Megalomania*, and the wall further right hosts other climbs that started two pitches below at the base of Pinnacle Bay. A useful reference point in the upper tier is the deep corner-line of *Seventy Foot Chimney*, which is located three-quarters of the way rightwards along the upper terrace.

Approach:
1. For two-pitch routes starting from the lower terrace, ascend Shoot Gully, turning right onto the lower terrace at the second main crossroads (two-thirds of the way up). A word of warning: Tree clearance and the banking-up of the terrace with debris has made traversing it a more delicate and exposed affair: even the goats fear the traverse of the terrace beyond *Dianthus*.
2. For the upper tier pitches, abseil from the cliff-top. Alternatively it is possible to approach the upper terrace by descending the gully between the two pinnacles of Castle Rocks (Gully of Creeps) and walking along the rock ledge beneath Spacehunter Wall. This is only suitable for routes right of and including *Seventy-foot Chimney*, since beyond it the terrace narrows and steepens uncomfortably.

Beneath the start of the terrace, just right of the *Genesis* ridge, is a rectangular wall with a huge white lichen patch, visible from the road. The

Stoned (E6, first ascent)
Castle Rocks
Climber: Martin Crocker
Photo: Carl Ryan

The Common Start (XS), Sunset Buttress
Climber: Martin Crocker (in 1973)   Photo: Dave Ford

next two climbs take this wall. They provide excellent climbing on good, compact rock. Approach them by abseil or by a reasonable goat track which descends to the top of Long Wall from 50 metres along the terrace.

Exiled!   18 metres   E3 6a   (3.11.85)
Climb the centre of the wall past a good flake-hold to a horizontal break (*in-situ* thread and good wires). A delicate section on tinies leads to a second break. Swing left into a shallow groove, which is followed to ledges at the top.

Disenchantment   18 metres   E2 5b †   (13.03.03)
Climb a narrow groove in the right-hand side of the wall, and pockets above to a break. Step up to reach good fingerholds in the white patch, and then take a shallow groove past a small sapling (sling) to ledges at the top.

Warlord   53 metres   E3   (11.65/26.6.78)
An impressive climb, wrought from a long and turbulent history. It takes the left-facing flake-line and crack in the left-hand side of the dome-shaped wall. The climbing is very sustained and the positions superb. Start 12 metres right of the *Genesis* ridge, below the flake-line.
1 25m. 5c. Climb the wall, past two breaks, into a groove. Follow the groove and the flake-line, which curves gently leftwards past several pegs. At its close, swing right to peg and nut belays at a small foot-ledge.
2 28m. 6a. Climb up above the belay into a shallow groove. Climb the groove to the deep, half-height break and move up left onto the upper wall. Continue directly up the wall and groove to a bulge. Make a difficult move right to start the obvious bulging crack and climb it and its continuation on the right to easier ground and the top.

Every Step of the Way   54 metres   E6 †   (16.9.84/22.2.86)
In its day, one of the most radical bolt-free routes on southern limestone. Underestimate it at your own expense! High up in the centre of the wall above the break is a leaning groove-system: the second pitch. Start 18 metres right of the *Genesis* ridge at the base of a long flake crack.
1 27m. 6a. Climb the crack and groove, which steepens and narrows before closing down beneath a smooth wall. Move up and leftwards to a small roof and pull around right into a shallow groove, which is followed for a few moves before an exit leftwards is made on jugs. Peg and *in-situ* thread belays just below the break.
2 27m. 6b. Swing left onto a ledge (peg). Climb the leaning groove (peg) to its end and then swing out right (peg) to better holds in a short crack in the overhung niche. From undercuts in the bulge (peg on the left), reach up for a good sidehold and continue over the final bulge (peg) to a resting-ledge. Finish up a crack and groove, exiting leftwards at the top.

The next two routes start from the first stance of *Every Step of the Way*, best reached as for that route or (during times when the long seepage line appears on its first pitch) by a 'keep bouncing' abseil from a good thread at the top of the wall.

Doc Martin's   27 metres   E6 6b   (15.10.88)
A super-steep and exposed pitch which stays free of seepage.
Climb up leftwards to an enormous jammed block in the break (*in-situ*
thread). Pull up onto the wall and move up and left (*in-situ* thread and
8mm bolt) to a short crack (peg). Sprint up the now dramatically leaning
wall and rush slightly rightwards (two 8mm bolts) to good jugs and a peg.
From a shattered niche above, cross leftwards (*in-situ* thread) to finish up
the top crack of *Warlord*.

Cerebral Paralysis   27 metres   E6 6b †   (26.11.89)
A mind-numbingly hard and sportingly-bolted derivative of *Brainbiter*.
Move right to the foot of an open, undercut groove. Climb into the groove
on the right (peg), but move back left (8mm bolt) into a much steeper
groove. Some very thin bridging (8mm bolt) gains good undercuts below
the capping roof. Climb diagonally rightwards from the roof (8mm bolt) to
reach a ledge on *Brainbiter* (peg). Climb the crack above to the top, as for
Brainbiter.

Brainbiter   54 metres   E2 (2 pts aid) (E4)   (13.12.69/15.10.88)
A 70s and 80s favourite, banned in the 90s, but destined to return to
stardom in the Third Millennium. Though free-climbed at E4 6b, the use of
two traditional aid points on pitch 2 keeps the route at a consistent E2.
Some large pieces of rock have been levered off the route, most notably a
10-metre-high pinnacle on the first pitch. Start 25 metres right of the
Genesis ridge, where the path is narrow, at a twin-pronged flake
embedded in the ground.
1 27m. 5b. Climb a short steep wall to an overhung ledge. Move left to
the base of the groove-line and climb it with increasing difficulty until a
crack leads to a ledge (the sad remains of 'the seahorse pinnacle'). Climb
the wall on the right to reach the extreme left-hand end of the upper
terrace.
2 27m. 5b. Use a threaded sling in a roof to place a wire (two *in-situ*
threads adjacent). Use this to gain a high pocket and move up and slightly
left to a horizontal break (peg). Climb a shallow groove past a deep slot to
a ledge on the left (peg). Move left and climb the obvious crack and
continuation groove on improving holds in a fine position to the top.

Hall of Fame   27 metres   E5 6b †   (23.2.03)
Technical face climbing on compact rock. The route takes the left-hand
side of the smooth face right of the second pitch of *Brainbiter*. Approach by
abseil.
Climb the overhang and pocketed wall of *Brainbiter* free! From the deep
slot, move up a metre, and then stretch up and right for a good hold
(*in-situ* thread). A second good hold up and right gets you truly established
on the compact face. Reach a thin crack above and follow it direct with
difficulty until some layaways out right bring a horizontal break to hand
(peg). Move up to a jug; then take the rib above to the top.

Medusa 54 metres E3 (17.9.78)

The inviting grey wall above the left end of the upper terrace provides a fine second pitch on excellent rock which is best approached by abseil. The first pitch has been affected by rock removal and is vegetated. Start as for *Brainbiter*.

1 27m. 5b. Climb up to the small overhung ledge. Make a hard move over the bulge above past a peg to better holds in a shallow groove. Follow the groove to the new ledge on *Brainbiter*. Climb the wall above to the left end of the terrace.

2 27m. 6a. Move up into a hanging flake and onto the smooth wall (peg). Climb straight up (two pegs) on surprising finger-jugs and slots, until a long, hard reach leads to a small ledge at the right edge of the wall. Move up to a break and finger-traverse leftwards along it (peg) to more broken ground. Finish up an easier groove.

Skid Row 66 metres E2 †† (25.10.73)

An exposed girdle of the *Warlord* wall, now scarcely worthwhile since the best approach to the substantive, second pitch (Hard Very Severe) is by abseil. Resident goats are still working on this as a link-up to their track between Shoot Gully and the top of Sunset Buttress — watch the press.

1 30m. 5b. Follow *Brainbiter* pitch 1 to the break, but traverse left for 3 metres to peg and *in-situ* thread belays on *Every Step of the Way*.

2 18m. 5a. Swing left onto a ledge (peg) and hand traverse left along the break to the point where it closes. Pull over a small roof to a ledge and nut belays.

3 18m. 5a. Climb the crack above until a step right can be made into a groove which is followed to tree belays. Scrambling remains.

The February Risings 54 metres E1 (2.70/28.10.83)

1 27m. 5b. Follow *Medusa* to the base of the shallow groove above the bulge. Now traverse rightwards, rising slightly, to another groove. Climb the groove to nut belays in a short corner at the back of the upper terrace.

2 27m. 5a. Climb the corner behind the belay to the foot of a steep crack. Follow the crack to its end; then step left and move up to a narrow corner. Climb the corner and accompanying flake crack to a steep grassy exit.

The remaining routes climb to the right of the Warlord Wall; the first starts at an open grassy corner 35 metres right of the *Genesis* ridge (a quarter-moon roof 10 metres up the corner's left wall aids identification).

Eddy Grundy 54 metres Very Severe † (28.10.83)

1 27m. 4b. Climb the corner – full of grass.

2 27m. 4c. Climb the wide crack and system of grooves behind the belay.

Winter Chimney 54 metres Hard Severe (2.70)

Lurid antics in the eye-catching deep chimney in the upper tier. It is probably better to approach the second pitch by abseil.

1 27m. 4b. Climb the corner of *Eddy Grundy*.

2 27m. 4a. Climb up into the chimney and emerge into the light just below the top. Finish to the right.

Dianthus   54 metres   E2   (28.10.83)
Biodiversity rules! Here is the route of the wild flower, the Cheddar Pink, as safeguarded by climbers for the nation. Start below an elegant white corner in the right-hand side of the arête, 6 metres right of *Eddy Grundy*.
1 27m. 5b. Follow the corner delicately until, near the top, one is forced rightwards onto the rib. Continue up the shallow groove above to the upper terrace.
2 27m. 5b. Above the belay and to the right of the deep chimney is a vague arête. Climb it via a groove immediately to its right, and then trend up and leftwards to finish on the arête itself.

The Usual Pornography   52 metres   Hard Very Severe ✿ (16.11.83)
Uncensored dirt and filth – even after the big clean-up! Start below a groove 4 metres right of *Dianthus*.
1 25m. 4b. Climb the groove to the upper terrace.
2 27m. 5a. Climb the narrow chimney on the right until a move left can be made to a parallel crack near the top of the pinnacle-flake. Climb the crack to the top.

In the centre of the upper tier is a clean conical face, with oft-vegetated cracks to either side. Approach the routes here by abseil from the cliff-top. The first two climbs take the arête left of the conical face.

Blockbuster   30 metres   E2 5b † ✿   (3.8.83)
A poor and loose pitch. Start 6 metres right of the top of the first, corner pitch of *Dianthus*. Climb cracks in the left-hand side of the arête.

Cool Hand Luke   30 metres   E2 5c ✿   (5.4.81)
Quite a good climb up the most prominent crack in the right-hand side of the arête, now relieved of its most precarious blocks. Start as for *Blockbuster*.
Climb over a small roof into the crack. Follow the steep crack and then the arête to the top.

The Perfect Game   30 metres   E3 5c ✿   (7.4.81)
A fine, solid, wall climb that feels serious on sight. Start below the centre of the conical face, above a narrowing in the terrace (awkward belays). Climb the wall and move slightly leftwards to a small roof. Trend rightwards (peg) and make difficult moves to better holds in a groove. Climb the groove to a point where the wall tapers into a blunt arête. Some committing moves up the arête lead directly to a break below the final nose. Either digress left with a leap for a tree, or finish over the nose.

Planet Perfecto   30 metres   E5 6a †   (22.2.03)
A brilliantly engaging face climb, one of the best of its ilk in the Gorge. Take plenty of small wires and draws. Start below a thin vertical crack

straight above a narrowing in the terrace (the first pitch of *Seventy Foot Chimney*).
Climb the thin crack to ledges. Reach good hidden fingerholds above and (with a good wire for protection on the right) gain a line of spaced finger pockets slightly right (peg). Take the pockets, and then pull out left onto a rickety flake. Move over a bulge to a small resting ledge. Continue straight up, delicately, and proceed past a peg to larger holds in a groove. Climb the groove and exit left past an obvious, but not obviously solid, horn.

Back on the lower terrace, the terrace steepens worryingly, and a cautious traverse gains the next route.

Seventy Foot Chimney   47 metres   Very Severe   (1972)
An odd name for what is, imperially speaking, a 90-foot corner! A good, and well-protected corner-climb, best approached by abseil. About 60 metres right of the *Genesis* ridge are vegetated cracks that form a break in the lower tier.
1 20m. Grovel up mind-warping vegetation to the upper terrace and a belay below the big corner on the right (or approach by abseil).
2 27m. 4b. Climb the corner using a variety of tactics, most of which are wholly strenuous.

Ten metres further right, along the lower terrace, is a shallow cave visited by *Megalomania*.

In Memoriam   55 metres   Very Severe ❀   (14.4.73/12.4.81)
The first pitch is plastered with grass; the second is probably climbable.
1 25m. 4c. Climb the thin crack 7 metres left of the shallow cave, passing a triple-pointed roof on its left.
2 30m. 4c. Climb the right-hand of two parallel off-width cracks above (6 metres left of *Seventy Foot Chimney*).

The Squint   57 metres   E2 †† ❀   (9.10.75)
The first pitch has been severely affected by rock removal. Start in the shallow cave.
1 27m. 5c. Take the left-hand crack out of the cave.
2 30m. 5a. Five metres left along the terrace, climb the left-hand of two off-width cracks (right of the conical wall of *The Perfect Game*).
Variation
1a Smart Combination 30m. Hard Very Severe 5a (21.2.81). Climb the grassy crack 3 metres left of the shallow cave.

The next two routes take the slender pillar left of the corner of *Seventy Foot Chimney* in the upper tier. Approach by abseil down this route and take a belay on a sloping ledge below a flake-corner 9 metres up its left wall.

Ban's Off   20 metres   E3 5c †   (16.2.03)
Steep and technical with good small-wire protection. Step left and climb
the rib via a thin crack and slim groove. At 15 metres, flat blocky holds
lead to a large sloping ledge just below the top. It makes sense to pull out
on the abseil rope from here.

The Dead Cold   20 metres   E4 6a †   (16.2.03)
Climb the rib on the left for 3 metres; good wire above. Move right to a
pocket, below a thin crack in a smooth wall. Hard moves up the crack lead
to larger holds. Take a flake crack on the left and, from its top, swing up
and left onto the front of the pillar. Finish up the last 5 metres of *Ban's Off*.

Both the following climbs on the upper tier are reached by abseiling down
Seventy Foot Chimney to a tree belay beneath the arête on the right.

In a Blink   30 metres   E3 5c †   (16.2.03)
The left side of the striking arête right of the corner of *Seventy Foot
Chimney*. Good wire protection for the most part, and cams are useful. A
dramatic pitch.
Climb the corner for 5 metres. Step right onto the steep face, and take thin
cracks and slots slightly rightwards to a recessed ledge. Climb a crack in
the left side of the arête until it ends. Continue up the steep committing
face, exiting on the left.

Babylon   30 metres   E5 6a   (19.9.82)
A superb pitch of high atmosphere on the edge of the arête right of
Seventy Foot Chimney, restored in 2003. Though not technically hard for
the grade the climbing is bold and blind.
Climb a shallow groove in the arête to a small block overhang at its close.
Step right (vital *Friend* ½) and grope blindly for a jug high on the arête.
Climb the intricate compact face right of the arête (old peg) to a footledge
on the arête. Layback the smooth rib above to another ledge; junction with
In a Blink. Finish up the steep face of that route, exiting on the left.

Ripping Yarns   57 metres   E3 † ❀   (13.5.80)
An entertaining climb. Start 6 metres right of the shallow cave of
Megalomania and just left of a vegetated groove.
1 27m. 5c. Climb the wall to a narrow roof (peg). Pull over and move up
to another small roof. Move left to a crack and climb it to the upper
terrace. Belay as for *Megalomania*.
2 30m. 5b. Climb shallow grooves on the right for 5 metres and then
work left onto *Megalomania*. Climb that route's left-facing groove for 5
metres to a break which leads right onto the wall. Swing right, pull over a
small overhang (peg), and gain a small ledge. Follow the enjoyable crack
to an exit on the right. (The start and finish of this pitch is shared with
Blagging Louts.)

The remaining four single-pitch routes are on the right-hand buttress of the
upper tier and are approached by abseil from the cliff top.

Blagging Louts   30 metres   E5 6a †   (2.3.03)
A great pitch up the arête right of the top pitch of *Megalomania*, with one
hard and committing section. The gear is reasonable throughout, but don't
try the route if you aren't versatile placing wires. Start from the terrace
beneath the major left-facing groove of *Megalomania*.
Climb shallow grooves on the right and bear rightwards on white rock
(*Flexible Friend 1* useful) to a small overhang (twisted wires in obvious
pockets). Using some large layaways, move up and then make a hard,
long move to a break (peg). Pull over an overhang (peg) to a small ledge.
A good crack now leads enjoyably to an exit on the right.

Reel Empty Feeling   30 metres   E4 6a †   (22.2.03)
Builds in difficulty; high in the grade. Start from the terrace beneath the
narrow chimney (of *Immunity Syndrome*) high in the wall.
Climb a flake groove right of the deep crack of *Immunity Syndrome*, and
then pull up slightly leftwards onto twin jugs below a narrow groove.
Follow the groove to the second of two blind breaks. Make hard,
committing moves over a bulge to some hidden finger-holds in a tiny
groove (peg). Strenuous climbing up the thin crack above gains an easier
flake crack, which leads to the top.

Immortals   30 metres   E4 6a †   (2.3.03)
An extremely interesting climb on a good line; this is the groove system in
the right-hand side of the wall. Low in the grade. Start from the terrace,
about 8 metres left of the back of Terrace Gully.
Climb the groove to a bulge (peg). Bridge up and left (*in-situ* thread), and
then make awkward and strenuous moves into a break on the left.
Re-enter the groove, move up, and then make a hard move right into
another groove. Follow the groove and the narrow corner above to broken
ground. Exit leftwards past ash trees.

Captain Morgan   15 metres   E5 6b †   (31.12.89)
A lot of potent moves distilled into a short measure. Start beneath a
smooth, black wall just left of the back of Terrace Gully.
Climb the black wall past two 8mm bolts and a peg, starting up an
awkward rib and finishing up a rightward-trending groove. Abseil from
trees on the right (cut down!).

Castle Rocks

The upper reaches of Horseshoe Bend, to the east of Sunset Buttress, are
dominated by a series of pinnacles forming a dramatic, serrated skyline. The
largest two pinnacles, which are actually linked to the main slope by narrow
ridges, are bounded by three gullies. The gully to the left that separates the
most impressive pinnacle from Pinnacle Bay is known as Terrace Gully. The
central gully, the Gully of Creeps, is similarly bottomless and runs up

between the two pinnacles. The right-hand and deepest gully, the Great Unwashed Gully, rises the full 100-metre height of Castle Rocks. The wall to its right, which forms the reverse side of Sunset Buttress, extends in a massive dark sheet to a striking arête overhanging the Horseshoe Bend. See page 57 for a general plan of Castle Rocks and page 46 for a map.

The cliff is large and complicated, and though it can remain vegetated in places, it also boasts two of the finest rock walls in the region. With high exposure and a remote feel, the deep and moody atmosphere of the climbing here represents the very soul of the Cheddar experience. All climbs are approached from Shoot Gully or the cliff top.

Access: Climbing is allowed from 1 October until 15 March inclusive. However, the routes *It Must Be the Russians* and *Doomwatch* (first two pitches only), together with all routes on Madrugada Wall from *Madrugada* to *Palo Alto* (Sunset Buttress) inclusive, remain banned. This is because there is no rock-catch fence beneath them, and any loosened rocks could fall directly into the road.

Terrace Gully (Spacehunter Wall)

The climbs of Terrace Gully are located on two walls in its right-hand side, which are the westerly extensions of the upper two tiers of Pinnacle Bay. The lower is an 18-metre-high wall, smooth, dark, and water-worn. The upper wall, Spacehunter Wall, which is the 40-metre east face of the left-hand pinnacle, is as splendid a piece of natural architecture as you can get. Above the narrow catwalk that divides the two tiers, the wall rears up as a neck-straining series of overhangs and bulges throwing its routes right out into 100 metres of space. Fortunately, the cliff is sheltered, quick-drying, and mostly free of seepage. Welcome to a small collection of the best single-pitch limestone routes in the region, and probably the country. Hopefully, good-quality renewed fixed gear will be there to greet you.

Approach the Spacehunter Wall by abseiling from the cliff-top or by scrambling or abseiling down the upper section of the Gully of Creeps between the two pinnacle ridges to the terrace and the rock ledge running between the two walls. There is ample room hereabouts for the most exotic of warm-up routines. The routes on the lower wall can then be reached by a short abseil to the steeply sloping terrace below (stay roped).

The following routes are on the lower wall.

Terrace Gully   15 metres   Severe 4a   (1961)
Definitely not worth the effort to get to it. From the small cave at the base of the gully, pull over a bulge and climb the easy chimney to the bay above.
Variation
The Prime Slime Climb   18 metres   E1 5b †   (26.10.86)
Pull over the bulge as for *Terrace Gully*, but climb the ramp-line in the right wall of the chimney (old *in-situ* threads) to gain the rock ledge.

Little Wing 18 metres E4 6b † (26.10.86)

A direct, yet subtle line up the compact and solid wall to the right of the gully. Start as for *Terrace Gully*.

Swing right from the small cave and pull up to a short crack. Reach up leftwards for pockets and continue directly to jugs over a tiny overlap. Move left and then straight up to the rock ledge. *In-situ* thread, 8mm bolt, and peg.

Make No Mistake 20 metres E4 6a † (2.11.86)

The series of grooves in the gully wall. Start 5 metres down and right of the small cave below *Terrace Gully*.

Climb the groove boldly (*in-situ* thread) to a good crack and runners at 10 metres. Move up (8mm bolt) and push on diagonally rightwards to jugs in the base of the second groove. Follow the groove more easily to the rock ledge.

The next routes are on the upper wall.

Beverley's Wall 40 metres E3 5c † (4.12.83)

A sustained and technical excursion onto the smooth wall forming the left-hand section of the pinnacle face. Start in a terraced bay in the gully and some 6 metres left of the top of the chimney of the route *Terrace Gully*. Climb a narrow corner and the bulge above; then trend rightwards to a good flat ledge below the smoother wall. Climb directly up the wall via a series of thin cracks and grooves until good fingerholds lead diagonally rightwards to easier ground. Scramble to the summit.

Spacehunter 45 metres E6 6b (4.12.83/2.11.85)

An unsung contender for one of the greatest traditional limestone pitches in Britain. This formidable climb forges an enormous, rightward-tending arc up the overhanging pinnacle wall to finish in incredible position above the big strip roofs. Start below the obvious short roof-capped corner in the left-hand side of the stepped, overhanging wall, above the top of the chimney of the route *Terrace Gully*.

Climb straight up the unprotected, bouldery leaning wall (*in-situ* wire at 6 metres) to a resting-place in the short corner. Swing around the arête on the right and climb a short crack (*Friend 2*) to undercuts below a roof (peg). Pull strenuously over using the hanging flake, and continue up rightwards to another rest in a shallow roofed groove. Traverse precariously rightwards (peg) and pull up immediately to good holds on a narrow leftward-slanting ramp. Now reach right to a thin crack in the wall (peg) and climb it and the groove above to easier ground leading to the summit.

Return of the Gunfighter 42 metres E6 6b F7c (17.10.93)

An outstanding sport route, the most sustained pitch of its type in the gorge, and 'one of the best 7cs in Britain'. The route is fully equipped with stainless-steel staple bolts; but be quick on the draw!

Climb the wall 2 metres left of the corner of *Star Spangled Banner*; then take the obviously powerful line through the tiered roofs to reach a projecting jug on *Star Spangled Banner*. Bear rightwards up the open scoop, but then gain jugs at the top of the huge undercut block. Swing right along the top of the block and forge a direct line through bulges to the hand-traverse of *Spacehunter*. Step left and balance straight up the shallow, smooth-walled groove to the capping roof. Swing right and climb the final wall to the *Spacehunter* exit. Twelve bolts and a peg.

Star Spangled Banner   27 metres   E6 6b F7b+   (26.10.86)
A fine companion route to *Spacehunter*, which traces a lower parallel sweeping line starting up the broad, open corner in the centre of the pinnacle face. Some of the fixed gear is old, but the route receives a fair number of ascents. Start at the left end of the rock ledge below the open corner.
Climb the corner to its close and make an awkward stride left to the obvious sharp jug. Move up and right into a shallow, bulging groove and climb it to a gravity-defying, undercut block roof. Undercut wildly rightwards beneath and around the roof until it is possible to climb diagonally rightwards to a resting-place below the upper strip roof on the face. Stretch over and lunge right for a jug, which enables a small groove and the break above to be reached. With back-up, lower off an old abseil station, or belay and move right to follow the top pitch of *Forbidden Zones*. Nine bolts and two pegs; some small wires optional.

SkyScrape   42 metres   E6 6b F7b+   (26.12.89)
An imposing line of fantastic quality. Perhaps the most amenable of the hard routes on the face; largely bolt-protected (but mainly 8mm) and supplied with good resting-places and holds. Aspirant redpointers need take only a few wires for the upper section. Start from the rock ledge, 3 metres right of *Star Spangled Banner*.
Take the smooth lower wall on tiny holds to reach a good ledge. Continue directly to jugs in the roof and pull around leftwards to reach an open groove (junction with *Star Spangled Banner*). Move up to good holds above the enormous undercut block, and progress strenuously up the overhanging scoop to gain a resting-place in the roof-capped groove of *Spacehunter*. Bear leftwards around the roof, and climb straight up the final wall to reach better holds on *Beverley's Wall*, which leads easily to the top. Five bolts and three pegs.

Fornicator Simulator   40 metres   E8 6c F8b   (22.3.70/10.97)
The last major aid climb to be free climbed, with some of the hardest moves in the region. At present, some of the fixed gear is in a poor state (though legalised all-year round climbing would soon put that right). Start from the centre of the rock ledge below the obvious weakness in the wall. Climb easily onto a ledge. Move up to the roof. Undercut around to gain hopeless holds on the face above, and make the move that no-one else can do. Continue up the face to join *Star Spangled Banner*, and follow that route to its old abseil station.

Spacehunter Wall

1	Captain Morgan	E5
2	Beverley's Wall	E3
3	Spacehunter	E6
4	Return of the Gunfighter	F7c
5	Star Spangled Banner	F7b+
6	Fornicator Simulator	F8b
7	Forbidden Zones	E5
8	Rear Entry (top pitch)	E2

Terrace Gully

ABSEIL

Gully of Creeps

Forbidden Zones   39 metres   E5 6a   (12.2.84)

Yet another superb route. After an unnerving start up the right-hand side of
the smooth wall, the climb offers an overdose of exciting climbing through
the roofs. Start from the rock ledge below a long black streak on the wall.

1 27m. 6a. Climb directly for 5 metres and then trend rightwards to a
narrow sloping ledge (poor thread). Now make a series of committing
moves slightly rightwards to a resting-place in a bottomless groove at the
right end of the big roof. Swing out left around the bulge (hidden peg) to
good holds and cruise on up over the next roof (peg) to a small ledge and
peg and nut belays.

2 12m. 5b. Climb the thin crack behind the belay and continue up
leftwards over loose ground to the summit.

Gully of Creeps

This is the central, bottomless gully which deepens above a large, brooding
wall and fans out to form a broad, grassy couloir between the two pinnacles.
The current quality of the climbing on the wall below and to the right of the
gully can only be guessed at. Much of the wall lay beneath ivy for two
decades, and substantial quantities of loose rock have been removed. Some
long and interesting climbs await rediscovery by pioneering teams – now the
ban has been lifted.

This fairly continuous buttress is divided by narrow terraces into three tiers.
The lower is a 45-metre-high wall, the left-hand side of which features three
vertical cracklines. These constitute the starting pitches of a number of climbs
that rise the full height of the cliff. The lofty corner in the right-hand side of the
wall was climbed by the first pitch of *Doomwatch*. The upper tier that forms
the east face of the right-hand pinnacle is divided into two smooth walls by
the second chimney of *Geronimo*, *Stone Warrior*, *Stoned*, and the top pitch of
Doomwatch accept the challenge of the arête of the pinnacle. The climbs
can dry quickly.

The routes that commence on the large, lower wall are reached from Shoot
Gully. Take the second of two paths out of the gully (20 metres above the
rock-catch fence), as for the approach to Long Wall, and continue rightwards,
descending slightly, to the climbs. The routes on the pinnacle walls can be
approached directly by abseil either side of the arête to the underlying terrace,
which is very narrow in places. It is also possible to walk in along the terrace
from left or right, although this will prove very intimidating and exposed,
unless you're a goat.

Rear Entry   97 metres   E2 🏵   (3.10.70/10.11.74)

Returned to its full-height stature following cleaning operations, this climb
finishes on the right arête of the Spacehunter Wall. Start at the base of the
left-most (corner) crackline, which is directly below the deep gully at half
height.

1 22m. 5b. Climb the corner past a huge semi-circular overhang on the left wall and with increasing difficulty (peg) until a bold swing left gains a tree stump.

2 22m. 5a. Climb the corner above; then trend leftwards to belay on a terrace to the left of the deep gully.

3 18m. 4c. Climb a groove in the wall above to tree belays on a large terrace below the final arête.

4 35m. 5b. Climb the groove just to the right of the pinnacle arête to an overhang. Take the overhang on the right to a continuation groove, and follow this until a swing left gains the short final arête and the summit.

The final pitches of the next two routes are situated on the right-hand pinnacle.

Super Creeps 99 metres E2 ❀ (28.10.78/6.4.81)
Worth a re-clean, or – at least – climbing the top pitch independently. Start below the middle crackline, 3 metres right of the *Rear Entry* corner.

1 22m. 5b. Climb the crack to its close. Continue over a bulge to good holds, and follow easier rock to an overhung niche. Peg and nut belays.

2 22m. 5b. Climb the left-hand crack out of the niche to good holds. Follow the crack and groove above to a steep exit into a wide bay.

3 25m. 4c. Gain the corner above and climb it to a roof. Exit left to belays on the narrow, top terrace below the right-hand pinnacle.

4 Elidor 30m. 5b (28.10.78). Between the smooth east face of the pinnacle (*Siouxie*) and the right arête (*Doomwatch*) are two groove-lines. Climb the left-hand groove with interest to the left end of a series of roofs. Pull over the bulge in the crack above and climb it, trending slightly leftwards to the pinnacle ridge.

Scary Monsters 101 metres E2 ❀ (28.10.78/5.10.80)
More than enough to give you the creeps. A similar beast to its neighbour. Start below the right-most crackline, 7 metres right of the *Rear Entry* corner.

1 22m. 5b. Gain the crack and follow it past a roof. Climb a short corner to the overhung niche. Peg and nut belays.

2 22m. 5b. Climb over the bulge on the right, and follow the groove above to a steep exit into the wide bay.

3 27m. 4c. Climb the crack in the right wall of the bay to the terrace below the pinnacle.

4 30m. 5a. Climb the broken crack just right of the arête of the pinnacle to the top.

It Must Be the Russians 54 metres E2 ❀ [PR] (10.9.80)
The route is banned due to the risk of rockfall onto the road from the section shared with *Doomwatch*. Two good pitches on a line that can be straightened out (and cleaned up), now that the cornice of hanging gardens has gone. The straightening would restore access to the route. Start below an open undercut corner 12 metres right of the *Rear Entry* corner.

1 27m. 5c. Climb easily to a niche and then pull through the overhang into the main corner. Climb the fine corner and continue on good pocket

holds above to a ledge. Move up and right to higher ledges. Peg and poor nut belays.
2 27m. 5c. Traverse 3 metres right and climb steeply to a good horizontal break below the line of roofs. The remaining climbing is beyond the protection of the rock-catch fence: make a long traverse rightwards below the roof to join and finish up *Doomwatch*.

Doomwatch   96 metres   E1 †† ✿ [PR]   (24/25.1.70/1970)
The first two pitches are banned owing to the risk of rockfall onto the road. Formerly a long and classic outing, the third pitch of which is still accessible.
1 45m. 5a.   The lofty orange corner near the right edge of the lower wall, and the groove above to the terrace.
2 24m. 4c.   The broken grooves on the right and then left of the arête to the upper terrace.
3 27 metres   5b. See page 79.

The remaining routes in the Gully of Creeps are situated on the walls beneath the cliff-top, from which they are reached.

Bonanza   30 metres   E5 6a †   (2.11.86)
The most obvious feature of the tower face that forms the left-hand extension of the pinnacle is a long groove rising above a very smooth wall at its base. This hard pitch, which is difficult to protect, takes a direct line up the wall and groove. Start at a tree below the wall and above the mouldering confines of a virgin gully.
Climb straight up the wall behind the tree to a small horizontal slot at 8 metres (vital wires). A thin, ragged crack above is gained by a highly technical sequence and leads, with the questionable security of an *in-situ* thread on the left, to good holds on the right. Move diagonally left to a big round pocket and a good rest below the groove. Pull over the bulge (peg) and follow the better protected groove until it is possible to escape easily left at its close to tree belays just below the pinnacle ridge.

Geronimo   54 metres   Severe   (21.1.68)
The pair of deep chimneys, the second of which divides the east face of the pinnacle. A route of character, good to see again. Scramble carefully down the gully between the two pinnacles, and then abseil down the deep gully to the next terrace. Roped-up, traverse right for 8 metres to the first chimney.
1 27m.   Climb the chimney to the grassy terrace.
2 27m.   Climb the second chimney to a shallow cave. Move left and continue up a wide crack to a vegetated gully and the top.

No Reservations   27 metres   E3 5c †   (3.11.85)
The groove right of the second chimney of *Geronimo*, which appears to have cleaned up nicely. A good route.
Climb the chimney as for *Geronimo* to the shallow cave. Pull around right into the groove and follow it on consistently good finger-jams to a small

roof. Move right and continue steeply up the groove to pull over onto the capping rock bridge. Finish up the broken wall above.

Siouxie   27 metres   E5 6c †   (2.11.85)
A plumb-line up the centre of the stark wall in the face of the pinnacle to the right of the second chimney of *Geronimo*. A despicably hard crux! Start from the steeply-sloping terrace, below the centre of the wall.
Climb the wall fairly centrally and without any special difficulty to the horizontal break at half height. Stretch up to undercuts and gain the thin groove above. Climb the groove (peg) until better holds lead rightwards to easier ground and the pinnacle ridge.

Stone Warrior   30 metres   E5 6a   (12.12.70/17.10.79)
A superb route which climbs the groove-line left of the arête to finish leftwards through the spectacular stepped roofs above. Start 2 metres left of the arête (good nut belays on the right).
Climb the left wall of the groove boldly, past spaced wire protection, until better holds can be reached in a slight niche up to the right. Make hard moves (peg) to an undercut flake, and then swing left and back up right (peg) into a small groove beneath the stacked roofs. Take the obvious line rightwards through the roofs to a rectangular block under the largest roof (peg). Escape bravely leftwards along the obvious hand-traverse to broken ground. Continue more easily, but scalped, to the top.

Stoned   30 metres   E6 6b †   (15.3.03)
Who needs chemicals with routes like these around? This is the awesome definitive line of the arête, with F7b+ climbing performed above 100 metres of space.
Follow *Stone Warrior* to the small groove beneath the stacked roofs. Take the obvious line rightwards through the roofs to a rectangular block under the largest roof. Undercut right (peg), stretch around the lip (peg), and make powerful moves up and left into a slim groove in the headwall which contains a vertical crack. With the road between your legs, climb the technical crack (peg) to the top.

Some big metal stakes bedded in the terrace by the cleaning teams provide good belays for the next three routes.

Doomwatch   30 metres   E1 5b   (24/25.1.70/1970)
A fine and airy route up the pinnacle arête, which was always worth doing as a separate pitch. The first two pitches of the original route are out of bounds.
Climb the thin crack-line in the tip of the arête to the top. Some awkward but well-protected moves at 9 metres provide the technical interest, while the position does the rest.

Deathwatch   30 metres   E3 5c †   (9.3.2003)
An absorbing route on generally good compact rock, needing care to protect in its upper reaches. Start 4 metres right of the arête.
Climb a good flake crack to just short of a sloping grassy ledge up right. Swing left into a thin groove, and take this to a thread and good

rock-spike slightly right. Stand up, and then move awkwardly left into another groove. Follow the groove past a hand-ledge (with small *in-situ* thread) until a series of good holds right of a bulge lead to easier ground. Scramble on the right to the top.

Crimewatch   30 metres   E3 5c †   (9.3.2003)
Elegant face climbing, always with good protection where it counts. Start 2 metres right of the flake crack of *Deathwatch*, below a small block overhang.
Pull over the overhang, and climb the steep wall above on layaways to jugs and then a resting-ledge. Take a slight groove to a vague break, and make tricky moves up a steep face to a second vague break. Above is an improbable rib; move up it, step left into a smooth groove (wire placement in left wall), and then take jugs to easier ground. Scramble on the right to the top.

Great Unwashed Gully (Madrugada Wall)

The climbs associated with the deepest and most westerly of the three gullies are based on its extensive right-hand wall which overhangs the upper leg of Horseshoe Bend. The wall offers some fantastically atmospheric hard climbs which are sheltered and found on good rock. A rock-catch fence in the gully should protect the road from any rockfall from the leftmost climbs. This is not the case for routes right of, and including *Madrugada*, which overhang the road and are banned.

In the gully bed lurk the squalid remains of **Dirty Dick** (30.9.78) and **The Great Unwashed** (7.59/18.4.73), both VS, both low in the popularity polls, and to both having taken a hammering during the landowner's cleaning spree. To the right, in stark contrast, is an immaculate light-coloured, rectangular wall, the home of the classic *Kephalonia*. The disjointed grooves in the centre of the wall are taken by *Madrugada*, while the smooth black sheet in between gives some hard climbs with fixed gear (8mm bolts and *in-situ* threads).

The erection of the rock-catch fence below Long Wall now precludes a three-minute approach straight up from the road. Approach either from Shoot Gully on the left, as for the Long Wall routes, or from the shoulder on the right beneath Sunset Buttress. Both ways involve tiptoeing along a narrow catwalk, now very exposed without underlying foliage, to get to the gully. Caution will be required. Exit from those routes not equipped with abseil stations is made by walking rightwards to a short gully leading up to the main cliff-top path.

Fountain of Arethusa   72 metres   E5 †   (15.10.84)
A charismatic route. The second pitch follows the long crease rising from the gully, whilst the third storms up the left-hand weakness in the final overhanging wall. Start in the base of the gully.

1 18m. 4b. Ascend the chimney and crack, and belay in the gully at an elderberry tree below a rounded rib. (Alternatively, reach the same point by starting up *Red Beretta*: 6a.)
2 27m. 6b. Step right onto the rib and move up a short leaning groove to a horizontal break. Enter the crease and follow it (two pegs) with more than a few surprises to a roof on the right. Pull strenuously over the roof and move up the wall to another roof. Swing right over this on good holds, step left, and climb easily to belays on a long, vegetated ledge.
3 27m. 6a. Climb the groove and crack behind the belay; move right along a break and then up to a small ledge where the wall steepens. Climb the wall (peg) to a small roof. Make hard moves into a bottomless groove and zap up it (peg) to exit leftwards on good holds. Finish up a tiny corner and short wall.

Red Beretta 25 metres E5 6b †   (11.10.87)
A very difficult eliminate that fails to take a direct line up the smooth wall immediately right of the gully. It does, however, stay dry in wet weather. Start at the base of the gully.
Climb the leaning right-hand wall of the gully to a bulge (*in-situ* thread). Pull over to jugs (8mm bolt), and follow finger-pockets up and leftwards (two *in-situ* threads) until forced into the gully. Move up, swing rightwards onto the wall at the level of another *in-situ* thread, and make a hard move straight up (8mm bolt) to twin rounded pockets. Continue (peg) with a long reach up left for a superb, hidden sidecut and the break (peg). Move right to belay as for *Kephalonia*. Continue as for that route or abseil off.

Kephalonia 75 metres E5   (11.3.84)
World class – when clean. A brilliant route, high on the hit-list of Cheddar Man. This classic gully-wall climb ascends the layback crack and slim groove in the sheer wall right of the gully and finishes up an exciting flake in the upper wall. The protection is tolerable throughout and the climb is fast-drying. Start at the base of the gully.
1 25m. 6a. Climb the right-hand side of the rounded rib to an overlap at 8 metres (peg). Pull over on the right (*in-situ* thread) to a thin crack (*in-situ* thread). Traverse back leftwards to a hidden pocket and continue straight up the wall to the obvious layback crack. Climb the crack to the half-way break (peg and thread belays).
2 25m. 6a. Step left and climb the slim groove to its close (peg). Move up and right to a niche (peg) and, from the break above, make an intrepid swing left over the large roof on a big jug. Continue more easily to the long, grassy ledge.
3 25m. 6a. From a ledge behind the belay, climb the obvious groove fairly easily (*in-situ* thread) to a double roof (peg). Follow the overhanging flake rightwards around the bulge (peg) until fingery moves (*in-situ* thread) gain a small slab on the left. Finish up the short, steep corner above.

Cruising the Med 30 metres E5 6a   (25.10.87)
Tracks torpidly across the black wall to the right of the gully. Start at the base of the gully.

Follow *Kephalonia* to the thin crack above the roof (*in-situ* thread) and continue to an 8mm bolt (on *The Scented Isle*). Traverse rightwards across the smooth wall to a junction with *Thermopylae* (8mm bolt). Move up and stride right to large holds (*in-situ* thread). Finish direct (8mm bolt) to an old abseil station.

The Scented Isle   50 metres   E5   (16.10.87)
A challenging route of great interest with two sustained pitches. Start at the base of the gully.
1 25m. 6a. Follow *Kephalonia* to the thin crack over the roof (*in-situ* thread). Make some extending moves up the wall (8mm bolt) to good holds above a bulge. Pull over, climb easily to the break, and traverse left to the first stance of *Kephalonia*.
2 25m. 5c. Step back right and move up a short, smooth wall to a break (*in-situ* thread). Pull over the bulge to a slim corner and follow this until a step right across a short, blind groove gains a good foothold on a rib (peg). Follow the shallow groove above (*in-situ* thread) and exit left to an easy groove and the long grassy ledge.
Continue up *Kephalonia* pitch 3, or sacrifice gear and abseil off.

Thermopylae   25 metres   E5 6b   (17.10.87)
Hard, sustained climbing with good rock and bolt protection. Start 3 metres right of the base of the gully.
Climb straight up the lower wall to a small ledge beneath the roof. Pull fancifully through the roof (8mm bolt) to reach a good resting-place over the lip. Now climb the wall and shallow groove above (two 8mm bolts and two *in-situ* threads) to finish on welcome jugs. An old abseil station is at hand.

Rape of the Sabine Women   25 metres   E3 6c   (17.10.87)
A fine route but with unbalanced difficulties – the crux roof could cause problems! Start 6 metres right of the base of the gully.
Climb rather boldly up the lower wall (*in-situ* thread) to a rest-position and bolt below the roof. Overcome the roof (*in-situ* thread and 8mm bolt) by means of a complex sequence, and press on rightwards to jugs on easier ground. Climb up (*in-situ* thread and 8mm bolt) to the ledge and old abseil station.

Screw Archimedes   25 metres   E4 6b †   (25.10.87)
An absorbing route with an inventive crux. The protection improves after a bold start. Start from the grassy terrace, 10 metres right of the gully.
The initial smooth wall is climbed direct until some moves slightly rightwards (two *in-situ* threads) lead to a foot-ledge below a small double roof. Pull through the roof with difficulty (8mm bolt) and follow jugs to a good rest (*in-situ* thread). Tricky moves up the thin, blind groove above (two *in-situ* threads) lead to an exit left to the ledge and old abseil station.

The remaining routes on the Madrugada Wall must not be climbed owing to the risk of rockfall onto the road. They have been degeared, though outline descriptions are retained for posterity.

Madrugada   85 metres   E4 ❀ [PR]   (16.11.74/9.9.80)
A significant piece of history, but rather outshone by its neighbours.
1 33m. 5b. The groove in the centre of the wall and a 'grass traverse' left to a poor stance below a prominent overhung crack.
2 27m. 5b. A short loose wall and the crack past roofs to the long grassy ledge.
3 25m. 6a. *Kephalonia* pitch 3.

La Del Gioconda   25 metres   E2 6a ❀ [PR]   (17.1.88)
Good rock and a few thrills made this route an attractive proposition. It took an intricate line to the right of the groove of *Madrugada*, before retreating from an abseil station.

The Golden Road to Samarkand   25 metres   E3 6b ❀ [PR](27.3.88)
This was also a good pitch that saw a brief period of homage. It started 3 metres right of the groove of *Madrugada*, climbed a large roof, and continued fairly directly to the abseil station.

The remaining three climbs started from the narrow catwalk which leads onto the grassy shoulder beneath Sunset Buttress. The first two shared a common start 10 metres from the right edge of the wall.

Potwalloper's Wall   25 metres   E4 6a † ❀ [PR]   (18.1.90)
This route gave sustained and technical climbing to the left of the large roof to an abseil station.

Speltershake   25 metres   E5 6b † ❀ [PR]   (18.1.90)
An intricate and exposed line over the large roof which dramatically overhangs the Horseshoe Bend. It retreated from the abseil station of *Potwalloper's Wall*.

Rufus Roughcut   25 metres   E2 + A0 5b † ❀ [PR]   (9.11.86)
A route that somehow escaped being free-climbed – but it's too late for that now! It climbed over the right-hand side of the large roof, before taking the buttress on the left to the shared abseil station.

Horseshoe Bend Buttress

The inside edge of the tight bend in the centre of the Gorge, the Horseshoe Bend, is lined by a steep 27-metre cliff rising from the road. The Horseshoe Bend Buttress does not offer any exceptional climbs, although you would be pushed to find routes any more accessible. The bouldering is good; and getting run over is probably the main hazard. Descent from the climbs is to the right, or by abseil from trees.

Access: Climbing is allowed from 1 October until 15 March inclusive.

At the left (upstream) end of the cliff is a small, undercut buttress featuring a prominent groove (and thread!).

Muchos Bebe   12 metres   E4 6a F7a   (21.2.93)
A big little route to the left of the groove. From a recess, bear rightwards through the bulge and finish direct. Two decaying 8mm bolts.

BBG   12 metres   E1 5b   (Late 1970s)
Low in its grade. Climb the prominent groove.

Consider This   12 metres   E3 6b   (3.71/20.2.93)
Roof gymnastics. Start under the large roof that undercuts the small buttress.
First undercut and then improvise through the roof to jugs and easier ground (stick-clip 8mm bolt). Climb the easy crack to a tree and abseil off.

In the east face of the buttress is a relatively sheer, grey wall above a Volvo-sized lay-by at the road-side.

Round the Bend   25 metres   E4 6a †   (20.2.93)
An old-style gripper giving archetypal Cheddar climbing.
From a point 2 metres right of a chossy crack, climb in a strictly direct line up the grey wall (peg) to good holds and runners in a break at 10 metres. Continue more easily to a commodious ledge; then, with a runner on the tree (stump!) on the left, climb boldly up the rounded rib to a roof. Pull over to jugs (peg) and an exit groove.

Tied in Knots   30 metres   E3 6a   (5.10.86)
You will be if you get it wrong! A varied route.
Climb up over graffiti to a small overhang at 4 metres. Pull over; then follow a leftward-leading series of holds to their end. Move right to the top right-hand side of a large flake that forms a slab. Hand-traverse the break rightwards to a leaning groove. Follow the groove up and leftwards with difficulty to the top (two pegs).

Wall of Trees   30 metres   Severe 5c ††   (c.1950s)
A misnomer, thanks to the landowner. A poor route, but worthwhile if you jump off after 4 metres! To the right of the sheer, grey wall in the east face is a stepped groove that used to lead up to yew trees. Start just right of a left-slanting groove.
A short, smooth wall is overcome by a classic boulder problem or by a human pyramid. From good holds above, follow the groove past ledges to a sole surviving tree. Finish up the wall above.

Return of the Bunfeaster   30 metres   Hard Very Severe 5b (9.12.94)
Follow the obvious and awkward crack right of *Wall of Trees* to its tree.
Finish up the wall above.

Don't Don't   30 metres   Very Severe 5a †   (9.12.94)
The flakes and cracks right of *Return of the Bunfeaster*. Move right along a
ledge and take the depression to the top.

Viper Crack   30 metres   Very Severe 5a ††   (5.65)
A venomous problem. The deep crack just left of the front of the buttress.
Jam painfully up the crack to a bulge. Continue up the wider crack in
discomfort to reach a ledge. Move left to belay. Abseil from a tree or climb
the wall above to the top.

Dodo   18 metres   E1 5b   (21.12.86)
More survivable than most. The pitch climbs the rib right of *Viper Crack*.
Climb *Viper Crack* for 3 metres and then step right on a good hold to an
angular niche (or approach it over the roof below – hard 6b). Move out
right and climb a groove (peg) for 3 metres. Trend slightly leftwards (peg),
passing a jammed nut with difficulty, to ledges and the tree belay on the
left.

The Pioneers   18 metres   E5 6b F7b   (20.2.93)
Good-quality climbing: sustained and on nice rock, with its crux where it
should be – right at the top! Start 5 metres right of *Viper Crack*, below the
right-hand side of a large bulge.
Climb with a long reach for good holds below a small roof. Work up
through the roofs (two 8mm bolts); then step up and slightly right (*Rock 1*)
to a semi-rest (on *Long Shot Kick-E-Bucket*). Above is a roof; climb through
this rightwards (two 8mm bolts), strenuous, and so reach a good break.
Either abseil from an *in-situ* rope thread (which will need replacing) or
scramble rightwards to the top.

Long Shot Kick-E-Bucket   25 metres   E4 6a †   (19.9.85)
The antithesis of its neighbours; serious climbing with marginal protection.
Start below a roof, 6 metres to the right of *Viper Crack*.
Climb the wall to the roof (*in-situ* thread). Pull strenuously around into a
slim groove, which is followed to its close. Trend diagonally leftwards to a
good handhold in the base of another shallow groove. Layback into the
groove and climb it and the rib above to the top.

Spotlight   25 metres   E1 5c   (10.12.72/4.3.79)
An excellent, reliable pitch that takes the leftward-curling corner left of the
slabby nose of the buttress.
Climb the corner to a roof. Traverse leftwards and continue up the main
groove to a larger roof. A trying but protectable sequence over the roof
gains a thin crack and easier finishing ground above.

Nose Climb   25 metres   E1 5b   (25.3.73)
A nice, technical start, but the climbing soon runs cold. Start below the
slabby nose of the buttress, behind a 'road narrows' sign.
Climb the steep slab via incipient cracks to a broken groove. The groove
and characterless wall above lead to the top.

By a Nose   25 metres   Very Severe 5a   (9.12.94)
Climb the crack right of *Nose Climb* over the left end of a roof, and finish
up the centre of the wall.

The remaining climbs on the buttress are located on the west-facing wall to
the right of the nose. The wall can seep after heavy rain.

Partners in Crime   15 metres   E4 6a F6c+   (13.2.94)
Start at the foot of the groove right of the nose (5 metres right of the road
sign). A scary third clip gives the route its grade; E3 with the quickdraws in
place.
Climb the awkward bulge right of the nose and continue up the groove
above to a stainless-steel bolted abseil station (shared with
Whippersnappers). Four stainless-steel bolts.

Whippersnappers   15 metres   E3 6b F7a   (7.11.87)
The smooth black wall around to the right from *Nose Climb* provides some
hard climbing (on 8mm bolts).
Step up and climb on the right before trending leftwards onto the face.
Move up to a bulge, pull over on poor holds, and reach the stainless-steel
bolted abseil station. Two bolts, two pegs.

Crème de la Phlegm   15 metres   E3 5c   (27.3.88)
Start below the tall groove 8 metres right of the road sign.
Climb the right-hand of the two initial grooves and continue to a bulge
(two *in-situ* threads). Move left and follow the groove (8mm bolt) to the
abseil station of *Whippersnappers* on the left.

British Summer Time   22 metres   E2 5b   (27.3.93)
A nice thought in winter's gloom. Start below a thin groove a metre right of
Creme de la Phlegm.
Bouldery moves gain good holds at the bottom of the groove. Follow the
groove and pull out onto a compact slab (*in-situ* thread). Delicate moves
gain good holds in a break (*Friend 2*) and a steep sprint to finish.

I've Started...   22 metres   E3 6b   (7.3.93/13.2.00)
So you'll finish. Start below a thin groove 2 metres right of *British Summer
Time*.
A boulder problem becomes a bolder problem until the groove, and wires
at six metres, can be gained. Continue up small grooves, trending left onto
the compact slab of *British Summer Time* (*in-situ* thread). Follow *British
Summer Time* to the top.

12000 Miles   22 metres   E1 5c   (13.3.93)
Gain and climb the bottomless central crack and finish steeply right.

Smooth Operator   25 metres   E1 5b   (4.10.86)
Enjoyable climbing that links a line of left-facing layaways and groovelets.
Start 3 metres left of the corner towards the right end of the wall.
Follow the line of least resistance (a novel concept), via the layaways, to
finish up a groove and the wall on the left.

Tourist Distraction   22 metres   Hard Very Severe 5a †   (28.2.93)
Climb the obvious corner towards the right-hand end of the wall. One
in-situ thread and a peg.

St Valentine's Day Massacre   22 metres   Severe †   (14.2.93)
'Ignored in the past and will probably be ignored in the future' concede
the first ascensionists. Climb the broken grooves right of the corner.

Fat Slapper   12 metres   E3 6a †   (9.2.00)
Start 6 metres from the right-hand end of the cliff beneath a rib containing
a crack. Take the crack and rib to a bulge. Make a hard move over to a
small sloping ledge (in-situ thread), and so gain a larger ledge above.
Finish up a short rock step.

Sunset Buttress

Sunset Buttress is unmistakable. In the centre of the Gorge, hanging above the
Horseshoe Bend is a dome-shaped buttress of brazen white limestone,
undercut by roofs, and thrust out into bulges, prows, and grooves in its upper
reaches. At one time thought to be the sole preserve of the hammer-wielding
elite, Sunset underwent a radical transformation in the 80s to become a
hardcore bastion of extreme free climbs. The buttress boasts positions and
exposure that are just about as out-of-this-world as this country can manage,
and it even receives the afternoon (and evening) sun as a winter bonus. That
may sound like some climbers version of paradise, but nervous sport climbers
will have to go through hell to get there. For the buttress sits on a slabby wall
that remains almost totally obscured by sheets of ivy: the way in! Clawing up
vertical ivy here is in a class of its own but is the 'old skool' way of accessing the
long narrow ledge, the starting-point for most of the routes on the buttress
proper. (The groove of *Utopia*, however lends a less eccentric means of entry
to the ledge for sceptics.)

Unfortunately, the buttress can suffer prolonged seepage after sustained
rainfall, which can take half of the routes out of circulation for long periods
of the winter. No other crag in the Gorge would 'benefit' more from
realization of the summer climbing dream.

Sunset Buttress

1 The Common Start XS
2 Irradiation E5
3 Afterglow E4
4 Road to Paradise E5
5 Paradise Regained E5
6 For Ever and Ever E6
7 Bird of Paradise E6
8 Paradise Lost E6
9 Touching the Void/
   The Midnight Run F7c
10 Gates of Eden E5
11 The Other Side of Paradise F7c
12 Edge of Eternity E6
13 Sunsations E5
14 Nirvana E2
15 The Man that Never Was E5
16 The Underground Influence E5
17 Utopia VS
E Possible entry from Utopia for
   routes 5-11

All the climbs are served by a common pitch through (!) the underlying, overgrown wall that starts from the grassy shoulder 35 metres above the Horseshoe Bend; this is the only means of access to *Irradiation*, *Afterglow*, and *Road to Paradise*. Alternatively, the routes between *Paradise Regained* and *Edge of Eternity*, which start from the narrow ledge below the buttress, can be gained by traversing left from the top of the first pitch of *Utopia*.

Approach from the infilled lay-by below the right-hand side of the crag. Follow a track leftwards in the direction of the top of Horseshoe Bend Buttress, and then switch back right through trees to the shoulder. To exit from the top of the buttress, scramble up a short gully to the left of the summit plateau to reach the main cliff-top path.

Access: Climbing is allowed from 1 October until 15 March inclusive.

Warning: Great care should be taken as any rock dislodged from parts of the buttress could land in the road below.

The left arête of the vegetated lower wall was taken, largely up cracks to its left, by what was once a fine, exposed route: **Palo Alto** (48 metres Very Severe 4c [PR] 27.3.65); now very vegetated (and banned!).

The Common Start   42 metres   XS ❀   (8.5.65)
This botanical masterpiece features all the thrills and spills of Cheddar vegetation but it is also the quickest approach to the long, narrow ledge below the buttress. Start at the grassy shoulder.
Climb up rock to the right of the arête and then tunnel up through a line of weakness in the ivy mass, trending rightwards beneath slabs to some blackthorn bushes at 25 metres. Now, either climb the pocketed slab above and traverse horizontally right to the belay ledge, or continue diagonally up ledges to the same point. Peg and nut belays.

The first three climbs take the isolated steep wall with a long roof in the lower left-hand section of the buttress. They finish on a large vegetated ledge on the edge of the buttress, from which escape is made by scrambling up the obvious gully to the summit plateau.

Irradiation   25 metres   E5 6a †   (18.1.90)
An unrelenting pump on good holds. Start from a muddy ledge 20 metres up *The Common Start*.
Climb up slabby rock right of a shattered corner to a small ledge. Step left onto the white wall (peg) and pull straight up (peg) to a long hand-ledge above a small roof. Continue (vital *RP3* and *Rock 3*) to a good crack and peg at the left-hand end of the dominant roof. Bear steeply rightwards over a final roof (*in-situ* thread) and finish up an easier groove.

Afterglow   20 metres   E4 6b †   (11.10.86)
A central line crossing the long roof. Start from a ledge beneath a
pocketed slab, 20 metres up *The Common Start*.
Climb easily up the pocketed slab and groove above the stance to the roof
(cams). Extend around the roof to a pocket supreme and pull up
strenuously into a groove. Climb the groove to tree belays on the
vegetated ledge above.

Road to Paradise   25 metres   E5 6b †   (13.10.94)
Sheer irony: a very committing lead. Start as for *Afterglow*.
Climb diagonally right across the slab to the right end of the long roof.
Move up to the lip and reach for a jug (*in-situ* wire). Trend quickly leftwards
to gain good holds on a rib and then continue up and back rightwards to
follow a slight groove to further good holds where the wall steepens. A
precarious, long reach (10mm bolt) leads to better holds, and a traverse
leftwards, below the ivy, gains the vegetated ledge.

The following routes start from the long, narrow ledge below the buttress.
Note: the first three have recently lost their jammed blocks.

Paradise Regained   45 metres   E5 †† ❀   (7.4.67/6.6.84)
The recessed groove in the left-hand side of the buttress lacks the exposure
characteristic of its neighbours but provides the basis for two good pitches.
Unfortunately the route is often under the threat (or cover!) of ivy.
1 24m. 5c. From the extreme left end of the ledge, climb a thin crack in
the steep wall (peg) to a wide horizontal break (peg). Tread very carefully
right over some monster blocks jammed in a groove (*The Visionary*) and
move up steeply to the roof above (peg). Swing into a crack on the left
(peg) and climb it (*in-situ* thread) to peg and thread belays in the recess: a
good place to hide for a while.
2 21m. 6b. Pull over the roof above (good cam and peg) and continue over
the next bulge by some extra-wide bridging (peg). Pull rightwards to better
holds on the headwall and climb straight up an easier groove to the top.
Variation
Strangler in Paradise   E5 †   (23.3.86)
The imposing crack in the bulging wall to the right of the upper groove.
2a 21m. 6b. Step right and climb the crack to its close (8mm bolt).
Climb the scoop through the bulge (*in-situ* thread) until it is possible to pull
onto the headwall (*in-situ* thread). Climb the groove for 3 metres, and then
move right to finish up a groove and easy rib.

The Visionary   60 metres   E3 A0 ††   (22.6.76)
A major breakthrough in its time and still not a route to be
underestimated. It is essentially a rising left-to-right sightseeing tour of the
buttress – but with one hell of a view. Start from peg belays on the long,
narrow ledge.
1 25m. 5c. Climb the angular groove above the belay until it is possible
to pull left into the thin crack of *Paradise Regained* (peg). Follow that route
to the top of the jammed blocks, (or, for the lunatic fringe, it is possible to

pull straight out onto the blocks from the angular groove). Break out rightwards across the steep wall between roofs to a break and short groove leading to good thread belays on the right, in the main upper break.
2 20m. 5c+A0. Traverse rightwards along the break (pegs), around a rib, to its end (peg). Reach up rightwards with difficulty to the first of a line of bolts on a narrow, leaning ramp (*Gates of Eden* climbs this free). Aid up the bolts to peg belays on a small ledge.
3 15m. 5a. *Nirvana* pitch 2.

For Ever and Ever   45 metres   E6 † ††   (12.6.86)
A technical but occasionally contrived first pitch is outmatched by a breathtaking and very difficult finale up the hanging arête on the prow of the buttress. A Sunset special. Start from peg belays on the long, narrow ledge.
1 25m. 6b. From the base of *The Visionary* groove, swing right onto the smooth wall (peg) and climb its left-hand side via a ragged pocket and thin flake (old bolt on the right) until a good spike is reached below the left-hand side of the big roof. Step up left onto the jammed blocks and continue straight up to the next roof. Step right and pull desperately over the bulge (*in-situ* thread) to peg and *in-situ* thread belays in the main upper break.
2 20m. 6b. Climb straight up the wild hanging arête above (two 8mm bolts) to a superb pocket and mid-air rest. A fierce pull over the bulge (peg) leads to the base of a shallow rightward-trending groove (vital *Friend* 2½). Follow the groove and crack above (jammed nut and peg) and exit leftwards to a final easy rib.

Bird of Paradise   45 metres   E6   (3.12.69/17.10.86)
The last of the big aid routes to go free provides an absolute masterpiece. The route follows the aided line almost exactly: the big roof above the belay ledge and the tapering groove in the prow of the buttress. Miraculously, the climbing is not as hard as it looks! Take some small wires for the first pitch; the second is fully geared (but with an eclectic mix of rusting ironmongery). Start from the peg belays on the long, narrow ledge.
1 25m. 6b. Pull over the middle of the roof to the right of the belay, and climb straight up the centre of the smooth wall (2 very old bolts) before trending slightly rightwards to the prow (peg). Traverse left until it is possible to reach over to a good flake (8mm bolt). Make a spectacular swing over the roof and continue with haste up the pocketed crackline to a break. Climb the wall slightly rightwards to the thread belays of *The Visionary* at the main upper break.
2 20m. 6b. A very technical series of moves up the leaning wall behind the belay leads to better holds beneath a roof. Swing around left on superb pockets into a bottomless groove and reach a monster jug below a higher roof. Move left again and climb the blind, tapering groove before stepping leftwards onto a rib (junction with *For Ever and Ever*). Climb the crack above and exit leftwards to a final easy rib. Five (8mm and less) bolts, four pegs, jammed nut, and *in-situ* thread.

Paradise Lost   52 metres   E6   (8.5.65/11.9.76)
The first of the big aid routes to fall, and deservedly the classic of the
buttress. This is the dominating central groove of the buttress. A magnificent
challenge, with two contrasting pitches, the first of which has a reputation for
stopping good climbers in their tracks. Some of the original bolts are now
wafer-thin. Start from peg belays on the long, narrow ledge.
1 27m. 6b. Walk rightwards along the ledge and climb the obvious flake
crack (peg) to a small ledge (peg). Climb intricately through the bulge
above (peg) until a desperate move gains the next break (peg). Undercut
rightwards (8mm bolt) to a blind pocket, and pull up (*in-situ* thread) to a
foot-ledge and stainless-steel bolt belays below the main groove.
2 25m. 6b. Climb the groove (peg) to a roof. Pull around on the left and
continue by sustained, technical bridging up the groove (*in-situ* gear is
always close to hand!) until it is possible to escape leftwards (peg) into a
loose groove that leads to the top.

Touching the Void/The Midnight Run
                    45 metres   E6 F7c † (25.11.89/13.3.95)
A superb combination that climaxes in some high-exposure cranking on
the left arête of the *Paradise Lost* groove: 'out there or what?' It is possible
to approach the second pitch independently by abseiling down the groove
of *Paradise Lost*; otherwise start below some obvious block roofs, towards
the right end of the narrow ledge (stainless-steel bolt belay).
1 25m. 6b. Move up the slab to the roofs (*Rock 5*). Make powerful moves
to get established on good sideholds, and then crank up and back left to a
good curved hold on the arête. Follow the wall and arête a few awkward
moves to reach the break. Rock up and move left to join *Paradise Lost*, which
is followed to its stance. Eight stainless-steel bolts, two *in-situ* threads.
2 20m. 6b/c. Swing left from the belay and, from an old peg in a break,
climb the narrowing groove in the overhanging arête until a desperate move
past a small roof must be made onto the face. Trend diagonally leftwards to
easier ground and a final broken rib. Four 8mm bolts and three pegs.

Gates of Eden   99 metres   E5 (2 pts aid) †   (16-17.11.69/19.2.84)
Largely superseded by *Edge of Eternity*, but with a little something on the
second pitch to tempt the jackal. It takes a cunning line around the
right-hand side of the biggest roof on the buttress. Start below the big,
slanting flake crack of *Utopia* below the right-hand side of the buttress.
1 50m. 4c. Climb the crack and chimney over a small roof and continue
up the ramp-line until a 5-metre traverse to the left gains bolt and nut
belays on small ledges below a smooth black-streaked wall (which can
also be reached by traversing right from the usual belay ledge).
2 25m. 6a. Move up to a shallow groove and climb it (peg) until good
holds on the left wall (*in-situ* wire) lead to the wide horizontal break (peg).
Pull up and use two very dodgy aid pegs to cross the bulging wall below
the big roof. Better holds to the right lead up a small groove to a stance in
a niche (bolt, *in-situ* thread and *Rock 6* belays).

3 12m. 6c. Swing rightwards into a short roof-capped groove (*in-situ* thread). An atrocious pull over the roof (8mm bolt) leads onto the narrow, leaning ramp. Climb it using a complex concoction of layaways on its right-hand edge until it is possible to exit right to peg belays on the stance of *Nirvana* (four bolts, one of which is reasonably trustworthy).
4 12m. 4c. Climb the rounded groove behind the belay and move right to join the finish of *Nirvana*.

The Other Side of Paradise   90 metres   E6 F7c   (26.3.94)
An incredible line up the hanging groove in the arête right of *Paradise Lost* provides the most heart-stopping positions on the crag, and the best equipped route. Take a few wires to augment the belays and to start the central section of *Edge of Eternity*; otherwise the route is well geared with stainless-steel bolts, and pegs. Start from the first stance of *Edge of Eternity* (reached via *Utopia* pitch 1).
1 50m. 4c. *Gates of Eden* pitch 1.
2 15m. 6c (F7c). Climb easily to the peg on *Edge of Eternity*; then step left and work thinly up the blue streak to the wide horizontal break. Explosive moves rightwards through the bulge lead to jugs and a quick heave into the groove (*Rock 3*) of *Gates of Eden*. Bolt, *in-situ* thread, and *Rock 6* belay. Five bolts.
3 25m. 6b (F7b+). Swing left and move up to a break (*The Visionary*: *in-situ* thread). Step left, then climb awkwardly into a shallow, white groove just right of the *Paradise Lost* corner. Gain undercuts in the roof on the right and head right to an arête 'on the edge of the universe'. Move up, and using a jug on the right, gain entry to the groove. Teeter technically up the groove and draw upon final reserves to surmount the final prow and reach the top. Stretch out on the summit plateau and savour that special Sunset moment (cigar not essential). Eight bolts and two pegs.

Edge of Eternity   99 metres   E6 †   (7.3.86)
A phenomenal 'mixed-ethic' climb, sustained at a very high standard, which forces a line up the steep black-streaked wall and through the bulges in the right-hand side of the buttress. Start below the big slanting flake crack of *Utopia*.
1 50m. 4c. *Gates of Eden* pitch 1.
2 25m. 6b. Step right from the stance and climb easily up pockets to a slim groove. Move up (peg), reach right for a jug, and continue blindly and boldly up the smooth wall to the wide horizontal break (peg). Pull over the bulge (8mm bolt); trend leftwards up the vague, slanting groove through bulges (*in-situ* wire) and climb more directly (peg) to an incipient horizontal break (peg). Hand-traverse leftwards to the *Gates of Eden* stance (bolt, *in-situ* thread, and *Rock 6* belays).
3 12m. 6c. *Gates of Eden* pitch 3.
4 12m. 6a. Move out left, climb a thin groove (good wires), and then stride left into a discontinuous crack (peg). Climb the crack to the capping roof (*in-situ* thread) and finish leftwards in a 'sunsational' position.

Utopia   100 metres   Very Severe ††   (22.3.68)
A route of great character with 'Jekyll and Hyde' situations up the big, slanting flake-line and chimneys in the right-hand side of the buttress. Get

your hot-shot mates on one of the Paradise routes for extra entertainment. Start below the flake crack.

1 25m. 4c. Climb the crack and chimney (peg) over a small roof to a stance on the right (nut belays).

2 25m. 4c. Move back left and follow the ramp to some large blocks at the base of a smooth, open corner. Climb the corner to the left-hand end of the terrace.

3 25m. 4c. An impressive pitch. Half-way along the terrace is a deep, undercut and overhung chimney. Climb over the bulge into the chimney and go up to good holds leading to its close. Swing out left and climb steeply into the thickly vegetated terrace at the top of the buttress.

4 25m. 4a. At the back of the terrace is an oft-vegetated groove; climb it to the top. Alternatively, quit the route by walking leftwards along the terrace to the summit of the buttress.

The following eight routes start from the large terrace on the right-hand side of the buttress at the top of pitch 2 of *Utopia*. They are probably best reached by abseiling from trees on the overlying terrace, in which case several of them may be climbed (in combination with routes in The Zawn, if desired).

The Horse Knows the Way   36 metres   E2 5b † †† (20.11.77/6.7.83)
A route of singular character which effects one almighty hand-traverse from right to left along the wide horizontal break beneath the roofs. Start at the left-hand end of the terrace at the end of pitch 2 of *Utopia*. Hand-traverse the break past miscellaneous fixed gear to the grassy ledge on the left edge of the buttress. (A stance could be taken on *Paradise Lost* half-way along the pitch.) Escape to the summit of the buttress as for *Irradiation*.

Sunsations   42 metres   E5 †   (8.3.86)
A short but punchy problem forcing a direct and very airy (scary?) start to *Nirvana*. Start from the left-hand end of the terrace.

1 27m. 6b. Launch out leftwards above the void along a line of finger-jugs (peg) and pull up to pockets (*in-situ* thread). Move left and up (8mm bolt) to a big pocket and then diagonally rightwards to bigger holds on the sloping ledge of *Nirvana*. Step left and pull into a shallow groove (peg) which is climbed to peg belays on a ledge on the left (shared by *The Visionary* etc.).

2 15m. 5a. *Nirvana* pitch 2.

Nirvana   42 metres   E2   (6.6.70/1970)
An indeterminate line at a reasonable grade that encroaches onto the main buttress. Care is required with the rock. Start 5 metres from the left-hand end of the terrace.

1 27m. 5b. Climb the slabby and poorly-protected wall leftwards past an aluminium wedge with string (a Dearman original!) and then move up onto a sloping ledge at the foot of a groove (peg). Traverse leftwards along the ledge and pull into a shallow groove (peg), which is climbed to peg belays on a ledge on the left (shared by *The Visionary* etc.).

2 15m. 5a. Move right into the crack which is followed (peg) before trending back leftwards to finish easily.

The Man That Never Was   20 metres   E5 6a/b †   (19.11.89)
A rather friable and committing crux, although the route as a whole is not that bad. Start midway between the left-hand end of the terrace and the deep chimney, 2 metres left of a rightward-slanting crack.
Climb the steep grey wall to the right of *Nirvana* to a slot at 5 metres, and gain a hollow white flake above. Surmount the bulge and follow a shaky flake-line up and to the right to a short, blind groove. Climb the groove tensely, past a peg and a small overhang, to an easier groove leading to an old abseil station below ivy on the right.

The Underground Influence   20 metres   E5 6b †   (19.11.89)
A steep, fingery, and unrelenting pitch that takes a direct line up the wall to the left of the rightward-slanting crack.
From the base of the crack, climb steeply past finger-pockets (*in-situ* thread) to a jug below a small overhang. Step right (8mm bolt) and climb the leaning wall (8mm bolt) to an incipient crack (good wires). Gain a hand-ledge up to the left (small cams), pull over the bulge, and continue easily to the old abseil station of *The Man That Never Was*.

Déjà Rue   27 metres   E1 5a †   (31.12.89)
Not a pleasant experience. Start at the base of the rightward-slanting crack. Climb the rounded rib to the right of the initial wide section of the crack, and move slightly leftwards to join the crack at half height. Follow the crack to a peg in the left wall and then climb diagonally rightwards beneath an ominous jutting block to the top of the chimney of *Utopia*.

The Perishers   25 metres   E4 6a † ✿   (1.3.86)
The smooth wall, roof, and groove in the buttress to the right of the chimney pitch of *Utopia*. Some worthwhile climbing in its first half, though protection is hard to arrange. Start from the vegetated ledge, 5 metres right of the chimney.
Climb the steep wall to the right of a cave on good holds, trending back leftwards to the roof. Reach over to a jug and break out leftwards to a resting-place. Climb the shallow groove above, and step left to finish up a narrow, tottering pillar.

Northern Lights   27 metres   E2 5b ✿   (31.12.89)
Potentially enjoyable, and well-protected, climbing up the orange-coloured wall and groove in the right-hand side of the buttress to the right of the *Utopia* chimney. Start from the vegetated ledge, 10 metres right of the chimney.
Climb, trending rightwards above vegetation, to good holds (*in-situ* thread). Climb up and then leftwards beneath a peg with sling to some good little ledges above the orange wall. Swing right on jugs (*in-situ* thread) and then pull left into the groove. Climb the groove for 5 metres before swinging leftwards to finish up a final short wall on superb holds.

The Zawn

Between Sunset Buttress and Great Rock is Sickle Gully, which once supported the jungle-bashing extravaganza of **Hammer and Sickle** (135 metres Very Severe 7.59). The uppermost section of the gully, named The Zawn, comprises a deep recess with two smooth walls.

The rock on most routes is fairly sound, but beware of some loose material on the exits. In windy conditions the climbs offer shelter, and there are no seepage problems. The crag is as remote as you can get from the hustle and bustle of the road far below.

Approach from the top of Shoot Gully by following the cliff-top path westwards for 130 metres until, immediately beyond the two pinnacles of Castle Rocks, a grassy slope descends slightly to a promontory overlooking the gully. Reach the bed either from the summit plateau of Sunset Buttress by walking down the vegetated terrace, or by abseiling from trees. The routes on the right-hand section of Sunset Buttress are within easy (abseil) reach from this terrace.

Access: Climbing is allowed from 1 October until 15 March inclusive.

The East Wall

Chukostkiy   27 metres   E4 6a † ❁ ❁   (9.12.89)
A good line, which takes the continuous vertical crack in the left-hand side of the wall. Start behind a tree at the foot of the initial groove.
Follow the groove to ledges below the main crack. Climb the crack with increasing difficulty (*in-situ* thread and peg) until better holds lead leftwards across a final bulging section to a ledge and a good exit.

Alaska   25 metres   E5 6a † ❁   (13.10.85)
Concentration and cool are needed on the very smooth groove in The East Wall.
Climb an initial flake crack, and bear leftwards over a bulge to an incut ledge. Move right and climb the groove to its close. Traverse rightwards around the rib to finish on the right.

The West Wall

The West Wall forms a broad, clean face of fine limestone cleft centrally by the tall layback corner of *Nice Crack* and terminated by the curved arête of *Don't Make Waves* on the right.

The shorter, left-hand section of the wall bulges smoothly, but features a number of thin cracklines.

Bearing Straight (E5, first ascent),The Zawn
Climbers: Martin Crocker and Matt Ward
Photo: Gordon Jenkin

Shinanikin   12 metres   E3 6b †   (26.10.85)

A lively little route up the left-hand crack at the top of the gully bed. The crack is strenuous, but soon leads past *in-situ* threads to a small ledge on the right. Step left and climb a groove on big holds to finish.

Kumquat   15 metres   E2 6a   (26.10.85)

Small but tasty: the wall and leftward-slanting groove between the cracks of *Shinanikin* and *Shadowlands*.

Climb straight up the wall on finger-pockets (*in-situ* thread) to a small ledge. Step left and follow the groove to another small ledge, where it is possible to finish out left as for *Shinanikin*.

Shadowlands   27 metres   E4 6a   (13.10.85)

Quality climbing based on the crackline immediately left of the tall layback corner. Sustained and protectable.

Climb the initial thin crack, and swing left on finger-pockets into the main crackline, which leads with continuous difficulty to a big flake. Continue up the steep wall above to a scoop (peg) and then bear rightwards to a short final crack.

Nice Crack   27 metres   E3 5c   (5.79/26.10.85)

A perfect line, but with an imperfect exit.

Climb the layback corner, taking care with blocks to start, to a resting-place next to a big flake on the left. Continue up the corner on positive holds until it fizzles out. Move over the bulge and then bear rightwards to the short final crack of *Shadowlands*.

Madonna   30 metres   E5 6b   (12.10.85)

A 'beautiful stranger', who saw quite a bit of action in her younger years. A monumental lead on the immaculate central section of The West Wall. Start at a small white groove 6 metres down the gully bed from the layback corner of *Nice Crack*.

Take the groove, step left (8mm bolt), and then climb via undercuts to a thin crack (peg), which leads with difficulty to a small ledge on the right. Trend leftwards to a good foothold (*in-situ* wire) at a point where the wall rears up. Continue thinly up a very slim groove (8mm bolt), and pull over the bulge above to gain better holds (peg). Climb the short final crack above to the exit of *Shadowlands*.

Don't Make Waves   30 metres   E5 6b †   (12.10.85)

The impending, undercut arête overlooking Sickle Gully offers some good climbing and a committing start. Start at the small white groove as for *Madonna*.

Climb the groove, but then traverse rightwards to good holds beneath a roof (wires). Crank decisively over and move up rightwards to the arête. Climb the arête for 3 metres, step left into a scoop, and continue more easily rightwards to a steep, square-cut groove. A couple of hard moves up the groove lead to a short, grassy wall and the top.

The following four exposed climbs (which steal onto the upper tier of Great Rock) are approached from the bed of The Zawn by traversing along the wide bedding-plane that runs beneath it (easy, but stay roped) or, alternatively, by abseiling to the tree at the base of *Arni's Arête*.

A New Siberia   30 metres E4 6a   (10.11.85)
The deeper, left-hand groove in a fine, sculptured wall; an exhilarating pitch on excellent rock. Some ivy streamers in the first groove are commonplace. Start 5 metres along the bedding-plane (bong and large cam or Hex belays).
Pull into the groove (peg) and climb it to a step left onto a small ledge (*in-situ* thread). Continue up the main groove and surmount a juggy bulge (*in-situ* thread). Bridge delicately up the steeper groove to larger holds on the face above, and then swing right into a short crack leading to a tree and a short grassy exit corner.

Bearing Straight   30 metres   E5 6a †   (10.11.85)
Free wheels the right-hand groove before nearly grinding to a halt at a disquieting overhanging wall. Start from the bedding-plane, as for *A New Siberia*.
Step right and pull over the bulge into the right-hand groove. Follow the groove, fairly easily at first (peg) but then more steeply and at a disturbing distance from gear, until a hard move (side-runner) gains the obvious undercut. Swing right onto the leaning wall (peg) and fight up it into the short corner above. Follow this to the tree and grassy exit corner of *A New Siberia*.

Arni's Arête   18 metres   E5 6b †   (12.10.86)
The spacey arête that marks the junction between The West Wall and the front face of Great Rock. Good low down, but rather friable higher up. Start from the large tree at the foot of the arête.
Climb straight up the arête (thread) to where it steepens – dramatically! An off-balance series of moves up the arête enables a good (but hardly obvious) hold on the right to be reached (peg). Continue up the scoop to the right of the arête to an old abseil station.

The Insidious Green   27 metres   E5 6b † ❀   (12.10.86)
Back where it belongs – beneath ivy! The shallow grooves and crack in the rectangular wall to the right of *Arni's Arête*, starting from a large tree at the foot of the arête.

Great Rock

To the right of Sunset Buttress and Sickle Gully is the enormous bulk of Great Rock, which, at 120 metres, is the highest crag in the Gorge. The buttress comprises three distinct tiers separated by sloping grassy terraces. The lower tier, The Burmese Wall, is an impressive rectangular wall, 55 metres high, that

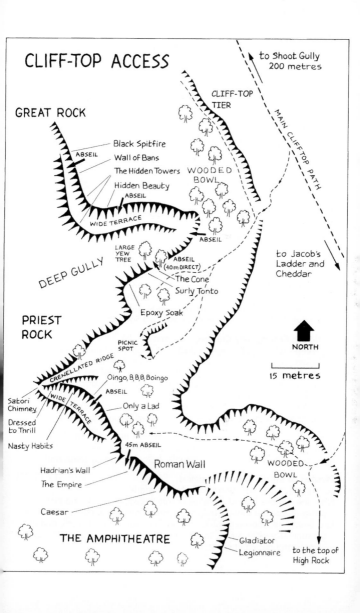

sports two prominent grooves, taken by *Burma Road* and *Avatar*. Unfortunately it missed out on the clean-up and is swathed in ivy. The rib bounding the wall to its right gives the first pitches of *Mourning Glory*. The upper two tiers, in common with the remaining rock right of, and including, *Mourning Glory* have had a face-lift and offer some cleaner climbing. Of the Upper Tiers, the exposed grey sheet in the top-centre of Great Rock is the home for *What a Bringdown*, and the isolated towers further right provide *The Hidden Towers* and *Hidden Beauty*. The towers overlook the upper reaches of Deep Gully, the broad gully marking the right edge of Great Rock. (A wooded bowl to the left of an obvious crenellated ridge between Priest Rock and The Amphitheatre marks the head of Deep Gully.) Finally, at the bottom of Deep Gully, right of the rib of *Mourning Glory*, is a slabby wall with three climbs.

Warning: Great care should be taken, as any rock dislodged may fall into the road or car-park below.

Access: Climbing is allowed from 1 October until 15 March inclusive.

The Burmese Wall

A vegetated catwalk runs along the base of the wall; the best approach is from the right (as for *Mourning Glory*), although it can almost as easily be approached from the left, from beneath Sunset Buttress. Escape from the overlying terrace is traditionally made by traversing rightwards along the terrace and making two abseils from trees down *Mourning Glory*. Some of the trees have now been felled, but anyone resourceful enough to have climbed any of the climbs in their current condition will find retreat plain sailing.

Instigate Emergency Closure   20 metres   E4 5c † ✿ ✿   (14.10.88)
The steep wall just to the right of pitch 1 of *Utopia* is often ivy-covered: no great loss. Start 3 metres right of the base of the flake-line of *Utopia*. Climb steeply up and slightly rightwards to a horizontal crack. Move up to another break and proceed directly to the right of an *in-situ* thread until a step left can be made below a small roof. Follow the difficult crack above (*in-situ* thread) to a small ledge. (Belay on *Friends 1* and *2½*.) Traverse leftwards to join *Utopia*, which can be reversed to the ground.

The next two climbs take the overhanging nose at the left-hand end of the Burmese Wall; both start below a shallow bulging groove 35 metres to the right of the *Utopia* flake-line. Unusually, both tend to stay clean and dry.

Pirates of Lamb Leer   20 metres   E4 6a   (12.11.89)
An ingenious little line; good value for the grade.
From the obvious hole at 3 metres (*in-situ* thread) move up and pull rightwards into the shallow bulging groove. Continue directly (good wires) to a 8mm bolt below a small overhang. Pull over (*in-situ* thread), and with a dynamic sequence gain a small leftward-facing corner. Follow the corner to ledges and an old abseil station.

Mercurian Sump Dweller   25 metres   E6 6b   (12.11.89)
Powerful climbing up the leaning wall to the left of the lower corner of
Burma Road, but low in the grade.
Follow the groove as for *Pirates of Lamb Leer* to a good wire-slot at 10
metres. Traverse rightwards, rising slightly (peg), to a good resting-ledge
on an arête. Climb the ever-steepening wall above (one peg and two
8mm bolts) and pull leftwards onto ledges and the old abseil station of
Pirates of Lamb Leer.

Burma Road   53 metres   E2 ✿   (3.12.69/1975)
'We were literally climbing vertical ivy on occasions, but this should not
detract from the brilliance of the first ascent concept.' The quote is even
more appropriate nowadays. A one-time magnificent route yearning to be
set free of its ivy captor. Start below the prominent corner in the left-hand
side of the wall.
1 20m. 5a. Climb the crack and groove over a small roof and continue
up the deeper corner to a small ledge.
2 33m. 5c. Traverse leftwards from the belay and move up to a ledge on
the arête. Climb up and rightwards into a groove entombed by overhangs,
and leave this for a big, detached flake on the right. Climb the wall above to
a small roof and make a hard traverse leftwards (peg) along the lip to better
holds. Continue more easily rightwards to tree belays on the terrace, or use
the old abseil station on the following route. (The original finish continued up
a corner-line in two further pitches [5a,5a]; now totally overgrown.)

Brazilia   47 metres   E5 † ✿   (8.11.87)
A direct assault on the massive central roofs is rewarded with exposed,
technical climbing on the headwall. Start 3 metres right of the foot of the
corner of *Burma Road*.
1 20m. 5c. Gain the obvious flake and follow it to a ledge. Climb the
rounded rib, pull up right over a roof, and continue up thin cracks in the
slab to peg and bolt belays on a good small ledge (three *in-situ* threads).
2 27m. 6b. Move straight up the smooth wall behind the belay (8mm
bolt) and swing right (peg) to a ledge. A stiff pull and a couple of long
reaches lead through the roofs (peg and 8mm bolts) to jugs above. Swing
airily left (peg) and move up to gain a break (*Friends 1½ and 2*). Continue
up a thin crack in the headwall (*in-situ* thread and peg) to a ledge and a
peg and 8mm bolt belay just below the jungle. Abseil 45 metres to the
ground.

Avatar   54 metres   E3 ✿   (27.5.70/14.3.76)
Potentially a great line, but ivy is wrecking the route. A machete-wielding
philanthropist with time on his/her hands is required. Start below and to
the right of a deep crack 10 metres from the right-hand edge of the
ivy-covered wall.
1 27m. 5a. Trend leftwards to the foot of the obvious deep crack. Climb
the crack to a roof, move left into a groove, and follow it to a stance and
peg belays on the left.

2 27m. 5c. Climb steeply into the bulging corner, which is strenuous to start but soon leads to a resting-ledge. Continue directly up the corner, mainly on good holds, until an easier crack leads to the terrace. Cams useful on this pitch.
Variation
2a Malaise 27m. E3 5c † ❀ (30.6.76). Climbed on sight and reputedly loose. Step down to the right and work diagonally rightwards across a steep slab to a corner (peg). Climb the corner to an overhang and swing up and right to a resting-place (peg). Move left and climb past a tree to the terrace.

The Prow   54 metres   E5 ❀   (9.4.81)
Not quite up to the standard of its northern namesake, this route can (if clean) offer some spectacular climbing up the crack in the prow of the wall.
1 27m. 5c. Climb trending leftwards as for *Avatar* for 10 metres and follow thin cracks in a steep wall to a small roof. Pull over this and continue in the same line until a hand traverse along the break leads to awkward belays on the right.
2 27m. 6a. Make a couple of difficult moves up the smooth scoop above the stance (peg) and climb the groove (peg) to the crack splitting the left-hand side of the prow. Power up the unforgiving crack until it is possible to exit leftwards to finish easily.

Mourning Glory   123 metres   Very Severe †† ❀   (3.70)
An all-time classic whose time ran out when it was dismantled in the late 90s. Its initial pillar is still just about in place but many of its trees have been felled, and most of its ledges have been covered by earth and grass. Those in mourning may consider allocating a day or three to its resurrection. In six pitches, the route climbed the rib (scarcely poking out of the ivy) at the right edge of The Burmese Wall, and the series of cracks, a corner, and a gully ('the couloir') to the summit of the Rock. The approach is from a track leading leftwards from the back of the large semi-circular car-park beneath Priest Rock.

The Upper Tiers
Approach: The choice of approach to the routes here is now reduced, owing to the unsavoury condition of *Mourning Glory*, the customary means of access. *What a Bringdown* and *Hidden Towers* start from the right-hand continuation of the big terrace running across the top of The Burmese Wall and can be gained by following the first three pitches of *Mourning Glory* (if cleaned up), or by two abseils from the top of the *Black Spitfire* wall. *Black Spitfire*, *Hurricane*, *Wall of Bans*, *Hidden Beauty*, and *Doomsday Machine* are situated on the top tier and should be approached from the top, by abseiling to the base of the routes.

What a Bringdown   69 metres   E2 †† ❀   (3.70/22.1.83)
A superbly positioned route up the grey wall below the summit of the Rock, now relieved of its dangerous rock (but not of copious vegetation). Ideally,

Great Rock and Priest Rock

1	Mourning Glory	VS
2	Pipped at the Post	F7a
3	The Hidden Towers	HVS
4	Hidden Beauty	E4
5	The Cone	E2
6	Ghosts at the End of the Line	E3
7	Irreverence	F7b+
8	Patitucci Bass	F7a+
9	Corea Elektrosound	F7a+
10	Ian Paisley	E6
11	The Ghettos	E5
12	Satori	E5
13	One Track Mind	E2
14	Dressed to Thrill	E4
15	Caesar	E4

HIGH ROCK

ROMAN WALL

The Amphitheatre

CLIFF-TOP TIER

Deep Gully

LOWER WALL, PRIEST ROCK

GREAT ROCK

the route needs recleaning, in which case the disjointed first pitch could be omitted. Start just above a depression in the terrace, some 15 metres to the right of the start of *Mourning Glory* pitch 4.

1 27m. 4c. Climb the short corner past a small roof. Follow the thin crack above and climb another corner, moving leftwards a touch, before climbing to the left-hand end of the upper terrace.

2 15m. 5b. Climb the crack behind the belay, surmount a bulge, and escape leftwards to a grassy ledge and awkward belays.

3 27m. 5b. Climb diagonally rightwards to the foot of a deep crack. Climb the crack to a bulge (peg) and pull over to scarred ledges on the left. Move up to a steep final crack but ignore it for the wall on its right.

Black Spitfire   38 metres   E5 ☘   (13.10.85)

A hard, bold route that aims for thin cracks in the centre of the grey wall below the summit of the Rock. The top pitch, which is brilliant, was recleaned in 2000. It is best reached via *Hurricane* as the first pitch is broken and covered in vegetation. Start at a large tree at the base of the wall.

1 18m. 5c. Climb the groove to the left of an overhang and then move up and rightwards onto poor rock. Climb up and leftwards to belay desperately on nuts and tree-stumps in a vertical hanging garden.

2 20m. 6b. Pull up to a flake and a vertical crack (peg), and make hard, blind, and bold moves slightly left and then slightly right over bulging rock to a small tree just below the top.

Hurricane   42 metres   E6 6b †   (5.3.00)

A mega-lead. One of the most sustained high-standard, technical face routes in the Gorge. Take several sets of small wires. Start at the large tree at the base of the wall.

Climb rightwards via a short crack to a grey rib undercut by a large white scar. Move up delicately onto the rib, and take the smooth grey streak above direct (peg) to a rest at the horizontal break. Traverse left along the break (peg) to a crack, and a junction with *Black Spitfire*. Pull up to a flake and a vertical crack (peg), and make hard, blind, and bold moves slightly left and then slightly right over bulging rock to a small tree just below the top.

Wall of Bans   39 metres   E2 † ☘   (13.8.83)

This breaches the right-hand side of the wall of *What a Bringdown* by a necessarily devious line. Some fragile rock and many weeds. Start at the large tree, as for *Black Spitfire*.

Climb the crack right of the overhung groove until it fades at a bulge. Swing left onto the wall and climb diagonally leftwards to gain a line of flakes leading to a tree stump. Move right and then back leftwards to finish.

The Hidden Towers   60 metres   Hard Very Severe ††   (4.4.81)

The isolated towers at the right edge of the Upper Tiers that overlook Deep Gully. There have been major alterations to the second pitch. Start some 45 metres along the terrace from the start of *Mourning Glory* pitch 4.

1 30m. 5a. Climb the corner in the first tower to a large tree on the sloping terrace.

2 30m. 4c. Climb the crack in the second tower and the orange corner above to the top.

The next two climbs take the steep grey right-hand face of the highest tower which overlooks the upper reaches of Deep Gully. Approach by abseil.

Hidden Beauty 36 metres E4 6a †† ✿ (8.8.83)
The thin, left-curling crackline right of the arête; too much green make-up often conceals her good looks.
Gain the thin crack from the left and climb it, steep and sustained. Curve left around the arête to finish up the orange corner of *The Hidden Towers*.

Doomsday Machine 36 metres E5 6b † (14.11.99)
Top-quality, technical, steep-face climbing; the sort that is unique to Cheddar. Start in the centre of the steep grey face, 2 metres right of *Hidden Beauty*.
Take an intermittent thin crack to its close. Move up to a small overhang (*in-situ* thread). Forceful climbing up a shallow groove above leads to larger holds. Finish leftwards, or move right to exit behind a large tree.

The next three (sport) routes are situated on the slabby wall, with a long strip roof at half-height, beneath Deep Gully. Unfortunately, they are threatened by ivy, and grass abounds. Approach using a track that leads leftwards from behind a 'pay and display' sign at the back of the large semi-circular car park underneath Priest Rock. A cave in the track is the site of a speleological dig. (The track leads leftwards to the foot of *Mourning Glory* and beyond to the Burmese Wall.)

The left-hand bolt-line, that starts 2 metres left of the cave, was a project.

Lost Cause 18 metres E4 6b F7a ✿ (10.3.95)
Great climbing; take a set of wires. Start at the cave; cavers' bolt belay. Climb a groove right of the cave to a horizontal break. Move up to the roof and surmount this with difficulty to gain a 'brilliant' jug in the groove above. Follow the groove to a flake; stainless-steel bolted abseil station on the right. Four stainless-steel bolts and a peg.

Pipped at the Post 18 metres E4 6b F7a ✿ (10.3.95)
Take a few wires. Start below a corner 3 metres right of the cave.
Amble up the groove and step up onto a ledge (*Friend 2*). Continue up on decreasing holds to where the wall steepens. Power through the roof to gain the base of the groove above, and follow this with some technicality to gain a stainless-steel bolted abseil station on the left. Four stainless-steel bolts.

Priest Rock

This is the extensive area of rock (and grot) between Great Rock and The Amphitheatre, which looms above the large semi-circular car-park immediately upstream of High Rock. A massive hollow descends two-thirds of the way down the cliff. To its left a lofty, slender buttress rises the full height of the Gorge, whilst to its right is a staggered arête demarcating the left edge of The Amphitheatre.

In the upper left-hand part of the slender buttress is a narrow, vaguely cone-shaped tower which forms the right wall of the upper reaches of Deep Gully. *The Cone* and clones occupy this tower and are reached from the cliff top by abseil. The top of the wall is 35 metres north of the obvious crenellated ridge between Priest Rock and The Amphitheatre.

By far the best and cleanest climbing is located on the more easily accessible lower wall. A distinctive feature high up in the centre of the lower wall is a huge overhung circular scoop. Down to the left of the scoop is the compact black wall of *Corea Elektrosound*. To the right, a groove-seamed wall is overhung by large roofs. The staggered groove leading up to the roofs is the line of *The Ghettos*. The vegetated corner at the extreme right-hand end of the wall is *Portal*.

Access: Climbing is allowed from 1 October until 15 March inclusive.

The Cone Wall

At the base of the cone-shaped tower is a large yew tree, gained by a short traverse from Deep Gully (or from the top by abseil). All three routes start from the tree. The wall has escaped disassembly, and odd bits of ivy and friends hang out here from time to time.

The Cone   43 metres   E2   (19.10.75)
An atmospheric and airy route with plenty of good climbing.
1 25m. 5b. Pull over the overhang on the left of the tree into a groove. Work rightwards across the wall to a flake crack and climb it to a ledge on the right (peg). Traverse leftwards along the break and climb boldly up a short wall to peg and nut belays in a niche below a prominent crack. (Beware, something with a huge beak and talons nests here!)
2 18m. 5a. Climb the crack and subsequent vegetation to the top.
Variation
Surly Tonto   E3   (17.4.81)
A sharper climax to *The Cone*.
2a 18m. 6a. Swing right onto the wall (peg) and struggle strenuously up the overhanging flake to a ledge. Continue very steeply up the groove above (peg) and finish up an easier crack.

Epoxy Soak   40 metres   E5 †   (24.2.90)
An ambiguous encounter with the front face of the pillar, right of the crack of *The Cone*.
1 20m. 5b. Follow *The Cone* as far as a small ledge where that route traverses leftwards. Peg and nut belays.
2 20m. 6a. Climb a short groove to a good ledge where the face rears up. Continue directly (8mm bolt) and then by using holds to the right to reach a break. Swing left (peg) and persevere up the pillar face on crumbling holds (*in-situ* thread) to exit easily on the left.

Lower Wall

The following three multi-pitch routes climb the high, slender buttress rising behind the car park. They lay dormant beneath ivy for fifteen years before being unearthed in 1991, and since then have not received any known ascents. Already, big patches of ivy are rematerialising, but you know what to expect by now!

Approach the following climbs via the obvious path behind a 'pay and display' sign that leads up to a cornice of overhangs below Deep Gully.

The Creaking Door   45 metres   Hard Very Severe ✿   (19.10.75)
A loose entry to Deep Gully, which follows the crack immediately to its right. Start 6 metres right of the cornice below a short, deep chimney 6 metres above.
1 35m. 5a. Climb to the foot of the (ivy-filled) chimney and traverse left above the cave to a peg below large unstable blocks. Climb up just to their right into a corner, and follow this for 3 metres until able to swing rightwards around the arête onto a steep wall. Climb the wall, a deep crack, and another short wall to a tree belay.
2 10m. 4b. Climb the narrow rib and steep ivy above to trees in the gully.

Hallowed Ground   96 metres   Hard Very Severe ✿   (28.3.76)
The rambling system of cracks and grooves in the buttress right of Deep Gully. Start below the chimney, as for *The Creaking Door*.
1 25m. 5a. Reach and follow the chimney (peg) to the bulging cracks. Continue steeply up the cracks to tree stumps, and gain a stance on the right (peg belays).
2 18m. 5a. Move left and climb a shallow groove until a projecting block on the right can be used to gain small ledges. Climb diagonally rightwards until a long step right can be made to a pair of spikes. Climb through the overhang above on good holds to a tree belay.
3 35m. 5a. Climb a crack for 3 metres; then move left around the corner, and traverse a line of flat holds to reach a small ledge. Climb up for 5 metres to some spikes before stepping left and up into a crack formed by a pillar. From the top of this, an arête leads easily to an ivy slope. Steeper gully scrambling gains a tree.
4 18m. 5a/b. Climb broken blocks on the left until a short traverse right gains a groove, which is followed to a rounded flake on the right wall.

Stand on this using holds on the right edge, move back into the groove, and climb it to the top.

Ghosts at the End of the Line   20 metres   E3 5c †   (12.10.95)
Technical climbing on surprisingly good holds up the black face between the adjacent crack-lines.
Climb easily between the two cracks to the foot of the black face. Work up a slight rib in the centre of the face (peg) with a delicate move to reach an undercut bulge (*in-situ* thread). Pull around on superb holds; then follow these slightly rightwards over another ledge to a large but dubious abseil bolt (back-up recommended).

Big Tower   104 metres   E2 ✿   (1972/11.1.76)
A major expedition necessitating jungle warfare. The first pitch to the abseil point of *Ghosts at the End of the Line* provides a worthwhile route in itself at E1 5b. Start below a slim bottomless corner 12 metres right of the cornice.
1 27m. 5b. A short steep wall, right of a vegetated crack, leads to the foot of the corner. Climb the corner to an overhang at its top. If not traversing left to the abseil point of the previous route, swing right and climb the wall, bearing right to a tree stump. Belay one step higher.
2 15m. 5b. Climb the wall just left to ledges that lead left into a short corner. Follow the corner to an undercut roof. Layback around the right end of the roof into a muddy groove and climb this to a tree belay.
3 25m. 4c. Climb the crack above over a bulge to a cracked groove. Follow the groove, moving right above a slight bulge to a small tree, and climb a short flake crack above to tree belays.
4 25m. Scramble up and left to a large yew tree, climb broken blocks above to a ledge, and move left along it to a stance on a large block.
5 12m. 5b. Climb the groove above the stance awkwardly to a bulge near the top. Swing left and climb loose grassy rock to finish.

Wake Up Dead   18 metres   E3 5c †   (12.10.95)
The subsidiary left-facing groove right of *Big Tower* pitch 1.
Follow good ledges right of the crackline for 10 metres (as for *Big Tower*). Move right and up to a bulge beneath the groove (peg). Climb the groove steeply and from its top, bear right to a stainless-steel bolted abseil station.

Irreverance   18 metres   E5 6b/c F7b+ †   (13.10.95)
A venerable sport pitch taking in the obvious jutting roof at 10 metres, right of *Big Tower*.
Use the *Big Tower* entry, and step right beneath the roof. Surmount the roof direct on improbable holds, and make for the abseil station of *Wake Up Dead* straight above. Three stainless-steel bolts; take a few wires just in case.

Judas   18 metres   E5 6a †   (13.10.95)
Devious. Use the *Big Tower* entry, but traverse right for 2 metres to a short crack beneath the roof. Use undercuts above to pass the roof and gain the foot of the tiny right-facing corner (vital *Rock 2* in thin crack on right wall).

Climb the arête formed by the corner; then traverse left to the *Wake Up Dead* abseil station.

The following two clean and well-bolted sport routes follow open groove-lines in the scooped black wall 30 metres right of the cornice of overhangs.

Patitucci Bass   20 metres   E4 6b F7a+   (8.10.94)
Chic climbing with a butch start; a superb climb. Take a few wires.
Climb fairly easily slightly rightwards to the roof. Break diagonally rightwards through the roof to reach a thin crack and a resting position. Plough on through the bulge above and then take the thin groove and pillar face to the break. Stainless-steel bolted abseil station. Five stainless-steel bolts and two pegs.

Corea Elektrosound   20 metres   E4 6b F7a+   (8.10.94)
Techno-Cheddar climbing at its best, offering sustained improvisation on 'thinking-man's' rock. Take a few wires. Start as for *Patitucci Bass*.
Climb rightwards and up to the roof. Enter the right-hand groove above the roof and so gain a short, thin crack. Follow the groove and surmount the overlying bulge on deep holds. Move up and step left to finish up the short, pillar face of *Patitucci Bass*. Stainless-steel bolted abseil station. Four stainless-steel bolts and two pegs.

In the base of the wall, above the point at which a second path from the car park meets the cliff, is a short, roof-capped corner (this is directly below the huge scoop 30 metres up the cliff). A series of grooves in the wall right of the corner provides the lines for the next routes.

Ian Paisley   25 metres   E6 6c †   (24.12.86)
A route to shout about (actually, power-screams will help in the holdless groove)! A superb route on beautiful rock; technically advanced and very committing. Recleaned in 2000. Start below an open pink groove 4 metres right of the roof-capped corner.
Climb up the initial wall via thin cracks to the bulge. Extend up to place poor wires in an undercut flake and make a gnarly move straight up into the pink groove. High-intensity bridging directly up the smooth groove (wire on the left rib) leads to a rest below a small roof. Reach over to jugs, swing right to good footholds (rock scar below), and follow the shallow groove above on good holds to a small deep cave on the right. Swing right into a crack containing an abseil station.

Ten Hours BC   25 metres   E4 6a   (24.12.86)
The central of three grooves leads to fine climbing on the steep, grey wall above. Small wires give good protection. Recleaned in 2000. Start as for *Ian Paisley*.
Climb the initial wall via thin cracks and trend right to the foot of the groove. Follow the groove (peg), and where it disappears (*in-situ* thread) swing steeply right to good holds at the base of the grey wall. Climb the wall and small rib to a break. Traverse leftwards to the crack and abseil station of *Ian Paisley*.

Into Dark   25 metres   E4 6b †   (23.1.00)

A more energetic start to *Ten Hours BC*. Start below an obvious block ledge
3 metres up, 8 metres right of the roof-capped corner.

Climb the easy initial wall to steeper rock. Climb slightly rightwards to a
flake in the bulge, reach up with difficulty, and step left to a large side-hold
below a roof. Move up to join *Ten Hours BC* at the good holds on the grey
wall. Follow *Ten Hours BC* up the wall to the abseil station.

The next four routes start below the staggered groove, 10 metres right of the
roof-capped corner.

Oh! To Be Young Again   25 metres   E5 6a †   (12.3.00)

Technically not too bad, but requires a little care to protect.

Climb easily up the initial wall 2 metres right of the block ledge to the
groove. Climb the groove to the first roof (peg). Traverse left 2 metres and
make a hard move over the overlap using a thin crack. Climb up for 3
metres and reach right to the base of a flake crack. Climb the crack
(junction with *The Ghettos*, peg) to the roofs (peg). Traverse left 3 metres
and step up to the abseil station shared with *Ian Paisley*.

The Ghettos   30 metres   E5 6a   (21.12.86)

A big, atmospheric lead that uses the elegant staggered groove to get to
the overlying roofs. By omitting the section through the roofs and
traversing leftwards to the abseil station of *Ian Paisley*, a clean and much
more amenable route of E3 5c results.

Climb easily up the initial wall two metres right of the block ledge to the
groove. Climb the groove, side-stepping the roofs to their right (three
pegs), until it is possible to make a delicate traverse leftwards to a flake
crack. Climb the crack (peg) to the horizontal break (peg). Make
committing moves rightwards over the bulge and traverse easily rightwards
below the next roof to a short, deep groove. Climb the groove (*in-situ*
thread) and the roof above to jugs, and an abseil station.

On the Right Track   32 metres   E5 †   (12.3.00)

An impressive route with a very difficult roof section. High in the grade.

1 8m. Climb easily up the initial wall 2 metres right of the block ledge,
bearing rightwards to peg and nut belays on a ledge in a niche.

2 24m. 6b. Climb a short flake crack and move right into a narrow
V-groove. Follow the groove with difficulty (vital *Rock 5*) to better holds and
a short crack which leads onto poor rock but a no-hands resting-ledge
(you may need it). Move up to the small roof (peg) and enter the groove
above by powerful moves (peg). Swing left (*in-situ* thread) to the short,
deep groove of *The Ghettos*. Climb the groove (*in-situ* thread) and the roof
above to jugs, and an abseil station.

Off the Beaten Track   32 metres   E5 6b   (31.1.87)

A climb of great impact that takes the white groove and roofs right of *The
Ghettos*. The climbing is absolutely riveting, but the fixed gear is rundown.

1 8m. *On the Right Track* pitch 1.

2 24m. 6b. Climb the groove on the right (8mm bolt and *in-situ* threads) to jugs at its top (*in-situ* thread on the right and old peg above). Proceed straight up the wall (8mm bolt) to the first bulge (*in-situ* thread). Cross the bulge (peg and *in-situ* thread) to the top roof (*in-situ* thread on right). Now pull around the large roof with a long reach (*in-situ* wire and threads) to easy ground and an old abseil station.

The remaining routes on the wall are being climbed by ivy. Any prospective gardener should bear in mind the vulnerability of the road at this point.

Satori   35 metres   E5 6a ❀   (24.1.70/10.80)
A sad sight at the moment, but beneath the ivy cowers a brilliant pitch. A major re-clean is needed, together with an abseil station to replace the belay and retreat trees that have been removed. For what it's worth, here's the full description. Start below a short groove under a large slabby wall. Climb the groove to a narrow roof. Pull boldly around on the right to better holds, which lead leftwards across the wall to a blunt rib. Climb a groove and the wall above (pegs) to a horizontal break. Traverse rightwards to a short, sharp groove piercing the roofs. Climb the groove (peg) and break strenuously through the roofs on their left-hand side to easier ground leading rightwards to who knows what?

Greenfinger   35 metres   E3 5b/c ❀   (27.9.79)
At one time a sustained and interesting climb with an air of seriousness, *Greenfinger* took the wall and obvious groove through the capping roofs near the right-hand side of the wall. However, it is in the same condition as *Satori* and the same advice applies. Start 10 metres left of the corner of *Portal*, below a small sapling at 6 metres.
Climb a short crack past the sapling to a small roof. Move left and climb the wall, bearing rightwards to a horizontal break. Climb the steep groove through the overhangs until it is possible to exit to the right. Traverse rightwards across ivy (too weak for Tarzan antics!) to trees.

One Track Mind   15 metres   E2 6a ❀   (15.10.88)
The ivy-clad face left of *Portal*. Start 5 metres left of the corner at the right end of the wall (8mm bolt belay).
Climb the wall (crux to start) to a strip roof, which is surmounted to reach an old abseil station. There are three 8mm bolts and two pegs under there somewhere.

Portal   18 metres   Severe 4a ❀   (8.4.76)
The corner at the extreme right-hand end of the wall is now under ivy: a shame as an amiable route lies beneath.

Cliff-Top Tier
Stretching from the top of Deep Gully to the top of High Rock is a long tier of short cliffs and buttresses. These offer some peaceful climbing/soloing that is very sheltered in windy conditions.

Approach the tier from the cliff-top path or by contouring left from the plateau above the top of High Rock. The corner of *A Life of Grime* is to the right of the steep muddy break in the cliff at the top of Deep Gully. The first eight climbs described are to the left of the break.

Near the left edge of the tier, and above The Zawn, is a prominent arête.

Prickles Numb   7 metres   E2 5c †   (28.10.99)
Starting 4 metres left of the arête, climb a bulging rib and the face above to exit immediately right of a projection. Lay your crashmat over the underlying hawthorn!

Bread and Jam   7 metres   Severe   (28.10.99)
The corner left of the arête.

Sunset over Exmoor   7 metres   Hard Very Severe 5b   (28.10.99)
The very edge of the arête; protection at half-height if needed.

Daylight Robbery 1999   7 metres   Very Severe 4c   (28.10.99)
The steep crack right of the arête.

After Work   6 metres   Very Difficult   (28.10.99)
The groove and rib 3 metres right of the arête.

After Dark   7 metres   E2 5b †   (28.10.99)
Long reaches between positive holds on the solid grey pillar left of the chimney-scoop. A night-time ascent mitigates the exposure.

The next two climbs take the smooth face and arête 20 metres left of the break in the tier. Both are little gems, and well worth the trek.

Drinking in LA   10 metres   E4 6b †   (26.10.99)
Pull up from a block embedded in the ground (peg), and climb a faint line of weakness in the centre of the smooth face. Exit rightwards. Very technical.

Weekends of Rain, Weekdays of Sun   10 metres   E4 6b †   (26.10.99)
The right arête of the face: superb. Boulder up the left-hand side of the arête for 3 metres, and make a hard entry into the hanging V-groove. Climb the groove, swing left around the arête, and exit using jugs to the left of the large block.

The muddy break in the tier now intervenes.

Audience of Goats   9 metres   Severe †   (26.1.94)
The fault and groove 5 metres left of the corner of *A Life of Grime*. Finish to the right of the large tree.

It's a Dirty Job, But...   9 metres   Very Severe 5a †   (4.2.94)
Climb the bulging crack to the left of *A Life of Grime*.

A Life of Grime Left-hand 9 metres Difficult † (31.1.94)
The left-hand weakness of the corner.

A Life of Grime 9 metres Very Severe 5b (13.2.94)
Scottish 'VS'? Climb the right-hand side of the corner over a desperate
overhang and finish up the crack.

Zugzwang 10 metres E2 6a (4.2.94)
The left-hand side of the impressive undercut arête.
Pull over the overhang of *A Life of Grime*. Traverse very thinly rightwards
along the lip, and climb the left-hand side of the arête to the terrace.

Der Hinter Zug 10 metres E3 5c (14.11.99)
The arête direct: fine climbing, if bold.
Climb slightly rightwards to the right end of the overhang before pulling
up to good fingerholds right of the arête. Take the right-hand side of the
arête and swing left on a jug to reach the terrace.

The Unacceptable Face of Unacceptability
                                  10 metres Very Severe 4c † (27.3.94)
Climb the front of the isolated white buttress 10 metres further right, past a
tree at the top. Unashamedly tautological: the route looks more like E1!

To the right of a wide grassy gully is another wall.

9.81 The Old Enemy 12 metres Very Severe 5a (27.3.94)
A Grimm start with a fairy tale ending. Climb an overhanging groove
(*in-situ* thread) to an awkward exit into a large niche. Move left, surmount
the overhang, and finish up the short groove on immense holds.
Variation: From the niche, step right and climb the arête/face to the finish
of *Could It Be the Mild Humble Janitor?*

Could It Be the Mild Humble Janitor?
                                  12 metres Hard Severe 4a † (27.3.94)
A chance to use your neglected *Hex 10*! Gain directly, and climb awkwardly,
the wide, left-slanting crack. Alternatively, climb the crack in its entirety.

Solitaire 12 metres E3 5c † (10.4.00)
Climb the face right of the slanting crack to a small roof. Reach a
projecting hold above, pull over, and follow positive holds to the top.

The Blue Brothers 12 metres Very Severe 4c (13.2.94)
The capped leftward-slanting groove in the centre of the wall has a
leftward exit onto a ledge. Avoid the large block.

The Passion 9 metres Severe † (31.3.94)
The pleasing flake on the right.

Fifteen metres right of *Could It Be…* is a short steep wall behind some ash
trees.

Rationale   7 metres   E2 6a †   (10.4.00)
A good solo up the grey scoop in the wall; good holds to finish, pull out on the tree.

Hugh's Who?   6 metres   E2 6a †   (10.4.00)
Using holds on the left, solo up the left-slanting groove in the right-hand side of the short wall. Much harder than it looks. Reverse down the crack on the right.

The edge now becomes broken, but re-emerges on the far (west) side of The Amphitheatre, and extends above the top of High Rock. Right of a wide gully are a red, north-east facing wall and an arête below the cliff top.

Pull Pit   6 metres   E1 5a †   (10.4.00)
Take the obvious line of holds up the centre of the red wall. Awful landing.

DJ Post Mortem   6 metres   E5 6a †   (10.4.00)
The essential cliff-top solo. From the very narrow terrace, climb the red arête direct with great commitment. The reason for the grade will become clear when powering the crux and realising that the true landing point is 9 metres below.

A little further right is a clean grey pillar, between wide cracks.

In the Balance   8 metres   E3 5c †   (19.10.99)
Climb the unprotected left arête of the pillar: smooth and precarious.

In the Red   8 metres   Hard Very Severe 4c †   (19.10.99)
The pleasant right arête, starting up a short groove.

Behind the summit of High Rock is a blunt white nose.

Shattered   8 metres   E1 5a †   (19.10.99)
Take the left arête of the nose to finish using an obvious short finger-crack.

Rovers' Return   8 metres   E2 5b †   (19.10.99)
An optional top pitch to *Coronation Street* (!). Climb the steep front face of the nose and exit immediately right of a shattered bulge. A good landing, but take care with the rock.

Inverted-V   7 metres   Severe   (19.10.99)
Climb the inverted-V recess with a wide crack in its left-hand side to a loose exit.

Right-On-Sight   7 metres   Very Severe 4c   (19.10.99)
The enjoyable thin flake-crack in the face right of the inverted-V.

The Amphitheatre

The walls of the Amphitheatre are set at the back of the huge wooded bowl between Priest Rock and High Rock. They are divided centrally by a vegetated gully into a west-facing left flank, which comprises The Terrace and Roman Wall, and a north-east-facing right flank.

There is a rock-catch fence at the bottom edge of the Amphitheatre, constructed to protect the left-hand side of the High Rock car-park from rockfall from the walls, or slope, above. It will not protect against rockfall from The Terrace, however.

Approach: The most satisfactory approach is by abseil from trees at the top. In all cases it is sensible to leave a fixed rope and take jumars. In emergency, however, it is feasible to scramble down the bed of The Amphitheatre and abseil 50 metres from the rock-catch fence or trees. A purer means of access would be to (clean and) climb *Portal* to reach the base of The Amphitheatre, but this approach is not recommended, especially for the trail-blazer in Autumn, when the indigenous nettles can reach head height!

Access: Climbing is allowed from 1 October until 15 March inclusive.

The Terrace

To the left of Roman Wall and slightly elevated from the bed of The Amphitheatre is the large vegetated ledge of The Terrace, above which rises a shorter wall running leftwards to the top of the staggered arête of Priest Rock. Keeping the ivy under control here seems impossible, though it is easily stripped on abseil – if anyone can be bothered.

Satori Chimney   27 metres   Very Severe 4c   (24.1.70)
An incongruous pitch, though nicely positioned. Climb the chimney and squeeze up past two chockstones until it closes. Swing right and climb the short final wall to the top.

Dressed to Thrill   27 metres   E4 6a   (17.11.84)
Absorbing, technical climbing centred on the face of the rounded tower to the right of *Satori Chimney*. Start 3 metres right of the chimney.
Climb directly up the face over a tiny roof. Step left at 8 metres, and then back right with a blind grope for a hidden jug in a small niche. A thin vertical crack above leads to easier climbing on the summit tower.

Nasty Habits   20 metres   E5 6b † ❀   (18.2.90)
The fine white wall just to the left of the central groove provides testing sequential climbing with 8mm bolt protection.

Take the white wall (two bolts) and strenuously gain a break above the block overhang. Continue more easily in a direct line to a small tree just below the top; retreat from this or scramble to the top.

Oingo B,B,B...Boingo!   20 metres   E5 6b/c † ❀   (23.2.85)
Strange name, deranged band, dead-hard route. The groove in the centre of the wall goes at endless 6b until, at half-height, good holds appear and a crack leads to the top (two pegs).

Only a Lad   20 metres   E4 6a † ❀   (18.2.90)
The slabby wall to the right of the central groove is climbed on small holds. Start up a slim groove, and continue past a peg and 8mm bolt to good holds over a bulge. Step up to the right (*in-situ* thread) and then bear leftwards to a tree at the cliff edge. Better tree belays just above.

Roman Wall

Roman Wall is the tantalizingly smooth 35-metre face just to the left of the central vegetated gully. By Cheddar standards, the rock here is excellent, the location feels natural and quiet, and the climbs are sheltered. Here lie some of the finest traditional high-standard face climbs in the Gorge, which are easily worth the slog up the hillside.

In the centre of the wall is a left-slanting crack and groove, climbed by *Caesar*.

Hadrian's Wall   40 metres   E3 6a ❀   (5.10.80)
The rounded left-hand arête of the wall; exhilarating climbing on excellent rock. Start below a roof at 4 metres.
Move up and left below the roof until it is practicable to pull over to a small ledge. Trend rightwards to meet a thin crackline (*The Empire*) and climb it (crux) to a horizontal break. Traverse left along the break onto the blunt arête. Climb thin cracks fairly easily (peg) until delicate moves can be made rightwards past a further peg to easier ground and the top.

The Empire   35 metres   E5 6a   (15.10.84)
A tremendous, clean wall climb; one of the best of its kind anywhere. It follows the long, thin crackline rising up to the apex of the cone-shaped wall left of *Caesar*, and offers a technically sustained undertaking with good small-wire protection. Start 3 metres from the left end of the wall. Climb up to the base of a rightward-slanting flake-line, which is followed to a bulge (*in-situ* thread). Pull leftwards to the base of the crack. Climb the crack to a ledge at its top. Finish up the short wall.

Caesar   42 metres   E4 6a   (29.4.76)
The classic of the wall and a wonderful natural line. The route has proved popular (for Cheddar), despite the character-building traverse to gain the crack. Don't let rope drag spoil the fun. Start 3 metres from the left-hand end of the wall, as for *The Empire*.

Climb the flake-line as for *The Empire*, but continue rightwards past the *in-situ* thread to a good nut-slot. Now make a long, precise, and bold traverse horizontally rightwards, past a good jug after 5 metres, to reach a small sapling at the base of the leftward-slanting crack. Climb the crack and groove (peg) to a niche. A few moves up the wider crack above lead to a move left to the ledge at the top of *The Empire*. Finish up the short wall.

Backstabbers   35 metres   E6 6b ††   (1.11.84/25.1.87)
Yet another very high quality pitch, having for its victim the thin well-protected crackline left of *Caesar*. Start 3 metres right of *The Empire*, below a shattered flake.
Lunge for the break and move left to the flake (*in-situ* thread). Climb the flake past a peg and some poor rock to better holds. Move up to the good nut-slot on *Caesar* but press on to the leaning crack. Climb the strength-sapping crack to jugs after 8 metres. Stretch up leftwards to a pocket (crux) and pull up into the *Caesar* niche. Follow *Caesar* to the top.

Caesar Direct   12 metres   E5 6c F7c †   (11.1.87)
A beautiful pitch on superb and compact rock, 'subjugated by bolts' (but in need of a rebolt). Start below a shallow undercut groove and bulge directly beneath the sapling on *Caesar*.
From the break, gain the groove by some desperate moves. Continue smoothly into another shallow groove, which leads to the sapling at the base of the *Caesar* crack and an old abseil station on the right. One peg and two 8mm bolts.

B 'n' B   14 metres   E6 6b   (21.11.99)
Brutal and Bold, but at least the plummet is into space. A big-buzz climb. Start below the higher of two disjointed orange, roof-capped grooves at the right end of the wall.
Gain the break and power straight up over a small overhang containing a ragged undercut into the higher groove (blind *Rock 3* placement in the overhang). Make precarious and scary moves up the groove to the roof (peg). Swing right onto the rib (hand-placed knife-blade) and follow good holds onto a small ledge above the roof. Lower off a pre-placed rope.

The Right Flank

The Right Flank comprises a series of vegetated buttresses divided by deep grooves and cracks. These have been neglected for all of two decades, and, to cap it all, they then missed out on the Gorge's clean up. A complete lack of attention in perpetuity seems guaranteed.

Caligula   35 metres   E1 5b † ❀   (22.4.78)
The first groove right of the vegetated gully is climbed by *Gladiator*. This route climbed thin cracks in its left-hand wall.

Gladiator   35 metres   E2 5c ❀   (6.4.76)
The once-attractive (and visible) groove right of the gully was probably the best route hereabouts.

Legionnaire   35 metres   E2   5b   ❀   (11.4.76/5.6.77)
The cracked pillar between *Gladiator* and the deep chimney of *Gaul*.

Gaul   35 metres   Very Severe   4c   ❀   (19.1.75)
The deep chimney in the centre of the cliff.

Boadicea   35 metres   E4   6a   ❀   (8.9.79)
Even if regardened the second half of the route will remain poor and
broken. The groove, roof, and crack right of the chimney of *Gaul*.

Nero   45 metres   Hard Severe   4a   ❀   (8.3.76)
The long, wide crack 10 metres right of *Gaul*.

Forum   45 metres   E2   5b (1 pt aid)   ❀   (27.5.76)
The steep wall to the right of *Nero*.

The remaining three routes take the white tower at the right edge of The
Amphitheatre (effectively borrowed from the upper left section of High Rock).
All commence from a vegetated platform reached by abseil from trees on the
summit of High Rock. They are not afflicted by ivy to the same extent as the last
few routes, but will probably require some safety-conscious re-cleaning.

The Pict   40 metres   E3   5c   ❀   (1.5.81)
Ivy currently messes up the start. Gain the base of a long groove in the
left-hand side of the tower and follow it slightly rightwards to the
half-height roof. Pull through the left-hand side of the roof on jugs and
continue up the exposed thin crack in the headwall to the top.

Bird of Prey   42 metres   E5   6b   †   (3.3.90)
A monstrous pitch that preys on the innocent. Sustained face climbing up
the front of the tower is topped with a spectacular battle through the
dominating roof. Treble up on wires.
From deep pockets, climb the narrow face to better holds and good nuts
on the right. Continue boldly but on positive holds to an incipient crack
and then swing left around an arête (*in-situ* thread). Gain the lip of the
roof with a long stretch (8mm bolt) and haul over (peg) to a resting-place
in a small corner (junction with *The Scarecrow*). Swing left to jugs and
follow a crack to the top.

The Scarecrow   42 metres   E3   6a   ❀   (27.6.79)
An adventurous route that features a dramatic transition into positions of
terrifying exposure.
Move right and climb the large corner to a roof. Pull over into a small cave
(scare the crows and they'll scare you!). Climb the steep crack above to a
pedestal (possible stance). Traverse left along the lip of the roof (peg) and
move up to a small corner. Swing leftwards to jugs and follow a crack to
the top.

High Rock

*The cliff rises as a great unbroken wall, on which practically not a shrub can
find a root hold…*
(H E Balch, 1947)

Towering majestically at the mouth of the main Gorge is High Rock, a massive
sheet of limestone rising 100 metres above road-level and capped by a
rectangular headwall with a slender, knife-edged pinnacle, The Sceptre, on its
right.

To many, High Rock, with its unparalleled sweep of unbroken limestone,
epitomizes – through the length, exposure and character of its routes – that
unique 'Cheddar quality' which still attracts climbers from all over the country.
Most, however, come only to do the most famous climb in the Gorge,
Coronation Street, leaving the remaining wealth of quality climbing vulnerable
to revegetation. In the 90s many of the climbs seriously degenerated, a sorry
situation compounded by descaling operations that left some formerly
world-class routes in a weed-infested shambles. Now, although High Rock is
clear of ivy, some of the climbs, even the once-popular ones, will need
re-cleaning and re-opening.

High Rock consists of a tall central wall with supporting wings gradually
decreasing in height to either side. In the centre of the crag is an obvious
huge flake crack rising from road-level, which is the starting-point for
Coronation Street and *Sceptre*. To its left is the groove of the first pitch of
Crow, which continues up the centre of the main wall before it is deflected
leftwards into the big corner in the left-hand side of the headwall. The thin,
vertical crack deadly centred in the headwall is *West Route*, whilst the
groove-line in its right-hand side gives the finishing pitches of *Coronation
Street*. The Sceptre pinnacle to the right of the headwall offers its crest to *The
In Spire* and the crack in its centre is taken by *Crown of Creation*. A squat,
rectangular tower below the pinnacle marks the final corner-pitch of *Sceptre*.

The quality of the rock is reasonable but the occasional friable patch and
loose holds do occur. With the exception of *The Wishing Wall* area, seepage
problems are very limited, and some of the roadside lines barely get wet at
all. The multi-pitch routes, however, are very exposed to the wind.

Access: Climbing is allowed from 1 October until 15 March inclusive.

Warning: The utmost care should be taken as any rock (or gear) dislodged,
including from *Coronation Street*, will fall directly into the car-park below.
The safety of anyone using the car-park beneath you is your responsibility.

Descent from climbs reaching the top of High Rock is either via the main
cliff-top path, or by following one of a number of sketchy tracks diagonally
down rightwards through trees and scrub to the main descent couloir.

High Rock

1	Play the White Man	E4
2	No Slings Attached	E4
3	Bigfoot	E5
4	Bad Dog	E5

5	Desert Rat	E5
6	The Wishing Wall	E6
7	Shangri La	F7b+
8	The Wrecking Crew	F7c
9	Still Waters Run Deep	F7b
10	Bird of Prey	E5

11	Scarecrow	E3
12	Crow	E3
13	Hallucinations	E5
14	West Route	E6
15	Lionheart	E5
16	Osiris	E3
17	Coronation Street	E1
18	Sceptre	VS
19	The In Spire	E5
20	Take the Bull by the Horns	E4

21	The Twilight of Imperialism	E2
22	Crown of Creation	E3
23	Shakin' Like a Leaf	E5
24	The Fall	E5
25	Roadshow	E2
26	Dada	E4
27	Plastic Bullets	E2
28	Hot Lanta	E2
29	Eat a Peach	VS
30	Morituri	E1
31	RPs Out, Matt Ward's In!	E5
32	Jill	S
33	Jack	VS
34	Dig This, People	E4
35	Soopa Doopa	E3
36	The Blighter	E5
37	Knight's Climb	D

Carrying a head torch may help stragglers. Consult descent information on page 16.

At the extreme left-hand end of the left wing and some 15 metres right of *Portal* is an ivy-covered slanting corner-crack: **Forced Entry** (30 metres E2 5b ✿ 16.4.78)

The lower-left wing rising above an earth bank at road-level features a strip roof 12 metres up, which undercuts an expansive grey wall. The following seven climbs start from a ledge that rises leftwards from the foot of *Crow*.

Play the White Man   25 metres   E4 6a ✿   (5.10.86)
A fine route, when clean and dry, that offers sustained and technical climbing up the narrow, slanting groove bounding the left-hand side of the wall. Start at a tree near the left end of the ledge.
Climb a vague ramp rather boldly up rightwards to the obvious horizontal break. Traverse left for 3 metres, and work intricately up the steep wall (peg) to the base of the groove (peg). Nice, sustained climbing up the groove leads to an old abseil station on the right.

No Slings Attached   25 metres   E4 6b ✿   (15.2.86)
Strenuous climbing over the roof on suspect holds is relieved by bolt protection (with slings!) and the prospect of good climbing on the overlying wall. Start near the left end of the ledge; tree belay on the left.
Climb straight up the wall to the horizontal break and a ledge on the left (peg). Continue up the wall (10mm bolt) and pull over the roof, using a shaky spike (10mm bolt) to get established on the grey wall. A series of shallow grooves leads slightly rightwards and then back leftwards to the old abseil station of *Play the White Man*.

The next two routes start three-quarters of the way along the leftward-rising ledge, 3 metres left of an ash tree stump, and directly below a short right-facing corner in the roofs at 12 metres.

Bigfoot   25 metres   E5 6b †   (19.10.95)
An extremely direct line, with very hard climbing through the roofs.
Follow *Bad Dog* to the corner over the first roof. Make a hard move over the next roof using the overhead pinch-grip and so gain jugs leading to foot-ledges (peg). Continue deliciously direct to the obvious undercut roof, pull over, and reach a break with a single 8mm bolt from which it is *possible* to retreat. (Two holes were drilled in preparation for an Eco-bolt abseil station.)

Bad Dog   25 metres   E5 6a ✿   (26.4.75/11.4.82/19.10.95)
Bad Dog was re-climbed subsequent to alterations arising from loose rock and vegetation removal by landowners. Unfortunately it still goes to the dogs from time to time. If it is clean, interested parties should not be put off by the reputation of boldness up to the roof; this is fairly straightforward and on positive holds (which will not be wet if drainage streaks are less than a metre high).

From the ledge, climb easily up the wall for 7 metres to a good break (*Friends* ½ to 1½). Climb straight up to the roofs on reasonable holds (vital *Rock 4* placement in base of corner over first roof). Pull into the corner (peg) and then undercut rightwards between roofs (peg) to gain the foot of a long shallow groove. Climb the groove without deviation (sufficient small wire protection) and, at its top, reach left to a single 8mm bolt from which it is *possible* to retreat, as for *Big Foot*.

Desert Rat   30 metres   E5 6a ❀   (16.10.85)

Potentially a fine pitch, but not in the best of condition. It can give rise to epics, even to masters of epics. Protection on the crux is almost entirely reliant on the solitary 1985 knife-blade. Start 15 metres along the ledge at the ash tree stump.

Climb the wall to the horizontal break, and continue to the roof. Make hard, committing moves over the roof just to the right of the peg and climb over the bulge above to a resting-place. Follow flake cracks until moves rightwards gain a horizontal break below a small roof (*in-situ* thread). Pull over the roof to a ledge and sapling and an old and withered abseil station 3 metres higher.

The Wishing Wall   30 metres   E6 6b † ❀   (16.10.85)

Inherently exceptional, but is it worth sweating up the hillside, stringing three ropes together, and dangling from the top of High Rock to check it out? Alternatively, attempt it on-sight: Dave Pickford did. Start 10 metres along the ledge, and 5 metres right of the ash tree stump.

Climb easily up the wall (can become ivy-covered) to the horizontal break. Gain the scoop above and climb steeply to the roof. Pull round on a jug and proceed up the smooth wall with increasing severity (peg and *Rock 1*), trending slightly rightwards to thin cracks. Traverse leftwards for 2 metres using a hidden flake, and work back right into a grey scoop. Move up, swing left onto the face, and climb directly to the horizontal break. Step left to a junction with *Desert Rat* (*in-situ* thread) and follow that route to the old abseil station.

Shangri La   25 metres   E6 6b F7b+   (22.11.69/23.10.85)

The first pitch of the old mixed route goes free to provide a very strenuous problem, questionably protected by fixed gear, some of which dates back to the original aided ascent. (This may not put off featherweight climbers, but others might consider rebolting the route.) Start 5 metres along the ledge, below a broken crack that leads up to the left end of the roofs.

Climb easily up the crack to the horizontal break. Move left and follow good holds to the roof (two pegs). A very difficult sequence through the roofs (one peg and three (Paul Nunn) bolts) gains a small resting-ledge. Continue more easily up a thin crack to peg belays. Abseil off.

The Wrecking Crew   25 metres   E6 6c F7c   (5.11.89)

Brilliant, but in need of a rebolt to regain its fan club. Start below a white roof at 14 metres, with the leftward-rising ledge at head-height.

Ascend easily on good holds to flat ledges. Climb steeply to the white roof, which is surmounted to reach a resting-jug on the lip of the second roof. Pull over onto a smooth wall and climb up to a larger roof and a bolted abseil station. (It is possible to extend the route through the roof to a higher (older) abseil station: the original line). Seven (mostly 8mm) bolts.

The following three climbs start below and to the left of a groove leading up to the right-hand end of a large roof at 20 metres, 15 metres left of the huge flake crack of *Sceptre*.

Still Waters Run Deep   25 metres   E5 6b F7b   (10.12.86)
This elegant and very technical line, which dries very quickly after wet weather, traces a leftward-arcing line up the smooth wall to the left of the groove of *Crow*. The 8mm bolts are well-used, but the route still attracts delighted ascents.
Climb a leftward-slanting crack (*in-situ* thread) to a horizontal break and then a useful no-hands rest where the wall steepens (peg). A series of very extending reaches leads directly up the wall (three bolts) to an easing next to a peg in a pocket. Traverse ambiguously leftwards, rising slightly (bolt), until it is possible to inch up a small slab to the abseil station of *The Wrecking Crew*.

Stone the Crows   30 metres   E3 5c   (21.2.81)
This is what's left of a major four-pitch route up the main face of High Rock. Although enjoyable, the pitch falls a long way short of the stature of the surprisingly short-lived parent route, which took a direct line (138 metres E4) based on the old mixed route *Shangri La* to link up with the top pitch of *Scarecrow*. Of course, the whole thing could be recleaned!
Climb *Crow* pitch 1 as far as the large roof. Make a long traverse leftwards beneath the roof to peg belays on *Shangri La*. Abseil off.

Crow   122 metres   E3 †† ❀   (17/18.10.70)
Alas the 'age of the Crow' is no more. What was once one of the greatest E3s in the country has suffered progressive neglect and, more recently, heavy bombardment by debris from descaling operations. Aspirants should take care, and expect to do a fair amount of cleaning en route. The top two pitches are commonly run into one.
1 25m. 5b. Make a few moves up the leftward-slanting crack, and swing right into the groove. Follow the groove past pegs to the roof. Swing right onto the rib (peg) and climb up to a stance in a short corner (peg belays).
2 25m. 5a. Follow grooves to a ledge (peg) and continue up the steep slab and rib above (pegs) to a large ledge.
3 27m. 5b. The smooth wall may be tackled in a number of places, but gone are the days when you could cheat by tugging on a big ivy root. From the highest of a series of grassy ledges above, make a hard move right into a thin crack and climb it until, after 6 metres, a line of good holds leads leftwards to peg and nut belays just below the horizontal break that undercuts the headwall.

4 25m. 5c. Traverse leftwards along the break to a line of flared cracks. Climb the cracks with increasing difficulty until a strenuous move gains a resting-place on good footholds above (peg). Move right and climb a steep crack to a ledge below the final corner.

5 20m. 5a. Climb the corner above the stance, initially up cracks in the right-hand wall, and then directly to the capping roof. Exit right (peg), or left, to the top.

Sherryland   20 metres   E5 6b F7b   (2.1.93)

More than a merry little tipple, this is a hard line through the spectacular, roofed groove to the right of the first pitch of *Crow*. Start 4 metres right of *Crow* at a short, shallow groove topped by a bulge.

Climb the groove and tricky bulge (peg) and then bear slightly leftwards to foot-ledges immediately next to *Crow* (*in-situ* thread). Make a hard move to enter the hanging groove (8mm bolt); then proceed energetically (peg, 8mm bolt) to engineer a retreat from pegs on the first stance of *Crow*.

Going up four storeys, the next two routes provide high-altitude acrobatics on the headwall above *Crow*. They start from the stance at the end of pitch 3 of *Crow*, best reached by fixing a rope to trees 6 metres back from the edge of High Rock and making a nerve-tingling 35-metre abseil – tie a knot in the end of the rope!

Hallucinations   40 metres   E5 6b   (23.2.85)

Impressive climbing on good rock in positions of mindless exposure! The route follows a system of grooves and cracks in the headwall to the right of the final corner of *Crow*.

Climb the steep wall behind the belay, making very hard moves leftwards via the obvious pocket into a shallow groove (peg). Pull over the small roof and trend rightwards to good holds and a resting-place. Move up a short groove and make a difficult stride left (peg) to twin cracks, which lead quickly to a ledge and possible stance just to the right of *Crow* (cams useful). Jam up the crack above and bear rightwards across the wall to finish easily up a grassy rib.

The incipient seam above the 'stride left' is an unresolved plum project: trad 8a+ climbing with 8c+ exposure!

West Route   35 metres   E6 6a   (10.4.65/8.10.78)

An outstanding line in masterful situation. The perfectly-centred thin crack in the headwall offers perhaps the loneliest lead in the Gorge. It still gets climbed. Take many small wires (and check that the placements are clear beforehand). It is possible to belay at a small sapling directly beneath the line 3 metres to the right of the *Crow* stance (better for the leader).

Climb the initial groove (often wet) to the roof, swing out right onto the arête (peg), and pull over the bulge with difficulty to gain a small ledge. Now climb the sustained crack past three rusting bolts from 1965 and an *in-situ* thread, until hard moves can be made slightly right into a shallow scoop (peg). Continue up the thin crack, taking the bulge to its left, and climb the broken final wall, trending rightwards past three pegs to the top.

Lionheart   112 metres   E5   (25.10.85)
'Without doubt one of the finest routes in the whole of the South-West'. Or
in the country, even? There's a catch of course: weed-life. *Lionheart* had a
major re-clean in 1994, and a welter of ascents, but the route can still
revegetate very quickly. The route is a big undertaking, which follows a line
up the smooth walls and crack-systems in the right-hand side of the main
face. Reserve some power for the crux at 100 metres! Start 10 metres left
of the flake crack of *Sceptre*, below a break in the roofs 12 metres up.
1 27m. 5c. Climb a broken groove and the wall above (peg) to the roofs
(peg). Pull rightwards around the overhang on prominent jugs and climb
straight up the wall above to a small ledge (peg). Move up and diagonally
rightwards to peg and nut belays on a pedestal stance.
2 20m. 6a. Climb easily up the blocky wall and then with more difficulty
up the smoother wall above (*in-situ* thread) to reach a good pocket. Move
up right and then directly to ledges. Peg belay high on the left.
3 30m. 6a. Climb rightwards across the wall (peg) to pull straight over
the bulge on superb holds. Trend rightwards up the pocketed wall to a
ledge below a short right-facing corner. The corner and the fine crack
above lead to peg belays on the fourth stance of *Coronation Street*.
4 35m. 6b. Climb the awkward corner above the belay to a ledge. Move
left to a flake and climb up slightly rightwards to a resting-place and
thread. Power up to the left on pockets (peg), and make a tricky move with
the aid of a small pocket on the left to reach a thin crack. Climb the crack
to easier ground and the top.

Spiritualize   40 metres   E7 6b †   (23.10.94)
A formidable route of derring-do. Extremely sustained, it takes a
super-exposed, leftward-rising journey across the headwall of High Rock.
Start from the fourth stance of *Coronation Street*.
Move up left into a shallow scoop, cross a bulge, and then bear diagonally
left to reach a good hand-ledge (peg). Make a very difficult and bold
reach up right for a good finger-pocket (just right of a peg), and rock up
leftwards to reach better holds and a good rest just above (two pegs).
Climb up for 3 metres (peg) and swing left into the crack of *West Route*.
Climb the crack to a bulge (wire the old bolt-head), and (instead of
moving right on *West Route*) head slightly left up a desperate, rejecting
groove (peg) to pockets (*in-situ Rock 6*). Pull over a bulge on jugs, balance
left across the void to a small right-facing groove (peg), and then follow
this (peg) to an easy rib and the top.

Rameses   113 metres   E4   (2.10.88)
Links some good climbing on a long and ambitious expedition. Weeds
and grassed-up holds will add to the commitment. Start 6 metres left of the
flake crack of *Sceptre*, below a hanging block 6 metres up.
1 33m. 6a. Climb a crack left of the block, aiming for a little
roof-capped groove in the overhangs (peg on the left). Move up the
groove (two pegs and an *in-situ* thread) until able to move left to a good
rest above the overhangs (junction with *Lionheart*). Traverse left along the

lip to a peg and make a committing move left to reach better holds (*in-situ* thread). Trend slightly rightwards for 15 metres, passing to the left of a tree to reach a small stance and peg and tree belays.
2 15m. 5b. Climb up directly (*in-situ* thread), and bear slightly rightwards (peg and *in-situ* thread) to gain a series of ledges. Scramble up broken ground on the left to gain a peg belay on *Lionheart*.
3 30m. 6a. From the left end of the stance, climb the wall (peg and two *in-situ* threads) to a resting-position under a bulge. Climb with difficulty (*in-situ* wire) to gain a grassy ledge (peg: optional belay). Move up into a scoop on the left and exit it on the right (peg). Continue slightly rightwards (peg) and climb the fine pocketed wall (*in-situ* thread) to reach the obvious break. Traverse right to a small ledge and peg belays at the fourth stance of *Coronation Street*.
4 20m. 6a. Follow *Lionheart* to its resting-place and thread. Step right into the crack of *Coronation Street* which leads to peg belays on a small ledge on the right.
5 15m. 5a. *Danger Bird* pitch 3.

Osiris   114 metres   E3   (4/17.10.87)
A prodigious route that gives consistently enjoyable technical climbing on a line that crosses and shares several stances with *Coronation Street*.
1 27m. 6a. Follow *Rameses* for 12 metres to the resting place above the overhangs. Move right and climb directly (*in-situ* thread) until easier climbing enables peg and nut belays to be reached on the left, below an obvious band of small overhangs.
2 15m. 4c. Climb over the overhangs from the right. Continue until it is possible to move right (*in-situ* thread) to an obvious nose of rock in the flake-line of *Sceptre*. Follow *Sceptre* for 3 metres to its small stance on the right (peg and nut belays).
3 25m. 5c. Move up and left via a slab to a break. Climb up on pockets (peg) until a move left can be made into a corner. Climb the corner to reach a small ledge on the right. Now trend slightly leftwards with a hard move to gain good holds (*in-situ* thread). Move rightwards a little and follow a faint groove to gain a narrow ledge on the right (left of the chimney of *Coronation Street*). Climb up past a peg, and bear rightwards to the chimney, which is followed to the third (pedestal) stance of *Coronation Street*.
4 12m. 5c. From the right-hand side of the pedestal, climb the wall (left of a left-facing corner) past a peg and *in-situ* thread to gain a good ledge, and peg and nut belays above the horizontal break.
5 20m. 6a. Climb a short, deep crack to another horizontal break, which leads leftwards to gain a very exposed position on the lip of the overhang (as for *Danger Bird*). Climb up and rightwards (peg) and then straight up (*in-situ* wire and peg) to a poor thread. Step right and move up more easily (peg) until a leftward traverse below a high peg gains the final stance of *Coronation Street*. (Clip an *in-situ* thread on the right to protect your partner on the traverse.)
6 15m. 4c. *Coronation Street* pitch 6.

Coronation Street 115 metres E1 (5.65)

This great climb, which remains a celebrated British classic, follows the magnificent and exciting system of cracks and grooves in the right-hand side of the main face. It has been climbed in the dark, rain, and snow, as well as solo. Nonetheless, the route is very committing, and retreat from beyond the Shield can prove problematic. (Benightments and rescues are not uncommon: there are more pro-active ways of climbers working with the local media. Set that alarm clock early!) Start at the foot of the huge flake crack in the centre of the cliff.

1 33m. 4b. Climb the crack-system to a stance on a small ledge.

2 12m. 4a. Continue in the same line past a small roof to peg and nut belays in a triangular niche.

3 20m. 5b. Climb diagonally rightwards past a small cave to the base of a groove leading to a triangular roof. Climb up to and past the roof on its left (peg) and tackle the groove and awkward overhanging chimney above to reach peg belays on a pedestal.

4 15m. 5a. Climb a steep crack to the horizontal break below the headwall (peg). Hand-traverse leftwards in a sensational position past the resonating Shield (of rock) and an original machine-nut runner to peg belays on a small ledge. An intimidating pitch – in 2002 part of the Shield fell off with climber attached!

5 20m. 5b. Step right into the right-hand of two corners and climb it, quite technical, to a ledge. Continue strenuously up the bulging crack above to suspect peg belays on a small, exposed ledge on the right.

6 15m. 4c. Climb a short crack on the right to a ledge. The slab and broken rock above lead to the top and tree belays 6 metres back.

Project X 45 metres E5 (7.11.94)

Like getting spaced out? Then sample this. A daunting line that takes on the roofs and arête above the Shield on *Coronation Street*, effectively absorbing *Danger Bird*. Start from the pedestal (third) stance of *Coronation Street*.

1 30m. 6a. From the pedestal, traverse horizontally left on hidden, finger-sinking pockets to a thin crack. Climb the crack and bear right beneath the Shield to the hand traverse of *Coronation Street*. Extend over the roof above (peg) and pull into the bottomless groove (*Danger Bird* comes in from the right here). Pull up past the right end of the roof (peg), and trend leftwards to a crack in the crest of the arête which leads to the final stance of *Coronation Street* (as for *Danger Bird*). (The original route undercut left at hard 6b beneath the second roof, but it is reported to have lost a hold… worth having a blast though.)

2 15m. 4c. *Coronation Street* pitch 6.

Sceptre 78 metres Very Severe (2.6.53)

A classic, unfortunately overpowered by its more illustrious neighbour. It was the first intrusion upon High Rock, and is still a good and popular initiation. Start at the base of the huge flake crack, as for *Coronation Street*.

1 33m. 4b. Climb the crack-system to a stance on a small ledge.

On the Right Track
(E5, first ascent)
Priest Rock
Climber: Martin Crocker
Photo: Carl Ryan

2 12m. 4a. Continue in the same line past a small roof to peg and nut belays in a triangular niche.

3 15m. 4a. Climb diagonally rightwards past a small cave and then traverse rightwards below the groove of *Coronation Street* across a short, steep wall to vegetated ledges. Follow the ledges carefully up and right to peg and nut belays at the base of a vertical crack (*Crown of Creation*) just to the left of the final corner.

4 18m. 4c. A strenuous pitch. Traverse rightwards to the base of the corner. Climb the wide corner-crack to a big ledge at the top of the squat, rectangular tower. Descent is best made by abseiling from a tree just to the right of the belay to gain the grassy shoulder below *Acid Rock*. The loose and vegetated gully above is a less attractive option.

Variation

Sceptre Direct   25 metres   Hard Very Severe 5a †† ❀   (16.3.64)
A serious direct finish to *Sceptre* that takes the obvious twin cracks into the gully. Start midway along the vegetated traverse of *Sceptre* pitch 3, below twin cracks.
Climb the cracks fairly easily for 6 metres. Now climb the right-hand crack and continue into the gully. Peg and nut belays on *The In Spire* to the right. Finish by scrambling very carefully up the gully.

The next three routes commence from the vegetated traverse of *Sceptre* pitch 3. They can be also be approached from the shoulder of *Acid Rock* on the right at 4c (*High Rock Girdle* pitch 1).

Danger Bird   60 metres   E3   (7.7.76)
The prominent left-facing corner right of the pedestal of *Coronation Street* is combined with high-anxiety climbing up the right-hand side of the headwall. Start from a narrow foot-ledge on the *Sceptre* traverse, 6 metres right of *Coronation Street*: good horizontal crack at shoulder height for wires.

1 20m. 5b. Climb diagonally leftwards over blocks and move up into the off-width corner-crack. Thrutch up the crack to peg and nut belays on a good ledge above the horizontal break (shared with *Osiris*).

2 25m. 5b. Climb a short, deep crack to follow another horizontal break that leads back leftwards above the roofs into a bottomless groove. Pull over the roof above and trend leftwards to a crack in the crest of the buttress. Climb the crack to the final stance of *Coronation Street*.

3 15m. 5a. Climb the crack above the stance to the top.

Kind of Hush   54 metres   E3 †   (4.2.95)
Two fine finger-cracks in exhilarating positions to the left of *The In Spire*. High in the grade but protectable throughout. Start from a narrow foot-ledge on the *Sceptre* traverse, as for *Danger Bird*.

1 27m. 6a. Step right to a ledge below a groove which becomes a distinctive dog-leg crack in the arête right of the wide crack of *Danger Bird*. Climb the groove and crack, with hard moves to pass the roof, and continue straight up the tip of the arête, delicately, to reach a break. Swing right to the foot of the gully, and move right again to the peg and wire belay of *The In Spire*.

2 27m. 5c. Step left and climb a groove, before exiting left onto a ledge below the smooth east face of The Spire. Step left again to the superb finger-crack and follow it (sustained) to the top of The Spire.

The In Spire   47 metres   E5   (7.11.85)
Superb climbing of high atmosphere on the alluring knife-edged arête of The Sceptre. A striking silhouette against the Somerset Levels awaits a rent-a-star photo-shoot. Start on a small, vegetated ledge 3 metres down and to the left of the third stance of *Sceptre*.
1 20m. 6a. Climb the face past a small roof on good but well-spaced holds to a sinuous, thin crack. Climb the crack and its deeper continuation to a short groove leading promptly to the horizontal break. Swing left to a small ledge and peg and nut belays.
2 27m. 6b. Climb straight up the tip of the arête, swing left to good holds, and then bear rightwards to its edge again (*in-situ* thread). Hard moves above (peg) lead into a bottomless groove, which is followed to a pedestal below the final facet of the spire. Teeter left onto the knife edge (poor peg) and layback to easier ground and the summit. (If the top 7 metres is too lichenous an escape can be made to the right.)

Back at the road-side, the right wing of High Rock commences with a steep rectangular wall, interspersed with roofs, to the right of the flake crack of *Sceptre*. The following three single-pitch routes are served by an over-used and under-funded fixed belay and abseil station at 25 metres; check its condition before launching back down.

Take the Bull by the Horns   24 metres   E4 6a   (29.11.86)
A wandering pitch. Start 5 metres right of *Sceptre*, below a bottomless groove capped by a triangular roof.
Climb the initial wall and pull over the bulge (poor peg) into the bottomless groove. Undercut leftwards below a roof (8mm bolt) and climb directly up the bulging wall (thread and wire) to better holds and a resting-place. Traverse 5 metres right above the triangular roof and then make an awkward move up to peg belays in the horizontal break. Abseil off.
Direct Start E5 6b † (8.3.87). Vicious. Start 3 metres right of *Sceptre*. Climb straight up the shattered wall (*in-situ* thread and peg) to black bulges. Move up right and pull over the roof into a tiny white groove (*in-situ* thread and peg). Continue desperately to the undercut and bolt on the parent route.

The Twilight of Imperialism   27 metres   E2 5b   (1.5.70)
A superb pitch, very popular in this form, which snakes its way through the roofs in the rectangular wall to the right of the flake crack of *Sceptre*. It is one of the few routes that stays dry in wet weather. Start 5 metres right of the flake crack of *Sceptre*, below the bottomless groove.
Climb the initial wall and pull over the bulge (poor peg) into the bottomless groove. Climb the groove to the triangular roof (peg). Make a difficult traverse right to a layback crack and climb it briskly to the horizontal break. Swing left to the peg belays. Abseil off.

Silent Night   25 metres   E4 6a   (6.12.86)
A deceptive eliminate that bisects the line of *The Twilight of Imperialism*.
Start 8 metres right of *Sceptre*, below a jagged roof at 8 metres.
Climb directly to the roof and pull over on buckets (*in-situ* thread). A very
awkward section up thin cracks in the smooth wall above leads to the
traverse of *The Twilight of Imperialism*. Pull up and left over the bulge, and
climb the crack to the horizontal break and peg belays. Abseil off.

Crown of Creation   97 metres   E3 ❀   (1969/13&24.5.76/23.6.76)
An impressive climb of character, which reaches the crack in the centre of
The Sceptre by a direct line up the buttress below. Unfortunately, the
second pitch is prone to vegetation, which usually heightens the
excitement. The first pitch is worth doing in isolation.
1 25m. 5c. Climb up to the roof as for *Silent Night*, but step right to a
groove. Follow the groove with interest to the layback crack of *The Twilight
of Imperialism*. Climb the crack to belay as for that route on the left.
2 25m. 5c. Move back right and pull over the bulge leftwards to a small
ledge. Climb up (peg) to a slim groove and follow it steeply until it eases
and leads past a small overhang to peg and nut belays on a grassy ledge.
3 12m. 4c. Climb the vegetated wall and ensuing ivy to peg and nut
belays on the third stance of *Sceptre*.
4 35m. 6a. Climb the face-crack behind the belay, take the right-hand of
the two cracks where it branches, and move up to the horizontal break. Step
up left and then move back right into the crack, which leads strenuously to
ledges. Ignore the vegetated wall above and bear rightwards to tree belays
in the gully. Scramble carefully up the gully to the top.

Shakin' Like a Leaf   25 metres   E5 6a   (29.11.86)
Exquisite climbing on an intricate line up the superb, smooth grey wall 10
metres right of *Sceptre*. Bold on the crux and consequently high in the
grade. The route was re-cleaned in 2000 and led bolt-free. Start 10
metres right of *Sceptre*, behind a 'pay and display' sign (did you?).
Climb the broken wall for 8 metres to the base of the smooth wall. Using
good sideholds, pull up a shallow scoop onto the wall; now boldly stretch
up to a good fingerhold before stepping delicately left to enter a thin
corner (*in-situ* thread). Climb the corner to a bulge and pull over to
finger-pockets (full-stretch wire placement). Tiptoe up on the wall, trending
rightwards to the horizontal break and a peg. Hand-traverse leftwards 3
metres to the abseil station of *The Twilight of Imperialism*.

The Fall   25 metres   E5 6a †   (13.2.00)
Good climbing up the right edge of the smooth grey wall; a less taxing
companion to *Shakin' Like a Leaf*.
Climb *Shakin'*... for 6 metres, traverse 2 metres right, and then step up to
undercuts below a thin overhang. Make long, thin moves direct up the
grey wall (peg) to better holds. Take a slight groove on the right; then
swing back left onto the wall. Climb the flake-line above to the horizontal
break and peg of *Shakin'*... Hand-traverse leftwards 3 metres to the abseil
station of *The Twilight of Imperialism*.

The central portion of the right wing of High Rock is prone to vegetation, but parts of this were removed during scrub and ivy clearance operations in 1990, and again during a minor new routes renaissance more recently. There are two large vegetated depressions at the same level, 25 metres up the wall.

Roadshow   20 metres   E2 5c   (12.6.79)
An excellent line, recleaned and reclimbed in this form in 2000. Start below a prominent orange groove that leads up to the left of the left-hand depression, 15 metres right of *Sceptre*.
Climb a broken groove with care to a shaky pedestal ledge. Step left and pull over a small roof on finger-curling holds into the groove (peg). Climb the groove to its top and an old abseil station on the right.

Dada   20 metres   E4 6a †   (5.3.00)
Unusual climbing above the roof right of *Roadshow*. Hard for E4. Start as for *Roadshow*, 15 metres right of *Sceptre*.
Climb a broken groove with care to a shaky pedestal ledge. Move up right to the widest part of the roof (good wire placement in roof). Layback powerfully over (peg) to an undercut rib. Step left onto overlapping slabs, and climb direct to the old abseil station of *Roadshow* on the left.

Shem Shak   54 metres   Hard Very Severe †† ❀   (19.4.75)
This route was only semi-exhumed, so the usual health warning applies. A line up the salad-infested groove in the buttress between the two depressions.
1 27m. 5a. Climb the wall to a small roof (peg). Climb into the groove above and follow it to a stance below a distinctive triangular roof.
2 27m. 4c. Move left and climb a short wall above the overhang to regain the groove. Steep climbing leads to the top.

Below the right-hand vegetated depression is a prominent circular niche at 10 metres.

Plastic Bullets   20 metres   E2 5c   (22.2.87)
A reasonable pitch up the clean, slender grey pillar left of the circular niche. Start diagonally down left from the niche, 20 metres right of *Sceptre*.
Climb straight up the wall past an old peg to a small roof at the base of the pillar (peg). Pull up onto the sandwiched slab and continue over a second small roof to a resting-place on the arête (peg on *Shem Shak*). Reach back right onto the face and break through twin overlaps to gain an old abseil station.

No Mnemonics   20 metres   E5 6a †† †   (8.3.87)
Powerful climbing through the roofs to the left of the circular niche. Start at the foot of a vegetated groove leading up to the circular niche.
Climb the groove to the base of the niche. Step left to a thin crack in the left wall. Blast directly up the leaning wall (*in-situ* thread) to the roof (peg). Pull over and, from a good jug up left, move into a broken groove above (*in-situ* thread); follow it easily to belays in the depression. Either abseil off,

scramble out on the left, or traverse right to exit up the top pitch of *Eat a Peach*.

Free Enterprise   33 metres   E4 5c † ❀   (8.3.87)
The technical and run-out white ramp rising out of the circular niche only needs a quick re-clean.
1 24m. 5c. Climb into the niche as for *No Mnemonics*. Follow the ramp rightwards on small holds until steep moves gain a scoop. Move right to the stance of *Eat a Peach*.
2 9m. 5a. *Eat a Peach* pitch 2.

Hot Lanta   35 metres   E2 ❀   (5.5.75)
Good climbing and normally clean enough. Start below the circular niche, as for *No Mnemonics*.
1 25m. 5b. Climb a slight groove on the right to a small overhang at 8 metres. Climb steeply up the thin crack and groove until strenuous moves enable a shallow scoop to be reached. Step right and climb up to a grassy ledge.
2 10m. 5a. Climb the steep crack behind the belay for 3 metres (as for *Eat a Peach*). Move left onto the undercut face and climb it to the top.

Eat a Peach   36 metres   Very Severe   (3.5.75)
The most distinctive feature of the buttress right of the circular niche is a leftward-leaning ramp and crackline. This gives palatable climbing, although the finish is tough for the grade. Start below the foot of the ramp-line.
1 27m. 4c. Climb the broken wall to the horizontal break and the lower end of the ramp (peg). Follow the ramp and crack with continuous interest until a step right and a short wall lead to the grassy ledge of *Hot Lanta*.
2 9m. 5a. Climb the steep crack behind the belay to the top.

Morituri   27 metres   E1 5b ❀   (1.1.73)
A good climb up the thin crack in the steep face to the right of *Eat a Peach*. Unfortunately some of the holds tend to grass up.
Climb the broken wall for 5 metres, as for *Eat a Peach*, and step right below a narrow roof under the steep face. Pull up over a bulge (peg) and follow the twin cracks (past vintage pegs) to ledges. Move up and then step right to the top of the groove of *Jill (Left-hand)*.

RPs Out, Matt Ward's In!   27 metres   E5 6a †   (26.12.92)
The arête with a dark streak on its right, just to the left of a short narrow chimney 8 metres up. Great moves, pumpy, and protectable.
Climb the easy lower wall in line with a vague crack to foot-ledges below the bulge at 10 metres. Pull straight over the bulge (peg) and layback the arête (good wires), finishing direct (peg) to ledges. Step right to finish up the final groove of *Jill (Left-hand)*.

Choss   27 metres   Hard Severe   4a   (26.10.72)
What you read is what you get. Climb up to the short, narrow chimney
and ivy. Climb the chimney to ledges and continue to finish up the groove
of *Jill (Left-hand)*.

The right wing of High Rock terminates in a fine promontory that overhangs
the road. The following four climbs are located here.

Jill   25 metres   Severe   4a   (1954)
Sadly a portion of this popular route has come tumbling down, and the
upper corner is probably now someone's rock garden. Nonetheless, the
climb is still very satisfying, particularly with the new direct finish. Start
below the corner crack immediately left of the promontory.
Climb the corner crack quite steeply to a large ledge at 15 metres. Climb
cracks in the steep wall above to the top. The easier finish is **Jill
(Left-hand)**, which follows the grassy, leftward-slanting groove to the top.

Jack   25 metres   Very Severe   4c   (5.65)
An excellent but very steep and taxing climb that takes the crack in the
left-hand side of the promontory. VSs don't get much harder.
Climb steeply up the nose and step left into a scoop beneath the bulging
crack. Climb the crack strenuously and move rightwards to finish at a tree.

Dig This, People   25 metres   E4   6a †   (13.2.00)
The dramatic arête right of *Jack* is not as constrained as it looks.
Follow *Jack* to the base of the crack. Step right onto the arête and make
elegantly dynamic moves up its edge (vital *Rock 2*) to good holds. Follow
the easier arête to the top, and get your partner to pass a hat around.

Sense of Doubt   25 metres   E2   5c   (8.1.78)
The crack in the narrow front of the promontory provides a problematic
pitch which is entertaining for onlookers.
Climb the nose as for *Jack*, but continue directly past a peg to the foot of
the right-hand crack. Pull over a bulge with difficulty and climb the crack to
the top.

Around the corner from *Jack* and *Jill* is a flat 12-metre wall above the
left-hand side of the car-park below Acid Rock: Cheddar's very own version of
The Embankment. The wall is split by four prominent cracks, each of which
provides good climbing on solid rock. From left to right, these are: **Fool's
Overture** (E1 5c 13.11.77); **Finefinger** (E1 5b 13.11.77); **Shaved Fish**
(E1 5b 11.77); and **Right Crack** (Hard Very Severe 5a 1977).

The following three climbs commence from the grassy shoulder above the
right wing of High Rock, which is reached either by following exposed ledges
rising leftwards above the *Finefinger* wall or via the Acid Rock approach
(page 137).

High Rock Girdle   117 metres   E1 †† ✾   (1967/21.6.76)
The deep horizontal break below the headwall of High Rock. Sensationally
exposed, but no place for those with nerves (as opposed to nerve).
Unfortunately, the first pitch can be vegetated; *Sceptre* provides an
alternative approach, which is advisable given the major alterations to the
start. Start from the grassy shoulder beneath the Main Face of Acid Rock.
1 27m. 4c. Stroll left along a ledge and climb up to the base of the squat,
rectangular tower (*in-situ* thread). Move left and scrabble up a dirty groove
to the corner-crack of *Sceptre*. Climb the crack to a grassy platform.
2 25m. 5a. Traverse horizontally left along the break (peg) past the
corner of *Danger Bird* and the Shield of *Coronation Street* to peg belays on
the latter route's fourth stance.
3 25m. 5a. Continue leftwards along the break past the third stance of
Crow until easier climbing leads to the ivy ledge below the tower of *The
Pict* and *Bird of Prey*.
4 20m. 5a. Move right and climb a large corner (*Scarecrow*) to a roof.
Pull over and, from the ledge above the small cave, traverse down and
rightwards to the final stance of *Crow*.
5 20m. 5a. *Crow* pitch 5 (p. 125).

Soopa Doopa   25 metres   E3 6a ††   (15.11.86)
The crack and left-hand arête of the squat, rectangular tower on the
right-hand edge of High Rock. Start from the grassy shoulder.
Stroll left onto a ledge and climb up to a flake crack leading up into the
centre of the tower (*in-situ* thread). Climb the flake and short groove (peg)
to a roof, which is taken awkwardly. Move left to the arête and follow its
very edge fairly easily until it is possible to swing left below a small roof to
the final moves of *Sceptre*. Abseil from a tree on the right.

The Blighter   25 metres   E5 6b † ††   (14.10.90)
A rewarding pitch up the right arête of the rectangular tower. Difficulties
are considerable.
Stroll left onto a ledge and move up to a flake crack (*in-situ* thread). Take
the cracks in the smooth wall on the right and then a tiny groove to the
roofs (peg and *in-situ* thread on the right). Lunge for an invisible jug
around the bulge and then make precarious moves straight up the arête
(8mm bolt) to a resting-place. Continue up the arête (8mm bolt) to a tree
belay. Abseil off.

Wind Rock

At the lower end of the car-park below Acid Rock, a flat-topped pinnacle,
Wind Rock, projects towards the road. The pinnacle, known locally as
Sugarloaf Rock, is clearly identified by a smooth and narrow slab in its

roadside face. Apart from *The Slab*, the climbing is fairly nondescript and unattractive.

Access: Climbing is allowed from 1 October until 15 March inclusive.

East Slab   15 metres   Difficult   (1931)
Start from just inside the deep little gully left of the pinnacle. Climb a short wall and continue up more broken rock to the summit.

Easy Way   15 metres   Difficult   (1950)
From the edge of the gully, climb a short corner and the wall above slightly rightwards to finish just to the left of the summit.

Central Route   18 metres   Severe 4a ††   (1985)
Climb the bulging groove in the nose of the pinnacle to finish up a short crack.

The Slab   18 metres   Severe   (1950)
A delightful pitch, the best on Wind Rock. Climb the narrow slab with little in the way of protection, and move left above it to finish up a short crack. Fall off and you will be on the roof of a passing car!

Mike's Party Piece   18 metres   Very Severe 5a   (6.53)
A local curiosity. Just to the right and around the corner from The Slab is a narrow ledge 3 metres up. This may be gained via several amusing problems. Climb the crack and bulges above the ledge to the summit.

West Wall Climb   18 metres   Very Severe 5a ††   (1985)
Start 5 metres right of the base of The Slab. Climb a thin diagonal crack to a niche. Step left and climb the cracked wall above to the top.

Windy Crack   15 metres   Severe 4a ††   (1985)
The short crack just to the right of *West Wall Climb* leads to the niche on that route. Climb the groove above to the top.

Pinnacle Route   15 metres   Difficult ††   (1931)
Climb the huge flake which lies beneath the far right-hand side of the pinnacle and continue up short walls to the top.

The Fearless Four   20 metres   E4 6a   (15.2.86)
A difficult line up the black bulging tower 15 metres right of *The Slab*. Climb a thin flake crack to good holds and runners in a horizontal break. Pull over the bulge onto a sloping ledge and move up to another break. Take the shallow groove above (peg) to the top. Strenuous.

Positively Bunky   20 metres   E1 5b †   (28.9.78)
A broken groove bounds the right-hand side of the tower. Climb the groove for 12 metres, before a line of pockets on the left leads more steeply to the top.

Just Like Art   12 metres   E3 6a ††   (4.89)
Climb the bulging wall 6 metres right of the black tower on pockets (two *in-situ* threads). A worrying exit.

Acid Rock

To the right of High Rock is Acid Rock, a 55-metre cliff that rises above a wooded slope behind the car-park next to Wind Rock. The crag is split into two by a diagonal gash that contains the series of chimneys taken by *Knight's Climb*. The open slabby wall to the left is the Main Face, and the bulging wall right of the lower chimney of *Knight's Climb* is Freaky Wall. Right again are the two tiers of Sunnyside Terrace.

Acid Rock faces west and often basks in the sun long before many other parts of the South Slope; for this reason, the climbs dry quickly after showers, and they also remain largely unaffected by seepage. All of the routes on the Main Face are worthwhile, while Freaky Wall offer a good collection of mean yet convenient desperates. Virtually all of the climbing on the cliff is underwritten by a rock-catch fence making the climbing less stressful than it used to be.

Access: Climbing is allowed from 1 October until 15 March inclusive.

Approach: The safest approach is by the path that rises diagonally leftwards behind the rock-catch fence above the car-park to the right of Wind Rock. Gain the right-hand end of the fence by scrambling up easy rock right of a short chimney above the right-hand side of the car-park. Squeeze through a gap in the fence and walk left behind it. A sloping wooded terrace runs beneath the cliff and leftwards to the grassy shoulder overlooking High Rock. **Descend** from the top of the Main Face by following a faint path rightwards along the cliff edge through scrub to the main descent couloir (see page 16).

Main Face

The Main Face is divided just below half height by a break with a grassy ledge on its left. The bulging white wall beneath the ledge, and just right of the grassy shoulder above the right wing of High Rock, is the home for the following five single-pitch climbs, which include some clean, well-equipped sport routes.

Fingerboard Crack   25 metres   E5 6a †   (4.2.95)
The glaringly obvious crack at the left-hand end of the Main Face; a challenging pitch with a plyometric entry. Start 2 metres right of the edge of the shoulder.
Climb easily to a break at 4 metres. Move up the bulging wall above (peg) until a series of finger-ledges lead dynamically past a vital *Rock 5* placement to a small rib and a step left to the foot of the crack. Follow the crack over a bulge and finish via an unusual pod. Tree belay; abseil off.

Yup, Yup and Away   25 metres   E6 6b F7b+   (12.2.95)

Steep fingery facework, but interrupted by a good rest: hence low in the grade. A few obvious wire placements should not prove too onerous. Start 6 metres right of the edge of the shoulder below a hanging block-roof at 8 metres.

Climb easily to the break at 5 metres. Take the wall direct; then from the third bolt bear slightly rightwards to a break and rest on *Farewell...* Pull into the shallow groove and climb it (*Rock 2* then *Rock 3* in pockets) to easier ground. Place another nut at the top of a short crack, and make a short traverse right to the abseil station on *Farewell...* Four stainless-steel bolts and an *in-situ* thread.

Farewell to the Working Classes   20 metres   E5 6b F7b   (22.2.87)

Sheer class. The original sport route: rebolted and reworked. Start 8 metres right of the edge of the shoulder and 3 metres left of a shattered flake (*The Clingon*).

Gain the break at 5 metres. Reach up to a good hold, and pass a tiny roof above to reach a good rest in the break above. Step right and climb the fine black wall to reach the shared abseil station. Four stainless-steel bolts and an *in-situ* thread.

Do or Dole   18 metres   E5 6c F7c †   (12.2.95)

Well worth queuing up for; possibly easier for light fingers. Start a metre left of the shattered flake of *The Clingon*.

Gain the break at 5 metres. Improvise up the wall past a mono and, from a good slot above, proceed to the rest and break of *Farewell...* Finish as for that route. Five stainless-steel bolts and an *in-situ* thread.

The Clingon   18 metres   E4 6a   (21.7.83)

Steep and trying climbing up the thin hanging groove and flake cracks in the lower wall. Start at a shattered flake, 8 metres left of the first chimney of *Knight's Climb*.

Climb up and pull into the hanging groove. Follow this strenuously to a small ledge on the right. Now trend slightly leftwards to thin flake cracks and the small broken groove of *Farewell...* Abseil off.

One Dry Sunday   45 metres   E5   (12.2.95)

A climb with great variety, which confronts the left arête of *Thor*. Take medium cams for the second pitch.

1 25m. 6b. Follow the flake of *The Clingon* to the resting ledge on the right at 12 metres. Delicately climb the wall above and reach a crozzly flake on the right. Now make a very difficult move (vital *Rock 2* in obvious pocket) to reach jugs and the terrace 3 metres above. Step left to a sapling and thread belay below the obvious white corner.

2 20m. 6a. Boldly climb the corner (*RP3/4* in slot on left wall) to reach a short jam crack. From the top of the crack, strike right and surmount the bulge (thread and *Rock 2*) to gain a spiky jug and a rest. Follow easier cracks (peg on the right) to a sloping ledge and the (optional) old abseil station of *True Colours*.

Acid Rock

Direct Start

1a 25m. 6b. From the break at 5 metres on *The Clingon*, step right and attack the wall and rib passing an obvious side-cut to reach the resting ledge on the present route. Problematic, rather squeezed-in, and often featuring a weeping hold.

True Colours   47 metres   E3   (28.12.86/28.4.87)
The second pitch offers interesting wall-climbing up the white tower. Start 5 metres left of the first chimney of *Knight's Climb*, at the foot of a narrow corner.
1 27m. 5c. Climb pitch 1 of *Ahimsa*; then walk left to nut belays below the central, and shortest, of three corners.
2 20m. 6b. Move up the short corner (peg) to a ledge. Bear leftwards past an 8mm bolt to gain a scoop (*in-situ* thread). Climb intricately up shallow runnels above (8mm bolts and *in-situ* threads) to a resting-ledge. Step left and climb a thin crack to an old abseil station 6 metres below the top. Either abseil to the ground or continue up a rib to the top of the cliff.

Ahimsa   54 metres   E3   (1.3.70/16.6.76)
A magnificent second pitch on superb rock: considered by some to be the best route of its grade in the Gorge. It heads for the slabby, open groove in the centre of the Main Face. Take plenty of small wires. Start as for *True Colours*.
1 24m. 5c. Climb the narrow corner to a bulge (peg). Cross this leftwards to a good hold and peg in the base of the shallow groove above. Haul strenuously over into the groove and follow it and broken rock to the right until it is possible to move leftwards more steeply to gain the right end of the grassy ledge above. Belay on nuts below the first (main) corner.
2 30m. 5c. Climb the corner to a ledge. Break out rightwards onto the wall (thread) and move up into the groove. Follow the increasingly steep and technical groove to reach a small roof (peg). Move left into a continuation groove and climb this (peg) before exiting out right by an awkward mantelshelf onto a projecting ledge. Finish more easily.

Bon Voyage/Dream Cruise   52 metres   E2   (20.2.88/27.12.87)
Reasonably engaging climbing at an amenable grade. Start 2 metres left of the base of the first chimney of *Knight's Climb*.
1 25m. 5c. Climb the wall past a thread before trending rightwards to a junction with the first pitch of *Thor*. Climb the groove above to a horizontal break, traverse leftwards to the grass ledge, and belay in the corner as for *Ahimsa*.
2 27m. 5b. Climb directly past a small sapling and move rightwards onto the obvious ledge. Continue to a bulge, which is taken on good holds. Go up the wall above for 6 metres (peg), and then trend rightwards with more difficulty (peg) to join the final corner of *Asina* at a small roof. Climb the crack above as for *Asina* (two pegs) to the top.
Direct Finish
2a 27m. E3 5c (25.2.95). The logical finish to *Dream Cruise*, which makes it independent of *Asina*. Mantel onto the obvious ledge 3 metres right of the corner and gain another ledge at a break. Pull straight over the

black bulge (left of a sapling) to reach good pocket holds. Climb the slabby wall (peg) to a difficult thin crack which leads to the top.

Thor   52 metres   Hard Very Severe   (2.66/1969)
The tall crack in the white tower gives a staunchly traditional crack climb. Large nuts or camming devices will prove invaluable. Start at the first chimney of *Knight's Climb*.
1 25m. 4c. Climb diagonally leftwards past a sapling to a small ledge. Gain a flake above, step left, and climb the groove to the horizontal break. Traverse leftwards to the grass ledge and belay in the corner as for *Ahimsa*.
2 27m. 5b. Climb the corner, as for *Ahimsa*, to the foot of the steep crack. Climb this (strenuous) and the wider crack above to a ledge. Traverse left along the ledge to the arête, which gives an exposed finish.

Asina   55 metres   E2   (28.2.70/23.3.75)
The climbing is sustained, the situations feel big and exhilarating, but the best feature of the route, however, is the wonderful position of the stance at the end of pitch 2. Start at the first chimney of *Knight's Climb*.
1 25m. 4c. *Thor* pitch 1.
2 18m. 5b. From the right end of the ledge, climb a short, steep wall to small ledges. Follow the broken crackline above, which leads to the left-hand side of a (now decapitated) flake in the middle of the face. Pull up to take a stance on the ledge on top of the flake.
3 12m. 5b. Make thin moves up the steep wall above the flake (quite committing) to a crack and a small roof. Pull round into the upper crack and follow this more easily to the top.

Baseline   45 metres   E5   (11.10.79)
The disjointed series of thin cracks in the right-hand side of the Main Face. The second pitch is sustained, technical, and a little awkward to protect. Start as for *Knight's Climb*.
1 25m. 6a. Climb up the left wall of the chimney via a thin ramp, until bold moves over the bulge lead to easier rock and the horizontal break. The thin crack in the leaning wall above (peg) is followed very strenuously until better holds in a broken groove slightly to the right can be reached. Move up to a small stance. Nut belays.
2 20m. 6a. A diagonal crack runs rightwards into the smooth slabby wall; follow it to its close and fix good gear. Now make hard moves up the wall above (peg); then traverse right to better holds leading to a steep, shallow corner. Enter the corner and climb it, exposed, to the top.

Backhander   30 metres   E5 6a †   (25.2.95)
Thirty metres of intricate face-climbing. Take an extensive collection of wires: good protection can be arranged throughout the main difficulties. Start from the tree at the top of the first chimney of *Knight's Climb*. Pull into the undercut groove on the left. Swing left onto the face, and move up to superb flake-holds. Climb a vague scoop to gain a small scooped ledge. Bear slightly rightwards before using finger-pockets on the

left (good wires) to make hard moves up an open white groove to reach a good slot. Climb the slim corner of *Baseline* to the top.

The next two routes are *slab* climbs – a rarity at Cheddar. They climb the shorter, slabby, right-hand section of the upper Main Face and commence from a tree belay 5 metres left of the top of the second (*Raven Chimney*) pitch of *Knight's Climb*.

Electronic Eye   18 metres   E4 6a †   (25.2.95)
Intriguing manoeuvres on a subtle line; modern technology may improve your game.
From the tree, step left and climb a narrow groove to its close. Pass the smooth wall above and enter a compact grey groove with difficulty (*in-situ* thread). Leave the groove using a hidden jug on the right wall and pull up to the easier-angled slab which leads past an overlap to a short exit groove.

Bouncing Back   15 metres   E4 6a/b †   (25.2.95)
Technically tricky, smooth and sly, one to floor climbers high in the sky.
From the tree, step right and mantel onto the obvious ledge. Pull up into the white scoop above (not the time to have forgotten your *RPs*); then, using a good pocket on the left, climb straight up the smooth slab to exit past a large but weak shrub.

Knight's Climb   52 metres   Difficult   (1931)
A fascinating climb, steeped in history and period charm. The finest route of its standard in the Gorge. Start at the lower chimney in the centre of the cliff.
1 20m. The Rowan Chimney. Climb the chimney, mainly on its right wall, until a swing right gains a small tree and ledge. Scramble across to a good block belay below the second chimney.
2 12m. The Raven Chimney. The chimney is tight at first and just plain hard work. From its top, exit on the right and scramble into a broad gully. Tree belays.
3 20m. The Knight's Pinnacle. Step right and climb a broken and somewhat loose crack in the face of the pinnacle above to its summit. Fix a runner and do the 'splits' to cross the gap to the mainland. Climb compact rock to finish. (This pitch is easily avoidable.)

Rook's Climb   55 metres   Very Severe   (11.3.96)
Variations on *Knight's Climb*. Start at the foot of the first (Rowan) chimney.
1 20m. 4b. Step right onto the rectangular rib and climb it to bush belays.
2 15m. 4b. Step down and left, across the top of The Rowan Chimney, to gain a continuation groove. Follow this (old peg) and exit right at the top to ledges. Scramble to tree belays on *Knight's Climb*.
3 20m. *Knight's Climb* pitch 3.

Freaky Wall

Hard climbs of character predominate on the bulging buttress right of the first chimney of *Knight's Climb*. Some of the routes have the bonus of staying permanently vegetation-free. **Descent** is by abseil from the terrace or by down-climbing the first chimney of *Knight's Climb*. It is also possible to thrash rightwards along the terrace to the descent couloir.

A distinctive landmark is a pyramidal pedestal of blocks, often ivy-covered, which includes a flat-topped, upward pointing, 2-metre high flake, next to the path. The flake is 8 metres from the left end of Freaky Wall.

Boo   27 metres   Very Severe 4b 🏵   (23.10.73)
An interesting pitch on which the holds, if they haven't grassed over, appear startlingly out of nowhere. It climbs the grooves at the extreme left end of the bulging buttress, right of the chimney of *Knight's Climb*.
Climb grooves in the wall and trend leftwards to the upper of two horizontal breaks. Pull around the bulge above to a short crack and move up this to the start of the main groove. Follow the groove, and either trend up and leftwards to a vegetated finish or, cleaner and more exposed, tiptoe right across the right-hand wall and finish up a short groove.

Manic Depression   27 metres   E5 6b †   (30.11.86)
Psyche up big-time for this difficult and bold line. Start 5 metres left of the 2-metre flake.
Climb directly through bulges to a ledge (*in-situ* thread). Pull into a short overhung corner (peg), move right, and make some distressing moves to gain a resting-place up on the right. Step back left above the roofs and climb a frustrating slim white groove (*in-situ* thread) until an escape can be made to the left. Finish up a short groove on the right.

Scarred Mind   27 metres   E6 6b F7c   (31.10.93)
A demanding bolt-protected super-direct with two contrasting cruxes. Start 3 metres left of the 2-metre flake.
Take an intermittent flake-line to a horizontal break. Improvise straight through the bulge above, harder for the tall; move right and then up to a reasonable resting position. Climb the shallow groove above on widely-spaced, positive holds, amongst some unsettling flakiness; then use the arête on the left to finish over a small overhang. Seven stainless-steel bolts.

Schizoid   27 metres   E5 6a   (23.10.73/27.3.84)
Most who have done this climb rate it highly. It forces a very sustained line up the open groove in the centre of the bulging buttress. Some of the protection on the first half requires tenacity (or luck) to place. Start a metre left of the 2-metre flake, below a roof-capped corner.
Climb a short crack and the open corner to a good horizontal break. Stretch up to the roof and make an off-balance move rightwards to a jug. Step up to the left above the roof (good but difficult-to-place wire) and work up the steep wall to a thinner break. Make delicate moves up a short,

smooth groove (8mm bolt) to reach better holds in a thin corner, which leads steeply to a terrace.

Manchmals   27 metres   E5 6b   (8.10.89)
A testing eliminate up the slight pillar between the grooves of *Schizoid* and *Speedfreak*. Start at the 2-metre flake.
From the top of the flake, step up on the left and balance boldly up the flat pillar face to a good break. Pull over two tiny overhangs (8mm bolt) to reach a good 'shakeout' jug on the left (on *Schizoid*). Now make a very fingery move up to the right (*Eco-bolt*) to reach good holds (peg). Clip the bolt on *Schizoid* to the left before climbing the front of the rib to the final corner and exit of that route.

Speedfreak   27 metres   E5 6b   (17.11.84)
A stunning route. The severely overhanging groove in the right-hand side of the bulging buttress. Very strenuous: E5 doesn't get any tougher than this. Start at the right side of the blocky pedestal, 12 metres from the left end of the wall.
Climb a short groove onto the pedestal. Step left and make hard moves up the leaning wall (*Eco-bolt*) to enter the groove. Cruise up the groove, passing a peg (with sling), until improving holds lead to a good ledge on the right. With a long reach for a jug, pull over the bulge (peg) and get established on the upper wall. Move up, and climb carefully to the terrace.

Bored of Pies   27 metres   E6 6b F7c   (7.10.89)
Pun-time. Sequential climbing with a stopper crux. Start as for *Speedfreak*. Step right from the top of the pedestal onto a ledge beneath bulges (*Eco-bolt*). Follow the sinuous groove-line with a monodigital crux span past a second *Eco-bolt*. Exit directly on better holds (peg) to the ledge of *Speedfreak*. Finish as for *Speedfreak* – if you've got the bottle.

Half-way along the wall is a broad, rightward-tending ramp with a tree growing out of its base; this is the line of *Paranoia*.

Sheer Lunacy   25 metres   E5 6b †   (29.11.86)
For nutters only. A threatening pitch! Start at a small groove just to the left of the base of a ramp and 3 metres right of *Speedfreak*.
Climb the groove to a ledge. Continue up the shallow groove above to a break. Proceed more steeply up the wall (keeping left of the flake-line) to a good hold (8mm bolt above). Lightning-fast moves diagonally leftwards across the wall gain a jug and peg. Pull back to the right using the obvious finger-pocket and climb thin cracks (old jammed nut) trending leftwards on steep rock to the terrace.

Paranoia   50 metres   Hard Very Severe †† 🌸   (8.11.70/14.4.84)
If the loose rock doesn't get you, the prickles will. A strong line, yet very rarely climbed.
1 25m. 5a. Climb up the ramp, which narrows and becomes vegetated. Continue on the right to the terrace and belay on the left.

West Route (E6), High Rock
Climber: Gordon Jenkin   Photo: Martin Crocker

Coronation Street (E1), High Rock
Climber: Unknown   Photo: Nigel Coe

Project X (E5), High Rock.
Climbers: Dave Pickford
& Thuli Whitehouse
Photo: Carl Ryan

Dig This, People (E4), High Rock
Climber: Martin Crocker
Photo: Carl Ryan

Acid Rock
Freaky Wall

1	Manic Depression	E5
2	Scarred Mind	F7c
3	Schizoid	E5
4	Manchmals	E5
5	Speedfreak	E5
6	Bored of Pies	F7c
7	Sheer Lunacy	E5
8	Paranoia (pitch 1)	HVS
9	Nonplus One	E5
10	Shock of the New	F7c
11	On Radio	E6
12	The Numb Ones	E3
13	The Babbler	F7b
14	Tarmac Terminator	E4
15	Little Gem	E3

2 25m. 5a. Three metres right of a flared white groove in the second tier
(*State of Mind*) is a scoop in the slabbier wall. Pull around into the scoop
with difficulty and move up to a bulge. Drop down left to the foot of a flake
crack and climb this to tree belays. Scramble up to the left and climb the
short wall behind The Knight's Pinnacle to the cliff-top.

Around a broad rib right of the ramp of *Paranoia* is an impending white wall.

Nonplus One   25 metres   E5 6b   (7.10.89)
Short-lived, but fairly heinous. Start 3 metres right of the broad rib.
Gain a brambly shelf via a short groove. Move up and make an
enormous reach past an *Eco-bolt* to gain good holds. Climb strenuously
(*in-situ* threads) to easier ground via a hard, rejecting scoop. Move up and
rightwards on ledges (vital *Friend 1* in a slot) before making a few steeper
moves to reach broken rock and the terrace.

Shock of the New   25 metres   E6 6b F7c   (8.2.86/30.3.93)
A great route up the centre of the impending white wall; arduous throughout
and with a particularly malicious crux. Start as for *Nonplus One*.
Climb the short groove to a sloping ledge on the right. Swing right on a
good pocket and make some digit-destroying pulls up a slight rib
(*Eco-bolt*) to gain a sloping hand-ledge (*in-situ* thread). Climb pumpingly
direct (*Eco-bolt*) up a shallow groove to grasp a massive but hidden jug
just to the left of a peg. Reach leftwards to good pockets left of a rib and
continue awkwardly to easier ground and the terrace. (An excursion right
to a rest and thread in the corner after the crux rib drops the grade a little:
the original line.)

On Radio   25 metres   E6 6b   (8.10.89)
The corner to the block overhang in the right-hand side of the impending
white wall is followed by a direct line above. A wild, blind crux at the top
should guarantee plenty of airtime.
Move up, overpower the corner (*Eco-bolt*), and undercut leftwards beneath
the overhang to gain a good rest above in a corner (*in-situ* thread). Step
right and climb straight up the thin black streak in the smooth wall (8mm
bolt) to the left-hand end of a thin rising overlap. Continue on typical
Cheddar edges (8mm bolt) until a leap (vital *RP4/Rock 1* in pocket to the
right) gains proper holds and the terrace.

The Numb Ones   25 metres   E3 5c   (8.2.86)
A severe frost, or unseasonable warmth, is often needed to dry up the
tearful first section. Start 10 metres right of *Paranoia*.
Climb a dirty scoop right of an overhanging corner to a small roof.
Undercut over, and reach up for a big pocket (long *in-situ* thread). Move
right and back left, and pull into a small groove. Follow the undercling out
to the left; then pull over into a shallow groove which leads with difficulty to
tree belays on the terrace.

The Babbler   25 metres   E5 6b F7b †   (3.95)
A damp squib: get in early before the winter rains.

Climb an overhang right of *The Numb Ones* to a large scoop. Make hard moves above to gain a large pocket. Continue on better holds, and take the crack above to a step right to the exit of the next route. Three stainless-steel bolts.

Tarmac Terminator   25 metres   E4 6b   (8.10.89)
A varied and enjoyable line. Start 15 metres right of *Paranoia*, below a short crack.
Pull steeply up the crack and, with protection from a peg (with sling), swing left to good holds and a constricted rest beneath an undercut overlap. Initially perplexing moves up the bare wall above lead past a 8mm bolt to better holds and good resting-ledges. Step right (peg) to a slim groove and climb this and the wall above (peg) to the top.

Little Gem   27 metres   E3 6a   (2.4.81)
A climb of considerable interest, which takes the enticing, leftward-rising overlap in the right-hand side of the wall.
Pass a small roof at 3 metres to enter a vague groove on its right. Climb up; move left and then straight up to gain the right-hand end of the overlap. Follow the crack up and left and, where it fades, make hard moves over the bulge to gain the finish of *Tarmac Terminator*.

Just to the right, the wall has provided three poor pitches, the most significant being **Ten Years On** (15 metres Severe 10.12.80) – an extinct line up a corner once formed by a massive flake.

Sunnyside Terrace

'…we were eventually confronted by 100 feet of man-eating brambles, and had to escape up a loose tower of tot (which will probably be written up as a new route by the bloke who led it). This cannot be the correct approach?!'
(A satisfied guidebook customer)

The right flank of Acid Rock comprises two tiers separated by a bushy terrace that narrows to the left and eventually joins up with the stance below the second (*Rowan*) chimney of *Knight's Climb*. The terrace walls are bounded on the right by the descent couloir. They supply quite a pleasant range of climbs in a relatively sunny setting, including a number of reasonably geared sport routes. Climbs on the lower wall are of lesser quality, but at least some stay dry in rain. On both tiers **the climbs are described right-to-left**, as the normal approaches are from the descent couloir on the right. The base of the couloir is situated above the right end of the car-park right of *Wind Rock*. The initial gully is best avoided by a zigzag path immediately on the right. The rock-catch fence above, attached to the left-hand side of a 20-metre tower, should be passed via a hole on its right-hand side. (This rock-catch fence extends below the entire lower wall.)

Sunnyside Lower

Walk left below the initially ivy-covered wall from just above the rock-catch fence in the gully. The first two routes occupy a sheer white pocketed wall 20 metres left of the couloir; they require a pre-placed rope to retreat (fixed at the foot of *Sport for All* on the tier above).

Never Forget a Face   8 metres   E2 6a †   (27.11.99)
Climb direct to a tiny groove. Make hard moves up and then left to jugs and the lower-off rope. Protectable.

Lest We Forget   8 metres   E2 6a   (11.11.93)
Desperately attain a standing position on a small sloping ledge beneath an undercut that weeps rust. Using the undercut (good wire) make a long reach to fingerholds and jugs above; lower-off.

Does Rock Dream?   12 metres   Very Difficult ✿   (9.3.94)
Of gallons of weedkiller perhaps: the rightward-slanting groove is extremely vegetated.

Stripped for Action   12 metres   Hard Very Severe 5b †   (4.3.93)
The series of cracks in the white-stained rock to the left of *Does Rock Dream?* Climb the cracks with escalating interest and swing left to the stainless-steel bolted abseil station of the next route.

Best of Things   11 metres   E4 6b †   (27.11.99)
A slab – of sorts. The first ascent was soloed (E5), though there is a good wire placement just below the crux that could prevent a deck-out.
Climb the right-hand side of a blunt rib to an undercut. Make very thin moves onto the slab above to better holds. The abseil station is 2 metres higher.

The Best Things in Life Aren't Things   12 metres   E2 5c   (4.3.93)
'Moves that are sure to bring a smile to your face' (!). Start just left of the blunt arête, below a small overlap 6 metres up.
Climb steeply into a scoop beneath the overlap. Pull delicately and boldly up and right to a flake-crack under a second overlap. Swing right and gain the stainless-steel bolted abseil station.

A Pinch of Thought   12 metres   E2 5c † ✿   (4.3.93)
A hard crux, and with weeds seriously infesting the finishing holds. Start at an arch in the rock just above ground level.
Climb a crack on good holds to small, twin pockets (high peg), whereupon a sequence of slopers and pockets (and weeds) lead to a ledge left of a tree. Continue past two further ledges to a bolted abseil station hidden above a small overhang on the left.

Just Another Sunday   12 metres   E2 5c   (10.93)
Climb leftwards to a curving crack (*in-situ* thread) and follow it to a peg before moving left to ledges. Finish slightly rightwards, following the cleanest line to a bolted abseil station.

Cleared for Take Off   13 metres   E1 5b   (4.3.93)
Start behind a large tree. Follow a curving crack to its end and make a
long reach to a great little flake hold and a ledge beyond. Continue
rightwards along the obvious line to a bolted abseil station hidden above a
small overhang on the right (shared with the previous route).

Just to the right of Sunnyside Terrace, the following climb takes the open,
isolated tower 25 metres up the descent couloir.

Quicksnake   18 metres   E1 5b †   (1.1.95)
From the rock-catch fence left of the arête of the tower, climb an earthy
groove, and move right along a break to the arête. Delicately follow the
arête to the top.

Sunnyside Upper

Reach the right end of the wall by following a faint path leftwards from a point 40
metres above the rock-catch fence in the gully. The right end of the wall is only a
few metres left of the couloir; two large yew trees aid navigation hereabouts.

Wiggly Park   10 metres   Severe   (22.11.93)
Start at the extreme right end of the wall, behind the right-hand of two large
yew trees. Climb a short groove past a thread and continue up the headwall.

Gardeners' World   9 metres   E2 6a   (7.11.93)
Start between the two large yew trees. Quite tough. Climb a tricky wall
past a peg to good holds and a sapling. Finish slightly rightwards to a
single 10mm bolt abseil station.

Arson – A Burning Desire   10 metres   E2 5c   (27.2.94)
Good clean climbing on compact rock; committing to start (unless a
runner is fixed on the tree). Start behind the left-hand yew tree.
Strenuously gain a ledge at 5 metres. Move up slightly right (*in-situ* thread)
and step up onto a short slab (*in-situ* thread). Bear right to the single 10mm
bolt abseil station on *Gardener's World*. (A direct exit is over-vegetated.)

Microscopic   8 metres   E1 6a/b   (12.11.93)
Eminently soloable (but don't forget a rope to get back down). Start at a
large undercut hold 3 metres to the right of *Poached Eggs*. A
bolt-protected boulder-problem gains a large flake and a single 10mm
bolt abseil station.

Hang This – Sucker!   9 metres   XS 6b   (27.11.99)
Possibly the world's most dangerous boulder problem. The hanging flake
(the one that you don't use) is even looser than it looks and must weigh
about a ton.
From the 'ear' of *Poached Eggs*, stretch right for a finger-jug. Traverse
powerfully rightwards along the lip of a roof, and using the lower (and
slightly more attached) of the two undercut flakes, swing around further to
the flake crack and abseil station of *Microscopic*.

Poached Eggs   6 metres   E2 6b   (28.11.93)
Grapple with the obvious right-facing 'ear' of rock. One poor peg; single
10mm bolt abseil station, shared with *The China Shop*.

The China Shop   9 metres   E3 6a   (7.11.93)
A miniature-classic up the groove left of the obvious 'ear' of rock, 7 metres
left of the left-hand yew tree. Not as fragile as the name suggests.
Hard moves on undercuts and a steep pull into a short groove (*Rock 7*) are
followed by further steep moves, until a pull out right gains ledges and a
single 10mm bolt abseil station.

Abort, Retry, Ignore   10 metres   E5 6b F7b   (1.93)
A two-bolt sport route for frustrated cyberphobes. Very fingery. Start 10
metres left of the left-hand yew tree.
Pull into a slight niche and make hard moves up and leftwards to better
holds. Continue directly to a break (peg) before climbing more easily to a
bolted abseil station. Two 10mm bolts.

Sun Blind   12 metres   Severe †   (24.11.93)
Climb the obvious corner to a tree belay.

Green Man   12 metres   E2 5a †   (14.11.92)
An unpleasant climb. Climb the obvious corner (*Sun Blind*) and the wall
above to a prickly belay in the jungle.

To the left the cliff is undermined by well-populated badger holes (chances
are one will pop out while you're there) and, past a short section of poorer
rock, an undercut, grey rectangular wall marks the site of the next three
bolted face routes. They share the same bolted abseil station.

Sport for All   15 metres   E1 6a F6a   (2.93)
Start at the right-hand side of the undercut wall.
Make a hard move to good flake-holds at 3 metres (*in-situ* thread). Move
up past two 10mm bolts and an unexpected loose block; then continue
leftwards to reach the abseil station.

Parallel Lines   15 metres   E3 6a F6c   (28.2.93)
Excellent climbing. Climb the centre of the wall with a macro-stretch to
start. Four 8mm bolts to the abseil station. Short-arses may require a
sneaky rock pile to get going (or some serious finger strength!).

Chalk and Cheese   15 metres   E4 6a F6c+   (7.3.93)
A fine, technical pitch up the left-hand side of the grey wall. Low in the
(French) grade.
A tricky start is followed by easier climbing to another hard move to gain
an overlap. Pull over and move right to the abseil station. Four 8mm bolts.

Over Easy   15 metres   Hard Very Severe 5b   (26.3.93)
Start in a depression below a yew tree. After a loose start, climb cracks and
flakes to the tree.

Always on My Mind   24 metres   Hard Very Severe 5b   (12.12.94)
Climb onto the flake right of a narrow overhang (on *Dulled Sword*).
Continue via another flake and follow pockets to a crack. Climb the crack,
and step left over a slight bulge to a large pocket. Move left to a bolted
abseil station (shared with *Sunnyside Up*). Four *in-situ* threads.

Dulled Sword   25 metres   Hard Very Severe 5b   (15.4.81)
Slabby climbing with a tricky start. Start below a narrow overhang 3
metres up.
Climb up to and over the overhang with difficulty. Continue up the
pocketed slab above to a short groove and the top. Scramble off
rightwards.

Opt-Out   18 metres   E1 5c   (7.2.93)
An enjoyable right-to-left diagonal line near the left end of the tier. Start as
for *Dulled Sword*.
A disproportionately hard lock-off gains the narrow overhang at 3 metres.
From good holds above the overhang (peg), follow a leftwards-rising line
past two *in-situ* threads, (crossing *Sunnyside Up*), to steeper rock. Make a
blind move left, and finish past an *in-situ* thread to the shared bolted abseil
station

Fool's Bolt   15 metres   E4 6c F7b   (21.2.93)
Terribly thin climbing up the smooth wall just to the right of *Sunnyside Up*.
Rock up onto a good foothold; then smear and teeter on minimal holds
(two 8mm bolts and a *Rock 2* placement) to reach the ledge on *Sunnyside
Up*. Finish up the groove of *Sunnyside Up* (10mm bolt; abseil station).

Sunnyside Up   15 metres   E4 6a F7a   (12.2.93)
Lots of character on one of the wall's better climbs. It follows the
disconnected grooves at the left end of the tier.
Climb the initial groove past a nut-slot to its close (10mm bolt). Undercut
up to the right to reach buckets and slabbier rock. Continue slightly
rightwards (10mm bolt) and finish at the shared abseil station.

Prodigal Sun   12 metres   Hard Very Severe 5b   (29.3.94)
The prominent left-to-right line leading to the abseil station atop *Sunnyside
Up*. Start below a large, downward-pointing block, left of the disconnected
groove system.
Bouldery moves gain a series of small pockets. Follow the pockets to the
flake/ramp line. Travel the ramp more easily to the abseil station of
Sunnyside Up.

Fuzzy Logic   15 metres   E2 5b   (10.93)
A good route starting up the rib to the left of the groove system.
A hard start leads to easier and better climbing, which leads straight to a
bolted abseil station. The alternative left-hand start is **Neural Network**
(18 metres E2 5c 10.93), which has a peg runner.

The next three routes start next to a large flake below a large tree in a slabby section of the wall.

Wild Thyme   18 metres   E1 5a †   (11.93)
Climb the loose wall above the tree to the top.

Bent Spear   25 metres   Hard Very Severe 5a   (7.12.80)
Climb rightwards to a narrow arch (peg), and continue traversing for 5 metres to a rib. Climb the rib and move leftwards to a short groove to finish. Abseil from trees or scramble off rightwards.

Broken Arrow   20 metres   Hard Very Severe 5b   (30.11.80)
An amenable pitch that takes a line through the narrow arch.
Climb rightwards to the narrow arch (peg). Pull over the arch and follow the groove above before moving leftwards at the top to a vegetated ledge. Abseil from trees or scramble off rightwards.

The final two climbs take the extreme left end of the wall, right of the Rowan Chimney pitch of *Knight's Climb*, from which they are much more easily reached.

State of Mind   20 metres   E5 6b ✿   (7.11.85)
The compelling flared white groove. The protection is spaced and the climbing very strenuous. Babbling is guaranteed!
Climb steeply leftwards into the groove. Bridge up the groove on increasingly small holds (peg). Using a small hidden pocket in the right-hand rib (vital but blind wire placement), continue with difficulty over the bulge into an easier groove (peg). Climb straight up thin cracks to belays. Scramble to the top.

Clean Hand Man   20 metres   E5 6a † ✿   (12.11.89)
A vague series of grooves immediately left of the flared white groove. Solid but poorly protected. Start from a tiny cave at the left-hand end of the terrace.
Swarm up a friable flake on the right and continue directly into a scoop. Climb a difficult bulge into a shallow groove (*in-situ* thread) and proceed to a small ledge above. Move right to belays. Scramble to the top.

There are a number of small crags near road-level between Wind Rock and the Gough's Cave complex. The only recorded route, **Vanishing Point** (18 metres E3 6b 7.10.83), is a finger-stretching boulder problem out of the left-hand side of the railed-off cave at road-level. It has been usurped by the installation of a Cheddar Caves signpost. The crags above the cave and further to the west are strictly out of bounds, apart from the well-advertised Cheddar show caves climb (but then you'll have to pay for the privilege of using its bolt-on holds!).

Lion Rock

Access: This compact yet striking crag, the finest on the north slope, is poised at the mouth of the Gorge immediately opposite Gough's Cave and behind some cottages. Unfortunately its cherished lion-like profile has proved too close to civilization to allow climbers' activities to go unchallenged. The National Trust has banned climbing on the crag, following the long-term complaint of one adjacent resident. For the time being, therefore, consider the descriptions as hypothetical, and hope that circumstances change for the better (and we can restore entertainment for the Cheddar show caves management opposite!).

Access: Climbing is **banned**.

Lion's Share   24 metres   Hard Very Severe 4c †   (11.1.86)
A circuitous pitch up the broad, south-west rib of the Rock. Start at the extreme left end of the leaning south face.
Move up ledges to the obvious ramp and follow this leftwards to finish up a crack and broken ground.

Pussy Galore   15 metres   E4 6b †   (22.1.94)
The steep wall above the start of *Lion's Share*; short but tricky. Climb for 6 metres to an incut pocket on a sloping ledge. Swing right onto the face and from the second vertical wire slot bear right, precariously, to a proposed abseil station on *Human Zoo*.

Human Zoo   15 metres   E6 6b F7c   (22.1.94)
An impressive and sustained pitch on the overhanging arête left of the leaning south face.
Climb the fluted arête with big reaches between big holds (or smaller reaches between smaller holds) until a swing left at 7 metres gains a brief shake-out. Overcome the bulge above, direct or slightly right; then continue with no let-up to meet *Pussy Galore*. Five stainless-steel bolts. Proposed abseil station.

Cheddar Death Knell   15 metres   E6 6b F7b+   (20.3.94)
A precipitate eliminate, for climber and complainant alike. Start 2 metres left of *Taming of the Lion*.
Climb directly to the foot-ledge on *Taming of the Lion* and rock over awkwardly. Climb the difficult final bulge above. Four stainless-steel bolts. Proposed abseil station.

Taming of the Lion   24 metres   E6 6c   (26.1.86)
The sensational, leaning south face provides the setting for a very difficult pitch. Start at a small corner in the centre of the face.
Climb the corner and crack above (*in-situ* thread) and move up right on tiny, weak edges into a black niche (peg). Pull up leftwards over the bulge (8mm bolt) to small foot-ledges (peg). Perform an excruciating sequence

up onto the bulging headwall (8mm bolt), and then continue straight up with long reaches (*in-situ* thread) to the top.

Circus, Circus   24 metres   E6 6b F7c   (28.1.94)
A glorious variety of moves on a beautifully intricate line to the right of *Taming of the Lion*. Save some calories for the crux of *The Snarl*!
Starting 2 metres right of *Taming of the Lion*, muscle up through bulges to reach the obvious round hole at 6 metres. Continue deviously slightly left to undercuts below a small overhang. Now trend diagonally rightwards to share the undercuts and crux of *The Snarl*. Continue up the groove and juggy wall above to the top (as for *The Snarl*). Four stainless-steel bolts (and a peg on *The Snarl*).

The immaculate F8a+ unclimbed headwall, where *Circus, Circus* is forced right, awaits more settled times.

The Snarl   27 metres   E4 6b   (11.1.86)
The eye-catching V-groove in the left-hand arête of the corner of *Simba* gives a bouldery route. Start below the corner of *Simba*.
Climb up the corner for 7 metres. Arrange gear; then swing left around the arête and move up to a roof. Pull into a groove with great difficulty (peg) and follow it to finish up the right arête.

Simba   24 metres   E1 5b   (1965/4.2.73)
A classic route which climbs the compelling corner that offsets the south face. Climb up into the corner (crux) and follow it with good protection to the top.

Lion in Winter   27 metres   E3 6a   (11.1.86)
A seductive line taking the right-hand wall of the corner of *Simba*. Exhilarating climbing on superb rock. Start below the corner as for *Simba*. Climb up the corner for 6 metres. Step right onto the wall and make a long reach for a jug which enables a short crack (*in-situ* thread) to be reached. Climb the crack, pull out on big holds, and then finish up a small, triangular wall.

Valley of the Blind   24 metres   E6 6b F7c   (31.12.88)
A stupendous and brawny pitch that overpowers the dramatic, leaning arête to the right of the corner of *Simba*.
Start up a flake to reach undercuts beneath a bulge (bolt). Heave over onto the arête (peg) and gain a jug (and crucial *Rock 3* placement above). Pass a roof on the left (peg) to reach a projecting hold (peg) and pull up steeply to a slabby exit.

English Cheddar Gorgeous   18 metres   E5 6c †   (12.1.86)
A super-technical pitch on compact rock that climbs the very smooth groove in the east face. Start at the base of the off-width chimney.
Trend diagonally leftwards to a jug in the base of the groove. Bridge up (8mm bolt) to a bulge and then power out right to a short crack. Continue on good holds to the top.

ECG 12 metres E5 6a † (30.1.94)
An eliminate which has some nice holds (but some difficult wire protection). Start as for *English Cheddar Gorgeous*, at the base of the off-width chimney.
Climb up and left for 3 metres, as for *English Cheddar Gorgeous*; then pursue a direct line using pocket holds on the left to reach a couple of jugs. Step left to finish up *English Cheddar Gorgeous*.

Leadbelly 18 metres Very Severe 4c (1965)
Breathe out (or is it in?) and struggle up the narrow, off-width chimney in the right-hand side of the east face.

Rock Junky 9 metres E4 6b F7a+ (10.1.94)
Climb the short but powerful bulge to the right of *Leadbelly*, keeping on the front of the buttress. Three stainless-steel bolts. Proposed abseil station

The Forest 18 metres Very Severe 4b † (31.12.88)
Climb the shallow groove in the small buttress, starting 3 metres right of *Leadbelly*.

The Remnant

'The best place to start is by warming up at the Bristol Climbing Centre'
(Gareth Parry, 2000)

This is the short, overhanging crag situated 100 metres upstream from Lion Rock and approximately 50 metres above road-level. A 90s crucible of sporting endeavour, it is the home of the area's hardest bolt climbs, as well as some strong natural lines on good rock.

At one time The Remnant was one of the most dangerous (for the public) crags to climb on. Cleaning operations together with a protective rock-catch fence have changed all that, and it is now one of the safest. Ironically, its recent popularity did not suppress the growth of ivy and the great dense thickets of honeysuckle, hawthorn, and brambles at either end of the crag; but – stop press – in 2002 much of this was removed by The National Trust.

The crag faces south-east, gets the sun until early afternoon, and is exceptionally sheltered from the wind. Typically, some of the routes are affected by seepage after heavy rain, but, when dry, the crag qualifies for a Rockfax umbrella symbol.

Approach: Traditionally, this is from the six-car lay-by right of the *Friendly Cuppa* (opposite The Cheddar show caves complex), although there is technically no right-of-way. Scramble rightwards up the back of the bay, onto and up a short ridge. Follow the path leftwards and pass the left end of the rock-catch fence to reach the left end of the main crag. It is also possible to

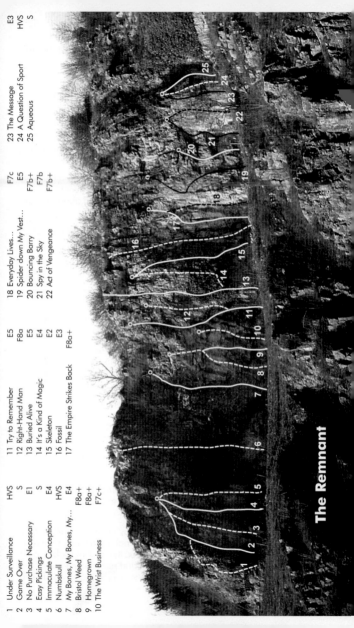

1	Under Surveillance	HVS	23	The Message	E3
2	Game Over	S	24	A Question of Sport	HVS
3	No Purchase Necessary	E1	25	Aqueous	S
4	Easy Pickings	S			
5	Immaculate Conception	E4			
6	Numbskull	HVS			
7	My Bones, My Bones, My…	E4			
8	Bristol Weed	F8a+			
9	Homegrown	F8a+			
10	The Wrist Business	F7c+			
11	Try to Remember	E5			
12	Right-Hand Man	F8a			
13	Buried Alive	E5			
14	It's a Kind of Magic	E4			
15	Skeleton	E2			
16	Fossil	E3			
17	The Empire Strikes Back	F8a+			
18	Everyday Lives…	F7c			
19	Spider down My Vest…	E5			
20	Bouncing Barry	F7b+			
21	Spy in the Sky	F7b			
22	Act of Vengeance	F7b+			

The Remnant

approach along the public footpath that leads up to the left of Lion Rock, and then by walking under Lion Rock. Although a number of routes have old abseil stations, it is possible to walk off from all routes left of *Everyday Lives of Ordinary People*.

Access: Climbing is allowed from 1 October until 15 March inclusive.

At the time of writing there are still big patches of ivy on the cliff; these may have dropped off by the time you are under the crag with this guidebook.

Under Surveillance 5/15 metres Hard Severe 5c ✿ (12.1.95)
Climb the undercut arête at the left end of the crag to a jumping retreat or a finish up the open corner on the right.

Game Over 15 metres Severe ` (11.1.95)
Climb the open corner near the left end of the crag past a small overhang and bulge (*in-situ* thread) to a rightward-rising traverse and the abseil station of *Easy Pickings*.

No Purchase Necessary 15 metres E1 5c ✿ (11.1.95)
The compact grey rib right of the corner leads to good holds. Move right and follow a groove to the shared abseil station.

Easy Pickings 12 metres Severe ✿ (15.10.94)
Follow a groove to the shared abseil station.

Immaculate Conception 12 metres E4 6b (15.10.94)
A rock anchor 4 metres up shows the way. Climb past the anchor and up the smooth groove above to an abseil station on the left. Note the very real risk of losing a finger in the crux mono-doigt (unless there is already one there!).

Numbskull 27 metres Hard Very Severe 5b ✿ (19.12.1978)
Next right is a pair of short overhanging cracks left of some block roofs. Climb the wall just left of the cracks and gain a groove with difficulty. Follow the groove and looser ground above to the top.

The cleaner and steeper main crag now commences with some block roofs at 4 metres above some blocks lying on the path.

My Bones, My Bones, My... 18 metres E4 6b (23.11.85)
This takes the wall and open groove above the block roofs. A bone-breaker start.
Persevere up the leaning wall to the right of the cave, swing left over its lip, and climb the slabby wall above to a slot. Pull out right into the groove and climb it to ledges and an optional old abseil station.

Old Bones 18 metres E5 6a † (27.3.97)
Serious. Make the first few moves of *My Bones...* up and left to an obvious two-finger-pocket above the block roofs. Rock up and right to rickety undercuts, step back up and left to a dodgy looking block (*Rock 1*), and finish at the old abseil station of *My Bones...*

Bristol Weed   18 metres   E7 6c F8a+   (3.97)
Heinous climbing up a friable bulging wall. Start 2 metres right of the
block roofs.
Climb bulging rock to a scoop at 8 metres. Pull right past a roof into a
hanging groove; climb this and easier rock above to an abseil station. Five
stainless-steel bolts.

Homegrown   18 metres   E8 6c F8a+   (3.97)
The hardest on-sight first ascent in Britain, and a major challenge for the
rest of us who can't climb this grade, let alone on-sight it. The climbing is
brilliant. Start 4 metres right of the block roofs.
Climb straight through ferocious bulging rock, past the obvious undercut,
to gain the blind hanging groove and finish of *Bristol Weed* on the left. Five
stainless-steel bolts.

The Wrist Business   9 metres   E6 6c F7c+   (14.3.95)
Power training of the left hand is a pre-requisite for the all-important pinch.
Start 3 metres left of a shallow cave.
Overpower a black overhanging scoop and, using that pinch, somehow
gain a jug above a bulge. Step up and finish at an invisible abseil station
in the headwall, i.e. jump off! (Alternatively, finish up the next route.) Three
stainless-steel bolts.

Try to Remember   20 metres   E5 6b   (23.11.85)
The magnificent and alarmingly steep crack in the centre of the crag. Very
strenuous. Only the super cool or sketching weaklings will not back up the
threads. Start in the shallow cave below the crack.
Bridge up the scoop and climb the crack to a square-cut niche (four *in-situ*
threads). Contort desperately over the bulge (above the thinnest of threads)
and continue more easily just to the left of the final crack to the top (old
abseil station).

Right-Hand Man   18 metres   E7 6c F8a   (20.3.94)
Archetypal power-endurance climbing on the white headwall right of *Try to
Remember*: a run of hard lock-offs with no rest.
From 5 metres up the scoop of *Try to Remember*, span rightwards to an
undercut pocket in the bulging wall. Break through the bulges and
continue up the headwall on positive finger-edges, keeping just right of the
final bolt to reach easier ground and the top (old abseil station). Five
stainless-steel bolts.

Buried Alive   20 metres   E5 6b † ❀   (1.1.86)
Still entombed by ivy. A nerve-racking pitch. Climb scoops and the friable
steep wall 5 metres right of *Try to Remember* to the top.

It's a Kind of Magic   15 metres   E4 6b ❀   (6.2.94)
'...the rate the ivy grows.' Ivy has regularly to be stripped from the base of
the route. From the scoop of *Buried Alive*, swing right and flow through the
bulge past two stainless-steel bolts. Finish up the groove above to reach
the old abseil station atop *Skeleton*.

Up a step, and right of centre, is the unmistakable leftward-slanting crack and groove climbed by *Fossil*.

Skeleton   15 metres   E2 5c ❀   (2.6.77)
A pleasing and technical route if the ivy hasn't muscled in. Start below the left-hand arête of *Fossil*.
Pull over the bulge and follow a ramp diagonally leftwards to the arête. Move up to retreat from an optional old abseil station.

Fossil   15 metres   E3 5c   (24.5.77)
A route of character and a great line. Start below the crack.
Climb the crack fairly easily until it steepens and narrows to fist-jam proportions. Follow the crack to a bulge (*in-situ* thread) and surmount this decisively to a short finishing-groove and an optional old abseil station.

The Empire Strikes Back   15 metres   E8 6c F8a+   (23.3.97)
The very impressive compact white wall right of *Fossil*. The current route quits the wall after the third bolt, leaving the main challenge for a super-superhuman.Climb the centre of the wall, and then trend right beneath a bulge into *Everyday Lives…* Six stainless-steel bolts.

Everyday Lives of Ordinary People   15 metres   E6 6b F7c (9.2.94)
An everyday favourite of the common man. A classic of the crag. The pocketed crack to the right of *Fossil* is just nudged into its French grade by a vicious entry. Start 3 metres right of *Fossil*.
Crank out the initial bulging wall to a shallow scoop. Continue, largely on pockets, until awkward moves over the capping bulge enable an abseil station to be reached. Four stainless-steel bolts, plus an obvious *Rock 1-3* cluster straight in front of your face at half-height.

Skullduggery   12 metres   E4 6a † ❀   (1.1.86)
An old route with a changed personality; it has not been reclimbed since some heavyweight blocks were taken out. Climb the right-hand side of the scarred rib and finish diagonally rightwards up the committing bulging wall to a bolted abseil station on the next route.

Spider down My Vest – Cardiac Arrest!   12 metres   E5 6a (26.3.94)
Arachnophobes beware. Start 2 metres right of the rib right of *Fossil*. Climb the groove (*in-situ* thread) to a ledge on the left. Finish rightwards as for *Skullduggery*, up the committing bulging wall above. Bolted abseil station on the left.

Bouncing Barry   12 metres   E5 6c F7b+   (1994)
Make a desperate move over a triangular roof to leftward-slanting slots. Continue to pull straight over roofs to an abseil station. Four stainless-steel bolts. (The need for bouncing around on the first bolt can be obviated by cheating up the preceding route [6b; F7b].)

Spy in the Sky   12 metres   E5 6b F7b   (19.2.94)

The superb white scoop-line towards the right end of the cliff is not just a 'warm-up' for the harder routes. Start 7 metres right of *Fossil*.

Climb the scoop with a long reach to jugs and an unbelievable thread-handhold. Pull over a final hard bulge to reach an abseil station on the right. Five stainless-steel bolts.

Act of Vengeance   9 metres   E6 6b F7b+ ✿   (5.10.94)

Possibly only F7b. Start 2 metres right of the white scoop-line of *Spy in the Sky*. Step up onto a ledge, and make a diabolical reach for a high pocket. Make rapid moves up the leaning wall on improving holds to gain a set of good jugs and a bolted abseil station above. Three stainless-steel bolts.

Star Wars: The Trilogy   44 metres   E7 † ✿   (24.3.97)

For those who were disappointed when girdle traverses went out of fashion, fear not: this is for you. Start as for *Spy in the Sky*.

1 17m. 6c. Climb *Spy...* to its fourth bolt before moving out left (bolt) and down into *Spider...* (Friend 2). Move left to good pockets and a thread, and continue traversing to the *Rock 1-3* cluster on *Everyday Lives...* Step up and work across *The Empire Strikes Back* via a very hard and blind sequence to gain a belay in the corner of *Fossil*.

2 12m. 6b. Move out left and step down to the second bolt of *It's a Kind of Magic*. Step down and left again to gain a poor belay in a scoop (often ivy-infected) on *Buried Alive*.

3 15m. 6c. With protection from the first bolt of *Right-Hand Man*, step down and traverse left to meet *Try to Remember* at its first thread. Continue left (two bolts) to a hard move down into the scoop of *Bristol Weed* (bolt). Summon up courage and head off leftwards past numerous loose holds to arrive at a hard-to-place *Rock 1* in a suspect block. ('If you fall off here, pick your feet up; if you fall off clipping, pray'.) Continue left by easier moves to gain the slot on *My Bones...*, and move up and rightwards to its old abseil station.

The remaining climbs occupy the less steep, vegetated right end of the crag. The corner here is climbed by *Aqueous*.

The Message   9 metres   E3 6a † ✿   (11.1.95)

Climb the short slab right of *Act of Vengeance* to an overlap. Reach good holds above, step over using the right-hand arête and continue calmly to an abseil station.

A Question of Sport   9 metres   Hard Very Severe 5a ✿   (12.1.95)

Climb the slab left of the corner, above a ledge, to a square-cut overhang. Pockets above enable good holds on the left to be used to climb a white groove to an abseil station.

Aqueous   9 metres   Severe ✿   (11.1.95)

The corner at the right end of the crag past an armpit-deep hole (*in-situ* thread) to an abseil station on the left.

Knight's Climb (Diff), Acid Rock
Climbers: Ivan Hoare
& Arthur King
Photo: Carl Ryan

Digit Wall (E2), Prospect Tier
Climber: Steve Monks
Photo: Andy March

Some distance to the right is the cave of Sun Hole. This is a scheduled monument and under no circumstances should climbing take place here.

Pride Evans Cliff

…the most recent cave dwelling in Mendip. Here, early in the last century, lived Pride Evans with his wife and children.   (H E Balch, 1947)

Immediately upstream of the Cheddar Showcaves complex is a tight bend in the road; above this are various crags, all of which are strictly out of bounds. Around the bend and rising from just above road level is the lower tier of Pride Evans Cliff, easily identified by its large arched cave – the onetime luxurious abode of a certain Mr Evans but now the home of the cave-boulderer. Superb hard climbs adorn the face.

There is a fence running parallel to the crag which should on no account be climbed over; it can be easily skirted on its left-hand side.

Access: Climbing is allowed from 1 October until 15 March inclusive.

The first four routes battle out of an overhung bay at the left end of the main crag, 15 metres left of the cave.

Ultra-Violence   15 metres   E6 6c F7c   (13.3.93)
An explosive power-line of undercuts through the left-hand side of the overhung bay. Start from a mega-thread belay in the centre of the bay.
Take the line of undercuts leftwards through the bulge to a jug in a scoop above. Follow the rib and overlying thin crack to a single-bolt abseil station on the right-hand side of a large, detached rock bridge (don't touch it for God's sake!). Four bolts (two *Eco*) and a peg. Retreat with care (a pre-placed rope is the safest option).

Secret Cabaret   15 metres   E6 6c F7c+   (27.2.93)
One of the Gorge's premier sports climbs; an immaculate fusion of technique and power. Start from the mega-thread belay
Enter the hanging groove and reach the pocketed break above and left. Continue up the rounded, leaning arête directly past a small useful spike to an old abseil station (on *Jewel in the Sun*). Four *Eco*-bolts and one 8mm.

Jewel in the Sun   15 metres   E4 6b   (23.10.85)
Precisely that (well, at least up to 3 p.m.!). The bulging pocketed crack and groove cleaving the centre of the crag is the line of this sparkling pitch. Start at the mega-thread belay.
Step right and muscle into the crack (*in-situ* thread) using good holds on the right wall. Continue with difficulty up the groove, until it is possible to gain and retreat from an old abseil station (or top out easily).

Jewel of a Son   18 metres   E5 6b F7b   (16.1.93)
A top-quality route; excellent rock and great moves (though some say it's
F7b+).
Pull through the bulge right of the crack and climb direct to jugs on the
right (and a no-hands rest on the arête). Swing left and climb straight up
the centre of the white face to a peg (plus maillon) runner, where a short
leftward traverse gains the *Jewel in the Sun* abseil station. Five 8mm bolts
and two pegs.

The remaining climbs start from Pride Evans Cave, which is reached by a
short, steep scramble. There is some beautiful and not too taxing bouldering
on the cave walls. **Piglet's Groove** (Very Severe 4c 9.1.72) used to climb
the open groove on the left of the cave, but it once again wallows in ivy.

Sing a Mean Toon, Kid   20 metres   E6 6b F7b+ †   (17.1.93)
The system of discontinuous cracks and slim grooves in the wall to the left
of the cave. A route of escalating difficulty, high in its French grade.
Too-obvious-to-miss, bombproof nut placements supplement the fixed
gear. Start at the left-hand side of the cave.
From the extreme left-hand end of the ledge, climb steeply (peg) to a short
crack (*in-situ* thread). Move right to another short crack and right again to
a short overhanging groove (8mm bolt). Contort into the groove and
execute a complex layaway-and-slap sequence (*Eco-bolt*) to reach an
optional single peg lower-off just below the top (which should not be
depended upon in isolation).

House Burning Down   25 metres   E6 6b †   (17.11.85)
Electrifying. The roof of Pride Evans Cave and the superb white headwall.
Climb a shallow groove in the left edge of the cave and trend rightwards
along the lip to a pocket (peg and *in-situ* threads). Wild moves up and
right could gain good holds at the base of the headwall (*in-situ* thread).
Move up (*Eco-bolt*), reach right, and continue up the wall to gain a short
hanging groove and old abseil station. (Full marks if you top out.)

Pride Evans Locker   20 metres   E6 6c F7b+   (6.2.93)
A harder but safer (sport) version of *House Burning Down* on mostly fine
rock save for the crucial 'jug', which changed shape three times during the
first ascent process! Start in the back right-hand side of the cave.
Follow a series of good holds until it is possible to bury your head in the
roof of the aven for a rest (*Friend 2* and long sling). Headjam rightwards
across the aven and 'hit the light' (*Eco-bolt*). Power around the lip
(*Eco-bolt*) and move up the trying wall above to join *House Burning Down*
at its shakeout ledge (peg and in-situ threads). Follow *House Burning Down*
up the headwall (*Eco-bolt*) past the old abseil station to the top. Tree
belays.

Privy Purse   20 metres   Hard Very Severe 5a   (19.2.76)
Starting a metre right of the cave, climb the steep crack past miscellaneous
foliage to the top.

The upper tier is of much less interest, being broken and vegetated, although three short cracks at the left-hand end, **Parallel Cracks** (Moderate 1931), and the corner to their right, **Hepatitis** (Very Severe 4b 9.1.72), may attract the less fastidious climber. Left again is a groove above a cave, **Solstice** (Hard Very Severe 5b/c † 21.12.93), and 20 metres down and right is a short buttress, the front of which is climbed by **It's Behind Yew** (Hard Very Severe 5a † 21.12.93).

Subsidiary Walls

Directly opposite the car-park on the Cheddar side of Wind Rock is a small broken buttress at road level, Subsidiary Wall. Above and to the right is Subsidiary Buttress, an east-facing wall which is sheltered and quick-drying.

Access: Climbing is allowed from 1 October until 15 March inclusive.

Subsidiary Wall   18 metres   Severe   (1972)
Distracting for motorists, and needing care. Start just to the left of a small cave at a crack. Climb the crack, step left, and take the broken rib above to the top.

The next four routes are situated on the Subsidiary Buttress, which is best reached by traversing leftwards from the main access path to the Tiers.

Grockles Super-Galore   18 metres   E3 6a   (8.10.93/21.12.97)
Quite good, despite tenacious plant-life. Start 7 metres left of the rock-catch fence, below a line of pink cracks.
Go up the pink cracks to a short right-facing corner. Move up and right slightly and pull back left over the bulge (*in-situ* thread) to foot-ledges. Make fingery moves straight over the bulge (8mm bolt) and, keeping a little right, ascend the steep headwall to finish through a nick in the skyline.

Tell-tales   18 metres   E2 5b †   (21.12.97)
The system of slim white grooves left of Subsidiary Buttress: pleasantly satisfying. Start 5 metres left of the rock-catch fence, at the foot of a thin crack.
Follow the thin crack and shallow grooves above to intersect a good break at 10 metres, right of a grassy hole. Step up into another small groove, and then proceed direct (avoiding a premature escape into *Subsidiary Buttress*) to finish at a tree.

Subsidiary Arête   18 metres   E1 5a †   (8.10.93/21.12.97)
Suspicions may be raised by the red-marked pairs of glued metal tabs en route. Start 2 metres left of the rock-catch fence.
Climb steeply past a horizontal slot to a break and traverse right for 2 metres – below the groove of *Subsidiary Buttress* – to the base of an arête, of sorts. Take the arête, exiting above a single red mark.

Subsidiary Buttress   18 metres   Very Severe 4c   (1.5.76)
A misnomer, but does it matter? Start at the rock-catch fence. Move up and
bear left to the most prominent groove in the wall. Enter the groove, and
climb it to finish on the arête to the right.

The Tiers

O'er the changed scene, and on the evening air
Came a wild fragrance from green ledge and cove,
That nourish those sweet flowers that blossom there
Like hidden worth, mid all that's desolate and bare.
                    (Mention of the Cheddar Pink in an extract from
                    Somerset and the Severn Sea by John Draper, 1867)

The crags on the North Slope opposite Acid Rock and High Rock are
organized in three distinctive tiers. The lower tier, or 5b Wall, (virtually
opposite Wind Rock) rises from the road. The middle and top tiers (Prospect
Tier and Heart Leaf Bluff) merge at their right-hand ends into the imposing,
blunt white prow of *Mescalito*, the dominating feature of the North Slope.
The cliffs are fast drying, receive sunshine up to mid-afternoon, and are
relatively free of seepage.

Access: Climbing is allowed from 1 October until 15 March inclusive.

Warning: great care is required as any rock dislodged could roll down the
slope and into the road below.

5b Wall

Climbing on the lower tier is scarcely justifiable, given that the crag
overhangs pedestrians, the road, and a busy pull-in. Besides, the routes are
fairly undistinguished, a trifle loose, and are currently returning to nature.

Super High-Intensity Micro Climb (15 metres E4 6b † 6.12.86) climbed
the smooth wall on the left end of the tier past fixed gear (but was instantly
dismantled by The National Trust!). **Stichtless** (15 metres Very Severe 5a †
20.10.85) was a poor route up a leftward-curving flake crack 10 metres
from the left-hand end of the wall. **Solo** (18 metres Very Severe 5a †
20.10.85) took the wall via the loose-looking pillar 12 metres from the left
end of the wall. **Jacko** (18 metres Severe 1954) surmounted an obvious
pedestal in the centre of the wall, and then followed a vague line of
weakness leftwards to the top. **5b Wall** (18 metres Very Severe 5a 6.53)
climbed a short, bulging corner and crack on the right-hand side of the wall.

Prospect Tier

Prospect Tier offers a variety of short and occasionally quite popular pitches at a variety of grades on variable rock. With caution, approach the left end of the crag by following a path diagonally rightwards above 5b Wall. As an alternative, the right end of the crag can be approached from the grassy couloir left of the quarry.

Adjacent to the left edge of the crag is a large circular hole 3 metres up.

Wham Bam Thank You Ma'am 12 metres Very Severe 5a (25.1.86)
Down to the left of the circular hole, a crack rises to a small roof. Climb the crack, roof, crack, and bulge to the top.

Hair Cut 12 metres Very Severe 4c (10.71)
Climb up to the circular hole and take the crack above to the top.

Mohican 12 metres E1 5b (28.12.82)
Climb the shallow, leftward-leaning groove to the right of the circular hole directly to the top.

'Gentleman in Red Trousers' 12 metres E4 6b † (22.10.87)
Climb the obvious blunt arête 5 metres right of the circular hole. The finish is committing.

Short Cut 12 metres Severe 4a (c.1950s)
An amenable little route, despite the plant life, which climbs the recessed corner 15 metres from the left-hand end of the crag. Climb trickily up into a niche, move left, and continue fairly steeply up the wall above.

Your Destiny 12 metres E4 6a (5.11.94)
The leaning wall immediately right of *Short Cut*: overall a touch nasty. Get established on a sloping ledge at 3 metres and step delicately (and gently) up to a good jug (wire). Make some difficult moves rightwards and back left (peg), to reach better holds. Continue to the top.

Centrefold 12 metres E1 5b (23.10.83)
Start 2 metres right of *Short Cut*. Climb a shallow groove for 8 metres; then step left into a narrow corner to finish.

At the back of a shallow grassy bay is a grassy gully (**Prospect Gully** 12 metres Difficult 1950), and to the left of this is a slabby grey wall.

Charge 12 metres Very Severe 4c (6.69)
An enjoyable pitch at the grade, and not too steep – for Cheddar! Start midway between the grassy gully and the recessed corner of *Short Cut*. Climb straight up the wall (peg), move up into a niche, and climb rightwards to finish.

In the centre of the crag, right of the grassy gully, is a broad overhanging tower.

Watching the Days Go By   15 metres   E4 6a †   (6.11.94)
A direct line up the face of the tower. Start below a rightward-facing flake
crack, 6 metres right of the grassy gully.
Step up onto a ledge, climb the crack, and move right (hard) to a large
ledge (*Rock 1* in a slot). Pull up onto the ledge and finish up the centre of
the tower face.

Digit Arête   15 metres   E5 6a   (3.84)
Forceful and committing climbing up the right-hand rib of the tower. Start
below an obvious pedestal 7 metres up.
Trend leftwards across the bulging wall left of the pedestal to reach good
holds at a break (peg). Make a hard move to gain an easier final groove,
and exit with care.

Digit Wall   18 metres   E2 5b   (8.2.76/13.1.79)
A north-side classic, regularly climbed. Right of the tower, a dog-legged
crack rises up the left-hand side of an otherwise featureless south-east-facing
wall. This is strenuous, well protected, and one of the better routes of its
grade in the Gorge. Start below the crack running up to the right side of
the pedestal.
Gain the top of the pedestal. Follow the crack before moving right into its
thinner continuation, which gives a tiring and thought-provoking finish.
Variation E1 5b. Give your digits a rest and escape left at three-quarter
height.

A Pot of Crock (18 metres E4 6a † 12.2.95) is a poor eliminate right of
Digit Wall which starts and finishes as for that route.

Wild Frontier   18 metres   E6 6b   (25.1.86)
A very fingery wall-climb, largely on infinitesimal holds. Widely-spaced
wires, some awkward to place, add only a modicum of security. Start
diagonally down rightwards from the pedestal on *Digit Wall*.
Stand up on a projecting jug above a small roof, and climb straight up to
finger-pockets. Crank away via a tiny groove to reach a short crack slightly
to the left (vital *Rock 2*). Step right and move up to the break, from which
easy climbing leads to the top.

A little over half-way along the tier, to the right of the sheer south-east-facing
wall, is a distinctive overhung hollow, the starting point for the next two
routes.

No Fit State   18 metres   E4 6b F7a+ †   (22.10.94)
An intriguing problem; the scoop above the curious hollow which emits
Fart.
From the left-hand side of the hollow, bridge directly up the scoop (useful
pocket on the right) and climb with sustained difficulty to easier ground
and the top. Two stainless-steel bolts.

Fart   18 metres   E2 5c   (14.3.76)
An idiosyncratic little route which is easy to fluff.

Pull out of the right-hand side of the hollow into a very steep crack and follow it strenuously to a niche. Traverse rightwards to a thin crack, which leads past an old abseil station to the top.

Vic Bond   18 metres   E4 6b   (15.2.86)
A move that expels many. An excellent pitch on good rock, which takes the open white corner right of the hollow.
Gain a ledge at 3 metres, below the right-hand side of the hollow, and then climb a short crack and the bulge above (*in-situ* thread) to the corner. A very precarious sequence may lead up the corner (8mm bolt) to the old abseil station and exit of *Fart*.

Maker's Nameplate   18/21 metres   E5 6b   (22.4.79/31.8.83)
A superb route; powerful and committing. Start in a shallow recess capped by a quarter-moon roof, 12 metres right of the rib of *Digit Arête*.
From the right edge of the recess, boulder boldly up the leaning wall to a short rightward-facing flake below the roof. Move up to the roof (vital small cam), and pull around rightwards on better holds (peg). Either bear leftwards to climb the groove to join *Fart* at the old abseil station, or climb the less-than-solid groove overhead to the top.

Jon Luke (18 metres E5 6b † 31.10.92) is a filler-in which argues with the bulge left of *Makers Nameplate*. Join and finish up *Fart*. One 8mm bolt, one peg (missing).

Rigorous Self Abuse   18 metres   E5 6a †   (22.10.87)
Tight, technical wall climbing with weak gear. Start 2 metres left of the overhanging crack of *The Wink*.
Climb straight up the wall (*in-situ* thread) to a peg and a good hold. Continue blindly (*in-situ* thread) until a swing left gains a very steep crack in the arête. Follow the crack to a massive thread on the right and either abseil off or finish up *The Wink*.

Towards the right end of the tier, and 25 metres right of the central tower, is a distinctive overhanging crack and groove that can't be missed: *The Wink*.

The Wink   20 metres   E2 5b   (20.4.75)
A compelling and strenuous line. Start below the overhanging crack 5 metres right of the roof-capped recess.
Climb the crack without much relief to a small ledge at 15 metres (peg). Move right into the upper corner and follow it past an old abseil station to the top.

The Nod   20 metres   E2 5b   (14.2.76)
Fairly difficult climbing up the compact open corner 3 metres right of *The Wink*. Possibly one of the most failed-on routes at Cheddar.
Climb the corner and, where it peters out, move left onto less steep rock. Climb up via a flake to a groove and follow this to the exit of *The Wink* on the left.

Mary Jane   20 metres   Very Severe 4c   (30.9.73)
Quite popular. Start below a deep, wide crack commencing at 5 metres,
right of *The Wink*.
Climb a thin crack and the wider crack above to ledges on the right. Climb
the corner above to a small roof, step right, and move up past an old
abseil station to the top.

Prospect Eliminate   20 metres   E4 5c   (12.10.78)
Normally entwined by ivy. Start at a smooth white corner 8 metres right of
The Wink.
Get off the deck, if able, and follow the thin, bulging crack above to the
ledges on *Mary Jane*. Move left beneath a bulge, pull over with some
anguish to gain better holds, and continue more easily up a thin groove to
the top.

Madcap Laughs   20 metres   Very Severe 4b   (1.4.73)
Good climbing up the obvious right-facing corner-crack 12 metres right of
The Wink. Start below a pocket just above head-height.
Pull through the bulge on the reassuringly polished pocket, move left, and
follow the corner to the old abseil station and exit of *Mary Jane* on the left.

The tier now turns around a rib and, immediately, there is a short overhanging crack left of a huge pedestal flake.

Asylum   25 metres   Hard Very Severe 5b   (15.4.73)
Climb the crack with difficulty before continuing over bulges to finish up an
easier, stepped rib.

Lonely Pride   25 metres   E4 6b   (15.11.86)
A fingery and technical pitch with some sad old threads. Start just left of
the huge pedestal flake.
Climb straight up the wall past two *in-situ* threads to a flake crack that
leads quickly to a leftward-sloping ramp (peg). Follow the ramp easily,
swing right (peg) into good twin cracks, and climb to the top.

Sub-Mescalito   25 metres   E2 5c   (25.1.70/7.83)
Formerly the first pitch of *Mescalito*, with which it has very little in common
now that the second pitch goes wickedly free. Start at the huge pedestal
flake.
Step right from the top of the pedestal, and climb a steep flake-crack (peg)
to small ledges on the right. Pull left into a thin crack and climb it steeply to
the right end of the terrace.

Heart Leaf Bluff

The white upper tier, which reaches 25 metres in height, provides a mix of
technical face climbs and a few classics, in a quick-drying and open setting.
Approach as for Prospect Tier (p. 165), but continue up a steep and rocky
depression to the left end of the terrace below the upper tier.

Near the left end of the tier is a prominent, square-cut tower with a corner on each side of it. A rock-catch fence across the top of the gully on the left ends in front of the left edge of the tower.

Forgotten Sacrifices   15 metres   Hard Severe   (11.11.94)
The grooves and cracks 2 metres left of the left-hand corner.

Brass Monkey   15 metres   Hard Severe   4a   (21.1.73)
Climb the corner-crack bounding the prominent tower on its left-hand side; a good pitch.

Weasel Words   18 metres   E4   6b †   (1.1.95)
Sneak up the bold left arête of the tower via an obvious sloping hand-ledge at 5 metres and join *ICBB* at its peg. Move up; then continue direct (*Rock 3*) to the roof (*in-situ* thread). Take the roof by moving slightly right and finish up the front of the tower.

Inter-continental Ballistic Bonzo   18 metres   E3   6a   (10.12.83)
Climb steeply up the centre of the tower to a resting spot (peg). Swing left and climb a shallow groove with difficulty to finish on the arête.

Condensation Canyon   18 metres   E4   6a † ††   (23.10.99)
The right arête of the tower; escapable.
Climb the arête for 6 metres. Use an undercut on the left and make tough moves up a short flake. Continue up the arête, avoiding the *Funny Bone* cracks on the right, and finish with care.

Funny Bone   15 metres   E1   5a/b †   (4.12.83)
Climb flake cracks in the left wall of the *Humerus* corner. More solid than it used to be, but not perfectly solid!

Humerus   13 metres   Severe   (1950)
A friendly old classic and engagingly steep for the grade. Climb the corner-chimney and crack bounding the tower on its right.

Riotsville   15 metres   E2   5c   (10.9.85)
Climb the wall and shallow groove 2 metres right of *Humerus* to the top. Definitely worth doing.

Greg's Little Wall of Horrors   18 metres   E2   5c   (4.12.83)
Hardly a horror-show, this route gives enjoyable but tough climbing on good rock. Start 3 metres right of the corner of *Humerus*.
Climb directly up the bulging wall and pass to the right of a small square-cut nose (peg). Ascend a flake crack and a rib above before moving left to the top.

Readers' Wives   20 metres   E1   5a   (16.1.93)
Eight metres right of *Humerus*, a slabby wall leads up to a narrow cracked pillar right of a cave. Poor protection.
Starting a metre right of a big flake, climb the slabby wall until forced rightwards beneath the pillar to good layaway holds. Reach back left to the

Prospect Tier and Bearleaf Bluff

1	Short Cut	S
2	Centrefold	E1
3	Charge	VS
4	Watching the Days Go By	E4
5	Digit Arête	E5
6	Digit Wall	E2
7	Wild Frontier	E6
8	No Fit State	F7a+
9	Fart	E2
10	Vic Bond	E4
11	Maker's Nameplate	E5
12	Rigorous Self Abuse	E5
13	The Wink	E2
14	The Nod	E2
15	Mary Jane	VS
16	Madcap Laughs	VS
17	Sub-Mescalito	E2
18	The Three Bombardiers	E2
19	Robertson's Jam	E4
20	Lean Burn	F7b
21	Me No Stereotype	F7c
22	Will Stanton	F8a
23	Still Wanton	F7b
24	Brass Monkey	HS
25	Weasel Words	E4
26	Inter-Continental Ballistic Bonzo	E3
27	Condensation Canyon	E4
28	Funny Bone	E1
29	Humerus	S
30	Riotsville	E2
31	Greg's Little Wall of Horrors	E2
32	Readers' Wives	E1
33	Letcher	E5
34	Craitor Traitor	E5
35	Consenting Adults	E2
36	Heart Leaf Direct	E3
37	Au Bout de Souffle	E5
38	Harley Street	E4
39	Driller Killer, Q'est-ce Que C'est?	F7c
40	Fettered Trajectory	F7b+
41	Air to Air Exit	F7b+
42	Concorde	E5
43	La Tour Noire	E5
44	La Tour Noire Super	E6
45	Dinner Date	E1
46	My Wife's Apple Crumble	E4
47	Mescalito	F7c
48	Sentinel	E3
49	Vanguard	E3
50	Editorial Axe	E3
51	Gubia	E6

Danemark Cliff

52	Danemark	HVS
53	Groundrush	E4
54	Assassin!	E6
55	Thriller	E3
56	Psycho	E1
57	Slow Return	E2
58	First a Fence	E6
59	Dead Stop	E5
60	Poisoned Ivy	E4
61	Free Fall	E2
62	The Dimming of the Day	HVS
63	Micawberism	E2
64	Cyclists Advised to Walk	E1
65	Avalon	VS
66	Mare's Nest	VD
67	The Grail	E2

crack in the centre of the pillar and climb this to a good ledge. Finish up the arête above.

Letter   20 metres   E5 6a †   (23.10.99)
Start beneath a 5-metre scoop, 10 metres right of *Humerus*.
Climb the awkward scoop to small pockets (difficult gear), and gain better holds above. Continue direct to ledges and the short vegetated groove of *Heart Leaf Climb* on the left.

Consenting Adults   20 metres   E2 5b   (30.11.86)
Interesting climbing, where ivy may need to be stripped on-the-job. Start 13 metres right of *Humerus*, below a narrow corner with a pocketed crack in the back.
Climb the corner to good ledges. Pull up onto a smaller ledge and take the wall above to a scoop. Step right and finish easily.
Variation
Craitor Traitor   E5 6b †   (5.11.94)
A chance to make good use of your crash mats in Cheddar. Start 2 metres left of the corner of *Consenting Adults*.
Boulder up the overhanging wall to good holds at 6 metres (peg clippable after the crux). Continue to a horizontal break and move right to finish up *Consenting Adults*.

Twelve metres short of the right end of the tier is a broad recess, often monopolized by sunbathing goats. The next route starts up the narrowing slab that slants leftwards from the left side of the recess.

Heart Leaf Climb   25 metres   Severe 4a   (1931)
A nice start, but the route soon becomes deflected into a leftward excursion.
Climb the slab with interest to ledges after 8 metres where it narrows. Make a long traverse left along ledges until it is possible to finish up a broken vegetated groove.

Heart Leaf Direct   20 metres   E3 6a   (10.9.85)
A difficult but natural continuation to *Heart Leaf Climb*.
Climb the leftward-slanting slab to the ledge at 8 metres. Continue out of balance up the narrow, leaning groove above (two pegs) to pull around the bulge using a small tree. Bear carefully rightwards to exit or to a retreat from an old abseil station on *Harley Street*.
Superdirect Start E4 6b † (7.4.87). Starting 2 metres right of *Consenting Adults*, climb straight up the black, bulging rib to the left of the slanting slab with a macro-stretch for a flat hold at 6 metres.

Au Bout de Souffle   20 metres   E5 6a   (2.94)
A moderately frightening eliminate starting as for *Heart Leaf Climb*.
Climb as independently as possible up the wall right of *Heart Leaf Climb* on big flakes to reach an undercut on the left. Arrange some good wires, make a long stretch to flat holds, and continue up and right to a subsidiary

arête. Move back left and forge steeply up past a weak *in-situ* thread to arrive breathless at the top (or at the old abseil station of *Harley Street*).

Harley Street   20 metres   E4 5c   (4.5.79)
A serious climb, on which protection is in short supply, that takes the groove to the right of *Heart Leaf Direct*. Start from the recess in the centre of the wall, as for *Heart Leaf Climb*.
Climb rightwards into a scoop with an obvious pocket (large cam). Pull up into the groove (hard), which is followed leftwards to an easier corner and the top or the old abseil station.

Driller Killer, Q'est-ce Que C'est?   18 metres   E6 6b F7c   (26.10.94)
A left-hand variant to the substantive sport route hereabouts, *Fettered Trajectory*. Low in the grade.
Follow *Fettered Trajectory* to its third bolt and make hard moves leftwards across the wall to a good jug. Move up to a small ledge. Continue up the wall, avoiding a loose bulge to its right, to reach a hand-ledge. Traverse right for 2 metres to the abseil station of *Fettered Trajectory*. Eight stainless-steel bolts.

Fettered Trajectory   15 metres   E6 6b F7b+   (8.11.86)
A contemporary test-piece, which challenges the leaning wall above the recess in the centre of the cliff. Start 3 metres right of the leftward-slanting slab.
Sustained fingerwork leads up and slightly rightwards into a small scoop at 6 metres. Climb straight up a grey streak until finger-pockets allow a resting-ledge on the right to be gained. Move up and then right to a short arête leading to an abseil station. Five stainless-steel bolts.
Variation
Air to Air Exit   20 metres   E6 6b F7b+   (22.10.94/3.10.82)
A dramatic continuation to an already pumpy pitch. A sit-down rest on the original line means no alteration in the french grade. From the abseil station, take off up the leaning wall, either to the top, or to an improvised retreat from the fixed gear. Overall: seven stainless-steel bolts and an *in-situ* thread.

Concorde   15/20 metres   E5 6b   (13.3.71/3.10.82)
The most obvious feature in the sheer wall between the leftward-slanting slab and the arête of *Mescalito* is a long black streak crossed by *La Tour Noire*. *Concorde* climbs the wall to the left of the streak via an obvious brown scoop. A good, oft-tried pitch (but beware the Ace of Spades!). Start 3 metres left of the streak, just left of a peg-marked crack.
Boulder out the lower wall, moving right (peg at 4 metres) to gain the crackline. Strenuously follow the crack past the poor 'Ace of Spades' peg into a brown scoop. Climb the groove above to the abseil station of *Fettered Trajectory* on the left. Retreat, or continue up the steep and interesting groove to the top.

Tumbletot   15 metres   E5 6b †   (20.3.94)

A bouncy addition to Cheddar's unassailable wealth of bold E5s.
Boulder straight up the blunt white rib left of the black streak to grasp a
good hand-ledge at 6 metres: awkward wires here. Continue straight up
to an assembly of jugs on *La Toir Noire* and follow that route to where it
swings right to a peg. Press on direct to easier ground and the abseil
station of *Fettered Trajectory* on the left.

La Tour Noire   18/25 metres   E5 6a   (27.12.83)

A superb, absorbing pitch on excellent rock. Take your time to protect the
route properly. Start 2 metres right of the black streak.
Using a short flake, rock up into a small scoop. Move up onto the flat wall,
where a series of pockets and finger-flakes leads leftwards across the black
streak to a small ledge in the centre of the wall. Climb up for 2 metres,
swing right (poor peg), and then up again (hard) to a big ledge. Climb
into a groove above and either retreat from an old abseil station here, or
continue to the top.

La Tour Noire Super   20 metres   E6 6b †   (23.10.99)

A high-risk run-out, but on perfect rock. One good runner at half-height
will need to be complemented by an even better runner on the ground.
Follow *La Tour Noire* to a finger-flake and good nut 7 metres up, at the
edge of the black streak. Take the blind left-slanting fault above, keeping
to the left of the small overhang, until one final hard move way above
gear gains a good undercut side-pull. Pull up onto the big ledge above,
and finish as for *La Tour Noire*.

Dinner Date   25 metres   E1 5b   (25.1.70)

A popular pitch with technical interest that climbs the exposed groove left
of the blunt arête of *Mescalito*. The infamous block roof at 6 metres no
longer poses a threat: it parted company in 1998 with a certain
'Himalayan guide' attached to it. Start 5 metres left of the arête.
Climb the groove and pull over a bulge to a recess. Step left and climb the
steepening groove and crack (past an old abseil station) to the top.

My Wife's Apple Crumble   25 metres   E4 6b ††   (22.9.87)

Choke on this! An extremely direct line up the blank wall to the left of the
arête. It currently awaits rebolting, following a 'clean-up' by the contractors.
From a flake crack, climb via a tiny groove to ledges at 10 metres. Intricately
surmount a bulge (8mm bolt) and continue with a jump for a jug (8mm bolt).
Bear more easily rightwards to the old abseil station at the top of *Mescalito*.

Mescalito   25 metres   E6 6c F7c   (25.1.70/20.4.85)

A wildly exposed trip, which is fully stainless-steel bolted.
Follow the very tip of the arête, sustained but amenable, to a projecting
hold at 15 metres. Step left onto a very smooth, leaning wall and climb
straight up, making the most of a two-finger pocket. From a
resting-foot-ledge above, move left and climb a thin crack to an old abseil
station or top out easily. Ten bolts.

Rave Party   25 metres   E5 6a   (28.2.93)
This takes the right edge of the *Mescalito* arête. Wicked positions
compensate for some hollow rubble here and there. Start as for *Mescalito*.
Climb the wall 2 metres right of the arête (two 8mm bolts) to a good
pocket (*Rock 4*) and a semi-rest above. Follow the short, pocketed crack
(*in-situ* thread and smallish wires available) to an incut foot-ledge. Now
'large' up the breathtaking upper arête (two 8mm bolts, one peg) to good
finishing holds and the top.

Nameless Bay

Above the left end of the quarry in the North Slope is a high bay of buttresses
and walls which form the easterly extensions of Prospect Tier and Heart Leaf
Bluff. To the right of *Mescalito* the tiers form a continuous wall, but this is
soon divided by a widening terrace slanting up to the head of the grassy
couloir that rises from the left-hand end of the quarry. The broad white
buttress in the lower right-hand side of the bay is Danemark Cliff.

Access: Climbing is allowed from 1 October until 15 March inclusive.

Lower Tier

Ten metres right of the pedestal flake at the right end of Prospect Tier, look up
and find a small roof at 15 metres split by a slight vertical crack. The next
three climbs all end at a belay above the roof. Here it is possible to retreat
from a 10mm bolt abseil station. The routes provide quality climbing on
compact rock, have satisfactory wire protection, and would attract stars – if
stars were being given.

Old Romantics   16 metres   E2 5c †   (14.2.03)
Climb to a ledge at 4 metres. Trend leftwards to the left end of a small
overhang. Take side-pulls in the compact grey wall above to a good
finger-pocket slightly left. Now make a committing move up the steep face
on the right and take a line of rightward-rising holds to reach the ledge
above the roof.

The Three Bombardiers   15 metres   E2 5c †   (12.2.03)
The obvious groove that leads up to the roof. Climb past a ledge at 4
metres to the groove. Move up the groove – very interesting – and just
short of the roof step right using a good pocket. Move up and step left to
the ledge above the roof.

Nameless Scoop   15 metres   E2 5c †   (12.2.03)
Climb up into a short left-facing groove and gain a horizontal slot in the
white face above. Make tricky moves over a narrow overhang into a
scoop. Climb the scoop and wall above, and step left to the ledge above
the roof.

The next two climbs just to the right both end at the left-hand end of the ledge beneath *Will Stanton*.

Just My Imagination   15 metres   E2 5c †   (14.2.03)
Start as for *Nameless Scoop*. Climb up a metre right of the short groove (rock-spike) and move up to two pockets on the face above. Continue to a narrow overhang. Follow undercuts, flakes, and pockets rightwards to the ledge.

Once Again   8 metres   E2 5c †   (14.2.03)
Start directly below an overhanging layback flake in the wall above the ledge (*Robertson's Jam*). Climb up to a good horizontal break left of a shallow niche. Gain a thin flake in the wall, and climb this direct with a hard move to reach the ledge. Needs care to protect.

The next batch of routes centre upon a bulging, roof-capped buttress that holds a narrow recessed ledge 6 metres up. Apart from *Still Wanton* and *Gorilla Tactics*, all commence either from the ledge, or from a point some 15 metres up and right of the pedestal flake at the right end of Prospect Tier. Thread and nut belays at the right end of the ledge can be reached via a number of fairly straightforward lines, or a belay can be taken at the cliff-base with a bit of rope drag thrown in (as if the routes aren't hard enough already).

The long-forgotten and vegetated **Nameless Horror** (Very Severe 4b ††
c.1950s), climbed diagonally leftwards from the ledge to the step in the arête of *Mescalito*.

Robertson's Jam   18 metres   E4 6a   (31.10.92)
Forceful climbing up the overhanging layback flake in the left-hand side of the buttress. Don't forget your *Friend 1s*.
From the left end of the ledge, climb the flake to bulges where it ends. Cruise straight up with two hard moves and two 8mm bolts to a good shake-out in a superb crystal pocket. Finish on good holds. Tree belay immediately.

Lean Burn   18 metres   E5 6b F7b   (30.1.94)
A curious pitch, weird in places, technical in others, but strenuous overall. It takes a rightward-trending line driving for the obvious open bottomless groove. Near the left end of the ledge (*in-situ* thread), climb rightwards on small holds to good pockets. Continue slightly rightwards, and enter and leave the groove with difficulty; bolted abseil station on the right. Five stainless-steel bolts.

Me No Stereotype   15 metres   E6 6c F7c   (3.10.94)
A test-piece of the grade, demanding a wide skills-base and a lorry-load of determination.
Climb the bulging wall, just to the left of the groove system of *Will Stanton*, and bear slightly rightwards through the capping roofs to the bolted abseil station shared with *Lean Burn*. Five stainless-steel bolts.

Will Stanton   18 metres   E7 6b F8a   (11.10.90)

A showstopper in its time, and still with only a handful of repeats; intricate climbing with a run of great moves that are all hard! The pitch tackles the central groove system, aiming for the hanging groove in the apex of the buttress.

Take the scoops above the belay, and make fierce moves over the bulge on the right to reach good fingerholds. Undercut rightwards beneath the roofs to reach the hanging groove and the final repulsing move that fixes the grade. Four new bolts, and a peg; bolted abseil station.

Still Wanton   20 metres   E5 6b F7b   (30.1.94)

A warm-up for *Will Stanton* or maybe a challenge in itself? Purists may be irritated by the no-hands rest, while the rest of us will be thankful. Start directly below the roofs 15 metres up.

Ascend fairly easily to a hole at 6 metres. Work through the white bulge with long moves, and pull onto a slab beneath the capping roof. Move left beneath the roof before making some very powerful moves through it to gain jugs just left of the protruding 'beak'. Bear left to the abseil station of *Will Stanton* or top out to the tree. Six stainless-steel bolts.

Gorilla Tactics   25 metres   E3 5c   (31.12.83)

Start below the vertical face right of the roofs. Climb diagonally rightwards to a shallow niche. Take the wall above directly to the terrace, passing the large roofs on their right.

Upper Tier

The Upper Tier extends rightwards from the blunt arête of *Mescalito*, gradually becoming more broken until a small buttress (Micawber Buttress) above Danemark Cliff marks its right-hand end. **Approach** up the steep grassy couloir left of the quarry and then traverse down leftwards along a narrowing terrace.

To the right of the arête of *Mescalito*, and above the left end of the terrace, is a sheer grey wall. The first five climbs start from the left end of the terrace, at the foot of a right-facing layback crack; tree belay.

Sentinel   25 metres   E3 6a   (28.3.65/1979)

A vertigo-inducing pitch that takes the crack in the smooth wall some 5 metres right of the arête of *Mescalito*.

Traverse leftwards and climb easily to the foot of the crack. Climb the crack with increasing difficulty until it is possible to swing left (peg) and pull over a bulge into a groove. Follow the groove, still hard and very exposed, to the top.

Variation

Sentinel Direct   25 metres   E4 6a †   (22.9.87)

Considerably harder and more strenuous than the original. From the point where *Sentinel* swings left, climb the shallow groove to its close. Pull directly over the roof above using the obvious finger-pocket and finish up a crack (*in-situ* thread).

Mix a Quick Fix   25 metres   E5 6b F7b †   (23.11.97)
Smooth, cool, techno-rock on the pristine grey sheet left of *Vanguard*.
Ascend the layback crack for 4 metres, swing left, and move up to a break
beneath the sheet. Pursue a line, inventive as needs be, up the sheet,
eventually pulling right over the undercut roofs and finishing direct; keep
away from *Vanguard*. Seven stainless-steel bolts.

Vanguard   25 metres   E3 6a   (13.12.70/9.11.78)
Technically stimulating wall climbing on good rock. A north-side favourite.
Climb the layback crack above the stance to a big jug at its end (peg).
Stand up on the jug; then make thin moves up leftwards over a bulge to
gain a crack beneath a roof. Pull around the roof on the right to finish up
a short corner.

Bollocks to Broccoli   15 metres   E5 6b F7b   (31.10.92)
Food for thought. Climb straight up behind the tree to a good nut-slot,
from where thin moves diagonally left (8mm bolt) gain a shallow niche
and an *in-situ* thread. Make hard moves straight up the smooth wall to
bigger holds (two 8mm bolts). Step up right around the rib and scramble
up the easy gully to tree belays.

Twenty-five metres right of the arête, the upper tier forms a steep and smooth
face that is split by a crack which commences at half height. The next three
climbs start below the crack.

Editorial Axe   20 metres   E3 6a   (31.12.83/19.10.91)
Follow the line of finger-pockets in the left-hand side of the smooth face
before making a difficult move right to more pockets (peg). Swing right
again to the crack, which leads more easily to broken ground and the top.

Pitchfork Rebellion   18 metres   E5 6b/c †   (19.10.91)
An unfriendly face climb with gear that is strenuous to place.
Climb straight up to a vertical slot in a bulge (*in-situ* thread). Pull up and,
with protection from an obvious *Rock 1* placement above, step left into a
shallow niche. Step back right and make very thin moves over the bulge
(*in-situ* thread) to reach the crack, which leads more easily to broken
ground and the top.

Gubia   18 metres   E6 6b   (19.10.91)
A sustained and enjoyable route; the best of the trio. Some wires required.
Climb a thin line of weakness just to the left of an overhung groove (peg)
and move up to undercuts in the second of two bulges (8mm bolt).
Surmount the bulge (8mm bolt and *in-situ* wire) to reach superb
finger-pockets. Bear leftwards with a huge lunge for a jug and step up
(*in-situ* thread) to the exit of the previous two routes.

In from the Storm   25 metres   E4 6b † ✿   (13.4.85)
Climb the right-hand rib of the short overhung groove to a bulge. Step
right, and extend or dyno for a massive jug and small ledge. Move left
and follow a friable crackline to the top.

Bikini Amber   20 metres   E4 6a/b F6c+   (28.3.93)
An interesting pitch which requires two ropes to make sense of the
horizontally displaced fixed gear. Start just right of *In from the Storm*, at a
bare wall beneath the conspicuous, upper groove.
Step off a tree stump and move up to a tiny overlap (8mm bolt). Pull
rightwards to a good finger-pocket and a resting foot-ledge (peg on *A Day
for Feet*). Continue straight up (or on the left at 6b) past an 8mm bolt and
an *in-situ* wire above, reaching leftwards to a good hole (8mm bolt).
Easier climbing up the groove above (8mm bolt) leads to a ledge and an
8mm bolted abseil station.

A Day for Feet   20 metres   E3 6a   (15.3.93)
An enjoyable pitch on mostly good rock. Start beneath a vague crack-line
leading to a distinctive hole.
Pull up and left onto a jutting block and follow the line of the crack (peg
and *in-situ* thread) to reach jugs and the big hole (8mm bolt). Stand up
and traverse horizontally left to improving holds at the base of a large
groove (8mm bolt). Climb the groove easily to a big ledge and an abseil
station shared with *Bikini Amber*.

Micawber Buttress

The compact little buttress above Danemark Cliff and at the top of the grassy
approach couloir gives the following routes.

The Great Dane and Other Tall Tales   20 metres   Severe † (23.12.94)
Climb the stepped groove on the left-hand side of the buttress and finish
with an awkward move onto a ledge.

Micawberism   20 metres   Hard Very Severe 5a †   (21.12.94)
The left-hand crack.

Cyclists Advised to Walk   20 metres   E2 5c   (21.12.94)
One of the better pitches of its grade on the north side. Strenuously battle
up the right-hand crack; dismount, and finish up the groove above.

Avalon   20 metres   Very Severe 4c   (23.12.94)
Well worth seeking out. Climb the fine corner and swing left just above a
sapling onto the final arête.

Sell Your Soul   20 metres   E1 5a   (23.12.94)
Climb the right arête and enter a vague shallow groove on the left. Follow
the groove to the top.

Mare's Nest Buttress

The remaining climbs tackle the buttress to the right of a steep overgrown
gully.

So This Is Christmas?   18 metres   Hard Severe 5a   (25.12.94)
A short steep flake and vague arête lead past a ledge to the top.

Another Year Over   18 metres   Severe 5a   (1.1.95)
Right of the flake is a niche; gain it awkwardly and follow the groove and
crack above past a large ledge to the top.

Mare's Nest   18 metres   Very Difficult   (1954)
The deep crack in the left-hand side of the buttress.

The Grail   20 metres   E2 5c   (21.12.94)
Search for holds on the troublesome arête right of *Mare's Nest* (peg).

To the right the cliff diminishes in height; half way along is a steep white
pocketed wall that supplies one morsel: **Can-Can** (5b 23.12.94).

Danemark Cliff

This is the broad, white buttress above the left end of the quarry which is split
centrally by twin overgrown grooves. It is a good-looking crag but unfortunately
the rock does not come up to expectations. None of the routes merits getting
excited about – unless you find yourself on one.

Danemark   20 metres   Hard Very Severe 5a   (14.11.76)
Start 5 metres from the left end of the buttress. Scramble up a short crack
to a shoulder. Traverse rightwards along ledges below a smooth slab, and
climb its centre and the short groove above to the top.

Groundrush   20 metres   E4 6a †   (7.11.93)
A reasonable addition to this unremarkable cliff. The grade assumes
success in placing a vital wire at 8 metres. Start at the base of a short blue
groove, 7 metres from the left end of the buttress.
Pull into the groove and reach out left to a prominent hold. Step up to the
break above (good gear and an ancient *in-situ* thread); then climb the
nasty leaning wall (vital *Rock 3* in a high pocket) to jugs and a rest ledge.
Follow the thin crack on outwardly unhelpful slopers to a big ledge up and
right. Finish carefully up the final wall.

Assassin!   20 metres   E6 6b †   (4.12.93)
Really mean. Start 10 metres from the left end of the buttress.
Improvise to an obvious bucket in a niche at 5 metres (*Rock 4*). Pull
through the bulge to reach fingerholds (peg) and, using a good jug on the
left (peg), move up into the tamer groove above (*in-situ* thread). Continue
up the groove to join *Thriller*, which leads to the top.

Thriller   25 metres   E3 5c   (15.4.83)
Ever climbed on Gordale West Face? No need to travel so far: just climb
this – one of the better climbs on the cliff. Start in the centre of the left-hand
buttress below a shattered leftward-rising flake crack.
Climb the flake to a tiny roof. Make a long traverse leftwards to a shallow
groove, which is followed to the top.

Psycho 25 metres E1 5b (8.3.76)
A strenuous pitch taking the narrow angular stepped corner 5 metres from the right edge of the left-hand buttress.
Gain the corner directly and climb it to a jutting ledge on the left. Climb the wall above, and scramble rightwards over loose, broken ground to the top.

Dividing the buttress are two major parallel grooves, the left-hand of which is climbed by the following route.

Kay 24 metres Very Severe 4c ❀ (4.74)
Freed of ivy in 2001, the groove has now been taken over by other plant-life. Climb it if you can.

Slow Return 27 metres E2 5b † (29.10.83)
The shallow scoop-line to the right of the right-hand groove.
Climb the line of scoops and the groove past a slight bulge and then trend rightwards across the pocketed wall above to reach broken rock leading to the top.

To protect Cheddar Pink on the cliff-edge from trampling (and you from unpleasant vegetated rock) retreat from the following four routes using a pre-placed abseil rope. Position the lower-off knot and krab at a short steep wall 7 metres from the top of the broad rib of the buttress.

First a Fence 18 metres E6 6b † (12.1.02)
Fingery, hard, and – most of all – bold. Starting 2 metres right of *Slow Return*, climb the bulging wall to a hand-ledge (two pegs, the first of which, at 6 metres, is your first protection). Take a short-lived flake-crack and grey groove to better holds. Climb a groove and vegetated ledges to the top, or trend right to the pre-placed lower-off point.

To the right, in the left-hand side of the broad rib, are two left-facing flake cracks that start at 4 metres.

Dead Stop 27 metres E5 6a/b † (12.11.83/12.1.02)
Very steep and exciting with just enough gear. Start below the left-hand flake crack.
Follow the flake to its end. Press on straight above with a very long move, and so gain an incut flake-hold (*in-situ* thread). Rock up onto the flake, and bear rightwards and either climb vegetated ledges above, or step up and right to the pre-placed lower-off point.

Poisoned Ivy 18 metres E4 5c † (12.1.02)
Climb the right-hand flake crack and rib above to a shallow hole, containing two small holes, on the right. Stretch up left for a good fingerhold and pull up to larger holds which lead slightly rightwards to a junction with *Free Fall* or the pre-placed lower-off point.

Free Fall 25 metres E2 5b (5.6.77)
The disjointed groove in the broad front rib; a good-looking line, though with poor protection in the second groove.

Climb the first groove to its end. Move right into the second groove and climb this on widely-spaced holds to a ledge (pre-placed lower-off point of the previous three routes on the left). Step right, climb to a second ledge, and swing left on the arête to exit.

The Dimming of the Day   25 metres   E2 5c †   (12.1.02)
Worthwhile, with a thought-provoking crux. Start 2 metres right of *Free Fall*, beneath a line of weakness in the wall right of the broad rib.
Climb the rib to a resting-place at 6 metres. Enter a slim groove, and move up steeply to a ledge. Now, as for *Free Fall*, climb to a second ledge and swing left on the arête to exit.

Peg Leg Crack   25 metres   Hard Severe 4a   (28.1.76)
Climb the corner and crack 5 metres right of the front of the broad rib.

French Pinnacle

High above the quarry, and 45 metres right of Danemark Cliff, is a quaint little pinnacle, which just protrudes from the surrounding trees. The pinnacle is the objective of a small number of short pitches of considerable charm.

Approach by a path which skirts the left-hand edge of the quarry and runs up a scree slope in the vague depression above (French Gully).

Descent from the summit is by reversing the steep step of *Elizabeth Route* and then the east side of the window.

Access: Climbing is allowed from 1 October until 15 March inclusive.

Ten metres left of the pinnacle is a see-through chimney, and a little to the left is a blunt white arête, which is climbed by:

Mon Dieu   8 metres   E3 5c †   (31.3.99)
Delicately follow the arête, at first on its left side and then up its edge, to a tricky finish. E4 for the solo.

Zut Alors!   8 metres   Very Severe †   (31.3.99)
Take the thin crack and corner to the right of the arête.

A tall, narrow 'window' is visible between the back wall and the pinnacle. The following four routes start at the west (left) entrance to the window.

Elizabeth Route   10 metres   Difficult   (4.51)
From the window, climb up and left to the *brèche*. A few steep moves up the back wall of the pinnacle lead to its airy summit.

North-West Arête   10 metres   E3 6a †   (31.3.99)
If the back wall were dismantled this would be a good route. From the
ledge at the foot of the corner-crack on the right, step left onto the arête
and climb it – balancy – to the summit. There is a nut-slot at 6 metres, and
only those missing the point (and grade) will use the back wall on the left.

Original Route   12 metres   Difficult   (4.51)
Step right onto a ledge beneath a short corner-crack, which is climbed to
ledges and the summit.

Mariette Route   15 metres   Very Difficult   (4.51)
An enjoyable climb that takes the south-west (front left) arête of the
pinnacle. Traverse right onto the arête. Step right and follow a crack and
then ledges to the summit. A direct start is awkward and 4b.
Variation
A Slice at the Wife   15 metres   E1 5b †   (7.4.99)
Take the knife-edged arête direct, hoping the rock clearance team had
good reason to leave the monster-block in place. Finish up the short-lived
crack on the left.

Emily's Dog   15 metres   Very Severe 4b   (12.11.00)
Poorly protected. Start 2 metres right of the arête. Climb to the roof of a
shallow, ivy-filled cave. Skirt the roof to its left, step back right, and finish
direct.

Burial Route   12 metres   Difficult   (4.51)
Climb the crack in the east face until a move left gains ledges and the
summit.

The Quarry

*...in the year 1906, one dark night a tremendous roar resounded throughout
the neighbourhood and next morning it was found that an enormous rock-slip
had occurred and many thousands of tons of mighty boulders had been hurled
to the roadway below.' 'The quarrymen had cause to congratulate themselves
that the collapse had taken place in the night, when they were sleeping far
away, and not a life was lost. Had it been otherwise, every man must have
been killed.*   (H E Balch)

This is the boulder-strewn quarry opposite High Rock. At the back of the
quarry are two short but drastically leaning tiers. The lower tier, The Wave, is
separated from the upper, The Tsunami, by a commodious sloping rock
platform.

Many of the climbs are bolted sport climbs with variable-quality gear; some
still support original 8mm bolts (and pegs), while most of the post-1990
routes have been bolted with resined stainless-steel staples. The difference

The Quarry

1	The Bloodshed Begins	E2	HVS
2	Ritual Slaughter	E4	20 Ebee G Bees	F7b
3	Millimetre War	F7c	21 Split Rambo	F8a
4	Tot-ally Wick-ed	E1	22 A Day Called Zero	E5
5	Billy Crystal	F6b+	23 Sophisticated	E3
6	Crystal Gale	F7a+	24 Psycho-Bobble	E4
7	Grope the Slope	F6c	25 Hell's a Hard Place	F7a
8	Minstrelation	E4	26 Joyride	F7a+
9	'Real Runners'	E3	27 Liquid Sky	E4
10	Mutant Frenzy Bug	E3	28 Les Trois Chèvres	
11	Toxic Shock	E2	29 One for the	
12	Islands in the City	E5	Northern Brats	F7b+
13	Greed	F7b+	30 Sweet Tufa	F8a
14	Insatiable	F7b	31 Ya-Boo Yorkie!	F7b+
15	Raw Deal	E4	32 Hard Bass Religion	F7c
16	Bursting the Wave	F8a	33 Moonmilk	F7b
17	Holdloss	F7b+	34 Bick Zoomhead	F7b
18	Waiting (Project)	F8b?	35 Velcro Wall	F7b+
19	Bee Keeping....	F6c+	36 Dope on a Slope	F7a+
			37 On Beachy Head	F7b

will be obvious from below. Although short-lived, the climbs are very pumpy and offer a feast of slopers. The crag receives all available sunshine but stubborn seepage lines on both tiers make many lines unclimbable for much of the winter. (It's just as well that wider access is now legitimate.)

With the exception of a few hanging blocks on The Wave, the rock has been quarried solid. However, great care should be exercised when moving about the cliff-tops, since there is a fair amount of scree, which is easily dislodged (just watch how the resident goats have mastered the art of trundling). The boulder-field beneath is a favourite sunbathing spot and a playground for children, and you will not always be able to tell if people are there when you are climbing or moving around the terrace.

Access: Climbing is permitted here throughout the year except from 1 July to 31 August inclusive, and on Easter and the two May bank holiday weekends.

The Wave

Like a Virgin   9 metres   E3 6b †   (25.3.88)
Surprisingly strenuous. The left end of The Wave is bounded by a short, bulging arête. Climb the thin crack just to the right of the arête.

The Bloodshed Begins   9 metres   E2 5b   (20.2.88)
Enjoyable climbing on good, clean rock. Start 5 metres right of the left arête. Climb straight up the wall to finish with a nicely sloping mantelshelf. Three pegs and a bolt, all stolen.

Just to the right is an obvious black 'overhanging slab', the discontinuous flake-line to the left of which supplies:

Ritual Slaughter   9 metres   E4 6a †   (26.3.88)
Climb the flake with mounting interest, and finish dynamically past a bolt (stolen) and a vital *Rock 7* placement.

Millimetre War   9 metres   E6 6b F7c   (21.2.88)
Short admittedly, but every millimetre must be fought!
Climb the centre of the 'overhanging slab' in line with a faint, sketchy crack, and finish via a good hold over the lip. Three stainless-steel bolts; one *in-situ* dogger.

Tot-ally Wick-ed   9 metres   E1 5b †   (26.3.88)
'Udge' timidly up the left-hand side of the enormous hanging block right of *Millimetre War* (no place for high-powered laybacks) and finish with a steep move. One *in-situ* thread and two pegs – stolen.

Billy Crystal   9 metres   E2 6a F6b+   (1.10.95)
One big crystal: one big move. Start 5 metres right of the hanging block. A short easy slab leads to a small roof. Pull over to a crystal undercut, and stretch for success. Two stainless-steel bolts.

One-third of the way along the tier are the remains of a massive rockfall, the left arête of the scar giving the start for the next two routes.

Crystal Gale   9 metres   E5 6b F7a+   (1.10.95)
Sustained finger-flailing, almost entirely on crystals. Climb direct with a hard move to a rectangular white crystal. Three stainless-steel bolts.

Grope the Slope   9 metres   E3 6a F6c   (27.3.88)
Most peculiar. Frantically gain the sloping ledge on the arête from the left, and finish more easily. Three stainless-steel bolts.

Minstrelation   9 metres   E4 6b †   (26.3.88)
A hard pitch taking the black and white wall right of the rockfall. From a short groove, move up (peg) and diagonally right (8mm bolt) to pull onto the sloping terrace past a good *Friend* 2 placement.

'Real Runners'   9 metres   E3 5b/c †   (28.2.88)
An unexpected chance to use *RPs*. Climb the first, thin groove right of the rockfall.

Mutant Frenzy Bug   9 metres   E3 6a †   (28.2.88)
The technical wall and groove right of *'Real Runners'*. Two pegs – stolen.

Toxic Shock   9 metres   E2 5b   (1.10.88)
The second groove right of the rockfall with the crux to finish. One *in-situ* thread and an 8mm bolt.

Islands in the City   9 metres   E5 6a †   (26.3.88)
Start 2 metres right of *Toxic Shock*. Gain a hand-ledge at 3 metres, pull over the roof, and finish above a small rib with a tense mantelshelf. One peg and 8mm bolt; *RP2* and 3 useful at the top.

Greed   9 metres   E6 6b F7b+   (28.2.88)
A compulsive problem. Very extending (or should it be distending?). Start below the obvious (only) roof some 15 metres right of the rockfall. Climb up to the roof, reach over, and follow the thin crack to a break and an abseil station (not *in-situ*!) on the right. Two 8mm bolts and a peg.

Insatiable   9 metres   E5 6b F7b   (27.2.88)
Superb climbing, hypothetically speaking. Start about 18 metres right of the rockfall. Climb the leaning wall with a crucial span to a short crack on the left. (Don't!) lower off as for *Greed*. Two bolts and a peg – awaiting a rebolt.

Right of centre of the tier and about 20 metres right of the rockfall are twin, overhanging cracks.

Raw Deal   9 metres   E4 6b   (28.2.88)
The left-hand crack gives a wild pitch. Feet are unnecessary. Three pegs.

Bursting the Wave   9 metres   E7 6c F8a †   (1.1.89)
The radical right-hand crack is desperately touch-and-go. Finish with a
joint-killing dyno and hideous mantelshelf. Three pegs, *in-situ* wire, and an
8mm bolt.

Holdloss   7 metres   E6 6b F7b+ †   (26.11.95)
Three stainless-steel bolts in the sheer wall to the right show the way
(stick-clip the first bolt). A broken-off hold in the headwall currently
necessitates reaching back down to the final bolt to retreat. Try and top out
if you can.

Project: *Waiting*   7 metres   E6 7a F8b   (2004?)
It's open and cheap: go for it! (If successful, make cheque for £10 payable
to…)

Bee Keeping in a War Zone   9 metres   E3 6b F6c+   (27.3.88)
To the right of the twin cracks is another crack featuring a pod at 3 metres.
Swarm up the crack past three pegs and an *in-situ* wire. Lower off the
double 8mm bolt belay or top out.

The Wave now sweeps around a broad rib. In the left-hand side of the rib is
an obvious layback crack.

Ebee G Bees   9 metres   Hard Very Severe 5a   (25.3.88)
The easiest route on The Wave. Follow the crack and jive diagonally
rightwards across ledges onto the scree bank.

Split Rambo   9 metres   E4 6c F7b †   (30.3.88)
Been to Chullila? Powerful climbing up the shallow groove in the
right-hand side of the broad rib. Gain the obvious jug in the groove at 5
metres by some gut-wrenching moves and finish with haste. Two 8mm
bolts and a *Rock 4* placement.

A Day Called Zero   9 metres   E7 6c F8a †   (15.5.90)
A power-hungry test-piece with some of the hardest moves at Cheddar
(but with bolts that have long turned to dust). Start 3 metres left of
Sophisticated.
Make an explosive dyno (dust) to a jug and then a 'bronto' for a handrail
(dust). Finish direct (dust) via a jug and swing left to exit.

Sophisticated   9 metres   E5 6b   (30.3.88)
Blood-pumpingly taunting. The crack which starts with a pocket at 8
metres. Attack a white streak (*Rock 3* vital at top of crack) bearing
desperately leftwards to the crack. Sprint up this to a good exit. Two pegs.

Psycho-Babble   9 metres   E3 5c   (30.3.88)
Good fun. Start behind a big block at the extreme right-hand end of the
tier. Climb the crack on big holds and swing out rightwards to the
characteristically sloping exit. Two pegs.

Hell's a Hard Place   9 metres   E4 6b   (15.5.90)
Start 2 metres right of *Psycho-Babble*. Using a poor layaway, climb past a
8mm bolt to a break. Make a difficult pull to another layaway (8mm bolt)
and yard off this to a jug and the exit of *Psycho-Babble* on the left.

The Tsunami

The remaining climbs in the quarry are located on the upper tier.

Joyride   15 metres   E4 6a F7a   (17.2.95)
Good varied climbing with interesting features. Take some wires. Start
below a conglomerate shield at the left end of the wall.
Climb up onto the shield and make hard moves up the wall to a ledge
and tufa pillar. Rock up onto a ledge on the right below the slab. Move up
onto the slab and follow a crack to a stainless-steel bolted abseil station on
the right. Three stainless-steel bolts and a peg.

Liquid Sky   15 metres   E5 6b F7a+   (6.3.95)
A slab climb of sorts. Start at a flake below the centre-left of the wall, as for
Les Trois Chèvres.
Step up onto the flake and, using a conglomerate pillar on the right, push
up for good holds above. A distinct lack of footholds requires some
foot-free work to gain the ledge above. Move rightwards up the wall, and
(somewhat artificially using the arête on the left), reach good holds at the
base of the slab. Rock up onto the large ledge on the right, and a
welcome rest. Climb up onto the excellent smooth slab, to finish with a
technical move for the obvious jug in the centre of the slab. Lower off as
for *Joy Ride*. Six stainless-steel bolts.

Les Trois Chèvres   15 metres   E4 6b   (4.10.87)
Even more obstinate than appearances suggest. Start at a flake below the
centre-left of the wall.
Zigzag up the wall on unnerving, sloping holds (8mm bolt) to a larger
ledge on the left. Jump past a peg for another ledge above, and finish
more easily up a thin groove to the top.

One for the Northern Brats   18 metres   E6 6b F7b+   (4.10.87)
A physically draining pumpout up the centre of The Tsunami. Start at an
obvious, sharp, sidecut hold.
Climb straight up the wall (without deviation for a rest on *Les Trois
Chèvres*!) until a precarious grey slab leads directly to a small exit scoop.
Two pegs and two 8mm bolts.

Sweet Tufa   12 metres   E7 6c F8a   (1997)
A brilliant, if desperate, route up the shallow tufa. Three stainless-steel
bolts and one peg; bolt belay.

Ya-Boo Yorkie!   18 metres   E6 6b F7b+   (23.2.88)
Thuggish climbing up the white 'channel' in the centre of The Tsunami. A
great route.

Hot-dog the white rock via two good hand-ledges and a crucial stretch for a good resting-ledge at half height. Pull up onto a large flake, and traverse easily leftwards to finish up the scoop of ...*Northern Brats*. Four 8mm bolts and a peg.

Hard Bass Religion   10 metres   E5 6c F7c   (18.11.89)
More power-packed pumping, and some slamming hard moves. Start beneath a series of small sloping ledges in the right-hand side of the wall. Follow the ledges past a debilitating crux reach at half height and continue briskly to the good ledge and an old abseil station. Two bolts (8mm and 10mm) and a peg.

Moonmilk   10 metres   E5 6b F7b   (13.10.90)
Difficult climbing on stuff normally contained in chalk bags. Start below a short crack at 8 metres.
Rock over to crinkles (8mm bolt) and extend past a small roof (8mm bolt) to reach the crack (*Friend* 2½); easier climbing leads to the half-height ledge and an old abseil station.

Bick Zoomhead   10 metres   E5 6b F7b   (13.10.90)
A spectacular finish up the white headwall; it can be combined with any of the three previous routes.
From the half-height ledge, clip the 8mm bolt of *Ya-Boo Yorkie!* on the left; step right and continue forcefully up the weakness in the headwall to the top, past two 8mm bolts.

Velcro Wall   10 metres   E6 6b F7b+   (3.12.94)
Four really sticky moves, only just meriting the grade. Start 8 metres left of the chimney/cave.
Climb the overhanging wall, at first using stuck-on concretions; then bear right and up to a stainless-steel bolted abseil station. Three stainless-steel bolts.

Dope on a Slope   7 metres   E4 6b/c F7a+   (7.11.94)
A cute and perky problem up the right-hand side of The Tsunami. Start on a block 5 metres left of the chimney/cave.
Gain a hand-ledge, and from a sloper (to end all slopers), reach some big crozzly holds, the half-height ledge, and the stainless steel-bolted abseil station. Two stainless-steel bolts.

On Beachy Head   8 metres   E5 6b F7b   (7.11.94)
Wild and wacky climbing on bizarre rock formations that look like an import from the south chalk coast! Start from the double-bolt belay of *Dope on a Slope*.
Climb on deep pockets and follow some big (solid) encrustations left to a thread beneath the headwall. Strenuously climb the headwall and complete the experience with a flying finish to slopers. Three stainless-steel bolts and a thread.

Secret Solo Bluff

A fresh perspective on short hard routes in the Gorge; all the first ascents were soloed. This is the 8-metre crag of solid, compact rock 100 metres right of, and level with, French Pinnacle. The landing is flat, but crawling down for help after a sub-terminal crater would be problematic. The grades assume solo ascents, though protection looks to be available on some of the routes.

Night Vision   8 metres   E6 6a †   (9.4.99)
Climb a very shallow grey groove in the left-hand side of the wall and progress on pumpy slopers to a block overhang near the top. Swing right into a short jam crack and pull around on a small ash sapling that could be stronger.

Hard Lime   8 metres   E5 6b †   (9.4.99)
Pad the rock platform; then launch up from the sloper at head-height via layaways to a sharp jug. Continue very steeply on large holds to the top. Superb climbing.

Dangerous Dusk   8 metres   E5 6a †   (7.4.99)
Hard moves right to the top of the left-hand of two overhanging grooves. Some of the better holds are hidden: beware!

Thin Towers   8 metres   E4 6b †   (25.4.02)
Follow layaways up the bulging rib to the top. Holds in the adjacent grooves are not used. Contrived but flows well.

Above and Beyond the I'm So Pathetic Barrier

                                            8 metres   E1 6a †   (7.4.99)
The far-more-powerful-than-it-looks right-hand groove. Easy and straightforward above half height.

Secrets of 2002   8 metres   E4 6a †   (23.4.02)
Excellent. Starting a metre right of the last route, climb the bulging wall and rib straight to the top. The hardest moves are low down and the finishing holds are positive.

No Gear – Oh Dear!   7 metres   E3 5c †   (23.4.02)
Step up onto the left-hand end of the scooped ledge, and reach a dubious block-hold above. Ignoring the broken niche on the left, stretch up to the right for good holds and trend right to the top.

Secretly Barmy († 29.4.02) is a French 8a (English 6c) left-to-right traverse of the wall, based upon the line of footholds at or just above half-height. Start with a reach for a flake left of *Night Vision* and follow the footholds rightwards. When they disappear, a shoulder-wrenching set of moves is needed to access *Dangerous Dusk*. Now pull off the crux of *Secrets of 2002* and finish up *No Gear – Oh Dear!* The author will eat his chalkbag if this doesn't become one of the most popular pieces of hard climbing in the Gorge.

Hounds Bluff

A short but steep series of walls situated high on the hillside to the right of the quarry, opposite Priest Rock.

Access: Climbing is allowed from 1 October until 15 March inclusive.

At the left end of the tier is a compact, overhanging buttress with a narrow rightward-rising ledge 3 metres up.

Torn Limb from Limb   10 metres   E1 6a †   (5.5.99)
Dedicated to Pete. From a small white undercut flake above the left end of the ledge, climb steeply to buckets above a small double roof. Finish up the easy rib.

Leader of the Pack   10 metres   E6 6c F7c   (30.6.99)
A load of moves packed into a short space. From the left end of the ledge, pull hard to reach a sloping break. Improvise through the headwall and exit on a sharp jug. Twin 8mm bolts and drilled peg.

Fox Bites Back   10 metres   E4 6a †   (5.5.99)
Gain the sloping ledge and shuffle rightwards to a small left-facing corner. Climb straight up a line of weakness to a bulge (good wire). Finish strenuously up the thin crack and exit awkwardly left using a jug that you could yank off onto your mate below if you want.

The Hunt   8 metres   E2 5b   (19.4.99)
Starting below the broad right-hand rib of the buttress, climb to a small left-facing corner. Follow good holds up the rib on the right to a sloping ledge. Exit up the easy groove.

The Hunted   8 metres   E4 5c   (19.4.99)
An obligatory solo. Climb the steep grey wall left of a conglomerate patch, taking positive finger-holds past a short, thin crack to an awkward manoeuvre onto the sloping ledge. Exit up the easy groove.

Bramblebed   10 metres   E2 5c †   (15.4.99)
In the centre of the crag is a grey wall with an overlap above. Climb straight up the grey wall, in line with an intermittent thin crack, to the overlap. Trusting in the gods, pull over the resonating overlap to the top.

Snow in April   10 metres   E1 5b †   (15.4.99)
Climb the cracks right of the grey wall and finish strenuously.

Hounds in the Moonlight (12 metres E1 5b † †† 15.11.86) climbed the front face of the right-hand buttress to a bulge (*in-situ* thread – missing), which was passed with difficulty to reach the top. It appears that the boulders under the crag are all that remain of the route.

Arch Rock

The steep, south-west-facing wall overlooking the uphill edge of the Horseshoe Bend is distinguished by an undercut arch of rock in its centre and some good sports routes with mainstream appeal. Unfortunately, some of these were retrobolted without the first ascensionist's blessing. The crag seeps weepingly during winter. All-year round access rescues the routes from obscurity.

Access: Climbing is allowed all year round.

Get Kimitri!   12 metres   E5 6a   (26.6.85)
Short, boltless, and brilliant! A direct line up the perfect grey wall left of centre. Start 3 metres right of the right-facing corner.
Follow a groove and a series of technical layaways; step right, and climb to finger-pockets and an undercut flake just above. Move rightwards over the bulge and then go easily to the top.

No Time to Lose   12 metres   E1 5b   (21.12.86)
Worthwhile; start 5 metres right of the corner. Climb a faint crack-system and continue up the line of weakness to the top. Retrobolted in 2002 with 6 bolts and an abseil station.

Snug as a Slug on a Jug   18 metres   E5 6b F7b   (11.10.86)
Inspired by Paul Mitchell of 80s Grit fame, though the route bears absolutely no resemblance to its namesake on The Cowper Stone.
Climb blinkerdly up the face of the prominent white tower in the centre of the crag to finish over or at a small roof. Very precarious. Four stainless-steel bolts and a peg; abseil station.

Screwballed!   18 metres   E4 6a F7a   (30.1.94)
The overhang-rippled scoop immediately right of the white tower leads with increasing interest to a step up onto a black slab. Move left to the finish of Snug... One peg and four stainless-steel bolts to the abseil station.

Keystone Cop-Out   18 metres   E4 5c †   (26.6.85)
An unusual climb that toys dangerously with the undercut arch 10 metres up. Climb up and rightwards on good holds until a bold little groove leads to the right end of the arch. Undercut the arch leftwards; then pull over its left-hand side on disposable holds before trending rightwards to the capping roof. Exit over this on the right.

Playboys   18 metres   E6 6b F7b+   (4.11.90)
A fine eliminate right of the arch. Not as popular as it should be; perhaps the 6-metre hike-in deters? Start below a slim rightward-facing undercut corner-crack.
Climb the corner (gear) and pull up onto a steep black slab. Climb straight up the fingery wall and finish direct from a break. Five stainless-steel bolts to an abseil station.

Chulilla (F7b+), Brean Down
Climber: Lucy Creamer   Photo: Tim Glasby

rch Rock

Get Kimitri!	E5	5	Keystone Cop-Out	E4	9	Cascara Crack	HS	
No Time to Lose	E1	6	Playboys	F7b+	10	Hug the Jug	F4+	
Snug as a Slug on a Jug	F7b	7	All Hands to the Pump	F7b	11	Don't Fear the Bleater	F5+	
Screwballed!	F7a	8	Off the Wall	E2	12	As Happy as a Slug…	E4	

All Hands to the Pump   18 metres   E5 6b/c F7b   (28.9.86)
The smooth wall right again provides the best route on the cliff and its
hardest move. Some gear required. Start below a slim corner-crack, as for
Playboys.
Climb the crack, step right onto the wall, and wonder what to do next.
Move up, if possible, and gain a niche below the capping roof. Pull out
rightwards to top out, or leftwards to the abseil station of *Playboys*. Five
stainless-steel bolts.

Off the Wall   15 metres   E2 5b   (4.10.86)
A pleasant pitch that takes the line of weakness in the right-hand part of
the smooth, grey wall. Start 3 metres left of a large flake crack, where the
base of the cliff descends to road level.
Climb the face (or the flake on the right) and continue directly up a seam
to ledges and a finish on the right. Retrobolted in 2002 with 6 bolts and an
abseil station.

Cascara Crack   15 metres   Hard Severe 4a   (1954)
Follow the large flake crack 12 metres from the right-hand end of the cliff.
An abseil station was placed in 2002.

Hug the Jug   15 metres   F4+   (2002)
The bolted line right of *Cascara Crack* to an abseil station. Five bolts.

Don't Fear the Bleater   12 metres   F5+   (2002)
The final bolted line on the right to an abseil station. Five bolts.

An obvious flake crack 7 metres from the right-hand end of the cliff is an
un-named Severe.

As Happy as a Slug in Slime   13 metres   E4 5c   (24.12.86)
Spotters beware getting run over. Three metres from the right end of the
cliff, boldly climb straight up the smooth wall to the top. The original
starting pedestal has been plucked away, leaving an extra metre to fall.

Stepped Wall

Named after the rightward-rising line of steps in its left-hand side, this is the
steep, east-facing wall behind a lay-by 100 metres upstream from the
Horseshoe Bend.

Access: Climbing is allowed all year round.

Streamline   13 metres   E1 5b †   (8.10.94)
Rising leftwards from the first of the steps of *Stepped Wall* is a groove (also
a stream in winter). Enter the groove, and follow it to its end. Ignore easier
rock on the left and finish up the short wall past a good nut-slot.

Stepped Wall   18 metres   Very Difficult   (1954)
Amble up the line of steps until a short corner leads to a tree and the top.
There are less steps than there used to be, thanks to the rock clearance
team.

Matanuska   18 metres   Very Severe 4c   (1984)
Climb the narrow pillar face left of the corner of *Little Hopper*, starting up
an obvious layback crack.

Little Hopper   18 metres   Very Severe 4b   (28.11.70)
A good line. Climb the slim corner and wide crack 8 metres right of the
line of steps and finish steeply over a bulge.

Always Tomorrow   15 metres   E4 6b/c F7b   (31.10.93)
A challenge for French 7b flashers. A sprightly problem on the fine, white
headwall right of *Little Hopper*.
Climb the corner for 8 metres to cam placements. Swing right onto the
wall and take slopers straight up to a ledge 3 metres below the top. Finish
with a thin crank. Flashed it? Three stainless-steel bolts.

Odds against Tomorrow   18 metres   E5 6a †   (26.10.85)
An even bigger challenge for French 7b flashers; this is traditional fare
with thin wall-climbing devoid of any protection worth clipping. Start 3
metres right of the corner of *Little Hopper*.
Climb through a slight scoop to good finger-edges. Balance boldly up
rightwards to a small roof. Pull over on the left to a ledge, and finish up the
short crack above.

Cryogenics   18 metres   E5 6b F7b   (6.12.86)
Spaced bolt protection – the worst of both worlds? A difficult and sustained
pitch on all counts. Start 5 metres right of the corner of *Little Hopper*.
Climb a flat pink face to a finger-ledge. Freeze. If you can do it, a
desperate rock-up will get the first *Eco-bolt* clipped. Trend strenuously
rightwards to out-of-balance layaways to a 'why did you place it over
there?' *Eco-bolt* in a scoop beneath a roof. Pull back out left and finish
easily up the final wall to the right.

Bluepoint   18 metres   E5 6b F7b   (2.1.93)
A respectable bolt route up the vague pillar face and undercut arête right
of *Cryogenics*. Start 8 metres right of the corner of *Little Hopper*, at a small
roof at chest height.
Make a thin move over the roof and go up to a stopping place at
half-height. Climb the pillar face above on opposing layaways; then trend
left across the top of the arch to finish via a good jug on the left. Five bolts
of mixed race. A direct finish is slightly easier.

Bullsblood   18 metres   E4 6a   (23.10.86)
If the crag is allowed a classic, then this is it. A good route, bolted just
within the realms of safety. Start below a faint line of weakness, 9 metres
right of the corner of *Little Hopper*.

Stepped Wall

1 Streamline   E1
2 Stepped Wall   VD
3 Matanuska   VS
4 Little Hopper   VS
5 Always Tomorrow   F7b
6 Odds Against
   Tomorrow   E5
7 Cryogenics   F7b
8 Bluepoint   F7b
9 Bullsblood   E4
10 Decimation   F7a+
11 Subcutaneous
   Tissue   E2
12 Little M   E3
13 Stepping Back   E3

Climb fairly directly (*Eco-bolt*) until an intricate steeper section (*Eco-bolt*) leads to a good hand-ledge (peg). Finish steeply.

Decimation   15 metres   E4 6b F7a+   (2.1.93)
Starting 2 metres right of *Bullsblood*, climb to a break at 3 metres. Some long moves on poor holds lead up the steep wall above (two 8mm bolts) to a juggy hand-ledge. Finish leftwards on the exit of *Bullsblood* (peg).

Subcutaneous Tissue   15 metres   E2 5a †   (8.10.00)
Climb the streak past a low flake and use sloping hand-ledges to gain a narrow ledge up to the left (bold). Follow the shaky flake on the right to ledges and the top.

Little M   15 metres   E3 5c †   (8.10.00)
Nicer than her neighbours. Sustained climbing on reasonable rock. Follow the line of weakness right of the rock-scar streak, past a small overhang, to a move left to the previous route just below ledges. Scramble over ledges to the top.

Stepping Back   12 metres   E3 6a   (30.12.92)
To the right is a 4-metre-high slim groove in a compact wall. A tough little pitch, with a bolt that's hard to clip (and it's not even an 80s route). Move up and right into the top of the groove. Pull up (*Rock 2* placement and 8mm bolt) and continue up the wall above (peg), avoiding some loose material to its right.

Roamertherapy   12 metres   E2 5b †   (8.10.00)
Start below the obvious flake-crack that starts 4 metres up. Gain and climb the flake-crack to its close. Forage for reliable holds amongst bulges above, and continue to ledges and the top.

Overshoot Wall

Opposite the base of Shoot Gully and descending to road-level is a short and steep east-facing wall.

The first two routes take in the smooth and compact pink wall at the left end of the crag.

Access: Climbing is allowed all year round.

Whose Line Is It Anyway?   10 metres   E4 .6a/b   (1970s/5.94)
Start a metre right of a slight corner on the left-hand side of the smooth pink wall.
Climb the wall past two stainless-steel bolts and pull up to the capping roof. An awkward pull over onto a dirty ledge gives a disappointing finish (poor peg on *Airborne Attack*, hidden up right beneath the top overlap).

Airborne Attack   10 metres   Hard Very Severe 5b †   (27.9.86)
Misses the target. Start up the wall but trend rightwards around a bulge
almost into *Lucifera*. Move back to the left and pull over a bulge (peg) to
finish.

Lucifera   12 metres   Very Difficult   (7.59)
A good line but loose at the top. Climb the broken corner and narrow
leftward-slanting slab 6 metres from the road to a ledge. Finish up a short
square-cut chimney.

Eastender   12 metres   Hard Very Severe 5a   (6.10.86)
Climb the groove and arête near the centre of the crag to the capping
overhang. Step right and pull over on big holds. Abseil from trees.

Comfortably Numb   12 metres   E4 6b/c †   (25.1.86)
A mean problem. Protection is confined to the two old bolts. Start at a
block immediately right of the groove of *Eastender*.
Move up onto a good foothold below the smooth, leaning wall. A long
reach past a bolt is followed hard on its heels by a snatch sequence to big
handholds (bolt). Gain the old abseil station above. (The two monos en
route are not of Spanish extraction, but are unfilled holes for *Eco-bolts*:
shame they don't make them any more).

Berlin Wall   12 metres   E1 5c   (15.11.86)
The wall to the right of the groove of *Eastender*, starting 6 metres to its
right. Climb slabby rock to a short rightward-facing groove. Take the
groove, step right onto a ledge, and climb the blank wall (8mm bolt) to the
terrace.

The Niche

On the opposite side of the road from the pinnacle of *Consolation* in the
Reservoir area and some 12 metres above road level is a small bay. The bay
has a slabby grey wall on the left and a pocketed overhanging wall on the
right.

Goatoit (hard 6b 19.5.99) is a tiptoe boulder problem immediately right of
a hairline crack 4 metres from the left end of the wall.

Hairline   6 metres   E1 5c   (19.5.99)
Follow a sinuous hairline crack 5 metres from the left end of the wall, and
finish using the obvious block-hold on the right. Pad-out the scree before
setting off: this is a solo.

It's a Hard Life (Never Mind)   7 metres   E4 6b   (8.6.94)
Start in the centre of the slabby grey wall, below a thin leftward-slanting
crack. Climb past a pocket to where an extensive reach gains a further
pocket in the centre of the wall. Blindly grasp a good edge and exit left.

Absolutely Amazing Climb II   9 metres   E3 5c   (4.10.86)
There is a corner on the right-hand side of the wall. From immediately left
of the corner, reach and climb thin, discontinuous cracks to the top.

The remaining three routes depended variously on *in-situ* threads, all of
which have been cut or removed by persons unknown.

Peace, Love, Empathy   10 metres   E5 6b   (5.94)
Start as for the next route. Strenuous. Climb the steep pocketed crack for 5
metres (missing thread). Swing left and pull up on positive holds (two
further missing threads) to more good holds (*Rock 7*) and an evil top.
Belay on a pre-placed rope.

The Unrelenting Wit of David Turnbull   10 metres   E4 6b (9.10.93)
The pocketed crack in the centre of the short overhanging wall. High in its
grade and with the crux to start. Climb painfully on pockets (missing
thread) to a break (*Friend 1* useful). Pull rightwards on flat holds and finish
carefully.

Mean, Lean, Power Machine   10 metres   E5 6a   (9.5.94)
A line up the pocketed crack in the right-hand side of the overhanging
wall. Follow a sustained line of layaways and pockets (peg and missing
thread) to larger holds and the top.

Above and to the left of The Niche is a short sheer wall with a white patch.
The wall has three extended boulder-problems (solos) that merit E-grades.

Double-mono Wall   5 metres   E2 6b   (19.5.99)
Take the micro-pocketed face immediately left of a vertical crack. The
grade entertains the risk of bouncing off the end of the sloping ledge.

**The Peak Is Full of Gritstoners Humping Their Designer
Crashmats Around**   6 metres   E2 6a   (19.5.99)
Not to be underestimated. Follow the right-curving crack that bisects the
white patch above a sapling; then steeply climb the committing face.

Foam Roll-up (6 metres E1 6a 19.5.99) is a lightweight filler-in, which
gains and follows finger-holds above the white patch.

Blackrock Quarry   OS Ref 486 546

This is the small limestone quarry situated in the picturesque dry valley (Velvet
Bottom) immediately to the east of the Gorge. Approach it by a way-marked
trail branching off left from the eastern extremity of the Gorge where the
B3135 veers rightwards. The track leads through a wooded area to a quarry
in one kilometre.

The quarry wall is rather broken and, in places, very unstable, although a good-looking corner may make a visit just worthwhile. Note that there have been serious accidents here due to falling rock.

Access: Group use is not permitted, but use by individual climbers is not restricted.

Rachel's Crack   15 metres   Hard Very Severe 5a †   (28.8.84)
Gain the wide crack in the left-hand wall of the corner and climb it loosely to the top.

Black Rock Corner   20 metres   Hard Very Severe 5b   (c.1960s)
Climb the corner to the top with the degree of difficulty dependent upon finger size.

Killing Time   20 metres   E4 6a †   (28.8.84)
A committing pitch up the bare right-hand wall of the corner. Starting in its centre, climb the wall rightwards and then boldly to gain a series of ledges on the left. Step right and climb the arête to finish. A line of 8mm bolt stubs coincide with the line of the route (those cavers again!).

A Friend Indeed   18 metres   Hard Very Severe 5a †   (28.7.92)
Climb the line of edges and flakes right of *Killing Time* to the arête. Move left to a thin crack in a shallow groove and follow this to the top.

Cheddar Area

Sand Point

Along the north coast of the Middle Hope peninsula, 8 kilometres north of Weston-super-Mare, is a line of short limestone cliffs rising to 12 metres in height. Two crags here offer some recorded lines which are supplemented by beautiful bouldering on well-weathered rock. The base of the crag is tidal but generally only inaccessible for around two hours either side of high tide.

The headland is owned by The National Trust, and its use is governed by strict byelaws. A low profile will help to keep over-inquisitive walkers and children at bay.

Middle Hope

A minor venue next to a beautiful bay. From the car-park, take a path straight up to the top of the ridge. Walk eastwards for half a kilometre and then drop down to a semi-circular bay, with pebble beach, to the left. Four of the routes are situated on a steep buttress directly below a stone wall that traverses the ridge, just to the east of the bay. Adjacent craglets provide perhaps the best bouldering on the peninsula, all of which has been documented, but not here.

The buttress has a prominent left-facing corner left of a large slanting overhang low down. There are good tree belays above. Care is required with some hollow rock on both top-outs.

Peace Protest   10 metres   E4 5c †   (23.3.03)
Take a balancy line up the centre of the smooth yellow slab left of the corner. Two wire placements only, with a big, scary gap between.

Never to Go Back   10 metres   Hard Very Severe 5a †   (23.3.03)
Climb the left-facing corner. Enjoyable until its traverse left on dodgy flakes onto *Peace Protest* near the top.

Pedestal Overhang   10 metres   E3 6a †   (23.3.03)
A curious roof problem. Use the pedestal block under the overhang to its fullest extent to reach for holds on the lip. Pull around and then step left to finish up a broken arête.

Lip Slip   10 metres   E1 5b †   (23.3.03)
Tip-toe diagonally left along the lip of the overhang to finish up the broken arête. Good wire protection.

The remaining route here lurks in a gully 30 metres towards the bay.

Sub-marine Stubble   8 metres   E4 6b †   (23.3.03)
Climb to undercuts beneath a hanging rib in the west wall of the gully.
Break through an overhang into a groove in the rib. Easier rock leads to
the top. Tough if the stubble is wet or unshaven.

Swallow Cliff

The crag of principal interest is located a kilometre from the tip of Sand Point.
Approach from the car-park by taking the path westwards along the ridge
towards Sand Point. Soon after passing the triangulation point, drop down
the northern slope to a small pebble beach which faces down the Bristol
Channel towards Weston-super-Mare. The crag runs westwards from the
beach.

The cliff comprises a series of walls, prows, and an undercut buttress of very
solid rock. These offer some surprisingly good, if short, pitches of character;
all are worthwhile. The roof climbs are particularly special, as is the area's
madcap contribution to the 'deep' water soloing scene. Belays at the top are
scarce, and scrub cover makes the few stakes that are in place difficult to find
(the really keen could bring along their own stake to be on the safe side).

At the landward end of the beach and rising behind boulders is a violently
leaning wall, terminated on its right by a less steep, west-facing wall.

Underdogs   12 metres   E3 6a   (12.9.87)
A strenuous and unusual diagonal line across the leaning wall.
From a boulder, pull over a small roof and follow the line leftwards with
hard moves to finish up the smooth headwall (two *in-situ* threads). Bush
belay across the path.

Memento   12 metres   E1 5c   (8.5.96)
Climb the bulging blunt white rib just to the right of the start of *Underdogs*
to sumptuous jugs. From blocks on the left, take the short groove and slab
above to the top.

★Souvenir   12 metres   Very Severe 4c   (12.9.87)
A nice pitch up the centre of the slabby, west-facing wall. A problem start
over a roof leads to small holds on the wall. Follow these, trending left to
exit easily.

Ten metres to the right is a prominent crack in a bulging white buttress.

Drop a Clanger   12 metres   E2 5b †   (8.5.96)
Climb the eliminate left-hand side of the bulging white face to finish up a
small left-facing corner. There are long reaches between good flat holds,
one of which rocks.

The Soup Dragon Warbles   12 metres   E3 5c   (12.9.87)
A veritable pump. Climb easily to the bulging, rounded rib left of the prominent crack. Launch up the rib via a thin crack and jugs, and continue (*in-situ* thread) to finish over a projecting beak. Bush belay.

Broad Reach   12 metres   Very Severe 4b   (18.7.93)
Climb the obvious crack right of the previous climb.

Mister Fuzzy-wuz   12 metres   E1 5b   (12.9.87)
Gain the niche below the roof right of the crack. Pass the roof (*in-situ* thread) to finish up a thin crack. Bush belay.

Further right, the cliff-line is interrupted by three shallow caves with intervening prow formations. The next three routes occupy the leftmost cave.

Rugrat   8 metres   E4 6a †   (25.4.96)
A superb little route taking the very centre of the sheer left wall of the cave. Dyno for a projecting jug, reach right to a flake, and so gain a good slot at 6 metres. Continue direct until a swing left from finger-pockets gains the arête and slab. Better to fix gear; then descend the easy slab leftwards to the beach.

Sockthing   12 metres   E1 5a †   (8.5.96)
Exciting. Start in the back of the cave. Climb the front of the grey column to a bulge. Extend for jugs over the bulge and follow these rightwards, moving up and then right to gain the top move of *Seven Bridges*.

Seven Bridges   12 metres   E1 5a   (18.7.93)
Very steep climbing up the crack that rises out of the cave. A route that feels big for its size. Start up the chimney right of the grey column.

Weston Approaches   12 metres   Hard Very Severe 5b   (18.7.93)
Climb the overhanging chimney-crack in the buttress between the leftmost and the central cave. Scramble to the top.

Jutland   12 metres   E2 6a   (12.9.87)
Climb wildly up the underside of the left-hand and most overhanging of the prows (*in-situ* thread) to a ledge above. Scramble to the top.

Buoy Racer   12 metres   E1 5b   (11.7.93)
Enter the awkward hanging crack right of *Jutland*, step left above it, and take a short wall to easier ground and the top.

The next three routes start in the central cave.

Jocular Banter   12 metres   E2 6a   (18.7.93)
Boulder up the left wall and finish up easier grooves.

Gay Repartee   12 metres   E2 6a   (18.7.93)
From the back of the cave, link powerful and greasy undercuts leftwards to an easy finish.

Mass Debate   12 metres   E2 5c   (18.7.93)
The cleft in the nether regions of the central cave leads to a strenuous
jamming crack. Finish to the left.

Leaning Difficulties   12 metres   E2 5c   (18.7.93)
Climb the left-facing flake-line in the overhanging prow between the
central and the rightmost cave. Exit up broken rock.

The next two routes start from the rightmost cave.

Severn Bore   12 metres   E3 5c ††   (12.9.87)
Short, steep, and far from boring. Climb the leaning wall in the left-hand
side of the cave until missing flakes (now somewhere out in the Bristol
Channel!) lead left to a juggy slab and the top.

Second Severn Crossing   12 metres   E2 5c ††   (11.7.93)
From the back of the cave, clamber up to beneath the sloping roof 7
metres up. Launch out leftwards below the roof to finish as for *Severn Bore*.
Similarly affected by rockfall.

Immediately right of the cave is a fine buttress, characteristically undercut by
massive black roofs.

★Psycho 2   15 metres   E4 6c †   (6.9.87)
The virtuoso 3-metre ceiling in the left-hand side of the buttress.
Undercut out under the roof on painful finger-jams (*in-situ* thread) and
gain good holds on the lip by creative means. Continue to steep grass, or
move right to finish up the next route.

Sands of Time   15 metres   E3 6a   (6.9.87)
Start up the crack right of the 3-metre ceiling and, from a shallow groove
above (*in-situ* thread), follow a ramp rightwards to good holds and an
easy exit.

Too Big to Swallow   12 metres   E3 6a   (12.9.87)
An improbable line over the large roof at mid-height. Climb up to a
projecting block beneath the roof. Make a long reach for good holds over
the lip and pull over with great difficulty to join the exit of *Sands of Time*.

Then Chew on This   12 metres   E4 6a †   (12.9.87)
Jam for 4 metres up the rightward-curving crack splitting the buttress. Pull
straight over the tough roof above and move up left to the exit of *Sands of
Time*.

The Incalculable Cleft   15 metres   E4 6b †   (6.9.87)
Towards the right-hand side of the buttress is a large black roof split by an
evil cleft.
Struggle ham-fistedly into the cleft but evacuate it as soon as possible to
gain a niche above the roof on the right. Take the narrow groove on the
right and finish easily. Stake belay.

'I've Cleaned That'   12 metres   E2 6a   (6.9.87)
A hard problem through the roofs right of the cleft.
Gain a short rib between the roofs from the right. Pull over the upper roof
using a superb spike out right (*in-situ* thread) and climb (*in-situ* thread) to
the finish of *The Incalculable Cleft*.

S'all Yours   12 metres   E2 5c †   (25.4.96)
Start at the right end of the main crag, 3 metres right of *'I've Cleaned
That'*.
From an easy slab, make thin moves leftwards and up into the open
groove 2 metres left of the arête, and ascend this to an undercut bulge.
Pull over and exit with caution.

Forty-five metres to the right, the cliff forms a clean slab, with fluted vertical
cracks and a rugged rib leading up to the centre of the slab. The four climbs
here finish at the same point; there is a stake 2 metres back from the
cliff-edge. A pre-fixed rope attached to the stake will help with the slightly
loose exit, though it is not essential. All routes here provide enjoyable
climbing on great rock.

☆**Flute Elope**   12 metres   Severe †   (15.2.03)
Climb the sharp slab left of the rugged rib to a break beneath the slab.
Climb the left-hand vertical crack in the slab, step right, and take the
obvious exit.

☆**Pipe Music**   12 metres   Severe †   (15.2.03)
Climb the rugged rib to the break beneath the slab. A huge jug gives
access to the right-hand crack. Climb the crack to the common exit.

☆**Suggestive**   12 metres   E1 5c †   (15.2.03)
Climb easily to a sizeable roof under the right-hand side of the slab.
Undercut for a hanging flake over the lip, stretch for a finger-jug, and pull
over. Pockets above lead to the exit. Perfect protection.

☆**Ain't No Sunshine**   12 metres   Hard Severe 4b †   (15.2.03)
Climb to and enter awkwardly the V-groove right of the slab. Large holds
lead onto the slab above. Climb diagonally left to the exit.

Fifteen metres further right is a pebble-filled gully, the short, steep walls of
which provide the following climbs, sea moss permitting.

East Wall

There is a stake belay in the grassy spur above the wall.

☆**Elgar**   12 metres   Very Severe 5a †   (8.2.03)
An elegant little route up the narrow slab on the seaward rib. Move up
onto a slim pedestal. Climb straight up with a tricky move over a bulge,
and continue direct up the slab to the top.

Helga   12 metres   Severe 4c †   (8.2.03)
Climb the initial overhanging arête, and then continue to the top on large
holds.

Sterling Sea Moss   10 metres   Hard Very Severe 5c †   (8.2.03)
Start 2 metres right of the arête. Climb up to a flake with difficulty. Pass a
large thread above, eventually stepping left onto the arête.

Pomp   10 metres   Hard Very Severe   5b †   (15.9.87)
Excellent. Starting 3 metres right of the arête, climb into a niche 4 metres
up. Follow a rightward-curving crack on good holds; then escape leftwards
along a ramp.

☆☆**Circumstance**   8 metres   E3 6a †   (15.8.87)
One of the best routes at Sand Point. Use a flake and a mono to climb up
to twin jugs in the centre of the smooth face. Step up to the exit of *Pomp*.
Unprotected, but with the hardest moves low down and pebbles beneath.

Where Coral Lies   7 metres   E6 6a †   (8.2.03)
A short but very serious solo given the back-breaker boulder waiting at the
bottom. Make a move up a rightward-twisting crack, and take a vague
blunt rib above using two coral-stem projections to finger-pockets and a
sloping mantel exit. (The right-hand jug on *Circumstance* is off line.)

West Wall

There are two cracks in the slightly overhanging wall with another, shorter
and pocketed, to their left, which provides a highball boulder problem at 5c.

Rasp   6 metres   E1 5b †   (2.2.03)
The left-hand crack.

A Traction   8 metres   E5 6b †   (23.3.03)
Strictly eliminate, with long, hard moves above a big-bounce fall. Climb up
to a mono left of the crack of *Stomp* (wire in base of crack, and wire in slot
on *Rasp* to the left). Connect a series of finger-holds in the headwall above
and exit direct.

Stomp   8 metres   E1 5c †   (15.9.87)
The right-hand crack; well-protected after the hard start.

Fifty metres right, past a series of unusual fins with potential, is a boulder-
filled bay with an easy escape at the back. On its left-hand side is an
overhanging west-facing wall.

☆**It's Over**   8 metres   E4 5c †   (15.2.03)
It will be if you fall off. Superb rock though. Gain a ragged finger-jug, and
then undercut over a bulge to reach the left end of a high sloping
hand-ledge. A powerful final lock and it really is over.

Twenty metres right, beyond some foreshore blocks is a gully with a smooth left-hand wall.

Trench Town   7 metres   E1   6a †   (15.2.03)
Start in the centre of the face and, using the obvious pocket on the right, make hard moves to sharp finger-holds. Swing right onto a jug, and take black sawtooth cracks to the top.

Beyond, the cliff-line remains uninviting until the Point is reached. Here the limestone turns dolomitic and yields various clean slabs and cracks of up to 12 metres. Most of these will have been climbed in the 60s; unfortunately no records are available.

★★**Motorboat to Mars: The Re-release**   150 metres   XS   6a   (S2)   (7.7.98)
The area's premier deep (?!) water solo attraction, which crosses the main cliff on an intricate, very sustained, and fairly inescapable line. Although the climbing is generally only between 2 to 5 metres above the sea, various boulders lurk not too far below the surface and, in this respect, three trickier sections in particular demand care. All in all it could save you some serious grief if you check out the fall zones when the tide is out. This will reveal that the maximum depth of water above the predatory boulders is merely 1 to 2 metres. Any deeper than that and the line (and you) would be under water. Start by descending onto a projecting rib between two hollows, some 150 metres to the west of the pebble beach.
Traverse east, stepping down and fingering across the steep side-wall with difficulty. Continue around onto the seaward face and pursue a line of choice until after 60 metres of 4a-4c climbing you arrive at a short overhung corner that forms the right edge of the main cliff. The sea should now be lapping just beneath foot level. (If it isn't you'll either be drenched or be risking impalement on the boulders.) Traverse left beneath roofs, descending a little along a crack. Continue in the same line between roofs until a jug-rail leads into an alcove with an overhanging left wall. This will appear fairly intimidating, and since you know that boulders lurk below, you'll want to lose, rather than gain, height. Descend the wall strenuously leftwards onto a rib which provides a semi-rest. Either climb the flakes straight above or the groove slightly left to easier rock. Continue into an easier recess, reverse a ramp, and pull up a steep wall onto a rib. Traverse left into a third and final recess and get established on a square-cut column at its back. On the left is a steep undercut wall; again, aim to lose height and reach good finger-jugs 3 metres left just above the bulges. From here, make one final hard move to pull around onto slabbier rock. Continue more easily leftwards for 20 metres, eventually sewing up the experience with a nice section above a tilted rock platform leading to the pebble beach.

Wood Lane Quarry

The quarry lay dormant until 1970, when it was used as an amphitheatre-type arena for Weston's own 'Theatre in the Woods' productions. In July of that year, the first production, Hansel and Gretel, made the local headlines. It was seen by about 180 spectators on tiered wooden seats, and was lit by Calor Gas bottles. Its seasonal fortnightly productions ran for three years, all proceeds going to charity. (Wayne Gladwin)

Wood Lane Quarry is situated in Weston Woods, Weston-super-Mare. Leave the M5 at Junction 21 and, ignoring the town centre-signed new dual carriageway straight ahead, turn left on the Worle/Sand Bay road and follow it, skimming a roundabout, to a second roundabout (Homebase store on the right). Take the first exit to a third roundabout and then the Sea Front/Town Centre road on the right. Follow this for 2 kilometres to a mini-roundabout (church on the right). Turn right into Baytree Road (signposted Milton) and left at the lights into Milton Road. Follow this past the Bristol House pub on the right to a right turn into Manor Road. Go up Manor Road and park just before a crossroads; Wood Lane is opposite. Walk 30 metres up the lane and turn right at the second set of posts, immediately into the quarry.

The quarry supplies an interesting collection of climbs in a sheltered yet fairly sunny location. Steep rock, sparse protection, and endless pumping slopers make for committing climbing. A word of warning: on Wedgey's Wall in particular, the exits can be earthy and leaf-littered; a brief rap and brush will be excusable on the more serious routes, especially early in the season. The crag is not at its best during a wet winter when it can seep profusely after heavy rain. Once the crag has dried up, however, the combination of a canopy of trees and its steepness keeps most of the best routes completely dry in the rain.

The present owners of the quarry, North Somerset Council, do not object to climbing, despite the legally-required warning signs and fencing.

The Pit Wall
Upon entering the quarry, this is the short overhanging wall visible on the left above a dank pit which normally contains the remains of a few girlie magazines (and worse).

Fair Game   12 metres   E4 6a   (11.7.93)
For strong climbers. Start below a niche 5 metres up.
Climb up into the niche, move right and back left, and press on strenuously up cracks to a tree at the top.

Screaming of the Limbs   12 metres   E4 6a   (28.7.93)
For pain-resistant climbers. Start a metre short of the right arête.

Reach good holds 3 metres up and then layaway and slap past a funny peg to a hand-ledge (or do it statically). Climb the headwall (two pegs), finishing with care, if at all, through hanging ivy gardens.

Wedgey's Wall

The long wall, with a yellow hue, visible straight ahead upon entering the quarry is a 13-metre-high, leaning face of solid rock. It extends from the Pit Wall on the left to a blind cave on the right. It faces east and catches the morning sun. Unfortunately, since the routes were first climbed the wall has acquired various hangerless retro-bolt stubs (that need to be filled in).

Wedgey Went In   13 metres   Hard Very Severe 5a   (12.3.89)
The only obvious groove in the wall, starting 12 metres left of the cave. From a ledge 2 metres up, climb the lower bulging groove to a step right above. Step back left and climb directly to the top (two pegs).

★**Haggis Came Out**   13 metres   E1 5b   (12.3.89)
Two metres right of *Wedgey Went In*, a difficult start gains good holds (peg). Continue up on small but positive holds (peg) and then to the top (peg on right).

★**Teenage Mutant Snapping Turtle Head Soup**
                                    13 metres   E4 5c (14.12.89)
A lead of character. Start below what appears to be a turtle-head-shaped spike at about 6 metres.
Make long reaches to gain a good ledge just below the spike. Continue with difficulty past a small overlap to reach a jug on the left and easier ground. Bear rightwards to the top. Serious, since gear is restricted to a sling throttling the turtle.

★**Corporate Image**   13 metres   E3 5c   (22.7.90)
Good steep face climbing. Start 5 metres left of the cave.
Climb strenuously to a peg and move up to find a one-digit hold and a flat handhold. Clip a second peg and continue straight up the wall left of a small roof to an earthy exit.

☆**Smokey Robinson**   13 metres   E4 6a †   (15.11.89/28.6.99)
The very sustained narrow corner 3 metres left of the cave. Strenuous.
Climb the lower groove (*Friend 2* in borehole) to a jug and hidden peg at 7 metres. Make a hard move straight up the narrow corner (peg) and continue direct up bulging rock on undercuts to the top.

Chrality   13 metres   E3 5c   (15.11.89/13.5.90)
An unusual route; well worth doing. Bridge up the cave/chimney (peg), and pull up into the corner above. Climb the corner and move out left to exit with care.

The Buttress

The projecting lobe of rock to the right of Wedgey's Wall is not the best part of the quarry. It is terminated on the right by a shady gully.

The Clean Machine   12 metres   E2 5b †   (28.7.93)
The left-hand arête of the buttress; a poor route. Start in the cave. Climb rightwards onto a ledge on the arête. Continue up and left to a dirty finish.

Would You?   12 metres   E5 6a †   (28.6.99)
Seriously committing, without a lot of gear. Start 4 metres right of the cave, between the two arêtes of the buttress.
From a small sloping ledge just above head-height, span diagonally right across the leaning wall (watch for a decent landing) to a good hold (*Rock 7*). Trend steeply leftwards on sideholds into the centre of the wall. Move up and right over a bulge using the big block hold to easier solid ground and a tree on the cliff-edge.

Tour de Force   13 metres   Hard Very Severe 5a   (1.5.91)
Climbs the right arête of the buttress. Starting immediately left of a pair of boreholes, move up to a small ledge on the arête (peg). Climb the wall to the top (two pegs).

Georgy Girl   13 metres   Very Severe 4b   (12.3.90)
Relatively attractive. Follow the fairly straight line of boreholes and disconnected grooves (two pegs).

Thanks to the Nifl Hiem   12 metres   Hard Severe 4a   (21.3.90)
Thanks for what? Start on the left-hand side of the rock gully. Climb up to a tree 5 metres up. Pull up and step right onto a small ledge. Continue straight to the top.

Wedgey's Revenge   12 metres   Very Severe 4c   (22.3.90)
Layback the crack in the right-hand corner of the gully to a ledge. Trend left to exit.

Shield Wall

Right of the gully is a very steep white wall characterized by an ominously hanging shield of rock near its right edge.

Return of the Wedge   15 metres   Hard Very Severe 5a   (1990)
The loose left arête of the wall. Start 2 metres right of the arête.
Gain the arête over a pink patch of rock and follow it carefully to the top.

Men Behaving Badly   15 metres   E3 5c   (22.7.94)
A sustained pitch, well worth trying. Start as for *Return of the Wedge*, below a line of boreholes.
Climb a vague, slim groove 2 metres right of the arête, past a small roof and two pegs (one easy to see, one missing), to an overhang near the top (peg). Using underclings, reach good holds over the roof (peg) and exit up a groove.

★Hot Summer Nights   15 metres   E4 5c   (13.7.94)
This takes on the full might of the centre of Shield Wall. Low in the grade.
Start 4 metres right of the left arête, at the base of a shallow triangular
depression.
Pull up to the apex of the depression, to the left of a small roof, (bolt –
requires threading). Surmount the bulge, and get established on the
prominent narrow ledge above (three pegs). Finish decisively up the wall.

Whingeing Jimmy   15 metres   E2 5b   (27.7.94)
Fairly serious (and worthy of complaint). Start at the right edge of the
triangular depression, below a small roof at 4 metres.
Climb up and grope for good holds over a bulge (peg). Move up to big
holds below a pink area of rock (peg). Continue direct and then
rightwards to a loose finish.

Gannets Groanies   15 metres   Hard Very Severe 5a   (15.4.91)
Start below the left-hand side of the shield and reach its top via the wall
and a groove on its left. Continue to a tree on the right. Helmets
compulsory!

Wibbly Wobbly Wall   15 metres   Hard Very Severe 5a   (13.7.94)
Start at the right edge of Shield Wall. Climb diagonally leftwards to the
right side of the shield, swing left onto its face and mantel onto its top.
Continue to a tree and the top.

The Long and Short of Wit   13 metres   E1 5b   (13.7.94)
A short-lived moment of pleasure. Climb the square-cut groove in the
right-hand arête of Shield Wall.

In the centre of the wall around to the right is a poor, loose, and intimidating
route with a nightmare exit: **Watch the E7 Undergrowth** (18 metres Very
Severe 4c † 21.3.90) has been upstaged by E8 ivy.

Brean Down   OS Ref 290 588

'To say that Brean is an acquired taste is an understatement. The merest
mention of Brean Down to local climbers will send most hot-tracking it to the
climbing wall, shaking to the mixed emotions of terror and disgust. I guess
you can't blame them; the sight and touch of half of the routes is enough to
test the faith and beliefs of even the most trusting guidebook reader.'

                                                              (Anon.)

Brean Down is the whale-backed peninsula projecting into the Severn
Estuary just to the south of Weston-super-Mare, from which it is isolated by
the unbridged River Axe and its tourist-swallowing muds. The Down is the
westerly expression of the Carboniferous limestone ridge of the Mendips as it
disappears into the sea, pointing its finger at Wales. The crags intermittently

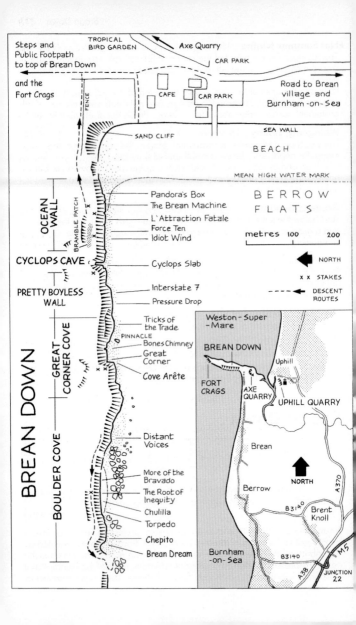

line the south-facing flank of the Down, rising to 30 metres above the northern end of the Berrow Flats, the vast sandy beach and shimmering mud flats frequented by sand-yachtsmen, horse-riders, and hordes of Brummy holidaymakers.

Brean Down is reached from the A38 or M5 (Junction 22) by taking the B3140 to Burnham-on-Sea and Berrow, where a minor road runs northwards to the Brean Down Café car-park at the roadhead below the Down. For a small fee one can park here, and for an equally modest fee Mr Mondeo-man and 4x4 owners can drive across the sand virtually to the base of the main cliffs. So much for their cool when their cars start sinking into the notorious local mud before a crowd who seem to be willing the tide to come in even faster. A local breakdown service makes a bomb out of hauling out the embedded cars of these humbled souls who can't tell mud from what the brochures market as 'sand'.

There are two main climbing sites on the Down. The first described is The Fort Crags, which are located close to the seaward end of the peninsula, about 2 kilometres from the roadhead. The established climbing site is The Beach Cliffs, which are close to, and clearly visible from, the roadhead and café. Between the two sites are occasional craglets and a sliver of low sea walls that offer some minor routes, and – more importantly – lots of potential to explore, boulder, and scramble around. The other minor venue is Axe Quarry, a sporty outcast which faces soulmate Uphill Quarry from the sombre north-east end of the Down.

Character

For the uninitiated, climbing at Brean Down may prove a major life experience. Many choose not to repeat it, but some do. The slight problem, you see, is the rock. On some parts of the main cliffs it's as exciting as it looks. And then there's the sand. Nature has really got herself confused here. Why is there more sand on top of the cliff than at the bottom? And how unfair it is that the dreaded Brean sand cornice should sometimes bar success to climbers pugnacious enough to get that far.

Poetic licence aside, the saving grace for *homo normalus* has to be a small oasis of top-calibre sport climbs on good rock at the eastern end of The Beach Cliffs, most of which are fully stainless-steel bolted and 'way powerful'. Yet there really is a lot more to tempt, even if there is no love at first sight. On The Beach Cliffs, a handful of historic mid-grade classics hold an ambience all of their own. And the Fort Crags is a new place to explore, returning the climber to a basic sea-rock experience with no other intrusion. And then there's the rest; a huge spread of rarely climbed traditional routes, on rock which is disturbingly compact and sometimes hard to protect. Some tips to help even the odds on these are:
• If the route is E5 or above, or appears neglected, and there is no queue, grab a soft brush and check out the top, at least, by abseil. (Unless there is a clean-cut top, finishing holds can get sand filled and will need to be cleaned.)

- Always take a nut tool on lead to clean out any sanded-up nut placements/pockets etc. (Brean can be a windy place; those winds can whip up the beach and throw it at the cliffs, leaving most of the sand *in-situ*.)
- Keep a sharp eye out for small wire slots and pockets (a useful by-product of the curiously crazed rock texture). Cams are useful too.
- Exercise caution while exiting onto and moving around the sand ledges and slopes. (Sandalanches do occur, particularly after heavy rain, when a slope reaches critical mass.) Sand skills, when learnt, can make the whole thing a lot more satisfying – and safe!
- Leave the goats alone – if you know what I mean.

Brean Down excels as a warm winter venue. All of the crags have an open, southerly, sunny aspect, and with little seepage, they can dry almost instantaneously after rain. On a crisp sunny mid-winter's day it is not uncommon to reveal considerably more of one's (tanning) body than normally possible on the international standard climbing wall.

Most climbs are accessible unless it is high tide. When approach along the beach is restricted, alternative ways in can normally be arranged without too much hassle. Wading isn't one of them. Tide timetables may be purchased locally and tide times are advertised in the Western Daily Press and on local radio and TV news programmes.

Brean Down is owned by The National Trust. No access difficulties have been encountered in the past; please ensure that this equable position is maintained. Climbers are asked to avoid the sand slope to the right of the main cliffs and the rock immediately adjacent to it, as recent finds of human remains from the Dark Ages and pottery from the Iron and Bronze Ages have rendered it a site of significant archaeological interest. In summer the place can teem with seaside folk who like to sit and sunbathe under the route that you've got your eye on. Do not place them at risk; find another climb.

The Fort Crags

These crags are not strictly a new venue, though it took all of 35 years to follow up John Hone's explorations (which were well documented in John Nixon's 1965 guidebook). The Fort Crags extend eastwards for a kilometre along the southern fringe of the Down from the Fort ruins at the tip of the headland. Brean Down Fort was constructed in the 1870s as a defence against the French, and was re-occupied and revamped during the Second World War. At the time of writing the Fort is being restored and made more accessible for visitors. There is no reason why climbing should be compromised.

Quite a variety of fairly esoteric climbing is on offer here, at most grades, and with scope for more easier routes. Virtually all the climbs soak up the sunshine and dry quickly. Their exits are straightforward, with several noted exceptions, and lack the overlying sandfields that require special care and occasional recklessness when climbing on the main cliffs. The climbing is of a traditional (i.e. adventurous) nature, calling for the degree of all-round competence demanded by the sea-cliff environment. It is perhaps the most remote and tranquil climbing venue in the Avon and Cheddar area.

Approach is simple and aesthetic: wheeze your way up the concrete steps behind the Bird Gardens, turn left at the top, and follow the footpath westwards along the spectacular ridge to the Fort at the end of the Down (about 3 kilometres).

Red Slab Wall

Climbed in the 50s and early 60s, this wall is a little-known treasure, now developed to its full potential. Though short, it offers some of the nicest quality rock on the Down and a relaxing location. A prominent line of roofs at two-thirds height provides some exciting cruxes.

Red Slab Wall is located approximately 60 metres south of the landward concrete gun emplacement. When approaching from above, the top of it is found 20 metres left (facing the sea) of an obvious hollow/zawn – the 'broken cleft'.

This is the most tidal crag at Brean, and access is not possible 1½ – 3 hours either side of High Tide. The routes on Red Slab are less affected. At highest tide conditions, this can be a viable deep-water soloing venue for strong swimmers – with strong stomachs.

Finger Crack   10 metres   Very Difficult   (c. 1960)
The prominent thin crack 6 metres left of the main crag.

Curving Crack   10 metres   Very Difficult   (c. 1960)
The deep hand-crack leading up to the left end of the roof.

Eavesdrop   20 metres   Very Difficult   (c. 1960)
From the top of *Curving Crack* (possible belay), follow the traverse-line rightwards beneath the roofs to the platform above Red Slab.

One False Move   12 metres   E5 6a †   (10.12.95)
Incongruously located on an otherwise convivial crag: a committing lead. Ascend the straightforward slab 2 metres right of *Curving Crack* to the roof. Fix copious gear (there is none above) and tackle the roof on slopers, 2 metres from its left-hand end, to reach an obvious downward-pointing spike and an easy exit.

Birthmark   12 metres   E1 5b †   (10.12.95)
Take the central line of weakness past a pedestal ledge at 4 metres to the roof. Using an obvious undercut, pull over to good holds and an exit groove: the roof can be protected well.

☆In the Soup   12 metres   E1   5b   †   (10.12.95)
The most consistent of the climbs which break through the roof. Start
below a thin crack diagonally down right of the pedestal-ledge of the
previous route.
Climb the vague crack past a jammed chockstone in a slot at 6 metres
(thread) and so reach the roof. Surmount the roof on good holds to an
easy exit.

Backstairs   12 metres   Severe   (c.1960)
A vintage route which climbs the left-hand of two grooves left of
Well-honed. A crack in the groove provides good protection and the roof is
skirted to its right.

Gone Fishing   12 metres   Hard Very Severe   5a   (10.12.95)
Climb the V-groove just left of *Well-honed*, strictly direct, to the right end of
the roof.

★Well-honed   12 metres   Hard Very Severe   4c   (10.12.95)
A superb little climb up the right arête of the wall. Climb the very edge of
the arête to the top.

To the right of *Well-honed* is Red Slab, which forms the left wall of a
prominent black corner.

Red Slab Crack   12 metres   Very Difficult   (c. 1960)
Climb the crack in the left-hand side of the slab.

Red Slab Central   12 metres   Hard Very Severe   4c   (c. 1960)
Take an eliminate line up the centre of the slab; effectively a solo (unless
recourse to the previous route proves necessary).

Red Slab Corner   12 metres   Severe   (c. 1960)
The prominent black corner: a strong feature.

In the right-hand, black wall of the corner are two cracks, which are taken by
the next two routes.

Red Wall Crack (Left)   12 metres   E1   5a   †   (10.12.95)
From 2 metres up *Red Slab Corner*, use shallow finger-pockets to traverse
right to a big hold at the base of the left-hand crack. The crack leads to the
top.

Red Wall Crack (Right)   9 metres   Very Difficult   (c. 1960)
The deeper, right-hand crack.

Broken Cleft

This is the open zawn 80 metres south-east of the landward concrete bunker
and 20 metres east of the Red Slab routes. With the exception of one line
through the massive cave roof at the back of the zawn, all the described
routes are located on the steep west-facing buttress which forms the east wall

of the zawn. The bed of the zawn is part-filled by two enormous flat-topped blocks, providing a convenient platform to access most of the routes except between one to two hours either side of higher tides. When walk-in access is not possible at high tides, the blocks can be gained by abseil either from rock outcrops 15 metres back from the cliff-edge or from good *Rock 8* and *Rock 5* placements in a small outcrop immediately above the exits of the routes on the east wall. The east wall climbs provide enjoyable climbing on compact rock with some extraordinary pocket-holds. Two cracked grooves in the left (west) wall offer unrecorded climbs of about Very Difficult standard.

☆**Dead Man's Handshake**   12 metres   E5 6a/b †   (27.1.96)
The monster (8-metre) cave-roof crack; unique in this area, and a good training aid for sterner stuff on the South Coast. Weird rock sculptures demanding weird and innovative climbing.
Stick-clip the first *in-situ* thread (and, from the right wall, place a *Rock 8* for the second rope in a crack to the right); then retreat to the back of the cave: headtorch desirable. From a boulder, pull up into the groove in the roof and contort around the drop in the roof (past the first thread) to a better fist crack. Follow the crack (passing two further *in-situ* threads) to the lip of the cave, and then climb up to retreat from a double 11mm rope-thread 3 metres higher.

The Big Chill   18 metres   E1 5a †   (27.1.96)
Start below the compact black slab 7 metres right of the cave-mouth, behind a pointed block.
Follow a line of pockets up the slab to a hole. Surmount the bulge above, and continue over another bulge on good holds to ledges leading right to the good nut belay.

Pint-handle Crack   15 metres   Hard Very Severe 5a   (27.1.96)
In the east wall are two obvious leftward-slanting cracks; this route takes the left-hand one. Start from the massive flat-topped blocks.
Move up to the foot of the crack and a pint-handle hold. Follow the crack, delicately at first, to a big spike. Finish carefully up a broken crack above to the ledges leading right to the good nut belay.

Save the Down from Mankind   15 metres   E1 5b †   (10.12.95)
The right-hand and finer of the two cracks, which starts as a narrow blind chimney. Start from the seaward edge of the outer, flat-topped block.
Scramble up to the foot of the bulging upper section of the diagonal crack (*in-situ* thread). Follow the crack, strenuous but perfectly protectable, and, from its end, tread rightwards across easy ledges to a straightforward exit and the good nut belays.

Honeycomb   15 metres   E1 5c †   (10.12.95)
An unlikely line up the steepest part of the buttress on some amazing holds. Start just left of the foot of the narrow blind chimney.
Climb easily to the foot of the bulging upper section of the diagonal crack of *Save the Down…*, (*in-situ* thread). Swing rightwards across bulges to

honeycomb pockets (threads), and crank up to a crack, which is followed leftwards to easy, solid rock and the exit of *Save the Down*…

☆☆**Me' Shell**   18 metres   E2 5c †   (10.12.95)
The strongest route on the buttress, which reaches the groove just left of the seaward arête.
Climb the narrow blind chimney to a ledge. In the bulging rock straight above is a big right-facing layback hold; gain it from an undercut and so enter the base of the groove (a fantastic two-finger coral-tube hereabouts should not be missed). Climb the groove (plentiful protection) to exit leftwards or direct to the nut belays.

The following two routes take lines either side of the seaward arête of the face, which is capped by a flying pillar.

☆**Apparition**   20 metres   Very Severe 4b †   (24.4.96)
A classic of its grade with a really nice line.
Climb the widening groove just to the right of the narrow blind chimney. Step right and take the steep stepped groove on big holds to the foot of the pillar. Slink left around the arête; then exit via the wide crack on the left side of the pillar.

True Identity   20 metres   Hard Very Severe 4c †   (24.4.96)
Not quite as memorable as its companion, though it bristles with jugs.
Start 3 metres right of the arête.
Take the most direct of three possible ways up the lower compact wall to reach the half-height break. From a short pink groove, climb direct until a swing left reaches a narrow finishing groove on the right side of the pillar.

The Ochre Strip

To the east of the Broken Cleft, the cliff maintains a height of around 25 metres until a grassy spur, with fisherman's track, intervenes after approximately 500 metres. The first (westernmost) 100-metre section comprises a fair amount of climbable rock and is called The Ochre Strip, after the widespread lichen coating (in the sunshine this brings the cliff to life with a yellow glow). Underlying the whole of the cliff, apart from the section between *Ochre Groove* and the unclimbed red corner, is a commodious shelf at 6 metres which gives access to most climbs at all tides as well as a quick and safe way along the cliff-base. At high tide the shelf can be gained by abseil from various points using nut/thread anchors in good rock outcrops about 15 metres from the cliff edge. Wild flowers abound, and care should be taken not to cause unreasonable disturbance. At high tide, especially with the sun out, the ambience of this sea cliff will be found hard to match locally.

OK Crack   20 metres   Severe †   (24.4.96)
In the lower left-hand wall of *Ochre Groove* is a hand-crack. Jam up this to the break and take the obvious layback crack above to the top.

Deception   20 metres   Very Severe 4b †   (24.4.96)
Climb the chimney at the back of the *Ochre Groove* to the break. Step left,
surmount the metre-wide roof (on a VS ?!) and follow cracks in the left wall
of the groove to the top.

Ochre Groove   20 metres   Very Difficult   (early 1960s)
This is the deep corner-chimney approximately 25 metres right of Broken
Cleft: an unmistakeable feature, and quite impressive for the grade.
Climb the compact slab just to the right of the chimney to a horizontal
break. Move left into the corner and follow it past a mighty chockstone
near the top. Beware of resident doves.

Bereaved   20 metres   E1 5b †   (13.1.96)
Good, solid climbing. Start 3 metres right of *Ochre Groove*.
Climb a short blunt rib and the crack rising from the left end of a wide,
projecting roof to a small roof at half-height. Step right, make a puzzling
move over the roof, and finish up a narrow groove.

The next two climbs take lines to the right of the 3-metre-wide projecting roof
6 metres right of *Ochre Groove*.

☆**Bequeathed**   20 metres   E1 5c †   (7.1.96)
Thoroughly enjoyable climbing on superb rock.
Go up a crack leading up past the right end of the roof, swing left over the
lip, and move left slightly to a double roof above a good horizontal break.
Make a hard move through the notch in the roofs (*in-situ* thread), and
continue up a short arête to an excellent finish.

Beholden   20 metres   E1 5b †   (7.1.96)
Climb a central line of weakness in the wall to the right of the projecting roof,
and so reach ledges at the break. Move left into a groove, and follow this
without duress, until a step left into a short crack leads to a reasonable exit.

Some 15 metres right of *Ochre Groove* is an unclimbed cheesy red-coloured
corner. Steep rock to the right offers a clutch of good-humoured climbs…
with one malevolent exception.

Cynical of Success   20 metres   E3 5b †   (13.1.96)
Climbers, meet thy doom. Serious slab climbing leads to a very intimidating
finish. Start 2 metres right of the unclimbed red corner. Climb the solid rib
just right of the corner to small ledges (where the character of the route
changes). Proceed straight up the dark slab and move delicately up onto red
rock beneath the capping roof (*in-situ* thread). Pull over the roof and the
ominously undercut bulge above, whereupon a series of carefully selected
(less detached) holds leads up the collapsing top wall to safety.

Blind Man's Paradox   20 metres   E1 6a †   (24.12.95)
A neat and clean climb. Six metres right of the corner a wide roof
commences just above head-height. Start below the centre of the roof,
after using a short cheat-stick to place the first wire over the lip.

Surmount the roof on finger-slots just to the right of a definite off-fingers crack. Take the golden pillar face above (*in-situ* thread) to half-height ledges. Climb past a bulge to finish up a nice compact slab.

☆**Travesty**   20 metres   E5 6a †   (24.12.95)
A fairly bold line up the smooth wall just right of a prominent deep left-slanting crack, 12 metres right of the red corner. Consistently good climbing. Start below a short groove 2.5 metres right of the deep crack. Balance up the groove and red vein above to a small roof. Make blind fingery moves (peg) straight up onto the slabby wall above and so reach small half-height ledges. Now much easier, climb on jugs to a white arête and follow this directly (*in-situ* thread) to a fairly straightforward exit.

The next five climbs take weaknesses in the long roof at 6 metres. Apart from *Black Comedy*, the climbs extend only to half-height ledges, at each end of which is a wire and *in-situ* thread belay. Retreat may be made from the right-hand thread which, at the time of writing, is solid and furnished with 11mm rope.

Theopolis   10 metres   E2 6a †   (24.12.95)
An eliminate pitch which crosses *Black Comedy*.
Using pockets just right of a blunt rib, climb straight up to the box-shaped chimney. Swing right into a thin crack above the right-hand side of the roof and climb it, with one perplexing move, to half-height ledges.

Black Comedy   20 metres   E1 5b †   (24.12.95)
An unusual climb, graded for a steep but surprisingly easy upper half. Fifteen metres right of the red corner, a good crack leads to a roof at 6 metres. Take the crack to the roof, and swing left into the short box-shaped chimney at its left end. Go up the chimney to half-height ledges. Continue straight up the wall above the chimney on big holds, before pulling onto the short undercut arête above (quite impressive, but comforting holds abound) to a simple exit.

☆**Satyre**   10 metres   E3 6a †   (24.12.95)
Maybe the best of the short routes, with a safe, problematic crux. Follow the next thin crack, 2 metres right of *Black Comedy*, to the most obvious break in the roof. Tricky moves into the groove above (*Friend 2*) lead to the half-height ledges.

Fun with Pyro   10 metres   E2 5c †   (24.12.95)
Take the pocketed wall 1.5 metres right of *Satyre* direct to the roof. Pull through the double roof with a long reach and finish easily up a shallow groove to half-height ledges.

Overgrade, Undergrade: Wobbling Free
                                    10 metres   E1 5b † (24.12.95)
Start below a groove leading to the right end of the roof. Climb the groove and pass the bulge using a downward-pointing spike (*in-situ* thread). A short groove above leads to half-height ledges.

Approximately 12 metres right of the *Satyre* roof, a fairly clean and steep wall, with bulges above half-height, emerges from intervening broken ground. The next two climbs take the wall.

Bongo Workshop Bash   20 metres   E2 5b †   (7.1.96)
Stand up in a grey niche, step right onto the yellow wall (committing), and reach a thin break above. Step back left and climb a short crack to bulging rock. Climb absolutely straight up through the bulges, nearly always on good holds, and continue on jugs to a good exit.

Ben Baddoo   20 metres   E2 5b †   (7.1.96)
The stronger of the duo; a little bold to start but safe and exhilarating once the steeper rock is reached.
Make a long move from undercuts in the centre of the yellow wall and reach a finger-jug and the thin break above. Continue up the slight scoop overhead to bulging rock. Plough through the bulges via an obvious undercut crack; then move left to finish up the top 4 metres of *Bongo Workshop Bash*.

At the extreme right end of this section of cliff, and immediately before a grassy gully, is a 3-metre-wide ceiling at 5 metres. The following two slight pitches circumnavigate the roof.

Pinnochio   9 metres   E2 5b †   (7.1.96)
Ascend an easy pink slab to the left end of the roof. Reach over to a jug, pull up onto a shallow scoop, and traverse rightwards to a good nut belay just to the right of the short arête. Lower off and recover the gear by abseil, or pre-place a rope down the left (west) side of the gully.

Nosejob   9 metres   E3 5c †   (7.1.96)
Climb a groove to the centre of the roof and finger-traverse rightwards (tape sling on small spike), until it is possible to make a long reach to a jug in a small groove. From here, climb diagonally left above the roof to the last route's belay.

Six metres right of the preceding route is a big boulder jammed in the access ledge; the next two climbs start either side of the boulder.

Purge the Week Away   20 metres   E2 5c †   (13.1.96)
Start a metre left of the boulder, below a yellow wall.
Use a good crack on the left to step right onto the yellow wall, and then take a short arête to the break. Trend left through the roofs to good pockets (*in-situ* thread) before proceeding up a small groove to good finishing holds. Exit with caution.

The Brean Bone Chamber   20 metres   E3 6a †   (13.1.96)
Varied moves on an interesting line. Start 2 metres right of the boulder. Climb the blunt slabby rib between two rightward-slanting cracks to the break. Fix gear in the undercut crack above, and then foot-traverse a metre right (along the edge of the chamber, a bone-filled hawk's larder)

until pockets above a small roof are gained. Enter the groove above, pass an enormous flake to its right, and exit easily.

Hotaches Buttress

Approximately 200 metres east of Broken Cleft is a white buttress, cleaner and steeper than the adjacent cliff-line, which hosts by far the best clutch of climbs hereabouts. It is located immediately to the right of an easily-negotiable gap in the non-tidal ledge which underlies the gully to the right of the projecting ceiling of *Pinocchio*.

Strong natural groove and arête lines, good compact white rock above the break at 8 metres, and stainless-steel abseil stations should attract at least some interest. Note, however, that endemic plant-life will compete for some of the holds. The routes may be started at any state of the tide from the narrow non-tidal ledge at 6 metres.

☆**Have-a-go Hero**   20 metres   E4 5c †   (10.12.95)
The only Bold (with a capital 'b') route on the buttress: the left-hand arête. Start below a shallow groove in the lower slabby wall.
Climb the groove easily to ledges beneath overhangs guarding entry into the left-hand corner-line. Pull over the roof into a small groove; then quit it immediately for a committing traverse leftwards to good holds above. Climb the steep arête (*RPs*) to an abseil station on the right.

☆**Hotaches**   18 metres   E1 5b †   (10.12.95)
The left-hand corner is possibly the most amenable climb on the buttress. Take care to protect the route adequately.
Follow *…Hero* for 9 metres, move over the roof, and then gain a monster-jug on the right. Climb the corner above to the abseil station of *…Hero*.

☆**Creak Machine**   20 metres   E2 6a †   (10.12.95)
The projecting roof and the central arête provide an excellent pitch with one problem move. Start as for *…Hero*.
Follow the shallow groove to the roof. Hand-traverse the square-cut block on the right, and then surmount the projecting roof (peg) to good holds on the right of the arête. Climb the arête to ledges and an abseil station above the central compact white wall on the right.

☆☆**Squeaky Clean**   18 metres   E4 6a †   (10.12.95)
The plum of the crag, which takes the thin line of weakness in the central, compact white wall. Impeccable, technical face climbing, if clear of plant life. Start 2 metres right of the shallow groove.
Climb the pink slab fairly easily (*in-situ* thread) to the roofs at 8 metres. Pull over direct, and then step up right onto a triangular projection (large sling). Move up onto the face, and follow incipient cracks up the white wall – sustained – until a finger-jug on the right enables a delicate step up left onto the slab containing the abseil station (shared with *Creak Machine*).

Chill Blane   20 metres   E2 5b †   (10.12.95)
The right-hand corner-line, accessed via the start of *Squeaky Clean* (in order to avoid an initial tongue of wild plants). Bolder than it looks. Start as for *Squeaky Clean*.
Follow *Squeaky Clean* for 9 metres to the triangular projection, but hand-traverse a little further right to pull up onto the white wall. Bear right into the corner and climb it before exiting right at its top to an abseil station.

Fruit Gum Company   18 metres   E2 5b †   (10.12.95)
A line up the centre of the slabby right wall of the right-hand upper corner. A tad bold in its upper reaches. Start 10 metres right of the *Hotaches* groove, below the centre of the wall.
Go up the easy-angled lower wall on good holds to the break at 8 metres. Pull up onto a prominent ledge; then continue straight up over a bulge to the abseil station of *Chill Blane*.

Everyone's Gone to the Moon   20 metres   E2 5b †   (10.12.95)
Lively climbing on the right-hand arête of the buttress.
Follow *Fruit Gum Company* for 9 metres and traverse right to gain the obvious horizontal crack on the arête (good small cams). Now ascend the arête quite steeply but always on positive holds until a reach left acquires the abseil station of *Chill Blane*.

Choc Ice Gully

This is the deep gully 30 metres east of Hotaches Buttress, the back of which comprises an unclimbed chimney with milk chocolate infill. The two climbs here, which start from a non-tidal ledge at 8 metres, may be reached either by a careful abseil from their metal belay stake or by extending the traverse from the Ochre Strip's non-tidal shelf at Very Difficult standard. The routes have atmosphere.

No Room to Run   35 metres   E3 6a †   (3.3.96)
A hard start leads to straightforward climbing up hollow-feeling flakes: serious. The belayer may like to bring a helmet (and cower to one side). Ascend easily up the lower wall 3 metres left of the brown chimney to a good break. Bear right through bulges via a pocket-line with undercuts until a hard reach gains jugs at the foot of an obvious groove in the left-hand rib of the gully. Swing left to pull into the groove and follow it to ledges. Continue up a (detached?) pillar and groove to exit with great caution over a small roof. Stake 10 metres higher.

Ice: a Tonic   40 metres   E2 5b †   (3.3.96)
A fine long pitch of sustained interest up the crack in the right wall of the gully.
From 3 metres right of the brown chimney, follow pockets and then good hand-ledges to the foot of the crack/shallow groove. Climb the crack over two bulges (good wires all the way) and bear left to pull onto an ivy ledge.

Take a solid, left-trending ramp before exiting delicately over loose rock. Stake 10 metres above.

The Central Crags

Between The Fort Crags and The Beach Cliffs is a succession of very minor crags up to 10 metres in height. A number of nice pocketed walls and slabs offer some short routes, though it is more relaxing just to explore and solo around. The rock is not too bad, being rough and gorgeously textured.

Approximately halfway along the cliff line is an 8-metre-high bluff behind the widest part of a pebble beach that projects out towards Hinkley Point. There is some recorded climbing here for those who have done absolutely everything else, everywhere else. The first ascents were soloed but note should be taken of the 2-metre band of rubble at the top and the appalling landing. A pre-placed rope to assist topping out would reduce the grades. The climbs are protectable.

Route 1 is the vague rib which starts 2 metres left of a low-level roof. **Route 2** climbs over a small overhang at 4 metres and continues straight up. **Route 3** pulls over the left-hand side of the low-level roof, **Route 4** takes the centre of the roof via an obvious pocket to reach larger holds, while **Route 5** crosses the right-hand side of the roof to jugs and a scary exit. All are E2 and climbed on 16.5.01, and all are 5a except *Route 2*, which is a grade harder.

Ten metres to the right is a good 5b problem up a short compact wall with an undercut.

One hundred metres further right is a bigger cliff with a rock-bridge at the top that looks ready to collapse.

Rap Stack   6 metres   E3 6a †   (16.5.01)
Make powerful moves through the twin-roof stack at the base of the wall left of the rock-bridge to a good pocket. Continue on fingery holds and gain a handrail. Swing right to descend a groove (or do something completely different if you happen to be roped up).

Nasty Piece of Work   10 metres   E4 6a †   (16.5.01)
Hard and serious climbing up the centre of the wall to the right of the rock-bridge leads to a break. Reach the second break and surmount the awkward little headwall to grass holds.

Two hundred metres right is a cave with an overhanging right wall and a relatively soft pebble landing. The pebbles won't be of any use on the first horror, however.

Completely Brainless and Aimless   6 metres   E5 6a †   (28.4.01)
From a ledge 5 metres up the left-hand wall, make a committing swing onto pockets on the right-hand wall. Reach a hollow flake above and exit on the right using handfuls of grass.

Groove Boat   7 metres   E1 5b †   (28.4.01)
Arm up flakes into the groove in the right-hand wall and climb it steeply to
escape on the right. Protectable.

Tired of Looking at Each Other   7 metres   E5 6b †   (28.4.01)
A good headpoint, with the crux comfortably at half height. Move up to the
centre of the vague leaning pillar immediately right of *Groove Boat*. Hard
moves gain a finger-jug, whereupon positive holds lead to a
straightforward finish.

Further entertainment may be had on the diminishing wall to the right,
though the underlying boulders make the 5-metre problems here feel more
like routes.

Approximately 500 metres west of The Boulder Cove there are a couple of
slightly taller, steeper sections of cliff. The following route takes a distinctive
white pillar, which is bounded on its right by an east-facing corner-crack.
There are good tree belays above all the routes.

Lone Shark   12 metres   E3 6a †   (16.12.95)
A fine little pitch up the arête of the white pillar. Climb easily to a roof at 5
metres which undercuts the pillar. From pockets above the lip (two threads
– one *in-situ*) stretch rightwards to a good (hidden) pocket on the arête.
Climb direct on positive widely-spaced holds (*in-situ* thread) to a simple
exit.

Lend-a-hand   12 metres   Hard Severe 4a †   (16.12.95)
Climb the corner-crack: loads of protection.

Borrowed Time   9 metres   E1 5c †   (16.12.95)
Six metres right of *Lone Shark* is a roof, the underside of which is a
purple/orange colour. A safe crux. Scramble to the roof at 4 metres, pull
over via a thin crack to pockets and continue direct to the top.

Twenty metres right of the *Lone Shark* pillar is a 10-metre-high, dark,
east-facing wall supporting a slab on its left.

Inwardly Extrovert   10 metres   Severe †   (16.12.95)
The slab; start 5 metres left of a broken chimney. Ascend to a bulge
beneath the slab. Pull direct onto the slab (good thread) and bear
rightwards on positive holds to the top.

LST   10 metres   E2 5b   (16.12.95)
Steep and solid climbing up the dark, east-facing wall. Start 3 metres left
of the broken chimney.
Ascend to a red-patched bulge at 5 metres and a flake on the right. Climb
straight up a bubbly wall on finger-pockets and finish on the arête.

Fifty metres left of the 'easy' descent from the top of the Boulder Cove Crag
is a stout, 4-metre high, inwardly leaning block – a sort of 'half-battleship'
with good bouldering. The following clusters of micro-routes make best use

of the short pocketed walls hereabouts. The first three are hosted by the slightly overhanging wall, which is 20 metres left of the half-battleship, and is bounded on its left by a brown chimney.

Seriously Scuppered Supertanker
                              9 metres   Hard Very Severe   5a †   (17.2.96)
Starting 3 metres right of the brown chimney, move up to and over an overhang on sinking holds; step right and go direct to the top.

Run Aground   9 metres   E2 5a †   (17.2.96)
The cream (flotsam?) of the cluster. Start 5 metres right of the chimney. Reach and follow a left-trending handrail and surmount the biggest bit of the bulge on good pockets. Continue direct (*in-situ* thread) to exit.

No Oil, We're Nuke   9 metres   E1 5b †   (17.2.96)
Start 6 metres right of the chimney, at a series of rightward-leading ledges. From 3 metres up the ledges, lock the obvious finger-flake on the wall on the left, pass the bulge, and climb straight up to finish.

The central clutch of routes wander over the slabby wall left of the seaward edge of the half-battleship.

Bow-out   9 metres   E2 5c †   (17.2.96)
An eliminate which conquers the blunt white prow in the slabby wall. Starting 6 metres left of the seaward edge of the half-battleship, climb easily to foot-ledges beneath the white prow. With (distant) protection from a good wire down left, use tiny holds to reach a bucket above the prow. Continue past an *in-situ* thread to a problem-free exit.

Look What the Tide Brought In   9 metres   E1 5a †   (17.2.96)
Start 3 metres left of the seaward edge of the half-battleship. Climb a line of weakness and scoop right of the white prow and finish up the simple solid slab just right of the prominent grassy ledge.

Turditz   10 metres   E2 5b †   (17.2.96)
Start behind the seaward edge of the half-battleship. Climb direct up a pink pocketed face to a good hand-hold and runners at 5 metres. Bear diagonally left to finish up the slab of *Look What the Tide Brought In.*

To the right of the half-battleship is a pocketed slab which yields the next pair of climbs.

Bolero Bar   9 metres   Hard Very Severe   4c †   (17.2.96)
From the left side of the boulder beneath the slab, climb direct to breccia holds (spike runner) and exit right at the top of the slope.

Shifting Sand Sorbet   9 metres   Hard Very Severe   4c †   (17.2.96)
From the right side of the boulder, climb straight up to a jug and *in-situ* thread. Continue past a good nut-slot to the top.

Serious but Stable   12 metres   E1 5a †   (17.2.96)

The 'El Cap' of the short walls; 30 metres left of the Boulder Cove descent is a pocketed white buttress. Follow the central line of weakness, step left, and take a short well-pocketed crack to a good exit left.

The Beach Cliffs

The principal cliffs at Brean Down run fairly uniformly for 400 metres from a shallow boulder-filled cove, the Boulder Cove, in the west to a vast sand slope close to the car-park in the east. To the east of the Boulder Cove and two-thirds way along this cliff-line is a prominent east-facing corner, *Great Corner*, at the back of another shallow cove, The Great Corner Cove. To its east is a short terraced wall, The Sandcastle, with a square white wall, Pretty Boyless Wall, on the right. Approximately 100 metres from the sand slope is an unmistakable narrow zawn and cave, Cyclops Cave. To landward of it, overlooking the beach proper, is the most impressive sweep of rock at Brean, The Ocean Wall. All of the climbs can be approached from the beach except within one to two hours of high tide, depending on its height. The routes on Boulder Cove Crag can be reached by abseil at any state of the tide.

Descent from the top of the climbs is by walking along a goat path near the cliff-top (too near in places!), either westwards to a steep gritty path immediately seaward of Boulder Cove Crag, or eastwards to the steps from the top of the Down. A safe bet for the less-than-sure-footed is to hike up the hill to the ridge of the Down to join the public footpath.

The Boulder Cove

This is the shallow boulder-filled cove at the left-hand end of The Beach Cliffs. At the back left-hand side of The Boulder Cove is a bulging, yellow-and-black-coloured wall: Boulder Cove Crag. This is the crag for lycra, toothbrushes, rope bags, and convivial cliff-base social interaction. And quite right too: the back wall provides a concentration of fine, hard, and mainly bolt-protected sport routes on solid rock. The unbolted routes do not need bolts and should stay as they are. Almost all the bolts are stainless-steel *Petzls*, *Eco-bolts*, or staples.

Most of the cliff-base is well above high-water mark, and virtually all climbs can be reached at any state of the tide by scrambling down a gritty path immediately to the west of the cliff or by abseil; various threads, nuts, and spikes in the overlying rock outcrops provide good anchors and belays for the routes. It is especially pleasant, in a sort of castaway sense, to climb here at high tide when holidaymakers are kept at bay.

The first batch of routes is located on the left-hand and highest part of the crag, a leaning yellow wall above a very nice little pebble beach: the *playa equipado*.

Boulder Cove

1 Brean Dream   F6b
2 Kraken   F6c
3 Bikini Atoll   F6c+
4 Coral Sea   F6c
5 Chepito   F7a
6 Pearl Harbour   E5

7   Tide Rising   F7b+
8   Three Snaps to Heaven E6
9   Torpedo   E2
10 Clashing Socks   F7b
11 Kamikaze   E5
12 Storm Warning   F7c+
13 Chujilla   F7b+

15 The Guilt Edge   F7c
16 Bullworker   F7c
17 El Chacco   F7c
18 The Root of Inequity E5
19 Casino Royale   F7b+
20 Yer Yella!   E5
21 More of the Bravado   E5

Brean Dream 15 metres E2 5c F6b (23.4.95)
A neo-classic which saw ten repeats on the day of its first ascent! Although a little raw, the route is well geared and is ideal as a warm-up for the harder routes.
Start at the left end of the cliff at a square block embedded in the wall. Climb direct with a hard move, and gain hand-ledges above. Reach left at the third bolt to large holds. Climb a slab to an abseil station. Five bolts.

Kraken 15 metres E3 6a F6c (7.11.93)
Start immediately left of a flake-crack.
Climb a short wall to a hand-ledge, step onto a second ledge, and move up and leftwards to a precarious clip at the third bolt. Make a difficult move to grasp a dubious layaway, from which easier climbing leads to an abseil station. Five bolts.

Bikini Atoll 15 metres E4 6a F6c+ (7.11.93)
An unappetizing and very blind pitch squeezed into the gap between *Kraken* and *Coral Sea*.
Climb the flake-crack to ledges. Pull straight up over the slight overlap and push on into a shallow shattered scoop. Escape left (rock permitting!) to join the finish of *Kraken* and its abseil station. Five bolts.

Coral Sea 20 metres E3 6a F6c (10.12.88)
A steep and rather fragile line. The first 'clip-up' at Brean, which effectively paved the way for its bolted compatriots. Recently rebolted.
Climb the wall left of a leftward-slanting pocket-line to a ledge at 5 metres. Make hard moves through the bulges and trend right on better holds before moving up to a horizontal break. Finish up the short crack above, or retreat from a single *Eco-bolt*. Four bolts.

★★Chepito 18 metres E4 6a F7a (19.12.92)
Probably the best of the sport routes on this wall; continuous and fulfilling. Start at a leftward-slanting pocket-line, below the steepest part of the cliff. Climb the left-slanting crack and then pursue a very direct line via a tiny left-facing groove and a glorious three-finger-pocket to reach the (optional) single *Eco-bolt* lower-off atop *Coral Sea*. One peg and four 8mm bolts.

★Pearl Harbour 20 metres E5 6a (10.12.88)
Many have made the attack. A pumpy climb, with more excitement than most – especially if the bolt is binned. Start at the leftward-slanting crackline below the steepest part of the leaning yellow wall.
Climb the crack to a large pocket 3 metres up, traverse right a metre, and pull up to the obvious hand-ledge (peg). Make a hard lock over a little roof to get the obvious jug-line (good cams). Move up into a shallow groove (8mm bolt) and follow it with trepidation (peg). Bear left to the break and finish as for *Coral Sea* up the short flake crack, or lower-off the single *Eco-bolt*. This route was retrobolted illicitly.

Tide Rising   18 metres   E6 6b F7b+   (23.4.95)
Forced between *Pearl Harbour* and *Three Snaps to Heaven*, this route
offers blind climbing that is hard to flash. Start 2 metres right of the
leftward-slanting crack of *Pearl Harbour*.
Amble up the depression to a ledge below the black, leaning wall. Move left,
reach a sharp layaway and a good hold above. A final hard move gains a
series of flat holds that lead rightwards to an abseil station. Five bolts.

Three Snaps to Heaven   20 metres   E6 6a   (25.11.90)
The thin curling groove to the left of the corner of *Torpedo*. A draining
lead, bereft of bolts and consequently not too popular! Start 3 metres right
of the leftward-slanting crack.
Climb the initial steep wall to a ledge. Enter the groove on black crud and
follow it strenuously past good wires to the abseil station of *Tide Rising* on
the left.

There are two traverses of this wall that mercilessly predate on its rich colony
of sport routes. Fortunately they aim in different directions, and are at slightly
different levels, which means that they both get the guidebook treatment.

Vets' Wall   27 metres   E6 6a F7b   (12.11.00)
A pump-infested, rightward-rising girdle-traverse of the leaning yellow
wall, based on the white band at half-height. Entirely bolt-protected, but
take some long slings to ease the drag.
Follow *Brean Dream* to its third bolt. Move up (past a bolt on *Kraken*) to
layaways. Traverse rightwards, descending slightly, to a good handhold on
Coral Sea. Continue horizontally rightwards using the three-finger-pocket
on *Chepito* into the shallow groove of *Pearl Harbour* (pausing to reach
down to clip its bolt). Swing right and, pumped brainless, finish up *Tide
Rising*. Ten bolts in all.

Sargasso Seamonster   27 metres   E5 6a F7a+   (19.5.00)
A good route to finish you off at the end of the day. Start as for *Three
Snaps to Heaven*.
Climb the initial steep wall to a ledge. Move left (bolt on *Tide Rising*); then
drop down slightly and move up to gain the good break on *Pearl Harbour*.
Traverse left across *Chepito* (bolt), and then make a tricky cross-over from
Coral Sea (bolt) to decent holds at the base of the crux groove of *Bikini Atoll*
(bolt). Follow *Bikini Atoll* to the abseil station.

Achtung Torpedo!   20 metres   E5 6b †   (17.12.88)
A wild alternative finish to *Torpedo*.
Gain the ledge below the corner of *Torpedo* directly (as for *Three Snaps to
Heaven*). Climb the corner to its close (cams). Now overcome the bulge
with great difficulty (peg), and make a dash up the headwall (peg) to a
ledge. Exit easily or lower off the single *Eco-bolt*.

Torpedo   20 metres   E2 5b   (18.7.76)
Strenuous but protectable climbing up the rightward-facing corner/flake in
the left-hand side of the wall leads to a rather worrying, vegetated exit.
Start at a large boulder below the corner/flake.
Step off the block and climb easily up the wall to the corner. Climb the
corner with increasing difficulty until it is possible to exit left onto a large
bushy ledge. Finish up the short wall with care (or pre-fix a rope from
which to lower off).

Clashing Socks   20 metres   E5 6b F7b   (25.11.90)
An eliminate, which hassles *Kamikaze*. Start amongst the boulders
diagonally down right from the base of *Torpedo*.
Go up ledges on the right and step back left to a big jug (*in-situ* thread).
Climb straight up the steep white scoop above on small positive holds to
reach a good rest at the break. Now make difficult moves up a thin seam
in the overhanging yellow wall (keeping out of *Kamikaze*) to gain a ledge
and the exit/*Eco-bolt* of *Achtung Torpedo!* Six bolts.

The remaining climbs on the wall start from the raised sandy platform.

Kamikaze   18 metres   E5 6a ❀   (10.1.87)
A route with an explosive impact, taking the obvious steep flake-line in the
wall to the right of *Torpedo*. Unfortunately there is a tenacious clump of ivy
pulling at its tail, and the starting block has collapsed onto the beach.
These are two good reasons for starters not to go and kill yourself.
From the left end of the platform, step left on shaky ivy ledges and make a
committing pull over the bulge to gain the flake. Climb the flake to the
break and move left to a resting-place. Launch up the second flake-line
and follow it on good, widely-spaced holds (peg on right) until strong
climbing over the final bulge leads to the top.

☆**Brean Topping**   18 metres   F8b †   (2002)
Probably the hardest piece of climbing in the area. Only an awesome
amount of power will see success on the headwall. Start below the
2-metre-wide black streak above the left end of the platform.
Boulder up the wall to good holds and a quick shake before moving up to
the main break. Now take the leaning headwall above, pulling as hard as
you can on its feeble holds. Seven bolts to an abseil station.

★**Storm Warning**   18 metres   E6 6b F7c+   (22.3.95)
A brilliant, if hybrid, climb. The route combines the black streak of *Brean
Topping* with the headwall of *Chullila*: pure power-endurance.
Follow *Brean Topping* to the main break. Swing right to the flake and then
follow *Chullila* up the headwall to its top-out/single *Eco-bolt* lower-off.
Seven bolts.

★**Chulilla**   18 metres   E6 6b F7b+   (10.2.90)
A modern classic. Spanish-style cranking across the overhanging sheet to
the left of the central groove. Start behind a massive block on the platform.

Climb a steep groove using an undercut flake on the right to reach a resting-ledge. Step back left and take a curving line leftwards across the wall to finish direct on big holds; top-out or lower off the single *Eco-bolt* belay. Six bolts.

★Prisoner of Conscience   19 metres   E5 6b/c F7b+   (4.2.90)
This reaches the prominent, central groove above half-height via some very bouldery moves. Start at the massive block, beneath the groove. Climb up and pass the left-hand end of a strip roof and continue with quite a stretch to good fingerholds and a resting-ledge beneath the groove on the left. Take the groove steeply on improving holds to a final bulge. Traverse left and then exit or lower-off as for *Chulilla*. Five bolts.

★The Guilt Edge   18 metres   E6 6b F7c   (13.8.94)
A fast-paced extension to *Prisoner of Conscience* up the overlying arête. Climb *Prisoner of Conscience* to a break. Continue straight up the arête with increasing difficulty to reach better holds over the bulge, and bear right to the exit/abseil station of *Bullworker*. Five bolts.

★★Bullworker   18 metres   E6 6b F7c   (1.1.89)
A gutsy test-piece that powers through the unlikely bulges 3 metres right of the central groove. Start at the massive block.
Climb a left-facing groove right of a roof, and its right arête, to better holds just below the break. Swing left to gain the break and then work over the bulges until a jug on the lip of a small roof enables an easy exit groove to be reached. Five bolts; top out or lower off a single *Eco-bolt* belay.

★★★El Chocco   18 metres   E6 6c F7c   (3.3.90)
Vibrant climbing with a floundering exit. Start 2 metres right of the left-facing groove of *Bullworker*.
Boulder up and leftwards and climb the face just right of the arête, until a delicate reach past a black patch gains a good ledge at the break. Flow up on pockets, reach left, and crank through the bulges to enter a 'holdless' scoop by a thoughtful move. Cross the final slab leftwards to a bolt belay. Six bolts. Lower off the single *Eco-bolt* belay on the left, or top out.

★The Root of Inequity   18 metres   E5 6b   (3.1.87)
A downright battle of brawn with the bulges in the centre of the cliff. Start at a line of weakness in the lower wall, 6 metres right of the massive block. Pull over the black bulge and continue to the break (cams). Climb straight up the leaning wall (peg) and surmount the roof above with great difficulty (*Eco-bolt*) to a good finish.

★Casino Royale   18 metres   E6 6b F7b+   (25.2.90)
Yet more bolt-protected power climbing through the unlikely yellow bulges right of centre. The 8mm bolts require renewing.
Start as for *The Root of Inequity* and from 3 metres above the black bulge, trend rightwards to a small jutting ledge beneath the break. Reach a large jug above (peg), overcome the bulge (bolt), and proceed directly up desperate overhanging rock (bolt) to finish on the left.

★★Yer Yella!   18 metres   E5 6a   (28.12.86)
Boltless, but with beautiful free air beneath the runout. A really exciting
pitch, both strenuous and technical, which climbs directly up the right-hand
side of the cliff via the obvious black, pocketed bulge. Start 10 metres right
of the massive block.
A boulder problem immediately right of a pair of incipient vertical cracks in
the initial bulge (the ledge narrows at this point!) leads to much easier
climbing and the break. Climb diagonally leftwards through the bulge on
buckets (two *in-situ* threads) into a large shallow black pocket. Fix
protection and climb straight up on much smaller holds until slabbier rock
leads to a single *Eco-bolt* abseil point or a grassy finish.

☆More of the Bravado   20 metres   E5 6b †   (3.1.87/2.1.89)
A choice of difficult starts leads to bold but superb climbing on the yellow
headwall right of *Yer Yella!* Start below an attractive rose-pink wall at the
extreme right-hand end of the cliff. A peregrine often nests on this route –
and may prefer to be left alone.
Climb diagonally leftwards across the pink wall to a ledge (and nest?) at the
break (*in-situ* thread on the left over the bulge). Climb the leaning yellow
wall left of a good nut-slot, committing but on marvellous holds, to the top
left end of a slanting crack (*Rock 6/7*). Traverse intricately left along the line
of footholds to a junction with *Yer Yella!*, which is followed to the top.
Variation
The Diabolical Start 6c. The leaning wall bounding the pink wall on its
left, starting 3 metres right of *Yer Yella!*

Police Training Route   22 metres   E4 6a †   (31.1.99)
Criminally strenuous climbing up the leftward-rising crack at the right end
of the cliff.
A difficult blind crack to the right of the rose-pink wall leads to the break.
Reach over the bulge for jugs, and pull up into the base of the main crack.
Follow the crack leftwards on undercuts to its end, and a junction with
More of the Bravado. Step up to the left and delicately traverse left on
improving holds to the abseil *Eco-bolt/top-out* of *Yer Yella!*

Anti-missile Missile   50 metres   E4 †   (20.1.91)
A tiring right-to-left girdle of the wall, via the half-height bedding-plane,
which eventually homes in on the *Torpedo* corner. Start as for *More of the
Bravado*. (The route can be climbed in one pitch by reaching the break via
The Root of Inequity.)
1 10m. 6b. Follow *More of the Bravado* up the pink wall to its ledge (and
nest?) at the break (nut and, on the left, thread belays).
2 40m. 6a. Step down and follow the break without difficulty (peg) to a
rib, after 12 metres, on *Bullworker*. Hand-traverse leftwards (*in-situ* thread)
to a constricted ledge on *Prisoner of Conscience* (bolt). With protection
from a bolt on *Chulilla*, continue with difficulty across the black wall to the
flake of *Kamikaze*. Easier traversing leads leftwards (bolt) to the top of the
Torpedo corner and its bushy ledge. Finish up the short wall above, as for
Torpedo.

In the right-hand side of the cove, above a pebble beach, is a series of walls, buttresses, and, at the far right-hand end, a 10-metre high pinnacle. This is Boulder Cove East, home of some of Brean's loosest and most esoteric routes. Some more conventional fun is to be had here too. The leftmost face is a steep pink wall with three shallow parallel grooves topped by the rarest of commodities at Brean – a slab. An ivy-consumed ramp in the left side of the wall was taken by **Quicksand** (27 metres E1 5a 18.7.76).

Comet Strip   25 metres   E4 6a †   (19.12.92)
A left-hand counterpart to *Distant Voices*; problematic but safe enough. Start midway between *Quicksand* and *Distant Voices*. Climb up to the widest part of the roof at 4 metres and surmount it direct (peg); then go up easier ground to a resting niche (spike runner). Make difficult moves through the bulge above (two pegs) and swing out beneath the grass ledge under *Distant Voices*. Follow *Distant Voices* up the conglomerate slab (8mm bolt, thread), but from the rising break finish direct up the small top slab.

★Distant Voices   27 metres   E3 6a   (1.1.89)
Quirky, even by Brean standards, yet fairly enjoyable, the final slab particularly so. The route takes in the left-hand and least obvious groove. Start 5 metres right of the boulder choke.
Climb up into a short corner-crack and reach large crozzly pockets above. Climb the black-streaked wall (peg) to a niche (peg). Make hard moves up the groove (peg) and pull out to ledges at the base of the smooth conglomerate slab. A 8mm bolt in an embedded stone offers suspicious protection for a run-out up the slab; trend diagonally leftwards from a half-height pocket (*in-situ* thread and *Friend 3*) to the top.

Loons of Pluto   30 metres   E4 5c †   (15.2.87/2.1.89)
Sub-classic esoterica. The central of the parallel grooves is followed by an engaging run-out on well-cemented pebbles up the left arête of the slab. Climb up over a small roof (peg) to gain the groove. Follow it (*in-situ* threads) until a long reach over the bulge (peg) lands one on strange slabby rock. Climb easily but somewhat seriously to the base of the smooth slab. Step left from the bolt and pad up the arête on knobbles to a good nut-slot after 6 metres. Move up to exit as for *Distant Voices*.
Variation
Enter Uranus   30 metres   E4 5c †   (17.1.99)
Climb the right-hand of the three grooves to a bulge. Traverse uncomfortably left into the top of the groove of *Loons of Pluto* (peg).

Strictly for those charmed enough to have survived everything else at Brean, the next two climbs harness the unprecedented looseness of the shattered white buttress at a high level, to the right of the slab of *Distant Voices*.

No Worries   27 metres   E5 6a †   (28.1.96)
Marginally the least bad of the dastardly duo. Start below a broad scoop right of the *Distant Voices* wall.

Scramble up the scoop to a good ledge at 12 metres, at which point the scoop opens into a broad grassy gully. Swing right to a big pocket and a slot; then take the over-steep thin crackline above to finish up a broken groove on shaky holds.

Nightmare Alley   27 metres   E4 5c †   (28.1.96)
A climb with terminal dandruff.
Climb as for *No Worries* to the ledge at 12 metres. Swing right to the pocket and slot, and hand-traverse this rightwards to a hard move to a crozzly hole. Step right into a groove (weak *in-situ* thread), which leads, amidst showering rock, to a grass ledge. A good wire protects the final short wall, but not the claw-out exit onto sand.

Right again is a small angular arête underlying a wide crack and groove high up. This gives two relatively solid pitches, the descent from which is down *Pinnacle Cracks*.

Span of Attention   10 metres   E2 5c †   (17.1.99)
Climb easily up and leftwards for 5 metres, and then follow pockets up the left-hand side of the arête, finishing with a nice span for its top.

Shattered Silence   10 metres   E2 5b †   (17.1.99)
From a good crack, take a thin groove in the right-hand side of the arête to a juggy niche; then step up left onto the top of the arête.

Pinnacle Cracks   27 metres   Severe   (Pre-1960)
In the far right-hand side of the cove are two deep cracks leading up to the top of a small pinnacle.
Climb either crack to the summit of the pinnacle. Either reverse the cracks or, more conscientiously, traverse left to an ivy-infected wide crack, which leads to the top.

Pinnacle Arête   10 metres   E2 5c †   (17.1.99)
Short and to the point. Follow the rounded arête of the pinnacle on good incut holds that tend to stay in place.

Scarface   24 metres   E3 5b †   (31.1.99)
Not quite as loose as it looks; the blunt arête above *Pinnacle Cracks*.
From the top of the pinnacle, climb the arête to semi-cemented jugs 6 metres up. Pull up to the left into a scoop, which is also a rockfall scar. Quit the scoop immediately by swinging right onto slightly more solid rock, and finish promptly before the rest of the cliff falls down.

Great Corner Cove

This is the shallow, pebble-filled cove which borrows the name of the huge, right-angled corner dividing the 30-metre cliffs centrally. The other un-mistakable feature is the vertical cleft of *Bones Chimney* in the right wall of the corner. Hereabouts, the rock can be friable, the exits not so hot, and the protection far from inspirational: all the motivation you need to stay on the

Great Corner Cove

1 Scarface E3
2 Scargil's Hairpiece E1
3 Castro's Corner VS
4 Lead Me to the Real World E4
5 Backdoor Beauty E3
6 Airy and Scary E4
7 Put 93 Behind E5
8 Cove Arête E6
9 Zeus E3
10 Great Corner E2
11 Eso Ego Wall E5

12 The Tennis E5
Elbow Club E4
13 Bones Chimney E5
14 Hot X Bones

Highball
Bouldering

Boulder Cove sport routes. There are good nut belays in the outcrop above *Great Corner*, but you will probably need to pull up one of your ropes to use them.

Scargil's Hairpiece   27 metres   E1 5b †   (17.1.99)
A slab climb! (but even this one has a bulge). Start 10 metres right of *Pinnacle Arête*, below slabs in the left side of the Cove.
A pocketed yellow wall leads to a ledge at 12 metres (thread). Take the slab above to an overlap, keeping left of a small ledge topped with a grass wig. Climb the bulge on pockets, and then trend rightwards to sand-ledges and a mystery peg in the wall behind. Finish rightwards with an awkward mantel onto a sloping ledge. Walk off to the left.

Castro's Corner   27 metres   Very Severe 4b   (c. 1960)
Rarely climbed, and indubitably serious. Ice tools would be useful for cleaning, and crampons for climbing. Start below the short right-angled corner in the left-hand side of the cove, 12 metres left of *Great Corner*. Ascend to the corner and climb it onto steep sand ledges. Continue up the sandy, grassy groove above, escaping left to finish.

Lead Me to the Real World   27 metres   E4 6a   (31.12.93)
A constantly surprising pitch up the white headwall right of *Castro's Corner*. Technically reasonable and not unduly bold (unless of course it's your first lead in the real world!). Start 3 metres right of *Castro's Corner*.
Climb a shallow scoop into a hollow and gain the ledge above by stepping right (junction with *Backdoor Beauty*). Arrange cam protection; then climb easily to a short pink groove left of the *Backdoor Beauty* crack. Move up the groove and onto the headwall with a long reach, and then follow finger jugs and pockets direct, passing a vital *RP3* placement, to a good small ledge. Exit leftwards with great care.

Backdoor Beauty   30 metres   E3 5c   (7.6.83)
Interesting climbing up the white wall left of *Cove Arête* is marred by a loose and precarious finish. Start 6 metres left of *Great Corner*.
Gain the obvious cavity at 5 metres and continue up left to ledges at the horizontal break. Climb the short, steep crack to a mantel onto a small ledge on the white wall. Traverse right and move up to a niche below thin cracks. Follow these to a grass ledge and an exit groove.
Variation
Airy and Scary   27 metres   E4 5c/6a   (13.1.93)
Strenuous, serious, awkward to protect; but worth doing.
Follow *Backdoor Beauty* to the break and then step up and right to the left-hand side of the huge block. Make a difficult and committing move over the black bulge (vital micro-wire) to better holds. Proceed direct (peg) to rejoin *Backdoor Beauty*. Follow the thin cracks and groove to the top, or – better – bear right to the easy (and solid) final crack of *The Fog*.

Put 93 Behind   27 metres   E5 6b †   (31.12.93)
A big route up the awesome, leaning black groove to the left of *Cove Arête*.
Difficulties can be adequately protected. Start 5 metres left of *Great Corner*.
From a small hollow at 4 metres, climb a vague scoop-line on the right to
the right-hand side of the huge block in the break. Step right (peg on *Cove
Arête* on the right), enter the groove powerfully (small wires and peg), and
make spectacular moves to gain buckets at the top of the groove and a
good resting ledge on the left. Climb the airy right arête (peg) until jugs
lead right into the crack of *The Fog*. Follow the easier upper crack of *The
Fog* to the top.

★★Cove Arête   27 metres   E6 6b   (2.1.94)
The stunning true left arête of *Great Corner*. Of south-west classic status,
and certainly the best and most sensational traditional climb at Brean
Down. Pumping, committing, but reasonably protected. Start immediately
left of *Great Corner*.
Climb steeply on pockets up the initial arête on its left side to the break.
Enter the hanging groove in the black arête by some fiendish moves (peg
and good wires) and continue hastily to a shake-out on the left. Swing
right around a black bulge (peg) onto the leaning white wall (peg). Make a
hard crank up left to a pocket and swing 'out of control' to a jug in space
on the very edge of the arête. Move up (peg), swing back right onto the
face, and climb the right-hand side of the arête past a break (peg on the
left) to a sound, easy exit.

★The Fog   30 metres   E6 6b   (18.12.85)
A menacing proposition: bold, strenuous climbing with the threat of friable
rock thrown in for good measure. It takes the crack in the left side of the
Cove Arête. Start as for *Great Corner*.
Climb the corner for 3 metres and swing left to a jug on the arête. Follow
the arête on good holds to the break (and junction with *Cove Arête*).
Follow the crux groove of *Cove Arête* (peg and good wires) to its shake-out
on the left. The overhanging crack above leads strenuously but with good
protection to solid ledges and a grassy niche. Break out right up a crack to
finish on the arête.

Zeus   30 metres   E3 5b   (24.6.78)
A great line, though few mortals choose it. The compelling crack-system in
the left wall of *Great Corner*; strenuous, and occasionally choked with
sand-life.
Climb *Great Corner* past the ledge at 12 metres (peg) to a bulge 4 metres
higher. Place good runners in the corner above and then make a wild
traverse leftwards to the base of the crack. Follow the very steep crack to a
slight groove on the right and a moderately frightening exit.
Variation
Crap Wall (30 metres E5 6a † 17.1.98) is a woefully tight eliminate
between *Zeus* and *Great Corner*, the traverse of the former being bisected
using side runners. It has a line of holds but no line.

★Great Corner   30 metres   E2 5a   (31.5.64/31.8.75)

Brean's most prestigious line. A climb of mixed reviews (and mixed terrain) where sandiness abounds and the gear does not match expectations: all the elements of an epic lead, no less.

Climb the compact and hard initial corner, mainly on its right wall, to an optional belay on the ledge at 12 metres (peg). Climb the awkward bulging black corner, and continue to the point at which it splits. Forget the left-hand crack (which will lead you to the nasty exit of *Zeus*); instead finish up the steeper but better protected right-hand crack to exit with handfuls of sand.
Variation

Not a Day at the Comp   33 metres   E5 6a †   (17.1.98)

A foolhardy excursion onto the right wall of *Great Corner*. Leave *Great Corner* at a good runner just above its crux bulge, and traverse right 2 metres to a pocketed line of weakness. Follow this for 12 metres to a grassy scoop (junction with *Eso Ego Wall*). Bear leftwards to the exit of *Great Corner*.

Eso Ego Wall   30 metres   E5 5c †   (25.11.90)

An adventurer's panacea: difficult route-finding, no fixed gear, long runouts, and a sufficient portion of loose rock and sand combine to make this a route worth staying at home to avoid. Start midway between *Great Corner* and a shallow cave, at the base of a huge featureless wall.

Gain large pockets at 4 metres and follow a series of good holds up and rightwards to a ledge at the horizontal break. Move up a short black corner on unwholesome rock (good wires) to reach a shallow recess. Swing left on a handrail and pull straight over the bulge on largely solid holds to a short thin crack and vital wires on the right. Press on directly with a long reach (crux) to good flat handholds, and follow these up an unprotected scoop to a niche on the left near the top (*Friend 3* in a pocket). Pull out over the sand cornice on the right and kick steps up the sandy gully to exit.

☆The Tennis Elbow Club   30 metres   E5 6a †   (3.3.96)

Irreconcilably good climbing on the left arête of *Bones Chimney*, though the approach may deter. Take long slings.

Follow *Bones Chimney* for 10 metres, and exit carefully left onto the long ledge. Step right onto a sand ledge and fix good wires in thin cracks left of the arête. Make hard moves to start, and continue on superb finger-pockets (two pegs), eventually pulling into a bottomless shallow groove in the arête. Reach buckets above, and follow the easier groove which trends rightwards to the exit of *Bones Chimney*.

★Bones Chimney   30 metres   E4 5c   (5.75)

The awesome vertical cleft. A memorable experience, like flying for aerophobics or caving for claustrophobics: where's the fun in being in total control anyway? Start below a shallow cave, 10 metres right of *Great Corner*. Climb strenuously out of the cave to a jug (peg) and work up the right wall of the crack on throwaway rock to gain a ledge. Mantelshelf up left onto a tottering sand heap. Intrude through guano into the solid speleological sanctuary of the chimney overhead and chimney up and out around the constriction to good holds. Continue with surprising normality to an exit better than many. Taking big gear will improve the odds.

☆**Hot X Bones**   70 metres   E5 †   (28.2.91)
A continually absorbing expedition which girdles the Cove. Best timed for high tide. The line cleverly seeks out the crag's soundest rock, above half height, and its finest positions; the first stance is particularly spectacular. Expect to do some hold-cleaning en route. Start as for *Backdoor Beauty*.
1 25m. 5c. Gain the obvious cavity at 5 metres and continue up left to ledges at the horizontal break. Climb the short steep crack to mantel onto a small ledge on the white wall. Traverse right and move up to thin cracks. From an obvious hand-ledge, make a tricky swing rightwards across the overhanging wall to a crack (*The Fog*) and a tiny stance on a projecting ledge on the undercut arête (peg, and a vital *Rock 9* some 3 metres above).
2 20m. 6a. Take the obvious hand-traverse into the crack of *Zeus*. Make one move down into the crack and cross into *Great Corner* at the level of a useful jug (crux – high runner for partner advised). Step down and traverse the *Eso Ego Wall* via an incipient horizontal break (good wires half-way across) to reach a slight groove in the arête. A bold and awkward move up this gains *Rock 7* and assorted poor belays at a hanging stance.
3 25m. 5c. Swing right into *Bones Chimney* (small cam). Traverse horizontally right to a short V-groove after 6 metres. Move up the groove and grope right to a large but hidden pocket. Continue rightwards below a bulge on curious holds, and pull over on jugs to less steep ground. Go directly up and then leftwards on sandy ledges to the top. Scramble to tree belays well back.

A brilliant bouldering traverse powers intricately right from the cave at the foot of *Bones Chimney* to a ledge above a rightward-slanting crack; **Cycle of Despair** (F8a+ 28.4.01) provides the best 8 metres of climbing on the Down. There are 5 classic vertical problems along this stretch, as well as two other traverses either side of it.

Nobody's Perfect   10 metres   E1 5b †   (30.1.99)
Of novelty value, and the rock is uncharacteristically good. Start at the base of the tower above the finish of *Great Corner*.
From a ledge at 4 metres, take a line up the steepest part of the tower face, past a small projecting overhang.

The Sandcastle

This is the 12-metre cliff rising from the pebble beach at the right end of the Cove. It is overlain by a steep sand slope, the result of a major rockfall in 1990 when the short upper tier collapsed onto the lower, leaving its four climbs in a sorry state. At long last they have improved, though exiting onto the sand field will not be a bundle of fun without re-cleaning. All things considered, this has to be a reasonable contender for cliff-top bolt belays. Until that time only the bare essentials are given. From left to right on the short steep wall are: **The**

Yer Yella! (E5), Brean Down
Climbers: Martin Crocker
and Terry Cheek
Photo: Carl Ryan

Cove Arête (E6), Brean Down
Climber: Martin Crocker   Photo: Carl Ryan

Pandora's Box (VS), Brean Down
Climbers: Terry Cheek and Martin Crocker
Photo: Carl Ryan

Chiming for You (F7b), Uphill Quarry
Climber: Steve McClure   Photo: Tim Glasby

Slow Sand (12 metres E1 6a † 3.1.87), the low scoop; **Tricks of the Trade** (12 metres E3 5c † 20.12.86); **Catbrain Lane** (12 metres E2 5c † 12.4.84), the original line up the obvious central crack; and **Sea of Sand** (12 metres E2 5b † 8.1.87), the wall and groove on the right.

Pretty Boyless Wall

To the right of The Sandcastle is a square-shaped, convex, white wall, with a promiscuity of lines, bounded on its left by the prominent scrappy crackline of the next route.

Pressure Drop   27 metres   E2 🏵   (31.8.75)
The pits: this route is not in a pretty condition. Start below the crackline in the upper wall.
1 13m. 5b. Climb easily to a bulge containing a short wide crack invariably guarded by a bramble at its base. Pull over with difficulty and continue to grassy ledges.
2 14m. 5b. Climb the weeded-up crack, sustained and strenuous, to an exit on the left.

Got the Drop on Me   27 metres   E4 5c †   (14.11.87)
A harder and bolder variation on the top pitch of *Pressure Drop*, though the rock is a lot better. The good climbing on the headwall can also be reached from the next route.
Follow *Pressure Drop* over the bulge and trend rightwards up the wall to the break at 13 metres. Now climb straight up the steep wall, 2 to 3 metres right of the crack of *Pressure Drop*, via an *in-situ* thread and a short thin crack.

The Unexpected Guest   27 metres   E5 5c †   (17.3.91)
High-stress climbing with a humbling degree of looseness initially; a shame because the upper wall provides fine, solid climbing. A shattered black crack leads up into the centre of the wall; the route starts here, but the second should stand well to one side.
Climb up to reach good holds over a bulge at 6 metres (rather dangerous). Swing right into the crack and follow it to a spacious ledge. Gain a shaky ledge 4 metres higher and slightly to the right. Climb a thin groove right of the obvious little roof (vital *Friend 2* in pocket), step left above it, and finish steeply on good holds.

The World's Worst-dressed Climber
                        27 metres   E4 5c † (20.12.86/11.2.96)
A harrowing lead with minimal margin for error; hence high in the grade. Starting beneath the widest part of a low-level roof, tackle the roof and slabby wall direct (*in-situ* thread) to gain the ledges and the break at 10 metres. Step left to a poor flake, and follow a slim groove on poor rock to better holds and moderate wires. Climb the steep (but solid) white wall 1.5 metres right of the tiny rightward-facing groove of *The Unexpected Guest* (small wires in short crack on the left), until a good hand-ledge is reached. Pull up carefully to the end of the rising traverse of *Pretty Boy Floyd* to exit.

Highball
Bouldering

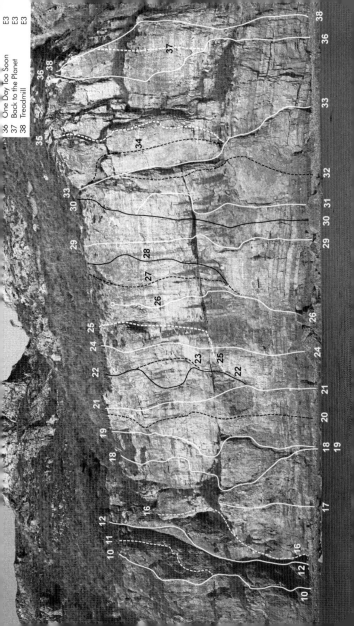

36 One Day Too Soon   E3
37 Back to the Planet   E3
38 Treadmill   E3

Pretty Boy Floyd   30 metres   E2 5a   (2.75)
Strong line, weak rock. This climb takes the leftward-rising diagonal
breaks across the wall. A committing lead, but oddly satisfying. Start below
the right-hand corner of the square wall, next to a pair of 'eyes' (pockets) a
metre up.
Climb a shallow groove to ledges and the break at 10 metres. Follow the
rising flake leftwards to its end. Climb the wall above boldly to connect
with the right end of the line of (wobbly) handholds, which lead diagonally
leftwards to the top.
Variation
In-a-state-again?   27 metres   E2 5a   (11.2.96)
A squeezed-in sequel guaranteed to squeeze out the fear.
Follow *Pretty Boy Floyd* past the break and continue up the flake for 3
metres. Step right onto a big flat foothold on the wall; then climb very
directly to finish up hollow, but static flakes in the white wall just left of the
big exit flake of *Interstate 7*.

★Interstate 7   27 metres   E3 5c   (14.11.87)
A direct line up the slabbier right-hand side of the wall provides a fairly
reliable route. Somewhat sparsely protected, but the rock is passable. Start
as for *Pretty Boy Floyd*.
Take the shallow groove to the break. Climb steeply up the wall above
immediately left of a black streak (peg) and gain a small, slanting
overhang with difficulty. Move slightly left; then follow good finger-ledges
to the obvious flake and a sound finish.

Tootin' Ska Moon   27 metres   E4 5c †   (24.2.96)
More of a line than most on the face, this run-out and sustained climb
provides good climbing up the ill-defined right-hand arête. The
seriousness is accentuated if the black drainage streak is active. Start 3
metres right of *Pretty Boy Floyd*, beneath a hole at 6 metres.
Climb steeply to the hole and continue to the large ledge system. With
protection from an *RP1* plus the (still sturdy) peg on *Be Bop Arête*, work
straight up the blunt rib (and black streak) to a step left, where a vital *Rock
7* can be placed (sideways) in a pocket. Move up to a roof (good wire) and
pull over on its left. Now bear rightwards to the top arête and follow it
boldly though with little technical incident.

Be Bop Arête   30 metres   Hard Very Severe 4c ❀   (18.5.75)
Very poorly protected, and clogged up with vegetation. The route takes the
grooved right-hand arête of the square wall. Start below the groove, 3
metres right of *Pretty Boy Floyd*.
Gain the foot of the main groove from either of two low grooves (peg).
Climb it with almost zero protection over a small overhang to a grassy
ledge. The crack in the steep wall above is harder and safer but soon
leads to the usual run-out into sand.

Cyclops Cave

This is the deep, boulder-filled rift and cave 5 metres wide which incises the cliff-line about 100 metres from the sea defence wall. It is capped by an enormous jammed boulder and is overhung in its left wall by the tall, tapering slab of *Cyclops Slab*. The cave is known locally as Reindeer's Rift after the ancient animal remains found within it, and is the habitat of a colony of white doves. Only very rarely is the lesser-spotted boulderer encountered here.

Care is required to secure satisfactory belays in small rock outcrops above the left wall, now that the original stake has been subsumed by the sand and the goats have eaten the tree.

Eye for an Eye   32 metres   E4 6a †   (14.11.87)
An oddball pitch up the blunt arête overlooking the rift. It is advisable to hang a rope down the sandy finish, which is about as bad as they come.
1 12m. *An Odd Sea* pitch 1 (5c) or *Cyclops Slab* (4c).
2 20m. 6a. Move up the arête a little before balancing left around it (*in-situ* thread) to pockets. Regain the arête (peg) and finish with a long reach past an *in-situ* nut. Pull up on the fixed rope or fast-paddle the sand to the top.

An Odd Sea   30 metres   E5 †   (20.12.86)
Challenges the thin crack in the leaning left wall of the *Cyclops Slab* corner. An excellent pump, but the route needs a brush from time to time. Start 3 metres left of a shallow, scooped chimney in the outer edge of the left wall of the cave.
1 12m. 5c. Pull through bulging rock on superb holds, swing left to pockets, and gain the ledge above. Move right and up a short crack to a ledge. Peg and cam belays.
2 18m. 6a. From a small ledge above the belay, climb the line of weakness in the wall to a good flat hold in its centre and a peg (hidden from below). Move up and right (jammed nut above) to gain the base of the thin leaning crack, and climb it with engorged veins to a leftward exit (two *in-situ* threads).

★Cyclops Slab   30 metres   Hard Very Severe 4c   (1961)
More of an anti-classic than a classic, this climbs the elegant and exposed slab above the cave. A serious lead (those owning a load of large cams should spare a thought for Pre-Cam Man!). Start below the shallow, scooped chimney in the outer edge of the left wall of the cave.
Climb the chimney strenuously on large holds to the base of the corner; optional peg and nut belay on the ledge on the left. Climb the corner for 8 metres to a narrow ledge (peg). Move out right and climb airily up the arête until a diagonal line of holds leads back into the corner (alternatively, climb the corner throughout). Exit direct.

Two Right Feet   30 metres   E5 6a/b †   (11.2.96)
Requires balls – metaphorically speaking. The blunt white arête right of the lower half of *Cyclops Slab*.
Follow the *Cyclops Slab* chimney for 4 metres and scuffle rightwards onto a projecting shelf (*Rock 7* at its right end). Swing right onto bulging rock; then make committing moves direct (poor peg) to big holds. Place a wire on the left before climbing the steep face (*in-situ* thread) to slabbier rock (peg). Step right and follow a scoop and broad rib to the exit of *Cyclops Slab*.

Brean Team Special   30 metres   E6   (21.12.86)
The bulging crack that slices formidably into the left wall of the cave. A powerful lead.
1 18m. 6b. Climb carefully up the shattered wall right of the slanting crack (*in-situ* thread) to a handrail (peg). Break through bulging rock (peg) and enter the crack precariously. Follow the crack to a ledge and continue more easily to belay next to the jammed boulder (thread in the groove above)
2 12m. 4c. Swing out left onto the rib (peg) and follow *Cyclops Slab* to the top; alternatively, scramble up the gully.

Psycho-death Drummer of Brean Café   18 metres   E6 6b † (13.6.96)
When this guy plays, the cliffs really rock and roll. One of those 'sort-of' sport routes (F7c) on pegs – though a few wires are needed for the start and finish.
Beat your way up the line of weakness in the overhanging wall 3 metres right of *Brean Team Special* (four pegs). Exit up *Brean Team Special* or retreat from a sling threaded around the huge jammed boulder (which doesn't look quite so well jammed from this perspective).

Pigeons of the Underworld   18 metres   E5 5c †   (2.3.96)
A scatological experience, clawing up sea-grease, crumbling rock, and – to cap it all – pigeon shit on the overhanging flakeline near the back of the cave. Start below the flake crack in the west wall.
Tackle the flake (warning superfluous) until large, faecal holds lure one to a juggy hand-ledge near the top of the cave. Laterally minded folk will, at this juncture, bridge confidently across the cave to de-pump. All, however, will need ultimately to hand-traverse left across rock excreta to a crawling escape through the hole beneath the huge jammed boulder. Exit as for the previous route.

Outside the cave, on the right (east) wall is a small pinnacle at half height dubbed The Giant's Fingernail.

The Giant's Fingernail   20 metres   E5 6a †   (2.3.96)
Short but nail-biting, and destined to slide into the sea.
Climb the overhanging right arête of the cave to a sloping grass ledge at 10 metres. Mountaineer right to the base of the 'fingernail' arête. With good gear to either side, ascend the crest past a knuckle-gnawing middle section to the top of the pinnacle. Thread belay.

Cyclops Gatepost   24 metres   Very Difficult   (c.1960)
Climb the corner right of the seaward arête to a grassy ledge, and then the
earthy gully to the top of the pinnacle (thread belay). Scrambling remains.

The Ocean Wall

This cliff, probably the showpiece of the Down, is the overhanging sheet of
rock, 20 metres high and divided just below half height by a horizontal
break, which runs between Cyclops Cave and more broken rock next to the
vast sand slope. The climbs here are as good as any at Brean; the rock is
excellent (above the break!) and the climbing is steep, technical, and
power-packed. Some of the most challenging traditional-style pitches in the
area are to be found on this wall.

In the left-hand side of the wall, below the break, is a rightward-curving crack
giving the first pitch of *Idiot Wind*. In the centre of the wall are two slim
grooves, the left-hand and deeper one being taken by *Sidewinder* and the
right-hand one by *Godspeed*. The right end of the wall is bounded by the fine
corner of *Pandora's Box*. When topping out from routes left of *Sidewinder*,
belay on nuts and a good metal spike in the back wall. For routes to the right,
nut and spike belays in rock outcrops well back can be augmented by a
choice of two stakes.

Spindrift   20 metres   E4 6a ††   (14.11.87)
Stressful climbing up the overhanging pocketed prow at the left end of the
wall. One of the original pegs has fallen out, and the grade is therefore
speculative.
Climb up onto the face of the prow on good pockets (*in-situ* thread).
Unfortunately the going now gets really tough and hard blind moves must
be made to a leftward exit (peg). Either belay on a sloping grass ledge or,
better, continue up the vegetated groove on the right-hand side of the
pinnacle to thread belays. Scrambling remains; or *Cyclops Gatepost* can
be reversed for extra danger.

Sail Close to the Wind   25 metres   E2 5b   (31.1.87)
Holds on the upper wall tend to become sand-covered. Start as for *Idiot
Wind* at the base of the rightward-curving crack.
Follow a ramp easily leftwards to a short groove, which leads more steeply
(*in-situ* thread) to a good ledge and optional stance. Move right onto the white
wall and climb it quite intricately on good, spaced holds to exit leftwards.

Idiot Wind   25 metres   E1 5a   (16.11.75)
An interesting, even weird, route with some large scale loose bits.
Ropework requires care. Start at the base of the black, rightward-curving
crack in the left-hand side of the wall.
Follow the crack up to the right past a rock spike to the break. The next
move is a sort of hand-holdless belly flop onto the end of the ledge on the
left (belay possible). Climb the steep crack on the right using widely spaced
and mostly wobbly holds to a short exit groove.

Sail on Past   25 metres   E5 6b   (18.12.85)
The wall and shallow leaning groove just right of the crack-system of *Idiot Wind*. A fine pitch, believe it or not, with a reachy and committing crux. Start 3 metres right of *Idiot Wind*.
Climb straight up with care to an incipient crack (*in-situ* wire); then pull leftwards round the bulge to the horizontal break and a good ledge on the right. From a horizontal slot, climb easily to the base of the shallow groove. Enter the groove (*RPs* vital) and stretch up to a resting-ledge on *Idiot Wind*. Swing immediately back right (peg) and make hard moves over the final bulge to finish.

War on Cocaine   25 metres   E4 5c †   (18.2.90)
Getting hooked on this sort of stuff is likely to be damaging to your health. Strenuous climbing up the tallest, black-streaked part of the overhanging wall right of *Idiot Wind*. Start 6 metres right of *Idiot Wind*, below a rightward-trending ramp.
Climb to the foot of the ramp, but continue up black Brean crud to the break and good runners. Climb straight up the blunt white rib above to a ledge on the left, below the leaning headwall. Launch up a juggy flake and, from a good block-hold above (*in-situ* thread), break out rightwards over bulges to an exit on the right.

★Force Ten   25 metres   E4 6a   (3.8.85)
A good route of mounting excitement; quite spectacular to finish. It aims for the rightward-diagonal line of weakness in the concave wall between *Idiot Wind* and the groove of *Sidewinder*. The route tends to stay in fine fettle, and the finish is on positive holds. Start 6 metres right of *Idiot Wind*, below the rightward-trending ramp.
Follow the ramp rightwards without incident to the break. Step over the bulge onto a slab (peg above). Move left onto a rib, and climb it to a flat hand-ledge below the headwall. Clip the peg overhead; then cut loose along the steep, rightward-rising traverse (peg) to a superb jug. Climb straight over the bulge to finish.
Variation
Tempestuous   E5 6b   (17.2.90)
A typhonic direct finish. From the peg before the traverse right, breeze up the headwall past twin pegs to good finishing holds on the left. Reaching the pegs is bold, passing them is very powerful.

★Galebird   25 metres   E5 6c   (17.2.90)
A dynamic pitch which targets the angular V-groove 5 metres left of the black groove of *Sidewinder*.
Follow the ramp of *Force Ten* to the break and step up onto the slab (peg above). Reach the foot of the V-groove on the right (peg). Using good holds on the right, climb the groove (peg) to the end of the traverse of *Force Ten* (peg). Climb straight over the bulge to finish.

Sidewinder   27 metres   E3 5c   (9.12.78)
Snakes into the left-hand and deeper of the black grooves in the centre of
the cliff.
Follow the ramp of *Force Ten* to the break. Hand-traverse rightwards on
crunchy rock to the base of the black groove (peg). Difficult, strenuous moves
lead up the groove to a resting place; the chimney above is much easier.

At the base of the centre of the wall is a concrete and iron structure, a
reference point for the following seven climbs.

★**One Man, One Island**   25 metres   E6 6b   (21.2.87)
An exhausting pitch of great quality with its crux right at the top. It takes the
line of thin cracks in the black-streaked prow immediately left of the
groove of *Sidewinder*. Start from a flat ledge 2 metres left of the concrete
and iron structure at the cliff base.
From the left end of the ledge, follow ledges and then a grim flaky wall to
the break. (*Force Ten* provides a more pleasant start.) Swing right and pull
up onto a smooth hanging slab below the cracks. Climb the cracks via a
good vertical slot (*Friend 1½* or large wire) until a frustratingly hard reach
(peg) gains a series of improving flat holds and the top.

★★**L'Attraction Fatale**   25 metres   E6 6b/c F7c   (18.12.85)
Bolted but beautiful; the white wall between the black grooves of
Sidewinder and *Godspeed*. A Brean masterpiece. Start at the concrete and
iron structure.
Climb a rightward-tending ramp to a short crack leading to the break
(bolt). Reach over the roof to good fingerholds (drilled peg) and make
sustained hard moves up to a jug (bolt). Crank up left to a thin crack (peg)
and gain the niche above (large wire or *Friend 2*). Pull out on good holds
to a bolted abseil station.

★★**Godspeed**   25 metres   E5 6b   (7.6.83)
A superb climb up the slimmer, right-hand groove in the centre of the wall.
Not to be underestimated technically. The route stays in good condition,
but check that the peg is in place beforehand. Start at the concrete and
iron structure.
Follow the rightward-trending ramp in its entirety to the horizontal break. A
fierce pull right next to the peg above gains a jug in the base of the
groove; thereafter the groove is followed strenuously to good holds above
the final bulge.

★**Going Turbo**   25 metres   E5 6c   (1.11.87)
A supercharged pitch that takes the first of the three parallel cracks in the
convex right-hand sector of the wall.
Follow *Godspeed* up the rightward-trending ramp to the break. Pull
desperately over the roof on the right (peg) to gain a one-finger-pocket
and (eventually) better holds in the crack above. Climb the crack (in-situ
thread) and move up slightly right where it closes (in-situ thread on *The
Brean Machine* to the right). Go back left to finish easily up a scoop.

★★The Brean Machine   25 metres   E5 6b   (3.8.85)

As classic a hard traditional route as you can get here! Brilliant climbing up the thin central crack that bisects the roof and bulging wall between the grooves of *Godspeed* and *Pandora's Box*. High in the grade. Start 5 metres right of the concrete and iron structure.

Climb pockets and a flake up and leftwards to a small pillar, and then move right to the break. Power out over the roof and climb the thin crack, very sustained but well protected, past a peg to a small foot-ledge (two *in-situ* threads). Finish up the wall.

★Iraqi War Machine   25 metres   E6 6b   (19.1.91)

The right-hand of the trio of cracks; major difficulties are next to gear, but the finish is run out. The exit holds may need to be brushed of sand before an ascent. Start 7 metres right of the concrete and iron structure.

Climb diagonally leftwards, step up into a hollow, and move right beneath an *in-situ* thread to a flake in a black niche. From the horizontal break above, make difficult moves to enter the crack (vital *Rock 4* in a pocket) and follow it speedily to a shakeout jug. Leaving a good nut-slot (and advisable *Rock 1* placement on the right), climb up the shallow groove before a reach right gains a series of jugs leading to the top.

The Beast Unleashed   25 metres   E5 6a   (3.8.85)

The black bulges and the right edge of the wall left of *Pandora's Box* promise a strenuous and exacting pitch with a bold finish. The exit holds may need to be brushed of sand before an ascent. Start below parallel cracks forming a shallow slot, 8 metres right of the concrete and iron structure.

Climb the evil, black-encrusted wall just left of the cracks, and move up into the overhung niche of *Iraqi War Machine*. Traverse rightwards along the break for 2 metres and climb up a thin crack for 2 metres to a jug. Make hard moves left onto the face to rejoin *Iraqi War Machine* (at the *Rock 1* placement). Move right to good hand-ledges and follow these to the top.

The Leveller   25 metres   E5 6a †   (5.12.93)

Solid climbing on the arête left of *Pandora's Box*.

Climb the slab to the base of the corner of *Pandora's Box* and fix a side-runner 3 metres up it (just below the level of the horizontal break on the left wall). From the foot of the arête, climb direct (with a useful layaway and pinch on the left) to gain the break (*Friend* ½). Continue up the arête and groove above to a junction with *Pandora's Box*; finish up this.

★★Pandora's Box   25 metres   Very Severe 4c   (1963)

Justifiably Brean's most popular traditional climb. The steep, smooth-walled corner in the right end of the wall provides a fine, well-protected pitch.

Follow a flake crack leftwards to a ledge at the base of the corner (peg). Climb the corner to the top.

★Crack o'Diamonds 25 metres E3 6a (17.5.83)
Steep and fingery climbing up the spidery thin crack in the smooth,
right-hand wall of the corner of *Pandora's Box*. Tough for the grade.
Follow the initial flake of *Pandora's Box* to the foot of the corner. With a
runner in the corner (not too high!), make steep moves to reach the crack.
Follow the crack with mounting difficulty to a ledge, and swing left to finish
as for *Pandora's Box*.

Throwaway Society 25 metres E5 6a † (15.12.93)
The right arête of *Pandora's Box*; not excessively bold.
Climb the initial flake of *Pandora's Box* and step right to ledges (vital *Rock
7* on the right). Pull up carefully to a small roof (peg) and, from a
pinch-grip at the base of *Crack o'Diamonds*, make tricky moves diagonally
right and round the arête (excellent *Rock 2* cluster) to small ledges on the
right. With protection from nuts in the crack on the right, climb the arête to
a big ledge and a wide finishing crack.

☆☆Hands across the Ocean 59 metres E5 † (14.3.87)
A tremendous left-to-right high-level girdle of The Ocean Wall with two
fine pitches, the second of which is especially demanding. Start as for *Sail
Close to the Wind*.
1 12m. 4c. Follow *Sail Close to the Wind* to the good ledge.
2 27m. 6a. Climb up right for 3 metres as for *Sail Close to the Wind*;
then swing right to the crack of *Idiot Wind*. Move right on good handholds
to the base of the shallow, leaning groove of *Sail on Past*, and continue
horizontally and down slightly right (peg) to the hanging slab on *One
Man, One Island*. Follow the cracks of this route to the vertical slot (*Friend
1½*), and make a hard move right into the *Sidewinder* groove at the level
of its projecting ledge. Bong, *Friend 2½*, and nut belays.
3 20m. 6a. Make fingery moves horizontally right across the smooth wall
of *L'Attraction Fatale* (peg) to the groove of *Godspeed* (*Friend 2½* above).
Turn the rib on the right to a good vertical pocket; then proceed boldly,
diagonally rightwards, to the foot-ledge and resting-place on *The Brean
Machine* (two *in-situ* threads). Make one move up, and traverse more easily
rightwards (*in-situ* thread) to finish on the arête as for *The Beast Unleashed*.

Two routes have been climbed up the chaos of loose sandiness right of
Throwaway Society: **Haven** (7.4.76) and **Elysium** (1960s), both Very
Severe 4a, climb the crack and the groove in the buttress respectively.

At the extreme right end of The Ocean Wall is a distinctive square wall
housing three climbs on unusually textured rock.

One Day Too Soon 27 metres E3 5c † (29.12.93)
Excitement guaranteed. Start 6 metres right of *Pandora's Box*, below the
right edge of the square wall.
Climb an open groove and make a disconcerting move to gain the right
end of the grass ledge beneath the square wall. Step up left onto small
ledges and climb the wall, bearing leftwards to reach the rounded left

arête. Gain a big grass ledge and climb the groove above (peg); or, finish up the arête on the right as for *Back to the Planet*.

Back to the Planet   27 metres   E3 5b †   (29.12.93)
Fear obligatory. Start as for *One Day Too Soon*.
Follow *One Day Too Soon* to the small ledges above the grass ledge. Swing right and climb the wall on good holds to the right of a thin crack, and then climb the thin crack itself, to exit onto a big grass ledge. With protection from small wires and a *Friend 2* in the groove on the left, climb the solid tapering arête to the top.

Treadmill   27 metres   E3 5b †   (2.3.96)
Death a possibility. The obvious groove in the front of the compact white wall climbed by *One Day Too Soon*. Start 3 metres right of *One Day Too Soon*, beneath the groove.
Ascend the line of ledges and gain the top of a block ledge from the left. Follow the whole groove past good gear, and then no gear, to disembark with care onto the grassy ledge at 18 metres. Finish up the arête.

Beach Buttress
This is the easternmost of the main cliffs before they (completely) degenerate into the fenced-off sand slope. Two atmospheric climbs of surprising quality (and no little adventure) take on the pair of solid walls above more broken ground. They are non-tidal, and should be avoided in the tourist season.

Adventure Route One   33 metres   E5 †   (24.2.96)
Start beneath a clean pillar face leading up to a pinnacle 18 metres up, and 15 metres left of the edge of the sand slope.
1 18m. 5a. Follow jugs to a crack which leads, with good gear, up the pillar face to a ledge. Traverse right across a vegetated groove and take a belay on nuts and threads in a black overhung alcove.
2 15m. 6a. A thrillingly exposed pitch. Pull up direct from a small cave to a juggy break beneath bulging rock (vital *Flexi-Friend 1½*). Swing right (vital *Rock 1* in obvious thin slot), and then make a hard lock to a line of superb holds leading to a rest (tape for big spike on the left). Bear slightly rightwards up the slabby wall almost to the arête; then finish direct over the capping bulge to exit onto a rabbit-furrowed sandy slope. Good nut belays 12 metres back.

Adventure Route Two   42 metres   E4 †   (24.2.96)
A little more serious than its neighbour, but steady nonetheless.
1 18m. 5a. *Adventure Route One* pitch 1.
2 24m. 5c. Walk right into the gully and follow a grassy flake up and right to a slight, shattered crackline in the right-hand upper wall. Climb the crack carefully (*in-situ* thread) and move up into the right-facing corner above. Reach right for a jug on the wall and (with more protection in the crack on the right) make steep moves up to foot-ledges. Follow a micro-seam in the headwall above, bearing slightly rightwards to finish on the arête. Good nut belays 12 metres back.

Axe Quarry
OS Ref 303 588

At the eastern end of Brean Down is a corrie-shaped inlet facing Uphill. The overhanging wall on its left has a clutch of four sport climbs with stainless-steel staple bolts. Elsewhere, on the broken back wall, are several old routes that await being plucked from obscurity. The crag is best avoided during a wet winter, when seepage can prevail. Approach either from the top of the Down via an easy track and a short scramble, or along the public footpath past the farm (not at high tide).

The Irrelevant One! 12 metres Severe (8.94)
Climb the small arête at the left-hand end of the crag.

Axe Attack 13 metres E2 5c F6b (16.4.94)
This climbs the loose-looking but solid arête at the left end of the leaning wall. Abseil station shared with *Brean Bunny Blues*. Three bolts.

Brean Bunny Blues 13 metres E2 6a F6b (31.8.93)
Climb the corner formed by the roof and traverse left along a ledge to an abseil station above. Three bolts.

See You Later, Renovator 13 metres E4 6a F7a (31.8.93)
Climb a hard wall to a ledge and finish up the wall above to an abseil station on the left. Five bolts.

Ego Trip to Mars 13 metres E3 6a F6c (31.8.93)
Climb the corner on the right-hand side of the face and finish up the wall above. Five bolts.

Uphill Quarry
OS Ref 315 585

'The Jimi Hendrix Experience has got to be about the best hard quarry wall climb in the area, perhaps in Britain, perhaps anywhere… If only there were more Uphills.' (Dave Pickford, 2000)

In its own way, Uphill Quarry is perhaps the most striking man-made crag in the Bristol area. Invisible from the north, this sheer windswept face slices the western shoulder of its hill, narrowly missing St Nicholas Church which stands spiritually defiant on the hilltop. Upholding traditional values in addition to God are a number of strong natural lines of moderate difficulty, though really the quarry belongs to the 80s and its remarkable batch of exceptionally sheer and sustained face climbs. Climbers operating in mind-expanding E grades will be in their element, though the crag's unique ambience of wind, sun, and boatyard percussion should be sampled by all.

Uphill village stands on the southern outskirts of Weston-super-Mare, from which it is clearly signposted and easily reached. The solitary hilltop church is

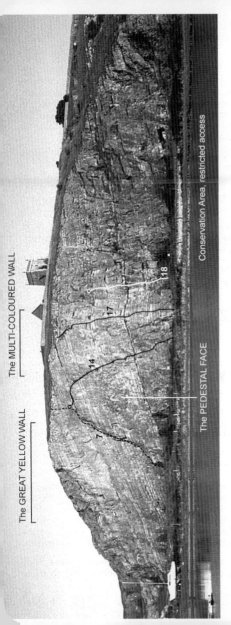

Uphill Quarry

The GREAT YELLOW WALL

The MULTI-COLOURED WALL

The PEDESTAL FACE

Conservation Area, restricted access

1 The Terminator	E3	
2 Images of War	E3	
2a Suburbia	F7a	
3 A Lesser Evil	E4	
3a Exhumed	E5	
4 Life and Times	E5	

5 The Enlightenment	E6	
6 The Jimi Hendrix Experience	E6	
7 Seven-eighths	HVS	
7a Boat Percussion	E5	
8 The Haunting	E4	
9 Uphill Racer	E5	

10 Living Dead	F7b	
11 Chiming for You	F7b	
12 Premonition	E4	
13 Subhuman	E4	
14 Tombstone	HVS	
14a Inhuman	F7b	

15 Turn in the Grave	E5	
16 Crematorium	E4	
17 Graveyard Gate	HVS	
18 Meet Thy Creator	E4	

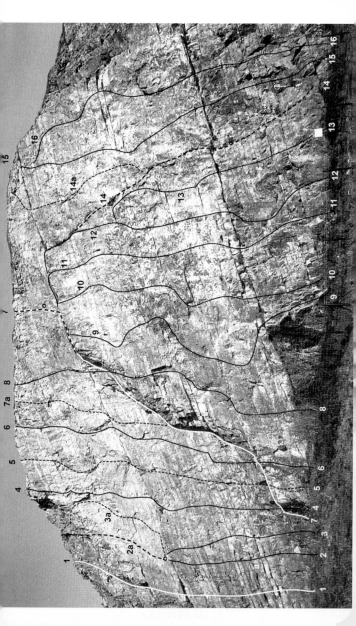

an unmistakable marker for the crag. **Approach** the quarry via an opening in the massive sea defence wall at the end of Uphill Way. The access lane is shared by Uphill boat centre and yard and must not be blocked; there is adequate car-parking space to either side of the sea wall. At high Spring Tides the sea gates are closed temporarily in order to protect against a repetition of the drastic flooding which devastated the village in the 60s.

The continual buffeting of the quarry by the elements means that much of the cliff-face is fairly clean and solid. However, the odd crystalline texture and occasional mudstone pancakes take some trusting at times, and several friable exits demand care. Stainless-steel bolts (mainly *Eco-Bolts*), and some pegs provide protection, albeit quite well-spaced protection, though small wires and *RPs* are useful on many routes. The overlying grassy slope is well furnished with stakes, a contrast to the previous practice of inserting pegs in the graveyard wall. The crag is probably the fastest-drying cliff locally and, as it faces west, is a reliable winter venue – provided the winds are not too strong!

Access: The quarry owners, North Somerset Council, have formally granted permission to climb. Such permission, however, is conditional upon climbers not venturing onto any climbs to the right of *Graveyard Gate* except *Meet Thy Creator*. The whole of the Quarry is a Site of Special Scientific Interest and English Nature has asked for this restriction to be placed on the more broken Right Flank in order to conserve its rare flora. The owners have erected a substantial chain-link fence, effectively cordoning off the Right Flank Conservation Area, and positioned warning notices below and at the cliff-top. Climbers are asked to respect these facilities, which have been provided to help secure the site as a safe amenity for visitors and to deter local children.

Behind the boat-yard shop near the quarry entrance is the isolated Gateway Buttress. An easy-angled bay (the quickest means of descent) separates the buttress from the main face to its right, a leaning 30-metre wall of unhealthily-coloured limestone. This is remarkably featureless, apart from two ramp-lines leading pyramidically in its centre to a ledge at 25 metres and delimiting The Pedestal Face, which lies between them. To the left of The Pedestal Face is the inhospitable blankness of the Great Yellow Wall, whilst to the right the narrower Multi-Coloured Wall terminates in the broad arête of *Graveyard Gate*. The (access-restricted) Right Flank of the quarry now falls back in a series of deep grooves and ribs of poorer rock until a short, steep wall above a shallow cave marks its right-hand edge.

Gateway Buttress

Overlooking the Uphill Boat Centre is an isolated 15-metre buttress. This provides some pleasant climbing, as well as a few idiosyncrasies.

Cave Chimney　7 metres　Hard Very Severe　5a　　　　　　　(1960s)
Scramble to the cave 10 metres up. Layback fiercely into the hanging chimney (thread runner), and invent a way to the top.

Shoot to Thrill (E4), North Quarry
Climber: Martin Crocker   Photo: Carl Ryan

Tiro's Crack (Diff), Churchill Slabs
Climber: J Bolton   Photo: Martin Whitaker

Behind the Boatshed   15 metres   E3 5c †   (30.1.99)
Essentially a solo. Starting below the right end of the cave, climb the steep, narrow wall using holds on the right at first to reach easier ground. Scramble to the top slab and finish near its left edge.

Groove and Slab   15 metres   Hard Severe 4a   (1960s)
Climb the left-hand groove, the continuation crack, and the delicate right side of the top slab.

The very smooth centre of the top slab can be climbed, immediately right of the obvious nut-slot: **Fast-track** (15 metres E2 6a † 30.1.99).

Summerfield   15 metres   Moderate   (1960s)
Popular with beginners. Climb the red right-hand groove and juggy crack to the top.

The Great Yellow Wall

The left-hand, graffiti-clad stretch of the wall is very broken and unpleasantly loose, and seems to have the capacity for only one route:

Uphill Corner   18 metres   Hard Severe
Targets the short right-facing corner near the cliff-top. Start 30 metres from the left end of the wall.
Follow a shattered groove leftwards to the corner 'whence the number of holds decreases and the difficulty increases with repeated ascents' (1964 guidebook).

The Terminator   20 metres   E3 6a   (5.9.87)
A line through the obvious (only) overlap left of a flat ledge at half height. Start below the overlap, 8 metres right of Uphill Corner and a similar distance left of the start of *Life and Times*.
Climb slabby, suspect rock with no protection to reach the break under the overlap at 12 metres. A series of hard moves up the smooth rounded rib (peg) leads to a ledge. Scramble to the top past an old bolt runner.

Images of War   15 metres   E3 5c   (5.9.87)
An interesting way to the ledge at half height. Start 3 metres right of *The Terminator*.
Take a fairly direct line up the grey slabby wall, with technical moves to gain the ledge (peg and bolt). Double-bolt belay.

★A Lesser Evil   15 metres   E4 6b   (29.11.87)
A perplexing initiation into the art of pulling on Uphill 'gnarlies': watch those flappers fly! Start at an obvious entry onto rightward-rising ledges, below the line of a narrow flake-groove.
Climb easily to the top of the flake-groove. Pull up right to a good handhold and then crimp straight up the smooth wall (two bolts) to the ledge. Double-bolt belay.

Two climbs commence from the flat half-height ledge.

Suburbia   13 metres   E4 6b F7a   (27.5.95)
Short but fully bolted. From the double-bolt belay, climb the smooth face
slightly rightwards to easier ground and a scramble to the top. Four bolts.

Exhumed   18 metres   E5 6b †   (27.5.95)
Seriously committing. From the double-bolt belay, step right and climb a
stubborn thin crack (two pegs) to a ledge. Saturate the flake crack above
with wires, and move right into a slight overhung corner. Pull up past a
flexing peg, and make troublesome moves to better holds. Escape off to
the left, or finish up *Life and Times*.

The right-hand side of the wall forms a sheer, yellow sheet in which three
incipient lines of weakness are subtly brought to light with hard-to-spot bolts.

★Life and Times   30 metres   E5 6a   (22.6.84)
The original frightener to breach the big yellow wall, via the definite line of
incipient vertical cracks. Show-stoppingly atmospheric climbing with a
spectacular finish. Every ascent merits a report in the local newspaper. The
protection is well spaced and if you do insist on falling off, do so close to one
of the *Eco-bolts*. Start at the obvious entry onto rightward-rising ledges.
Climb easily for 6 metres to the base of a vertical hairline crack. Follow the
crack (bolt) and cautiously gain a good ledge above at a rising break. Step
right and climb a thin crack to hand-ledges (peg). Move up on doubtful
rock to the base of a slight overhung corner; then swing right (bolt) and
climb the leaning wall on good but widely-spaced holds into a short
roof-capped corner. Make an outrageously exposed swing right to a steep
finish on good holds.

The next four climbs start 3 metres right again, below a 4-metre wall with a
black streak that leads onto the rightward-rising ledges.

★★The Enlightenment   30 metres   E6 6a   (5.9.87)
A challenging pitch up the centre of the yellow wall. It is distinctly run out, a
little fragile above half height, and will try the nerves (of those in search of
the light) to the bitter-sweet end. (As an aside, the climb gives a fantastic
five-minute aerobic workout on a top rope.) Start below the 4-metre wall.
Climb the wall and ledges above for 7 metres, to the centre of the smooth
wall. Reach up (peg on the right) and intricately follow a succession of
layaways and tiny holds (bolt), making bold moves to the half-height break
and ledge (peg). Move right and make a hard lock (peg) to reach the next
break. Work up left on worrying rock to a flake and then back right to a line of
jugs (two pegs), whereupon a sprint up the spacey headwall meets the end.

★★★The Jimi Hendrix Experience   30 metres   E6 6b   (17.9.87)
A wild, electric lead on a superdirect line up the right-hand side of the
yellow wall. In quality terms, feedback has likened it to full-on French 7b+.
The fixed gear is spaced-out; take a small rack in addition to quickdraws.
Follow *The Enlightenment* to its first peg, and move right a metre. Now
blast straight up the wall via a tiny rib and extremely tenuous climbing (two
bolts) to the rising break. Swing up right onto a resting-ledge. Pull up a

short groove (*in-situ* thread) and proceed directly up the headwall (bolt) to finish easily on good flat holds.

Boat Percussion   30 metres   E5 6a   (19.3.94)
A safe enough intro to the Yellow Wall set. Start below the 4-metre wall, as for *The Enlightenment*.
Climb the 4-metre wall, and follow rightward-rising ledges to a short corner at the foot of the ramp of *Seven-eighths* (belay advised to minimise rope drag). Climb the corner, and step left onto the steep wall (bolt). Move up to a rising break. Swing right to a good nut-slot above the break, and make thin moves up the face (bolt) to a niche below a small roof (bolt). Pull over to a pocket and finish on weak rock.

The Pedestal Face

All the climbs on this face, with the exception of *The Haunting*, share the finish of the following route:

Seven-eighths   33 metres   Hard Very Severe   (1963)
An unusual and serious climb with a trying finish. Start below the 4-metre wall; the ramp forming the substance of the route is up to the right.
1 27m. 4b. Climb the 4-metre wall, and follow rightward-rising ledges to a short corner at the foot of the ramp. Climb the slabby ramp (peg) to a bolt belay on the Pedestal.
2 6m. 5a/b. Find the easiest way up the short, final wall, and exit with care.

The Haunting   33 metres   E4   (26.6.84)
A devious and sparsely-protected excursion on the extreme left-hand part of The Pedestal Face is topped by a scary flake-line in the yellow wall. Can be done in one pitch. Start below a crystalline wall, 3 metres right of *The Enlightenment*.
1 24m. 5c. Climb directly for 6 metres, before moving right and up to a black-streaked niche capped by a small roof. Mantelshelf right and climb back left above the roof to the groove of *Seven-eighths*, which is followed to a peg belay below the prominent flake crack.
2 9m. 5c. Climb the crack to the double break above, and finish via a very steep groove, taking great care with the rock.

★**Uphill Racer**   30 metres   E5   (30.5.84)
Bewilderingly technical and bold: popular opinion now rates as E5 a route that started life as an E3! An excellent if convoluted pitch with its crux at the top. Start at the foot of a broken ramp and corner, 6 metres right of the remains of a fence.
1 24m. 6a. Climb the ramp to a sloping ledge on the left under a steep wall (peg). Traverse left, and then diagonally back right across the wall to ledges (peg). Climb up to a flake, and somehow get established on a sloping ledge (peg). Ignoring the temptation of a leftward escape (E4), climb a thin crack and the final wall, slightly right, to the Pedestal. Bolt belay.
2 6m. 5a/b. *Seven-eighths* pitch 2.

★★Living Dead   30 metres   E5 F7b   (16.6.84)

A classic. Sustained, crystal-tweaking fingerwork up the centre of The Pedestal Face. Start as for *Uphill Racer*.

1 24m. 6b. Climb the ramp to a block ledge on the right below a narrow roof. Move up to the left end of the roof (bolt) and then tiptoe back right along its lip to grasp a vertical seam (bolt). Follow the seam to ledges in the centre of the face (peg). Now take the left-hand of two vague depressions in the upper section of the face (peg and two bolts) until a very extending sequence leads to the Pedestal (bolt belay).

2 6m. 5a/b. *Seven-eighths* pitch 2.

★★Chiming for You   30 metres   E5 F7b   (29.6.84)

Those bells again… A superb and highly technical pitch, which is drawn to the right-hand of the two vague depressions in the upper section of The Pedestal Face. Start below a ramp, 5 metres right of *Uphill Racer*.

1 24m. 6b. Climb the ramp to a grass ledge. A crystalline matrix of red and white micro-holds on the sheer face above must be solved in order to gain ledges in the centre of the face (three ancient bolts and a peg). Climb the slightly leftward-trending depression (bolt) and steepening wall (bolt) to the Pedestal (bolt belay).

2 6m. 5a/b. *Seven-eighths* pitch 2.

The next three climbs start below a major, right-facing stepped corner, 8 metres from the right edge of the cliff.

★Premonition   33 metres   E4   (25.6.84)

A good if nervy pitch, technically not too taxing but bold, which climbs the left-hand of two prominent thin vertical cracks towards the right side of The Pedestal Face. Start below the corner.

1 27m. 6a. Climb easily up slabby rock to a break at 9 metres. Step left to the foot of the crack (peg) and follow it with increasing difficulty (*RPs* and small wires) to ledges. Climb the easier crack above to gain the corner of *Tombstone* which is followed to a traverse left onto the Pedestal. Bolt belay.

2 6m. 5a/b. *Seven-eighths* pitch 2.

Subhuman   33 metres   E4   (28.8.88)

Difficult but protectable climbing up the right-hand, snaking crackline.

1 27m. 6b. Climb easily up slabby rock to the break at 9 metres (peg on *Premonition*). Step right and attack the crack (two pegs) until trying moves gain a good hold on the arête. Follow *Premonition* to the Pedestal.

2 6m. 5a/b. *Seven-eighths* pitch 2.

Tombstone   33 metres   Hard Very Severe   (c.1960s)

The stepped corner and ramp demarcating the right edge of The Pedestal Face.

1 27m. 4b. Climb the rather vegetated corner which leads to the right-hand end of the Pedestal. Traverse left (peg) to the bolt belay.

2 6m. 5a/b. *Seven-eighths* pitch 2.

The Multi-Coloured Wall

The colourful expanse of sheer wall to the right of The Pedestal Face.

Inhuman 15 metres E5 6b F7b (10.5.92)
A suitable topping to *Subhuman*; a hard pitch up the upper left-hand section of the wall. Start from peg and nut belays at the right end of the long ledge at 15 metres that crosses The Pedestal Face (most easily reached via *Tombstone*).
Step across the corner of *Tombstone*, and move right onto the headwall at the level of twin rising breaks. Climb direct up the wall (two bolts and peg); then bear very slightly leftwards (*Rock 4*) to the top.

★★Turn in the Grave 30 metres E5 6a (10.9.87)
The archetypal Uphill face route; ruthlessly sustained and technical, particularly on the headwall, and only just adequately protected. Start at the base of the lower corner of *Tombstone*.
Climb the grey wall to a deep break 10 metres up. From a short flake above, climb the red face, shallow groove (peg), and rib above to a series of breaks at half height (*Friend 1½* and good wire-slot). Keeping cool, move up right onto the lip of a small roof to clip a bolt. Now proceed straight up the centre of the excellent headwall (bolt) on minuscule holds to gain a prominent jug (*Rock 1*), and a ledge just below the top.

★Crematorium 30 metres E4 5c/6a (5.12.87)
A big pitch up the right side of the wall. Committing but with gear next to most (!) of the hard moves. Start at a broken crack leading up the wall, immediately left of the Conservation Area fence.
Zigzag up the crack to a deep break 10 metres up. Move up to gain a steeper crack which leads to a large ledge. Pull straight up the caked-mud wall (bolt) to good breaks. A long reach up to the left (peg) gains a good handhold on the headwall. Climb direct (bolt and peg) until a move left leads to the steep finishing-moves of *Turn in the Grave*.

Traverses

★Taking a Line for a Walk 55 metres E2 (20.9.87)
A left-to-right traverse of the main face which, in following the prominent slanting break and ledge-system, enables the atmosphere of the quarry to be savoured without undue stress. Start below the letters HAR painted on the rock to the left of *The Terminator*.
1 20m. 4c. Climb up to meet the slanting crackline and follow this uphill to bolt and nut belays on the half-height ledge of *Images of War*.
2 20m. 5b. Move right to a scoop, drop down, and make a long hand-traverse across the break (peg) to the top of the ramp of *Seven-eighths* (peg). Bolt belay up to the right on the Pedestal. A strenuous pitch.
3 15m. 5a. From the right end of the Pedestal (peg) step down into the *Tombstone* corner. Follow the break across The Multi-Coloured Wall, pull up, and walk along the narrow ledge to finish.

★Get It While It's Hot   38 metres   E2   (28.8.88)
An enjoyable left-to-right girdle that tracks the diagonal break running
across the centre of The Pedestal Face and The Multi-Coloured Wall. Start
as for *Seven-eighths*.
1 18m. 5a. Climb up for 7 metres to a horizontal crack and follow this rightwards (peg) to a long ledge leading to a peg and nut belay at its right end.
2 10m. 5b. Step right into the corner of *Tombstone* and follow the rising
weakness across The Multi-Coloured Wall to the arête (peg above on
Crematorium to protect partner).
3 10m. 4c. As for *Graveyard Gate*: Climb a thin crack in a leaning wall
(pegs) to the top.

The Right Flank   (Conservation Area)

This is the restricted and fenced-off part of the Quarry; only *Graveyard Gate*
and *Meet Thy Creator* are permitted routes. Abbreviated descriptions are
given for all other climbs.

★Graveyard Gate   33 metres   Hard Very Severe 4c   (1963)
The best of the older climbs, which ascends the broad right-hand arête of
the main face. Start beneath a broken crack in the right-hand side of the
arête, 4 metres right of the Conservation Area fence.
Climb the crack to a roof at 12 metres. Move right; then step back left
above the roof to a good ledge. Trend up and right to a shallow groove
which leads to ledges below a thin crack in a leaning wall (possible
stance). Climb the crack (pegs) to the top.

A short steep crack in the wall right of the arête was the objective of the
interesting **Denzil** (33 metres E1 5a [PR] 1.62/8.6.84). The big corner of
Zombies (33 metres E1 5a [PR] 6.6.84), to the right of the broad arête, was
marred by a very loose finish.

Meet Thy Creator   18 metres   E4 6c   (12.12.87)
A three-move wonder on finger-splitting holds. Start below a pocketed wall
immediately right of *Zombies*.
Climb the centre of the pocketed wall (peg) to a roof, and pull leftwards over
this at its widest point to gain a good ledge. Move up to a small overlap
(peg) and continue up the centre of the headwall, via a hold of suspicious
origin and a bolt, to a good ledge. Double-peg belay. Abseil off.

Gorilla Groove (30 metres Very Severe 4a [PR] 1.62) started as for *Meet
Thy Creator* and climbed the arête and serious groove to its right. **The
Discrete Charm of the Bourgeousie** (33 metres E2 5b [PR] 5.12.87)
took the steep wall right of *Gorilla Groove* in two pitches. **Ape's Ascent** (30
metres Severe [PR] 1.62) followed the indefinite groove 6 metres left of the
large cave at the right end of the cliff. At the right end of the crag, a short wall
above the large cave provided the following two micro-routes: **God Bless
Celery** (12 metres E3 5c [PR] 12.12.87) on the left, and **Wot! No Meat?**
(12 metres E1 5b [PR] 20.9.87) on the right.

North Quarry

OS Ref 386 563

'The crag is worth a visit.'

(Francis Haden, 1994)

This is the limestone quarry on the side of Crooks Peak, an invariably dark and gloomy north-facing slab glimpsed by sun seekers Cornwall-bound on the M5, just 2 kilometres to the east. Here is the answer to their question: 'I wonder if there are any climbs there?'

North Quarry is located at the bottom of the north-west slope of Crooks Peak, the prominent mountain-shaped hill, 10 kilometres west of Cheddar. The crag is best approached from the village of Cross on the A38, some 25 kilometres south-west of Bristol. Turn west at the crossroads at Cross onto a minor road leading towards Loxton; then turn right at the Webbington Hotel. The quarry lies to the right of the road after 1 kilometre. Park with care, and keep an eye on your car.

The terraced wall at the back of the quarry has produced several easy but nondescript climbs. Its right-hand retaining wall, however, comprises a smooth and expansive slab up to 45 metres high which is divided into two sections by an area of more broken rock. The left-hand section, which is separated from the terraced wall by a tall, broken corner, is The Main Slab. To the right is the smaller Subsidiary Slab.

The quarry provides a nucleus of underrated slab climbs, with the usual accompaniment of nervy, balancy climbing between spaced (mainly fixed) gear. Here, bouldering skills are best substituted by plain old inner calm (even on a few of the 'sport routes'). All of the pre-1990 bolts were replaced with stainless-steel resin bolts in 1993, though the original and variously weak pegs are still in place and require care. Apart from the routes on the left-hand part of the Main Slab, which gravitate towards a shared double-bolt belay, the majority of climbs top out on occasionally poor rock. Fifty-metre ropes are required to reach tree belays on the hillside in these cases.

The Main Slab

The first two climbs start from a large, tree-laden ledge 25 metres up the broken corner on the left of the slab.

Condition Black   15 metres   E4 6b F7a   (12.93)
A pithy piece of pert toe-work. High in its French grade.
Climb the small roof and the face straight above the ledge. Top out or make a long traverse right to the double-bolt belay of Resin Resurrection. Three bolts and a peg.

North Quarry

1	Condition Black	F7a	7	Strong Safety	E4	13 Motorway Sheepdog F7a
2	Short Sharp Shock	F6b+	8	After Benidorm	E4	14 Tight End E2
3	Resin Resurrection	F7a	9	Journey Man's Wall	E3	15 By Pass E1
4	Head North	E4	10	Shoot to Thrill	E4	16 Quarry Squatter E2
5	Dickie's Downfall	E2	11	Free Safety	E4	17 Split End E2
6	Frank's Finale	E2	12	Bad Banana	VS	

★**Short Sharp Shock**   15 metres   E2 6a F6b+   (10.6.84)
Entertaining rather than punishing. From the right-hand side of the ledge,
take the slab past some surprising holds to a break. Traverse right to the
double-bolt belay. Three bolts and a peg.

★★**Resin Resurrection**   20 metres   E5 6a F7a   (3.10.93)
A modern quarry classic that forges a direct line up the blankest part of the
slab. A run-out on the crux complements the bolts. Start on a grassy ledge
20 metres up the broken corner left of the main slab; sapling belays
behind the ledge.
Amenable climbing lures one gently up across a break onto the smooth
slab. A sustained, blind sequence on smidgens (and less) makes the
run-out to easier ground well felt. Four bolts; double-bolt belay.

The next two climbs start from a narrow grassy ledge containing a small tree, 15 metres up the broken corner on the left of the slab.

Head North   30 metres   E4   5c   (17.6.84)
Extremely committing climbing, on rock that's not the one hundred per cent desired.
Climb a short, shallow groove on the slab and step right to a good foot-ledge. Move up (bolt) and trend diagonally leftwards following the best holds until a long stretch or an extra move gains the break and a peg. Swing right and then follow a shallow ramp to its end. A short traverse left gains the double-bolt belay of *Resin Resurrection*. A top-out is possible.

Dickie's Downfall   30 metres   E2   5b   (14.6.84)
Worthwhile, but not often climbed. Start from the ledge as for *Head North*. Climb a shallow groove on the slab and move right along the break. Climb diagonally rightwards (peg) and continue to a bolt. Gain the curving crack above and follow it to the top.
Variation
Frank's Finale   35 metres   E2   5c   (9.8.94)
Follow *Dickie's Downfall* to its bolt halfway up. Move left up a depression to a break. Climb straight up the slab (between *Head North* and *Dickie's Downfall*) to the top; three bolts.

★Strong Safety   42 metrest   E4   5c   (11.6.84)
One of the stronger lines on the slab, with a good central section. Start at the foot of the corner in the left side of the slab.
Climb the corner for 8 metres and then the broken groove on its right to a peg in a short, steep wall. Climb straight up to an arching crack: very bold in view of the state of the peg. Pull rightwards over a bulge to a hand-ledge on the upper slab. Reach up to another good hold (peg), and bear intricately rightwards to a break (poor peg). Take the bulge above, and climb up a slight scoop and slab to the top.
Variation
Under Pressure   42 metres   E3   5c   (21.4.94)
Fairly aimless. Follow *Strong Safety* to the hand-ledge on the upper slab. Step left (bolt), and pull over a bulge to a break. Climb up the slab above (bolt), to an easier but less well-protected finishing slab and a traverse right to exit.

★Journey Man's Wall   42 metres   E3   5c   (10.6.84)
A subtle, right-to-left sweeping line; one of the best in the quarry. Start at the foot of the Main Slab, 2 metres from its left edge, and directly below the right end of the prominent arching crack at half height.
Climb the initial slab over a small roof, and take broken rock to a smooth section. Work up the smooth slab (two bolts) to the foot of the arching crack on the left. Traverse leftwards along the crack and across the delicate slab (bolt). Climb the shallow ramp trending up and left to its end. A short traverse left gains the double-bolt belay above *Resin Resurrection*.

☆**After Benidorm**   42 metres   E4 5c †   (28.2.99)
A superdirect and optimal line up the tallest part of the slab. The crux is
high up and committing. Start at the foot of the Main Slab, as for *Journey
Man's Wall*.
Climb the initial slab over a small roof, and take broken rock to a smooth
section. Move left (bolt on *Journey Man's Wall* overhead), and climb a
broad rib past a small block roof to the right end of the arching crack. Pull
up rightwards over the bulge as for *Strong Safety* and reach its peg. Now
press on up the thin scoop to a jug (peg). Follow good fingerholds over the
bulge above and then thin cracks to a short traverse right to exit.

★**Shoot to Thrill**   42 metres   E4 5c   (3.10.93)
Essentially a (bold) link between *Journey Man's Wall* and *Strong Safety*, but
a big, consistent lead all the same.
Follow *Journey Man's Wall* to the horizontal break above its two bolts.
Balance warily up right above a small hawthorn tree to good fingerholds
(bolt). A substantial run-out straight above is mitigated by nice positive
holds, and leads to a break (poor peg but other good gear). Take the
bulge and slab above, as for *Strong Safety*.

Free Safety   42 metres   E4 5c †   (14.6.84)
A woefully serious line taking the right-hand side of the Main Slab. Start 5
metres from the left edge of the slab.
Climb the initial slab and a vague broken groove for 12 metres to a ledge
and small tree. Continue, to place your first runner on a large ash tree at
18 metres; then climb the slab on the left to a horizontal break. Move right
and climb straight up to a crumbling foot-ledge 5 metres higher. Climb up
with difficulty to a peg and trend leftwards over appalling, bulging rock to
the top.

The Never Ending Story   30 metres   E3 5c †   (9.8.94)
An enjoyable and nicely positioned right-to-left traverse of the Main Slab.
Start from the large ash tree 18 metres up *Free Safety*; roped or unroped –
it's a solo to this point.
Traverse left above a small hawthorn (bolt), move up (bolt on *Shoot to
Thrill*), and continue to the hand-ledge of *Strong Safety* (peg). Step down to
the left under a bulge (bolt), and continue across the slab to pick up the
ramp of *Journey Man's Wall*. As for that route, follow the ramp to its end. A
short traverse left gains a double-bolt belay.

Bad Banana   30 metres   Very Severe 4c †   (1965)
Start at the foot of the open depression between the two slabs. Climb the
ochre-coloured slab and the rotten, pocketed groove above to the top.

The Subsidiary Slab
Motorway Sheepdog   15 metres   E3 6b F7a   (3.10.93)
A very accessible bolt route at the left end of the slab, taking more traffic
than most. Just follow the bolts! Six bolts; double-bolt belay.

Tight End   18 metres   E2 5c   (17.6.84)
A good climb, when clean. Start 2 metres from the left edge of the slab,
below a modest arête.
Climb the arête (peg), and steep wall above (peg on the right) to finish up
pockets.

By Pass   18 metres   E1 5b   (11.6.84)
Start 5 metres from the left edge of the slab, below a slot with a lime green
stain 8 metres up.
Climb to the slot, and then trend leftwards to a large pocket, containing
(as you find out when you sink your fingers in) a wodge of mud. Proceed
delicately to exit via the obvious short crack.

Quarry Squatter   18 metres   E2 5c †   (7.3.99)
Better protected than most (non-sport) routes in the quarry. Start 6 metres
from the left edge of the slab.
Ascend broken rock, and then climb to a good vertical slot at 10 metres.
Trend very slightly leftwards to a slight break and finish with a long reach,
or a jump, to a good flat hold.

Split End   15 metres   E2 5b   (17.6.84)
Start below a pedestal low on the right side of the slab.
From the top of the pedestal, climb leftwards to the base of a very shallow
groove. Follow the groove to its close, and step right to finish with care.

Galapagos   18 metres   Hard Very Severe 4c   (12.6.88)
Climb the far right end of the slab past a grass clump. Bad rock; no
protection.

Sandford Quarry   OS Ref 420 590

'...surely with judicious landscaping such an ugly feature could be converted
to a most pleasing and well-used recreational area.'

(Richard Broomhead, 1984)

Although this quarry presents a barren wasteland of chippings, rubble, scrub,
and featureless north-facing slabs, the climbing more than compensates for this
somewhat cheerless outlook. A bank of uniformly- angled slabs provides fine,
but under-protected and often very bold, leads or solos on rock which almost
always requires at least a degree of care. Unfortunately, and unfairly perhaps,
climbers haven't taken to the place as much as the rampant buddleia has, so
it's hardly likely that you'll have to queue for the routes. A nice time to visit is a
summer evening, when the sun brightens the place up considerably and
charges the climbing spirit for that all-essential pad up the slabs.

Barely visible from the road, the quarry carves an immense scar in the
western flank of Sandford Hill, 8 kilometres north-west of Cheddar. When

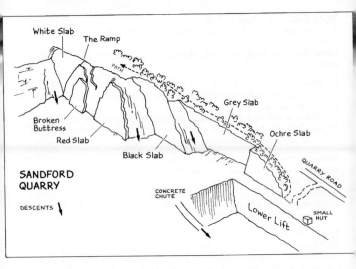

approaching via the A38 southbound from Bristol, turn right onto the A368 Weston-super-Mare road at traffic lights in the village of Churchill. Follow the A368 for 3 kilometres to Sandford, and turn left into Hill Road immediately before Sandford Church. Continue for 1 kilometre, turn left into Quarry Road, and park in a lay-by on the left after 100 metres. Approach to the quarry is via the main gated entrance a little way along the road on the left.

The quarry is owned by ARC who have erected warning signs in a futile attempt to keep away the hordes of local dog walkers, motor cyclists, boy scouts, bird watchers, ramblers, and – oh yes – the one or two occasional visiting climbers.

The Upper Lift comprises five broad expanses of slab, each readily identified by its own distinctive colour (although you may argue that early explorers were a little colour-blind or had their visual senses psychedelically enhanced). At the back of the quarry, far left, is the White Slab, which yields perhaps the quarry's best climb, *Le Poudin Noir*. To its right, a large broken buttress precedes the short Pink Slab at a high level. The grey rock of Red Slab follows, and this is separated from the tall Black Slab by a gravelly ramp. Beyond the Black Slab, at the back of a large recess is the Grey Slab. Finally, the short Ochre Slab is the first slab to be seen on the right when entering the quarry. Below and to the left as one enters the quarry is the Lower Lift.

The broad, earthy ramps to the left of the White Slab and to either side of the Black Slab provide possible descents. All require caution, even if you are an expert skier. A better option might be to pick up the path behind the cliff-top, which leads back down to the entrance track.

The Upper Lift
The White Slab

Some care is required with the broken and stony exits, but these won't be a problem for anyone with the bottle to get to them. There are two metal stakes to supplement the bush belays at the top.

Halfway up the earth ramp, at the base of a slab, is a shattered niche containing a buddleia bush.

Creep 24 metres E1 5a (28.7.85)
Better protected than it looks. Start immediately left of a shattered niche. Climb direct to join a thin seam and follow good, but spaced, holds to a gritty ledge. Climb diagonally rightwards along a narrow ramp to broken ground.

☆☆**Crawler** 27 metres E4 5b/c † (24.5.01)
Cool-headed and methodical climbing on sloping holds. Unprotected until 6 metres below the top, but at least the rock is solid. Start just to the right of the shattered niche.
Step up into the first scoop of *Brain Donor*, and move up left for 2 metres to a small overlap. Trend slightly right, and then climb up delicately to a good little ledge at 12 metres. Continue to a second ledge, and using cracks on the right, move up to the exit of *Creep*.

Brain Donor 27 metres E1 5a (23.10.83)
A natural line up the left-hand section of the slab, not over-endowed with protection. Start just to the right of the shattered niche.
Climb directly up the slab through the first two scoops to a peg in the third. Climb the crack above to the top.

★★**Le Poudin Noir** 35 metres E3 5c (5.8.84)
One of the area's 'quarry classics'. An excellent climb: sustained, delicate, and on good rock. Protection is widely spaced and a level head is required. Start at a flake on the slab, 5 metres right of the shattered niche. Step up onto a flake and make a rising traverse out right for 10 metres to a thin vertical crack (peg). Climb straight up, and then bear slightly left to a bolt amongst blankness. Progress direct (two pegs) to gain better holds and a careful exit. Stake belay.
Variation
★★**Le Poudin Noir Direct** 30 metres E3 5c (16.7.96)
As good as the parent pudding.
Step up onto the flake, and climb to a small niche 4 metres above (good wire). Tiptoe directly up the slab (8mm bolt) until hard moves gain a vertical slot. Move right onto a good foothold and a junction with *Le Poudin Noir* at its bolt runner. Follow *Le Poudin Noir* to the top.

Soixante-neuf 45 metres Hard Very Severe (25.7.85)
Dubious rock in a risqué position.

1 27m. 4c. From the unstable steepening on the ramp, follow the large scoop out rightwards until it ends. Climb the slab above, between two scoops, to a large vegetated ledge. Nut belays in a short corner on the left.
2 18m. 5a. Climb the bulge above the centre of the ledge (peg). Move up and right to gain the obvious crack which leads to the top.

The Ramp   45 metres   Difficult ❀   (10.7.82)
An obvious line. Follow the large scoop out right (as for *Soixante-Neuf*) and where it ends step right onto the ramp. Climb the ramp to the top past plentiful plant life.

Jez Arête   45 metres   E3 5b †   (1994)
An over-represented grade in the quarry. Start at the foot of the red/brown muddy gully right of the White Slab.
Climb the tall arête to the right of the gully to finish on a grassy ledge. Poor protection; poor belay.

The Red Slab

This is by far the quarry's worst and loosest bit of climbable rock. Apart from a good route at each end, its saving grace is the underlying jungle of buddleia and thorns that bars any attempt at bravery on its raw and shattered face.

Gaping Gill   24 metres   E4 5c †   (24.5.01)
An essentially unprotected climb on the slab left of the prominent left-facing corner. Start below a gaping hole in the slab beneath the corner. Scrabble up to the hole (a surprisingly deep rift). Stride left to a pocket, and take the slab above rightwards to crystalline pockets. Stand up on a suspect flake on the left (possible nut placement), and continue up the slab to a buddleia. Abseil from the tree if you've trailed a rope, or scramble leftwards to the top.

Semantic Deconstruction   33 metres   E1 5b   (15.7.95)
Sandford's claim to a real line; this is the striking left-facing corner at the left edge of the slab. A climb of character, with a committing finish.
Scrabble up to the hole, as for *Gaping Gill*. Climb the outside edge of the hole to a roof in the corner. Pull round into the main corner and follow it to a second roof. Swing around into the corner again, but cross right above the overhang onto an arete (good iron spike runner). From a sloping grass ledge above, make balancy moves up the short arête (peg runner) to a terrace. Belay, and scramble off to the right.

Dereliction   30 metres   E3 5b ❀ ❀   (14.8.82)
Deadly serious in its current condition. Start towards the left-hand side of the slab, below a roof containing a borehole.
Climb rightwards across a smooth slab to the roof and pull over just left of the borehole. Trend up and right to a thin, shattered crack, and climb this with difficulty to a scoop. The pocketed crack above leads to a second (larger) scoop on the right. Climb directly up the wall on poor rock to finish.

Isolation   30 metres   E3 5b † ❀   (20.8.82)
Horrendous, but fortunately inaccessible. The route took a seam and
scoops in the centre of the slab to a bold finish up the only part of the slab
that can be described as red.

Desolation   27 metres   E1 5a †   (7.8.82)
Seriously poor protection. Start just right of the centre of the slab below a
series of left-facing flakes.
Climb the flakes and thin groove to a scoop. Traverse left for 3 metres;
then climb pockets trending diagonally right across the slab to finish up a
short crack.

Graduates   20 metres   E3 5b †   (25.7.85)
Delicate climbing with appalling protection. Start 3 metres from the right
edge of the slab.
Climb slightly left and then direct with a bold move to enter a large
shallow scoop. Step left, and climb up the left side of the scoop past a
shothole above its lip to a ledge on the left (on *Desolation*). Move back
right and climb pockets above until a short traverse right gains the edge of
the slab. Peg belay in the block a little higher.

Annihilation   18 metres   E2 5c   (5.8.84)
At last a route worth trying! It also musters up a runner placement.
Climb the slab near the right edge of the face via a shothole, pocket
(cams), and a second shothole. From its top, scramble up to a peg belay
in a block.

The Pink Slab

The following three climbs all commence from a ledge at the foot of the slab
with indifferent wire and sapling belays. This is reached by a steep scramble
up the underlying rib.

Hellraiser   20 metres   E4 5b   (28.4.99)
A mega run-out with only rock to catch you.
Step left from a bolt near the base of the slab and pad up to a second bolt
(on *A Vision of Hell*). Step left to a tiny pocket (twisted wire). Now teeter
direct up the compact but rough slab trying not to visualise the
consequences of a fall. Finish up an easy rib and belay on the stout
buddleia above.

A Vision of Hell   18 metres   E3 5b   (8.93)
Step left from a bolt near the base of the slab and pad up to a second
bolt. Follow a slight line of weakness rightwards (wire placement) to the
top. Scramble to a stout buddleia.

A Date with Eternity   15 metres   E2 5a   (8.93)
Climb the right-hand side of the slab past hidden shotholes. A single wire
placement at half height cancels your appointment.

The Black Slab

Possibly the most impressive slab in the quarry, and certainly the most solid. The penalty for these attributes is an almost complete lack of protection amongst its ocean of ripples: you'll be lucky to find more than one runner on any of the routes! This is solo 'terror-tory'. All of the routes exit onto a narrow terrace 8 metres below the top. Scramble off rightwards from here to the right-hand descent ramp.

The first three climbs start from a grassed-over block 10 metres up the ramp that bounds the slab on the left.

Honky Tonk Highway   20 metres   Hard Very Severe 4c   (8.93)
From a point 3 metres left of the grassed-over block, invent a direct line up the slab to the top.

Scarcity   20 metres   Hard Very Severe 4c   (8.93)
Cruise straight up the slab above the grassed-over block to the top.

The Crush   20 metres   Hard Very Severe 4c   (14.8.82)
Climb slightly rightwards to a narrow ledge. Move up to a thin rightward-looping crack, and follow it past one meagre wire placement to a large shallow scoop.

E for Extermination   30 metres   E2 5a   (8.93)
Smooth rock: cool head? Starting 3 metres right of the grassed-over block, pad confidently up the slab while shutting out the name of the route that keeps ringing in your head. Finish directly above on larger, less solid holds.

★**Sensations**   30 metres   E2 5a   (28.7.82)
Sustained, elegant, and unprotected. An exercise in mind control. Start in the centre of the lowest point of the slab.
Climb easily to reach the tail of a thin, black vein. Follow the vein which curls back left into a large, shallow pocket. Finish directly above on larger, less solid holds.

Shit; What Have I Got Myself into?!   30 metres   E2 5a   (4.5.99)
Start as for *Sensations* but step right to a tiny sapling at 8 metres. Take a direct line above, eventually to gain a jug in a mauve and buff-coloured patch. Trend ever-so-slightly leftwards onto the headwall; then more delicately move up, and swing right to escape, babbling verbal diarrhoea.

The Grey Slab

Probably the quarry's most popular slab, despite miserly protection on many routes and still a smattering of suspect rock. As a means of descent, the loose earth ramp on the left is not very appetizing, and it is preferable to abseil or to pick up a good path several metres behind a cast iron pipe near the cliff-top (which used to carry steam to drive quarrying equipment).

Regular Boy Scout   13 metres   E1 5a †   (4.5.99)
Pretty much a solo. Start 12 metres up the ramp. Trend very slightly
leftwards to a small shallow recess. Now climb straight up the blankest
part of the slab passing a good finger-shothole towards the top.

Handbuilt for Speed   18 metres   E1 5b †   (5.8.84)
From a point 7 metres up the ramp, climb the slab with poor protection
and some suspect rock.

Blow Job   18 metres   E2 (E3) 5b   (18.7.82)
A nice, clean slab climb with one minimalist bolt miles up the cliff.
From 2 metres up the ramp, climb straight up the smooth slab past the bolt.

Softly Softly   20 metres   Hard Very Severe 4c   (2.9.82)
Above the base of the ramp rises a line of grassy pockets; start 5 metres
right. The line looks worn, but don't be deceived, this piece of rock is used
for abseil practice. Take an indefinite and poorly-protected line up the slab
via various breaks and pockets.

Première   20 metres   E2 5b   (28.7.82)
A good climb. Technically not too demanding, and the protection could be a
lot worse. Start 7 metres right of the ramp, at a blind incipient vertical crack.
Climb up to a break at 6 metres. Continue to just below the top, and then
traverse left to exit.

Sponsored by...   20 metres   E3 5b †   (4.5.99)
Leave your rope behind for this one: protection is non-existent.
Beat a superdirect path up the smoothest part of the slab right of *Première*
and exit over a rock garden fortunately enhanced with solid footholds. A
long reach at two-thirds height will feel much harder and more dangerous
to the vertically challenged.

Wo's On?   20 metres   Very Severe 4a   (10.7.82)
Climb the slab 10 metres right of the ramp, following a series of
expanding flakes and edges which curve slightly right. Where they end,
climb the slab just right of an insecure flake.

Dust   20 metres   Hard Severe   (8.8.82)
Towards the right-hand side of the slab, climb a short, pocketed crack and
a thin right-facing flake until a step right gains a shallow crack which leads
to the top. Not much gear.

...to Dust   20 metres   Very Severe 4a   (8.8.82)
Climb to the scoop on the right side of the slab and follow the cleanest line
above. Poor protection.

Fellatrice   48 metres   Hard Very Severe †   (7.8.83)
A traverse of the slab, starting as for *Dust*.
1 36m. 4c. Climb up to a faultline that rises leftwards across the slab.
Traverse the faultline, with a loose section to gain the bolt on *Blow Job*.
2 12m. 5a. Finish up the slab above, as for *Blow Job*.

The Ochre Slab

An amenable slab that offers enjoyable climbing when clean. The usual, but not necessarily safe, means of retreat from all three routes is to abseil off a single peg at the top of *Dead Glove*. An exit through the scrub is another possibility but not in T-shirt and shorts.

Marigold   12 metres   Very Severe 4b   (16.7.92)
Start at the foot of a rightward-rising black seam in the left-hand side of the slab. Follow the seam with care to a wobbly tree at the top. Traverse down rightwards to the abseil peg.

Dead Glove   12 metres   Hard Very Severe 5b   (5.8.84)
Very pleasant. Starting at a shothole at 1.5 metres height, climb the centre of the slab past a couple of prominent pockets to the abseil peg.

As Limp as a Wimp on a Crimp   12 metres   E1 5a/b   (21.7.92)
In the right-hand side of the slab is a vertical borehole near ground level and a shothole at 1.5 metres.
From the boreholes, climb the slab to a finger-pocket. Continue on scoops and broken flakes until a traverse left gains the abseil peg.

The Lower Lift

The climbs described here are situated on a broad low slab down to the left of the entry track into the quarry. Gain the base of the slab either by scrambling down next to a concrete chute at right-angles to the slab or by abseiling down the slab from trees just to the left of the track. There is some very worthwhile slab climbing here. Many of the lines left of *Big Bang Burger Bar* and at the far right-hand end were recleaned and reclimbed in 2001 and 2003 respectively. The remainder need similar treatment.

At the left end of the slab is a corner.

Mucky Pup   9 metres   Hard Severe 4b   (3/5.91)
Climb the vegetated crack that rises from the corner.

★First Offence   9 metres   E2 5b   (3/5.91)
Excellent, if bold climbing. Start 2 metres right of the corner. Climb the slab, mainly using holds left of a thin crack (peg).

★Captain Buddleia   9 metres   Hard Very Severe 5a   (3/5.91)
Starting 3 metres right of the corner, move up with difficulty to the first in a series of pockets. Follow the pocket-line slightly rightwards to pull out on a short iron spike.

Curvaceous   10 metres   Very Severe 4b   (3/5.91)
Often vegetated but still climbable. Start 5 metres right of the corner. Climb into the depression and take a good crack to the iron spike finish of the last route.

Six metres further right is a line of three blast scoops, and right again a line of two blast scoops.

Easy Route   10 metres   Severe   4a   (3/5.91)
Take the vegetated slab left of the three blast scoops.

Doinngggg   12 metres   Very Severe   4b   (3/5.91)
Climb up to and through the blast scoops, trending right from the third.
(The direct finish above the third scoop is a serious HVS 4c.)

Fridge Hid   12 metres   E1   5a   (22.5.01)
Start a metre right of the first line of blast scoops, and below a black crystalline pancake.
Mantel onto the pancake and trend rightwards to the left edge of the first of two blast scoops. Move up into the second scoop and finish direct past a good little shothole.

Boinnggg   12 metres   Hard Very Severe   5a   (3/5.91)
Climb into the second of the two blast scoops (peg runner), and climb diagonally rightwards to the top, finishing as for the next route.

Right again is a short vertical borehole at head height; *Don't Panic* starts here.

★Don't Panic   12 metres   E1   5b   (15.8.93)
Intricate and absorbing slab climbing with spaced protection to give it that extra edge.
Climb up and left from the borehole to a slot. Trend rightwards to the obvious left-pointing flake. Move up and left to horizontal cracks, and climb the final slab to the tree on the left.

★Microsoft   12 metres   E2   5b   (3/5.91)
Almost a solo. Start 2 metres right of a borehole. Follow fingerholds in a vague ramp rightwards, and finish direct on red rock.

After Dark   12 metres   Hard Very Severe   5a   (3/5.91)
Climb the rightward-trending line of pockets that are normally full of plant-life.

Flying Toasters   12 metres   E1   5a   (3/5.91)
Climb the slab via two large and grassy blast scoops. The only protection is near the top.

★Shot Down in Flames   15 metres   E2 (E5)   5c   (8.93)
Start 2 metres right of the first blast scoop of *Flying Toasters*.
Climb up to the right end of a ledge at 4 metres. Make very thin moves above (8mm bolt) and step left. Continue intricately (8mm bolt runner) to finish at a step in the upper edge of the slab

Icon   12 metres   E1   5a   (3/5.91)
Climb spaced holds to a large, shallow recess at two-thirds height (peg).
Bear rightwards to the top.

At the top of the cliff is a relatively large tree with a rectangular metal frame to its left.

★Polished Off   12 metres   E3 (E5) 5c   (3/5.91)
Very delicate slab climbing, which is much more satisfying as a solo. Start below the frame and behind an ominous concrete block (the landing). Follow small sloping holds to a positive finger-hold slightly to the right (8mm bolt). Continue direct and finish on good pockets.

Eco-line   12 metres   E1 (E4) 5c   (1990s)
The safest lead in the quarry? Start directly below the tree. From the right end of the concrete block, follow the line of four *Eco-bolts* and a peg, and step left to the tree.

Semi-redundant   13 metres   E1 5b   (3/5.91)
Enjoyable, with reasonable nut protection. Start 2 metres right of the concrete block.
Take thin cracks diagonally rightwards into two recessed concrete footholds. Move up into a scoop and pull through the left-hand of two notches in the concrete headwall to exit.

Mindwarp   12 metres   E2 5c   (1993)
Start 3 metres right of the concrete block, and follow a sinuous vertical seam to join *Semi-redundant* where it steps into the concrete footholds.

Mystery   12 metres   E1 (E3) 5b   (1990s)
A climb of mixed construction. Start 4 metres right of the concrete block. From a concrete plinth at 2 metres, step onto a brick and use iron 'phenocrysts' above to gain the concrete recesses of the previous route (8mm bolt). Finish as for *Semi-redundant*.

To the right is a huge square concrete block projecting from the centre of the slab. The 15 metres of slab beyond the block bristles with iron bars, girders and bolts; only one route probes the heart of this bizarre wasteland.

The Big Bang Burger Bar   13 metres   Hard Severe 4b   (12.8.93)
Start below the right-hand of two notches in the concrete headwall. Follow a rightward-trending line of pockets to retreat from iron spikes.

There are two bolts on a poor-looking line up a flaky pink slab immediately left of a line of metal clips (the route *Brackets*): still unclaimed.

Brackets   13 metres   Hard Very Severe 5a   (3/5.91)
Start below a line of metal clips below the right-hand end of the concrete headwall. Climb the slab using the clips for protection.

A Pensionable Question   15 metres   Hard Very Severe 5a   (3/5.91)
Climb the rightward-trending crackline 3 metres left of a black streak.

Black as the Ace of Spades and Twice as Tricky

15 metres E2 5a (8.93)

A big mental effort is required! Climb the slab left of the black streak fairly easily but boldly. One 8mm bolt.

Bonus in Retirement 15 metres E1 5a 🏵 (3/5.91)

Climb thin cracks in the slab right of the black streak to a step left onto a concrete capping wall.

Next follows 8 metres of jungle, beyond which is a clearing, left of a concrete hut at the right-hand end of the slab. A couple of the routes here are quite good, though the first isn't one of them.

The start for the following three routes is 5 metres left of the hut, below a horizontal slot just above head-height. Apart from the first route they share the same exit.

Designed to Kill 13 metres Hard Very Severe 4c 🏵 (8.93)

From the slot, move left 2 metres and climb the scrappy slab past saplings, trending rightwards to the top.

☆Emily's Six Tomorrow 13 metres E4 5c (12.1.03)

A quality eliminate with one runner. Step into the slot and take small holds straight above to easier ground (cam in pocket). Continue direct past a crozzley undercut flake and finish slightly right through a gap in the blackthorn topping.

★A Little Peace and Quiet 13 metres E3 5b (3/5.91)

Nervy climbing with no protection for the first 7 metres. From the slot, step right and climb intricately into the lower scoop. Move up its right edge to a pocketed break – your first gear. Gain the upper scoop, and finish more easily yet with care to the common exit.

Living Dangerously 13 metres E1 5a (8.93)

Pockets 2 metres right of the slot lead to a shothole and narrow ledge. Gain the pocketed break above (*in-situ* thread), stand up, and then step left to finish up *A Little Peace and Quiet*.

Ask the Tommyknockers 15 metres E1 5c (8.93)

Start behind the inner end of the hut. Climb the blankest part of the slab using a mono to reach a shothole and the right end of a rising break. Follow the break leftwards to the thread on *Living Dangerously*, up which the route finishes.

Ghosts of the Past 60 metres E2 5c 🏵 (8.93)

A two-pitch left-to-right girdle starting as for *Mucky Pup* and finishing up *Living Dangerously*.

Churchill Rocks

OS Ref 445 591

...a delectable slab rose serenely a hundred feet up from the roadside. It looked hard from a distance but on closer acquaintance it lay back to a disappointing extent. In fact, it seemed that all one had to do was to walk up...

(G Balcombe, 1936/37)

An impressive sweep of limestone slabs which are clean, compact, well worth visiting, but, unfortunately, banned. They offer a small selection of historic slab climbs of some length, at an amenable grade. And, when it's not raining over The Mendips, they attract lots of sunshine – a fair exchange for the infernal din of nearby traffic.

The cliffs lie a kilometre south of Churchill village, overlooking the A38. There is no parking immediately adjacent, and cars are probably best left in Churchill or in the Dolebury Warren car-park at the head of the valley off the east side of the A38.

Access: Churchill Rocks are privately owned. Although the owners have previously permitted climbing, they currently do not allow it. These descriptions are included in case the situation changes.

Churchill Slabs

The left wall of the cliff is broken and of little interest. The main face consists of three overlapping and relatively easy-angled slabs. The right wall overhangs the road. **Descend** via the easy central slab of the three, or by abseil.

Powers that Be   33 metres   Hard Severe 4a   (1993)
Climb the corner at the left margin of the slab, trending right up the slab above to the top. Seeps after heavy rain.

★Witching Waves   33 metres   Hard Severe 4a   (c.1930)
The left-hand slab is continuous. It may be climbed almost anywhere to the left of its central crack, keeping to the right of its left edge. The hardest moves lie in the last few metres.

★Tiro's Crack   33 metres   Difficult   (c.1930)
Climb the prominent crack in the centre of the left-hand slab.

★Dilemma Zigzag   33 metres   Severe   (c.1930)
On the left-hand slab; numerous lines are possible. Keep to the right of *Tiro's Crack* and left of the right edge of the slab.

The Right-hand Slab   25 metres   Difficult   (c.1930)
The overlapping slab may be climbed almost anywhere.

Oak Tree Wall (25 metres Very Difficult c.1930) is completely unjustifiable owing to the risk of rockfall onto the road. The oak tree at the top of the wall overlooking the road was reached via the rightward-trending ramp.

The Southern Outcrop

Almost hidden from view behind trees and a small, railed enclosure, this moulderingly green quarry comprises a wall and a series of deep grooves and copious amounts of vegetation. Climbing here is not an attractive proposition.

Captain Fishy's Fishy Fingers   18 metres   E1 5b   (12.9.92)
'Spade useful'. The obvious crack in the right-hand side of the steep wall. Follow the crack past a huge thread, and continue up the twin cracks to an exit on the right.

Ahoy There!   25 metres   Severe   (c.1930)
The left-hand groove is climbed direct.

Shipmates   25 metres   Very Difficult   (c.1930)
Climb the dirty groove and wide flake crack immediately right of the left-hand groove of the series.

Scurvy Crack   25 metres   Difficult   (c.1930)
The right-hand groove leads past an oak tree to a chimney and the top.

Rock of Ages   OS Ref 477 585

There is something dramatically grand about steep-sided valleys and rocky gorges, but how often do visitors to these landscapes consider the struggle for supremacy going on among the rock and scree by various plant, tree and animal species and their attempts to establish territory and dominance.

(The Weston Mercury)

Rock of Ages is the small, but very steep and compact, south-facing crag on the west side of Burrington Combe, a dry valley dissecting the northern slope of the Mendips. The crag immediately overlooks the B3134 running up through the Combe and is located 100 metres south of the pub. Burrington Combe is well signposted and easily reached from the A38.

Access: Until about 1990, Rock of Ages was in regular use for abseil instruction. Then English Nature instigated a climbing ban, which was mainly intended to control use by groups. The BMC are attempting to get this restriction, which is considered to be unwarranted for ordinary climbers, revoked. The easy-angled rock opposite Rock of Ages is used by groups.

★Cleft for Me   12 metres   E3 6a   (10.5.88)
An exciting and improbable finish. Start just left of the central and
shallowest scoop in the base of the wall.
Climb an intermittent thin crack via a slot at 3 metres to the ledge below
the headwall. From finger-pockets (bombproof *Rock 6*), reach up right to
an enormous jug and then press on direct (*in-situ* thread).

Kingdom's Throne   12 metres   E4 6b   (10.5.88)
Dynamic climbing, good rock, perfect gear. Start at the central and
shallowest scoop in the base of the wall.
From the scoop, climb the crack-system to a good hold on the right below
the headwall. Now climb straight up the crack in the headwall (peg) and
finish slightly leftwards.

Ebbor Gorge   OS Ref 525 487

The Gorge lies on the southern slopes of the Mendips, 4 kilometres
north-north-west of Wells. A footpath leads up the Gorge from Wookey to a
collection of outcrops where the valley narrows down. Eight climbs dating
from the 60s were made on the larger of the crags but climbing is not
entertained by English Nature.

Split Rock Quarry   OS Ref 539 471

'I make an attempt. At twenty feet the only reasonable hold snaps and
deposits me with a twisted wrist on the ground… Another attempt. This time I
make it only to fail a miserable few feet from the top because the pockets are
flowing with liquid mud. Two weeks later I hear the worst.'
          (Richard Broomhead in 1983, on discovering that he had been
          beaten to the first ascent of *Tricky Dicky*, the classic of the quarry)

An unlikely forcing ground it may be, but this bizarre cutting through the
centre of Milton Hill, just north-west of the city of Wells, plays host to an
outstanding concentration of tough traditional and sport climbs. For their
respective grades, the routes demand a high-powered approach as well as
stamina. The blankness of the rock to the right of *Certain Surprise* lends itself
to bolt protection; here solid *Eco-bolts* make the radical smearing and the
wincing bite of rasping finger-edges all the more bearable. The rock, while
mostly sound, is unique in composition, containing as it does a high degree
of haematite, which, apart from sabotaging smearing technique, tends to
stain those perfect tights an uncool shade of scarlet.

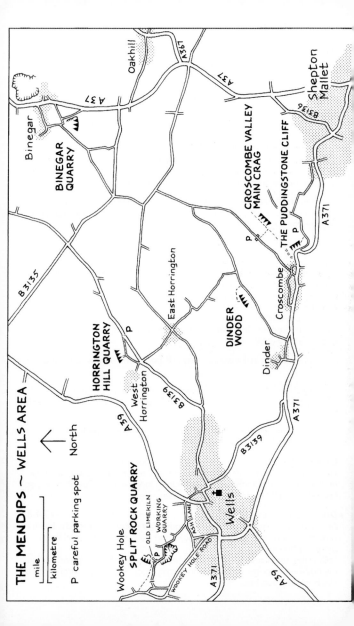

The quarry is the regular haunt of cavers who practise SRT, and hapless trainee managers on team-building events (you've been there?). The latter can be recognised by the aimless unstructured wanderings in the woods and the occasional scream of the inevitable strays who realise too late that teamwork ends where the cliff-edge begins.

Approach: Split Rock can be reached from the main Wells to Wookey Hole road. Just before the EMI factory, turn right into Ash Lane, which is followed to a crossroads. (Alternatively, Ash Lane may be entered from the Bristol road as it descends into Wells.) Turn left into Milton Lane and follow this uphill and around the perimeter of a large, occupied quarry on the left to a parking-area on the right. There is room here for about three or four vehicles. Note that vehicular access from the Wookey Hole direction is no longer possible.

The crag has been descaled by specialists, but there are still a few wobbly holds around. Take care with the rock generally, since a footpath runs beneath the crag.

Access: Climbing is not permitted on the right (east) wall of the cutting, which is very loose and overhangs the path.

All of the climbs described are contained on the left (west) wall, which is 25 metres in height, deep red in colour, and a glorious, quick-drying, winter sun-trap – since it faces south-south-east. Besides wet weather the only other conditions that might catch you out are during sunless winter days when cold, strong easterly or north-easterly winds are accelerated by the venturi effect of the canyon; in these conditions apply a chill factor of about −10° C, and climb in duvets.

A useful landmark in the centre of the cliff-base is the shallow cave of *Certain Surprise*.

Recently a line of *Eco-bolts* has materialized on the lip of *Red Rag to a Bull*. They appear to have been placed for top-roping, and are not referenced in the descriptions.

Fifteen metres from the left end of the wall a diagonal break rises leftwards from just above ground level.

Demolition Man   20 metres   Hard Very Severe 5a   (6.11.83)
Hand traverse the break leftwards to a niche at 4 metres. Gain the crack above and climb it to the left end of a long ledge system. Pull steeply (peg) into a loose groove and climb it to a good tree.

★Dune   20 metres   E5 6b   (25.4.84)
An uncomfortably strenuous climb requiring a decisive approach. There is wire protection, but it is hard to place. Start from the right end of the diagonal break.
Follow the tantalizing line of pockets straight up the sheer crimson wall to the half-height ledge. Step left, pull steeply (peg) into a loose groove, and climb it to a good tree.

Split Rock Quarry

1	Sahara	E5
2	A Magenta Smudge	E6
3	Crimson Dynamo	E5
4	Video Kills	E3
5	Rustic Wall	E3
6	Red Rag to a Bull	E5
7	Brazen Hussy	E5
8	Certain Surprise	E3
9	Corsican Days	E3
10	Chain Reaction	F7b+

Arrakis   20 metres   E5 6b   (5.1.91)
A suitable companion to *Dune*, though harder. Start 2 metres right of the
right end of the diagonal break.
Get established on a prominent large hold at 5 metres. Shuffle leftwards
across the hold before following awkward finger-pockets up the shallow
groove to the half-height ledge. Pull up onto a small ledge in the white
headwall (peg) and take the obvious diagonal crack to finish with a very
long stretch.

★**Sahara**   27 metres   E5 6b   (17.9.82)
A frustratingly hard start gives access to entertaining climbing and the thin,
bending crack in the upper white wall. Start as for *Arrakis*.
Get established on the prominent large hold at 5 metres. Swing right
across the wall to a small rib and balance up this to the half-height ledge.
Traverse right for 3 metres (peg) to the foot of the thin crack. Climb the
crack rightwards past a niche to the top. Exit on the right.

★**A Magenta Smudge**   25 metres   E6 6c   (19.2.89)
A very difficult and direct line up the left-hand side of the wall, which has
now found its true grade. Start 2 metres right of *Sahara*.
Boulder straight up on slippery holds to the half-height ledge, passing a
bolt with an especially hard move. From a peg, easier climbing up the
crunchy white wall above leads to a break (*Friend 2*), and an almighty
flying leap for the top (bolt).

★★**Crimson Dynamo**   25 metres   E5 6b   (9.9.84)
A brilliant route featuring sustained and dynamic climbing. Top of the
grade. Start below a line of widely-spaced pockets, 25 metres from the left
end of the wall.
Power up the pockets, and with a massive reach gain a bulge and bolt.
Bear intricately leftwards past the bolt, and then move up and right to the
half-height ledge. Pull straight up the leaning white wall above an *in-situ*
thread to a horizontal crack. Proceed straight up the headwall to the final
move of *Sahara*. Exit on the right.

In the centre-right of the cliff is a small shallow cave at ground level.

★★**Rustic Wall**   25 metres   E3 5c   (9.5.80)
An excellent, varied lead with some spectacular manoeuvres. Start 6
metres left of the shallow cave, below a thin, rightward-slanting crack.
Reach a ragged hand-ledge at 3 metres. Swing left and climb a pocketed
wall (bolt) to a deep horizontal break. Hand-traverse rightwards and take
the wide, overhanging crack and rib above to the top. Some big shaky
holds above the crack should get the adrenalin flowing.
Variation
★★★**Video Kills**   25 metres   E3 5c   (27.6.90)
Has become the normal (and better) finish. From the deep horizontal
break at half height, muscle straight up the leaning wall on pockets past
another break to exit as for *Rustic Wall*.

★Red Rag to a Bull   25 metres   E5 6b   (31.5.86)
High-quality pumping up the rightward-slanting crack left of the shallow cave
is tempered by a bold finish up the overlying slab. Start as for *Rustic Wall*.
Climb the intensifying crack (peg) to a 'got-it' pocket hold on the left.
Continue strenuously onto white rock (bolt) and reach a vague break
where the crack splits. A wild hand-traverse across the right-hand branch
leads to a short dog-leg crack and a rest in the right-hand side of a large
recess above. (Alternatively, the left-hand crack – on *Brazen Hussy* – can be
climbed to the recess: easier.) Pull out left above the recess to a small niche
(good wires). Now finish very delicately up the centre of the slab.

Medium Very Rare   25 metres   E6 6b   (5.1.91)
A filler-in, the destination of which is the right-hand side of the blank grey
slab which is taken centrally by the finishes of the two preceding routes;
this provides a courageous 6-metre runout on 'dinks'. Start 4 metres left of
the shallow cave.
Climb a short crack and pockets and tiptoe right to a thin crack. Powerfully
climb to a big thread runner below a tapering white corner. Make difficult
moves up the corner (peg) and follow its right-hand rib before trending
back leftwards (*in-situ* thread) to the ledge beneath the slab. A good
vertical nut-slot now points the way: climb directly above it and, ignoring
an escape jug on the right, reach and move very thinly up the diagonal
crack on the left to gain good finishing holds. Fortunately the potential
15-metre plummet from the crux is into thin air!
Variation
Brazen Hussy   27 metres   E5 6a   (10.8.83)
The original way up this part of the face.
Follow *Medium Very Rare* to finger-jugs at the base of the tapering white
corner (peg above). Traverse left to the point of bifurcation of the crack of
Red Rag to a Bull. Grovel up the ugly wide cleft on the left to the large
recess. Follow *Red Rag to a Bull* up the slab to finish.

★★Certain Surprise   25 metres   E3 5c   (9.5.80)
A quarry classic taking a natural line up the centre of the cliff. Strenuous.
The start is polished; the finish is bold.
Gain the crack above the shallow cave with a hard move, and climb it and
the steep, pocketed wall above (*in-situ* thread) to a broken niche (bolt).
Climb up slightly leftwards on jugs and then move rightwards across the
top of a depression to finish. It is also possible to climb straight up through
the depression – harder.

☆Corsican Days   27 metres   E3 5c †   (17.5.99)
A worthwhile addition with a hard finish on the headwall right of *Certain
Surprise*.
Follow *Certain Surprise* to its *in-situ* thread over the bulge, at 12 metres.
Step right into a shallow groove, and proceed up the wall onto a
prominent white sheet (pair of *Eco-bolts*!). From a big jug on top of the
sheet, traverse right 2 metres and pull up into a small cave. Step up (peg),
swing right (pair of *Eco-bolts*!!), and finish up the headwall (peg).

Polling Day Blues   27 metres   E4 6b †   (Polling Day 1987)
Start below a short arête 2 metres right of the shallow cave.
Climb the arête to a small, sloping ledge (bolt). Move up (bolt) to a poor
horizontal break and press on direct (bolt – missing) to bigger holds.
Climb diagonally rightwards past a smooth section to ledges and an awful
finish over rubble (hanging rope advised).

★★**Chain Reaction**   30 metres   E5 6b/c F7b+   (6.9.83)
A comic, right-on-the-edge sequence across the smooth, scooped slab
right of *Certain Surprise*. Start 2 metres right of the shallow cave, as for
Polling Day Blues.
Climb the arête to a small, sloping ledge (bolt). Move up (bolt) to the poor
horizontal break. Execute the crucial traverse rightwards (bolt) to a blunt rib
(peg) and some 'real' holds in a crack above. Climb the crack to the very
loose exit of *Polling Day Blues* (hanging rope advised), or stretch right to
the abseil station of the following route.

★★**Fact or Fission**   20 metres   E6 6c F7c   (10.5.86)
A fingertip-shredder on holds that wouldn't be holds even on *Rubicon Wall*!
Start 6 metres right of the shallow cave, just left of a large pocket a metre up.
Link well-spaced pockets and a puzzle of 'tinies' to get established on a
sloping foothold (bolt). Climb straight up the wall on more small holds
(bolt) until a savage reach gains a slot and a short, deep crack. Move up
the crack and wall above and then swing right onto a flake ledge.
Continue up the cracks to reach an abseil station on the right.

★**Red Snapper and Chips**   20 metres   E6 6b F7c   (12.1.91)
Fine climbing, despite the ancient chipped holds, of which only one at 5
metres remains. Extremely sustained. Start immediately right of the large
pocket, just to the left of the base of a rightward-slanting crack.
From a narrow foot-ledge, use the essential(?) 'chip' to jump for the
obvious large handhold. Move up onto the hold and then bear rightwards
up a precarious shallow ramp to a superb sidehold. Climb over a bulge
and, without recourse to the *Fact or Fission* crack on the left (a 'red
herring'), take a final shallow groove to reach the abseil station. (Five
bolts; *Rock 1* at top.)

★★★**Smashing of Amps**   26 metres   E6 6c F7c+   (19.4.86)
An 80s smash, holding strong for the Millennium. An irresistible diagonal
crack runs the full height of the right-hand side of the wall; start at its base.
Layback and smear up the blind crack to a welcome jug. Continue
strenuously up the crack to a resting-spot where the angle eases. An
'impossible' span left gains a good handhold and a no-hands rest on a
short ramp. Move up to a hollow flake and exit direct. Seven bolts.

★★**Tricky Dicky**   25 metres   E5 6a   (5.83)
A marvellous pitch; bold, technical, and sustained, which reaches the less
severe upper half of the diagonal crack via the prominent jutting ledge.
Start 5 metres right of the base of the diagonal crack.

Climb the pocketed wall with a very committing move to the jutting ledge at 8 metres (bolt). Mantel up and climb directly to join the diagonal crack, which leads to a good, flat ledge. The thin slanting crack provides a suitably tricky climax to the route.

Saboteurs of the Underground 25 metres E4 6c F7b+ (6.1.91)
A diabolically thin variation of *Tricky Dicky*, which was rendered even more holdless by descaling operations.
Gain the jutting ledge at 8 metres as for *Tricky Dicky* (bolt). Step down to the right and move up (bolt) to a shallow groove formed by the right-hand side of the grey 'pancake'. Climb the groove (bolt) to the good flat ledge of *Tricky Dicky*. From its right-hand end, climb the wall (bolt) to pockets. Traverse right (peg) and exit via a broken ledge.

★Smarty Marty 25 metres E5 6c F7b+ (19.5.86)
This climbs the smooth black wall just left of the obvious, shattered crack towards the right-hand side of the crag.
Climb the crack to a distinctive projecting handhold. Step left onto the wall (bolt) and make some fierce and fingery moves to a good pocket up left (bolt). Now climb straight up the vague rib on improving holds to a resting-place (bolt). Reach left to the flat ledge of *Tricky Dicky* and from its right-hand end climb the wall (bolt) to pockets. Finish steeply up and left to the exit of *Tricky Dicky*.

Gary's Gift 25 metres E2 5c (25.9.82)
Climb the obvious, shattered crack towards the right end of the wall, with difficult moves at 6 metres.

Open Invitation 25 metres E2 5b (31.3.84)
An uninviting climb! Start below a leftward-trending, overhanging groove 5 metres right of *Gary's Gift*.
Climb the groove to shattered rock above. Trend up and right across poor material until a traverse back left leads to the final steep crack of *Gary's Gift*.

End Game 25 metres E2 5b (26.6.84)
At the right end of the wall a narrow ramp slopes up to the left. Climb the ramp to the foot of a short, leaning corner. Climb the corner and crack above to the top.

The wall ends in some pleasant grey slabs, a favoured place of first contact for many groups of local schoolchildren.

☆Split Rock Girdle 64 metres E5 † (7.6.86)
A superb traverse of the central and right-hand side of the cliff. The second pitch takes the beguiling, horizontal line of weakness across extensive blank ground and is one of the finest pitches here. Start 3 metres left of *Rustic Wall*.
1 25m. 6b. Force a direct start to *Rustic Wall* and follow this to a deep jug above its bolt. Traverse rightwards around the bulge to join *Red Rag to a Bull* (bolt). Move up on white rock to the vague break and traverse right

below bulging rock to the hanging corner of *Brazen Hussy* (peg). Make a hard move up the corner and swing around the rib to take a hanging stance on nuts and cams on *Certain Surprise*.

2 27m. 6b/c. Step down and follow the horizontal break rightwards, together with the crux of *Chain Reaction* (!) (two bolts), to better holds around the blunt rib (peg). Move down and right to the pod of *Fact or Fission*. Reach right to a jug; then traverse horizontally rightwards (bolt) along a line of good footholds to gain the slanting crack of *Smashing of Amps*. Follow the diagonal crack (bolt) to the good, flat ledge on *Tricky Dicky*. Bolt and wire belays.

3 12m. 6a. From the right end of the ledge, move up (bolt) to a jug and traverse right along the break (peg) to the exit of *Gary's Gift*.

Horrington Hill Quarry   OS Ref 576 477

'You'll never find it – unless I tell you where it is!'   (John Watson, 1999)

One of the best-hidden crags on the Mendips; details were revealed just in time for inclusion in the guidebook! The quarry is situated in woodland on the southern slope of Horrington Hill, which overlooks the village of West Horrington 2 kilometres north of Wells.

The south-facing quarry reaches 16 metres in height at its left end and offers a handful of steep routes on very solid and superbly rough limestone. In winter it tends to seep in places after significant rainfall, but it does get all the sun going (that can permeate through the trees). Bring a mat, since the ground can get trampled and muddied by a herd of cows who come to lick salts from the rock surface (and eat any climbing gear going spare).

The crag is approached from the B3139 Bath to Wells road (Bath Road). Park in a large lay-by on the north-west side of the road at OS Ref 581477. Don't leave any valuables in your car. Enter the green lane (a public footpath) at the Wells end of the lay-by and follow it for 300 metres in the direction of West Horrington. After a leftward kink in the lane, take a path on the right that leads quickly to a limekiln in the wood and the quarry a short distance behind. It is also possible to approach from the village via the same lane, but parking is restricted.

☆The Cows Ate My Baseball Cap – Honest!
                            5 metres   E1 6a † (15.5.00)
A three-star boulder problem up the underside of the hanging prow at the left end of the quarry. Exit on the arête. Watch for cows beneath your feet. Add two E-grades for horns.

The next three routes takes lines up the back of the tall recessed wall at the left end of the quarry.

Smashing of Amps (F7c+),
Split Rock Quarry
Climber: Mike Weekes
Photo: Mike Weekes col.

Volume Eleven (E3), Fairy Cave Quarry
Climber: Ian Butterworth   Photo: Mike Raine

Outside: the Herd   15 metres   E4 6a †   (25.7.00)
Not the best route in the quarry. Start 2 metres right of the left-hand corner. Follow a blind right-facing flake to a good hold from which a peg (removed) in the break at 6 metres can be clipped. Make a very hard move to a better flake on the left and move up to an inset muddy ledge. Pass the ledge on the left and follow a good crack to a tree on the left.

★★Face Climb   16 metres   E3 5c   (1990)
A fine thin-crack climb, with good wire protection. Climb up to the base of the crack in the face. Pull over a small overhang with difficulty and follow the sustained crack (peg) to easier ground and the top.

☆☆Intimate Behaviour   16 metres   E4 6a †   (16.5.00)
The leading route of the quarry; intricate and technical climbing with just adequate protection.
Step up onto a ledge right of *Face Climb*. Reach sloping holds in a break above (peg), step left, and make hard moves past a small roof to reach better holds slightly right. Step back left and gain a good horizontal break above. Finish direct.

Horrington Crack   16 metres   Hard Very Severe 5a † ❀   (1990)
Currently overgrown, this route climbed the right-hand flake crack and corner of the recessed wall.

☆Faith in the System   12 metres   E5 6b †   (25.7.00)
Worth a star for the moves alone; this is the sheer, shallow scoop right of the corner. Eliminate, but at least the (limited) gear keeps you on line. Move up (wire) and accelerate to a projecting sloping hold slightly right. Make extending moves to a thin break (*Friend 1½* on the left), and go for the large projecting hold above. Pull up on the trees to get out.

Dick's Crack   12 metres   E1 5b   (1990)
The ubiquitous Dick strikes again. Start below the obvious crack in the yellow west-facing wall. Climb the crack!

'Lellow'   12 metres   E3 5c †   (15.5.00)
Climb the steep wall right of *Dick's Crack*, with a hard move from a slanting hand-ramp to a small ledge 6 metres up. Mantel onto the ledge, pull up onto a larger flake-ledge; then swing left and exit up *Dick's Crack*.

A Pat on the Back   13 metres   E3 5c †   (15.5.00)
Pumpy. Climb the yellow wall immediately left of the arête until committing moves gain a good finger-jug on the arête. Pull up onto a flake-ledge, and traverse left to exit up *Dick's Crack*.

The next two routes take the projecting face in the centre of the quarry.

Sod the Rope   9 metres   E2 5c †   (19.5.00)
Good, strenuous climbing with sound protection. Start below the right-slanting crack two-thirds of the way along the face. Follow the crack past a hard move at 6 metres. Pull out on a small hawthorn.

Bounce   9 metres   E2 5c †   (19.5.00)
An obligatory solo, though the crux is reasonably low. Climb the left-hand
side of the right arête via a shallow groove. Keep on the left and exit easily.

Corner-climb   10 metres   Very Severe ❀   (1990)
The scrub-infested corner at the right-hand end of the quarry.

Dinder Wood   OS Ref 588 454

An extremely quiet and private location, especially in summer and autumn
when a sea of nettles in the base of the valley prevents any casual visitation.
The cliffs here are tucked away at the head of a dry valley in Dinder Wood, 3
kilometres north-east of Dinder near Wells. They are not indicated on any
map, and are situated in (what is understood to be) private woodland, which
accounts for their very late development. The rock is steep limestone, which
is generally solid. Care will be required on some of the exits, however, due to
blocks that may have been loosened by long-term ivy growth.

Most of the climbs were established solo after cleaning and, in some cases,
top-rope practice. Most of the routes are open to leading (and graded
accordingly), but where they appear to be unprotectable by traditional
means, this is indicated in the text. As a consolation the landings are soft and
springy, excepting several bone-breaking trees.

The main cliffs face south-south-east, are open and sunny, and so steep
(and tree-topped) that they can stay dry even in heavy rain. All of the routes
are on the right-hand (north) side of the valley; the smaller cliffs opposite
could yield some (less attractive) climbing.

Access achieved so far has not led to any problems. Most of the recent
routes were climbed during weekday evenings of early autumn. Given the
private and unspoilt location, and the likelihood of nesting birds on the cliffs,
it is highly recommended that climbers are discreet and only visit outside the
nesting season (i.e. not between February and July). Also, the utmost care
will be required with parking. There is space for one small car next to the
approach stile, but large farm vehicles use the track opposite and may
require to turn here. The only safe alternative is on the slightly wider but soft
grass verge a short way down the valley.

Approach: On the A371 Shepton Mallet to Wells road, turn right just west
of Croscombe (signposted Dinder). Turn first right and follow the minor road
(Sleight Lane) uphill, until after a kilometre a parking/passing place appears
on the left at a stile. Go over the stile and follow the public footpath across
the field and down into the valley. There are now two options. For a first visit,
and when the nettles are down, follow the valley leftwards (over a fence),
and descend a bizarre cascade of huge concrete blocks (tank traps!) to a

cave. Now bear right to the main cliff on the opposite side of the valley. If soloing, or the nettles are in full bloom, continue leftwards up the other side of the little valley and though a gate into a second field (still a public footpath). The main cliff is beneath the fence and stone wall to your left: abseil in from trees.

The climbs are described from **right to left**.

At the right end of the crag is a short, sheer wall capped on its left by a prominent roof. The first three routes here exit via an ivy-filled chute on the right-hand side of the roof.

Dindergarten   9 metres   Hard Very Severe   4c †   (4.9.00)
Climb the obvious weakness on the right, and then swing left on jugs and exit up the chute.

☆**Fingernail Hell**   9 metres   E3 6b †   (4.9.00)
Starting 2 metres right of the arête, sear up crimps above an obvious finger-pocket to reach a second pocket. Continue steeply on larger holds to the exit chute. A superb boulder problem.

Choppers   10 metres   E2 5c †   (4.9.00)
Take an eliminate line right of the arête, past a distinct layaway, to a rest under a roof (first gear). Use a short jam crack to reach jugs above, and swing right to the exit.

Butcombe Buttress   12 metres   Hard Severe   (1991)
Climb the stepped white rib to the roofs. Traverse right below the roof to a crack and the exit chute.

To the left of *Butcombe Buttress* is a broad gully marked by two prominent cracklines.

Brewery Brake   10 metres   Severe †   (26.11.01)
Follow the central crackline to a block bulge. Climb over on the left with caution to a vegetated exit.

Pewter Pitcher   10 metres   Severe †   (26.11.01)
The twin crackline on the left-hand side of the gully gives a pleasant pitch with an ivy finish.

The gully wall develops leftwards into a tower, which is bounded on its right by the groove and crack of *Big Al's Silver Jubilee*.

☆**Fuel Crisis**   10 metres   E2 5c †   (20.9.00)
An absorbing eliminate up the smooth wall right of the groove and crack. Wire protection is available.
Climb straight up the technical wall, ignoring easier lines to each side, to a position below the right-hand side of the projecting roof at the top of the cliff. Swing left and mantel sensationally over the roof.

Big Al's Silver Jubilee   10 metres   Severe   (1991)
Climb the groove and crack; some care required with the rock.

☆**Elderburied**   11 metres   E4 6a †   (13.9.00)
Superb moves, exciting and steep (with the bonus of some protection – if
led). Start a metre left of the groove.
Make eliminate moves direct up the rib, with a hard move over an
overhang. From good sideholds slightly right, swing left onto a jug on the
face of the tower, and continue to a clean-cut finish.

The Plight of the Ordinary Working Man
                                     11 metres   E1 5b † (19.9.00)
Climb straight up the groove in the left-hand side of the tower with
difficulty. Swing left from jams onto jugs at the base of a wide crack, and
follow the crack to the top.

Forcible Retirement   10 metres   E2 5b †   (20.9.00)
Exhilarating. Climb up to a ledge on the west face of the tower. Reach
direct from good fingerholds to a side-hold up to the left, and take the
steep rib above to the top. Good cam protection can be arranged in a
crack right of the line.

Beyond hanging gardens rises an imposing clean arête, followed by a bay
marked by a number of undercut grooves and ribs.

★**For Cerberus**   10 metres   Very Severe 5a   (26.9.00)
Climb the obvious left-facing corner to the right of the arête. A technical
start gives way to easier, protectable climbing.

P45   10 metres   E2 6a †   (6.9.00)
Starting a metre left of *For Cerberus*, make a long move from undercuts;
then follow an easier line of weakness in the left wall of the corner to the top.

☆☆**Humble Origins**   11 metres   E6 6b †   (6.9.00)
The imposing arête: pumpy and dynamic. The grade reflects the
consequences of wrapping yourself around a gnarly tree at the bottom.
Looks unprotected. Start as for *P45*.
Undercut up, but swing left to a handrail under a roof (you're above the
tree now). Make athletic moves straight onto the arête above, and follow
positive but widely-spaced holds in an exciting position to the top.

Dripfed   11 metres   E4 6a †   (19.9.00/8.10.00)
Very steep and sustained climbing up the right edge of the first groove left
of the arête. Reasonable wire protection.
Take pockets to a jug and power up over the bulge with great difficulty into
the right-hand side of the groove. Continue direct up the leaning rib to
large holds and the top. (The first 6 metres can also be used as a
right-hand start for the next route.)

☆**Ivy Falls** 11 metres E2 5c † (19.9.00)
A direct line up the first groove left of the *Humble Origins* arête. A hard, bold start, but above a soft landing.
Move up on pockets and pull over a bulge into the left-hand side of the groove. Follow the well-protected crack in the groove to the top.

☆**Move All Mountains** 11 metres E4 6a † (6.9.00)
A strong, if escapable line; E5 if soloed.
The rib on the left-hand side of the first groove is reached from the left via spaced fingerholds until a swing right and step up gains an obvious little square-cut ledge at 6 metres. Using holds to either side of the rib (gear possible on the right), finish directly up its front.

Escape from the Lost World 11 metres E4 6a † (12.10.00)
Some protection, though the rock needs care. Climb the undercut rib, as for *Move All Mountains*, but pull up onto a small ledge beneath a hand-crack. Follow the crack to the top.

★**Bowl of Nettles** 12 metres Hard Very Severe 5a (26.9.00)
Good, safe bridging up the second groove. Climb steep rock to enter the groove. Bridge up past an undercut pocket and step right to exit.

Tumbling Concrete Dice 12 metres E1 5c † (26.9.00)
Take the slight blunt rib between the second and third grooves to exit up a short crack. Runners in a slot at 4 metres protect the crux but watch the underlying boulder.

Scoop of the Day 12 metres Very Severe 4c (26.9.00)
Climb the left-hand groove (and scoop) to a dirty exit and a tree.

☆**Cross Combe** 12 metres E4 6a † (12.10.00)
A strenuous solo-traverse at 5-6 metre level (which feels about French 7a+).
Climb up to the handrail under the roof, as for *Humble Origins*.
Hand-traverse left and stretch up left for the jutting square-cut ledge on *Move All Mountains*. Continue the dead-hang leftwards into the groove of *Bowl of Nettles*; then swing left around the final rib to descend (or ascend) *Scoop of the Day*.

At the left end of the bay are three climbs.

Jo Jo 12 metres Very Severe 4b † (19.11.01)
In the right wall of the corner at the left end of the bay is a groove. Climb the groove, and finish over the jutting prow to the right of vegetation.

Ellie 12 metres Severe 4a † (19.11.01)
Climb the corner to a ledge on the left. Continue up, using a crack in the left wall of the corner to avoid vegetation.

Walking with Crinoids 12 metres Hard Very Severe 5b † (19.11.01)
Climb the left-trending weakness to a good ledge above the bulge. The wall above leads more easily to the top.

The undercut bay is bounded on its left by another imposing arête, and then the ground rises to the foot of the wide *Cave Crack*. Left again is a fine wall, broken by several steep cracks, which ends at a lichenous yellow pillar.

Rattle Crack   11 metres   Hard Severe   (1991)
Climb the wide, bulging crack 3 metres right of *Cave Crack*, with an excursion to the arête on the right.

Swift Response   6 metres   E1 5c †   (27.9.00)
Pull over the bulge 1.5 metres right of *Cave Crack* using a small rib on the right. Reach the small tree above; then descend *Cave Crack*.

Cave Crack   10 metres   Very Difficult   (1991)
A good route up the broad cleft with a curious cave at half-height.

Mirror Image   6 metres   E1 5c †   (27.9.00)
Make difficult moves up the sheer wall 1.5 metres left of *Cave Crack*. At 6 metres, below hostile 'veg', swing right and descend *Cave Crack*.

Rob's Layback   11 metres   Hard Severe   (1991)
The flake-crack left again.

☆**Jamslip**   11 metres   Very Severe 5a †   (27.9.00)
A worthwhile pitch, despite some loose holds on the bulge. Follow the left-trending flake-crack 6 metres left of *Cave Crack* to the bulge. Pull over onto large, shaky holds, and exit left through a gap in bushes.

Rigor Mortis   10 metres   Severe   (1991)
Climb the wide crack, noticing that you can join hands two-thirds of the way up.

The next two routes are on the steep wall right of the yellow pillar.

The Reaper's Embrace   10 metres   E5 5c †   (12.9.00)
Unprotected. The loss of the underlying tree would reduce the grade to E4. Above the tree, link a series of layaways in the right-hand side of the wall and climb direct to a ledge. Swing left to exit up a fissure.

Down in Dingley Dell   10 metres   Hard Very Severe 5a †   (12.9.00)
Start 2 metres right of *Rosethorn*. Climb the line of weakness in the steep wall to a ledge. Exit up the fissure.

Rosethorn   11 metres   Very Severe 4c †   (13.9.00)
Climb the steep crack right of the yellow pillar, and escape left below prickles.

☆**Yellowstone**   12 metres   E5 6a †   (13.9.00)
A bulkier outing than most on the crag. Start below the centre of the pillar. Climb boldly to good holds (and assorted mediocre gear) in a bulge at 7 metres. Sustained hard moves above.

Easy Route   10 metres   Difficult †   (1.12.01)
The chimney on the left of the yellow pillar.

Spring Haze   10 metres   Hard Very Severe 5a †   (12.10.02)
Climb the white wall to the left of *Easy Route* on small edges.

Slash and Burn   10 metres   Hard Very Severe 5b †   (12.10.02)
Climb the groove at the extreme left-hand end of the cliff to a good
pocket, move right towards the arête, and continue up the wall on small
holds, exiting right.

Croscombe Valley Cliffs   OS Ref 601 449

Concealed in the small valley north of Croscombe between Wells and Shepton
Mallet, in Ham Woods, are some small cliffs with unique, pocket-pulling
appeal. The main cliff comprises natural limestone that can't be bettered: its
compact and highly pocketed character belongs more to the crags of central
France than to the Mendips. The climbs on the main cliff are generally short,
and all were soloed by the first ascensionists. Grades given, therefore, are
solo-grades, although on many protection looks available for leading. If
soloing, the best deal is to trail a rope to enable an abseil descent from trees at
the cliff-top. The landings are soft – with a few exceptions. The two other crags in
the valley are higher, and leading is the order of the day on them.

A good time to visit is spring evenings, when the cliff catches the sun. Like
many tree-capped cliffs, the rock can stay dry in the rain. After prolonged
heavy rain in the winter the crag seeps.

Approach from Thrupe Lane, the minor road that connects Croscombe with
Thrupe, which runs parallel to and just to the west of the valley. Park carefully
by some prefabricated agricultural buildings a kilometre north-east of
Croscombe. Take the wide, gated footpath that runs eastwards and down
into the valley bottom after five minutes. For the main cliff, turn left, and
follow the valley path for 150 metres until the cliff becomes visible up to the
right. The other two crags are situated downstream and are reached by
turning right and walking down the valley footpath.

Main Cliff
The climbs are described from **right to left**.

Thirty metres right of the main cliff, past ivy-covered crags, is a two-tiered
prow.

Director's Chair   8 metres   E1 5a   (7.6.00)
A nice feature. Climb the prow from the right on good holds to an
awkward mantel onto a large ledge. Finish to the right of the upper prow
(remembering the useful branch out in space behind you).

The Secret Existence of a Mendip Official
6 metres   Hard Very Severe 5b (21.3.00)
Start at the right end of the main crag, just to the right of a jutting prow.
Reach up to a slight crack in a groove, and take pockets in the wall above,
trending leftwards to trees. A well-used descent route.

The Prow 6 metres   E1 5c   (21.3.00)
Jump for jugs on the jutting prow, struggle up, and follow better holds
again to trees.

The Shelf 6 metres   E1 6a   (21.3.00)
Starting a metre left of the jutting prow, reach for the shelf and climb a
crack to trees.

★**Jump Start** 6 metres   E1 6a   (21.3.00)
Start below a crack up on the wall containing a forked tree at 6 metres.
Dyno for holds on the shelf; then powerfully stretch for finger-jugs and the
tree.

★**Deadpoint** 7 metres   E3 6b   (21.3.00)
Very impressive. Takes the smooth and impending wall. Reach jugs on the
shelf, swing right, and using monos on the wall stand up and crank for
jugs. Finish with a long reach for a tree root.

Mind the Primroses 6 metres   E1 5b   (7.6.00)
Get established on the thin jutting overhang from the right. Climb a crack,
and (doing as the name suggests) mantel onto a bouncy tree. Abseil off.

Dead-hanging Offence 10 metres   E1 6b (F7b)   (4.10.00)
A pumping traverse of the low-level shelf: perfect for those over-used
elbow tendons. Start from the overhang of *Mind the Primroses* and finish
up *The Prow*.

Next comes a vegetated groove, while the arête to its left is *Snowdrift*.

Snowdrift 10 metres   E2 5c   (5.4.00)
Climb a scoop, make hard moves up the bulging arête on finger-pockets,
and finish above a sapling more easily, pulling out on roots.

★**What's On?** 10 metres   Very Severe 4c   (4.10.00)
A good, well-protected climb. Make steep moves into a groove right of the
hanging yellow corner, and follow it to a pull out on holly tree roots on the
right.

★**Yellow Peryl** 10 metres   E4 6b   (3.5.00)
The hardest piece of solo-climbing on the crag: unprotectable. Start
beneath a hanging yellow corner right of the obvious left-slanting crack.
Climb to a flat hold over a bulge and make fierce pulls on small pockets to
gain entry to the hanging corner. Swing out left above it onto the rib and
follow good holds to trees at the top.

★★All Sown Up   10 metres   Hard Very Severe 5c   (4.10.00)
A climb of character, with protection.
Make a hard move to larger holds and a steep pull into the left-slanting
crack and groove. Follow the crack to a roof and, from a good jug on the
right, make an insecure-feeling move to trees and an exit on the right.

★The Drip   10 metres   E2 6a   (5.4.00)
Excellent pocket-pulling – if eliminate. Start below the large roof near the
top of the crag, at a small, sloping slot at head-height.
Get established on the slot using finger-pockets. Continue direct on
improving holds to the left end of the roof. Swing left and either retreat
from the tree on the right or the tree slightly higher on the left.

★Reasons to Be Cheerful   10 metres   Hard Very Severe 5a   (4.6.00)
Climb up onto a small ledge with difficulty. Follow the pleasant
black-and-green-streaked wall above to the exit of *The Drip* on the right.
(VS if led.)

No Mats Required   10 metres   Hard Very Severe 5b   (4.6.00)
Start below the little tree at 6 metres. Using a one-finger-pocket move up
to holds and the roof. Climb the line of weakness above, and either finish
up awkward muddy ledges or traverse right 2 metres to the exit of *The
Drip*. (VS if led.)

Two-thirds of the way along the crag is a pedestal at 3 metres, and to the
right an obvious roof.

★Angles-sur-L'Anglin   7 metres   E2 5c   (29.3.00)
A superb little climb. Starting a metre right of a dead tree, climb to a good
pocket below the roof. Take the widest part of the roof direct, and pull up
onto the wall on small pockets. Descend from the tree straight above.

Spear and Watson   7 metres   E3 5c   (29.3.00)
The grade accounts for the risk of being impaled! Start behind the dead
tree. Boulder up a smooth scoop, and continue direct until a swing left on
good pockets leads to a large tree.

Coward   6 metres   E1 5c   (29.3.00)
Starting a metre left of the dead tree, take a rib with a green streak straight
up to the large tree.

Role Reversal   6 metres   Very Severe 4c   (29.3.00)
Climb a slight groove to the top of the pedestal. Move up on pockets
behind a projecting branch, and swing right to a large tree.

Winter Approaches   6b F7b   (4.10.00)
An excellent bouldering traverse from *Role Reversal* to *Snowdrift*. The
difficulty climaxes below the hanging corner of *Yellow Peryl*.

Near the left end of the crag is a corner, with a hanging arête to its left.

Lightning Crack   8 metres   Hard Severe 4b   (5.5.00)
Climb the corner strenuously. Protectable if you have big nuts.

One-man Audience   6 metres   E3 6b †   (3.5.00)
Power up the impending wall left of the corner, keeping well away from the
corner-crack. A round pocket a metre right of the arête gives the line (but
is hard to reach).

★Death at Dusk   7 metres   E5 6a   (29.3.00)
A bold solo: blind and strenuous climbing above a poor landing. Climb
the overhanging arête using finger-pockets a little to both sides of the
edge. Pull out on the tree.

Lichen Wall

Approach. Turn right upon reaching the valley and follow the valley path
downhill for 400 metres; Lichen Wall is the north-facing wall high up to the
left

Backache   13 metres   E2 5b †   (25.5.00)
Harder than it looks, and needing care to protect.
Climb the square-cut corner on the left, and swing right onto a flat ledge.
Step up into the smooth groove, but immediately swing left to good
finger-jams in a crack around the rib. Climb the crack and bear steeply
right to a tree overhanging the top.

Headache   13 metres   E2 5c †   (25.5.00)
Follow a leftward-rising groove to the flat ledge. Take the thin crack in the
steep wall above to a swing left to the tree. The route can be started by a
contrived boulder problem below the flat ledge.

Fright of My Life   12 metres   Very Severe 4c †   (6.10.00)
The best route on the cliff, which will improve with use; well-protected.
Climb the narrow corner on the right, and carefully reach a large tree up
to the right.

Moss Pillar

This is the gloomy triangular pillar-face on the north side of the track, a little
further along the valley floor from Lichen Wall. There had to be one route on
it.

Slobodan   12 metres   E2 5b   (6.10.00)
Revolting when mossy and wet. Use a flake on the left to gain a rising
break. Strenuously follow the break and the questionably stable flake
above to a small roof. Reach jugs over the top to pull over. Abseil off trees.

The Puddingstone Cliff
OS Ref 597 423

An unusual place, with a brand of limestone similar in texture to Riglos in northern Spain (except that the 'puddings' sometimes leap out at you from their matrix!) In one spot this 'rock' has been quarried and here it provides some good bouldering. There are also three routes which are as obscure as they come.

If you've travelled the A371 Wells to Shepton Mallet road, you may have noticed the crag up in the woods on the left (north), immediately beyond the village of Croscombe. To reach the crag, take the first left (Ham Lane) after Croscombe and park (considerably) at the top of the hill, in a pull-in on the left near a field gate. Walk back down the road 60 metres to a point where an old track runs right (west) into Yewtree Wood. Follow this track for 300 metres past a shack to the crag. The partially quarried section is about two-thirds of the way along (westwards). The crag is southwest-facing and extremely sheltered.

The best bouldering circuit is the combination of a low and mid-level traverse on the partially quarried section (excluding several accommodating holds) at about F8a. There are a number of vertical problems here providing good plyometric exercise. The low-level traverse on the crag down to the left is also worth checking out, but elsewhere, being a traditionalist helps! Ownership of the crag and any rights of way are unknown.

There are two headpoint-solos on the overhanging and partially quarried section of the crag. Both provide powerful climbing, though their landing-site could be a lot better.

Scream Pudding   8 metres   E5 6a †   (1.2.03)
Immediately right of the black rock use a pocket and a layaway high on the left to get started. Gain fingerholds in the obvious little niche, and continue on positive holds to grab a small but solid tree. Scramble out.

Bleak Pudding   8 metres   E5 6a †   (1.2.03)
A metre right, launch up from a flat hand-hold at 2½ metres until, at 6 metres, you're left trying to decide whether to chance lurching onto the rotted tree on the right or swinging left onto *Scream Pudding*. Go for the latter: use holds above a bulge to traverse strenuously left to better holds and the tree on *Scream*…

The only other route climbs the tallest and steepest part of the cliff 25 metres to the right.

Life with Nancy Camel   10 metres   E3 5c †   (1.2.03)
Quite good climbing, surprisingly, but the ivy capping requires a pre-fixed rope. Start at a large tree and beneath a vague pillar under two huge puddingstones projecting from the face.
Climb very steeply up the pillar, and then swing left onto the puddings. Pockets above lead to a good hold beneath the ivy and the rope.

Binegar Quarry

'Quarries are once again the focus of attention. Mendip abounds with them and the future potential is vast...'
(Richard Broomhead, 1984)

Those who become closer acquainted with the vast acreage of rock in this little known quarry will soon understand why it is much better known for its illegal raves than its slightly less illegal climbing.

To approach the quarry from the Bristol direction, turn right from the A37 Shepton Mallet road at Gurney Slade towards Binegar. Take the first left and at a sharp left-hand bend park at the quarry entrance on the right.

Take a hike into the extreme far right (north-west) bay of the quarry; look left, and – between tottering walls of rubble – identify a clean grey face that shows some promise.

One Bullet 15 metres E4 6b † (9.6.99)
Start up a grass bank, below the centre of the face.
Scramble onto a solid ledge of blocks. Move up to an undercut pocket and make a very hard move immediately left of a pale streak to a break and a good vertical slot above. Continue much more easily (threads) on rock that's not altogether unpleasant. Belay on saplings 20 metres back.

The following two routes are to the right, where there is a brown wall split by an obvious crack.

Lithium Freedom 10 metres Very Severe 4b † (12.10.02)
Climb the slabby groove to the left of the brown wall and finish up the short layback crack.

Los Americas 10 metres Very Severe 4c † (12.10.02)
Follow the obvious crack splitting the centre of the brown wall. Pre-placed sling recommended on tree to protect top-out.

Ashwick Grove

An alternative venue for the local explorer, this is a tucked-away collection of small limestone crags in an attractive wooded valley near Oakhill, north of Shepton Mallet. Ownership is unknown, but a well-used public footpath runs along the bed of the valley.

The **approach** is straightforward and is achieved by a ten-minute stroll from the A367 Bath to Shepton Mallet road just north of Oakhill. Park in a lay-by on the east side of the road half a kilometre north of the cross-roads in Oakhill. Walk north along the road for 100 metres to a signposted public

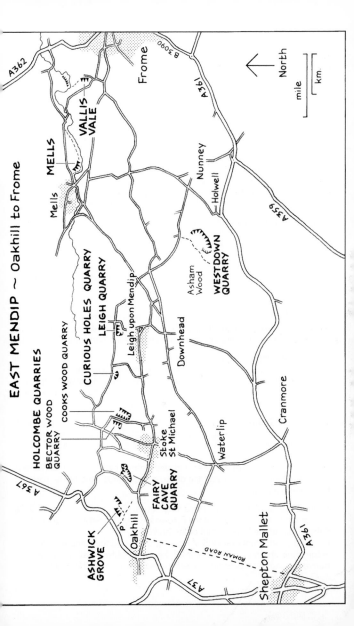

EAST MENDIP ~ Oakhill to Frome

footpath on the right. Follow the path across a field to the wooded edge of the valley. Go over a stile, descend the path to the valley floor, and turn left. The three craglets are within 500 metres of each other.

Raven Rock (The Nose)

Several hundred metres beyond the point at which the path alongside the stream is reached, the first craglet is encountered. It is anthropomorphized by a prominent nose which overhangs the path. A line of old bolts stubs up the front of the overhanging nose belongs to cavers.

Nasal Symphony   10 metres   E2 5b †   (11.4.96)
The left arête of the Nose. Grapple with an easy but leafy groove leading up the nose. Climb the left arête; then swing spectacularly along a series of jugs across the front of the Nose to finish up its right arête.

Paco Robanne   10 metres   E1 6b †   (11.4.96)
The right arête of the Nose hosts the Grove's hardest move.
Start up the right-hand and cleaner of the two grooves. Use the pinnacle on the right (*in-situ* thread) to place some good small wires in the face right of the arête; then descend to do battle. From the obvious undercut, take the arête to the top – simple once done (and so safe it's virtually a top rope).

Oakhill Pyramid

About 100 metres beyond The Nose, a crag should become visible through the trees, high up on the left (north) of the valley. This is the best crag in the valley, a 14-metre pyramid of solid, compact rock embellished with incut flake holds.

Tyson   14 metres   E3 6a †   (11.4.96)
A bit of a brute. Start just left of the lowest point of the buttress.
Gain a sloping shelf at 4 metres. Looming above is a big bulge; improvise straight over this immediately right of a short wide crack and pull over onto a ledge (with crevasse!). Finish up the juggy arête.

★★Stretch the Truth   14 metres   E2 6a   (6.3.96)
A pocket gem; well worth the drive from Bristol. This takes the left arête of the Pyramid on superb rock with plentiful protection. Start just left of the lowest point of the buttress.
Gain a sloping shelf at 4 metres and step right to below the arête. Make a steep and trying move to start the arête, and continue up a flake-crack in the arête to the top.

Period Piece   14 metres   Hard Very Severe 5b   (6.3.96)
The centre of the front face of the Pyramid; delightful climbing on incut flakes. Start at the lowest point of the buttress.
Go up a short, blunt arête left of easier ground and then step right to a ledge beneath an obvious small roof. Reach a rightward-slanting crack above the roof by a delicate move. Proceed to a small niche and finish easily to the top.

Weir Wall

A little further down the valley is a weir. One hundred metres further downstream on the right is a 10-metre grey wall not far above the path.

Groove of Relics   10 metres   E2 5b/c †   (10.4.96)
The distinctive left-to-right rising groove. Some objes d'art (actually three rusting pegs) are of historical interest only.
Follow the groove (useful flake on the overhanging left wall) and pass around a bulge to foot-ledges. Continue up the groove, making an exciting pull through the roof on jugs to a large tree.

The Weiring Way   9 metres   E2 6a   (10.4.96)
Small and hard. Start 2 metres right of a mossy scoop that leads up to the overlap.
From an undercut flake, extend for a fine, thin flake in the grey wall. Move right to pockets and an *in-situ* thread, and step up to finish up juggy rock. It is possible to rock straight up the blank grey scoop at definitive 6b.

Fairy Cave Quarry   OS Ref 656 476

Fairy Cave Quarry is a large limestone quarry which features a selection of very good quality 40- to 45-metre-high slabs, reminiscent of North Wales Slate. The slabs are natural limestone bedding planes which have been exposed by quarrying, giving an excellent solid climbing medium free of *in-situ* equipment. The quarry is very quick drying and whilst the main areas face north, they get the sun from May to August. There is also an assortment of areas facing west and east. Fairy Cave Quarry is an important addition to the climbing stock of the area. It is also known amongst cavers for containing some of the best-decorated caves on Mendip. These can only be acccessed on an approved leader system; contact a local caving club if interested.

Access: Following a long-term ban on access to the caves in the quarry, the owners, Hobbs, now appear to have relaxed their position in respect of both caving and climbing. Currently these activities appear to be tolerated.

Approach. The quarry is situated to the east of a small lane between Stoke St Michael/Oakhill and Holcombe, one and half kilometres west of the Holcombe Quarries. Fairy Cave is clearly marked on Ordnance Survey maps. There is road-side parking for four or five cars; be careful to pull in close to the verge as the lane is used by large animal feed lorries during the week.

After walking through the entrance 'zawn' the quarry is split into two main areas, east and west. The East End is on the far left as you enter the Quarry. The main feature of the East End is the large Rob's Slab with its distinctive line of stepped overlaps. The majority of routes are in the West End of the quarry

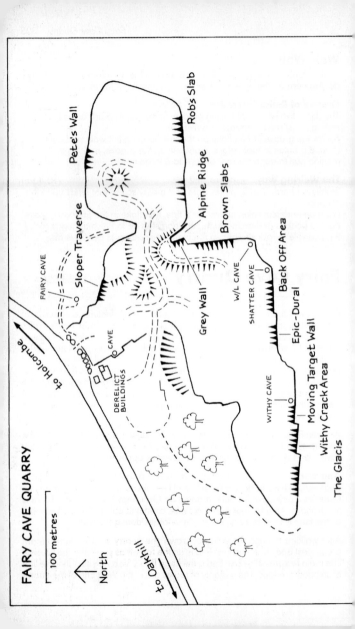

Balch's Slide (HS), Fairy Cave Quarry
Climber: Richard Nadin   Photo: Mike Raine

On a Mission (F6c),
The Holcombe Quarries
Climber: Lucy Creamer
Photo: Tim Glasby

Head Intrinseca (F7b+),
The Holcombe Quarries
Climber: Francis Haden
Photo: Tim Glasby

to the far right as you enter. The West End features several large areas of steep slabs identified by distinctive cave entrances along their bases.

Descents:
1. Follow the rim of the quarry in either direction back to the quarry entrance.
2. Descend the scree shoot at the West End of the quarry (not recommended in rock shoes)
3. Descend the Alpine Ridge between the East and West Ends. It is narrow in parts – take care on windy or damp days.
4. It is possible to abseil from trees in one or two places.

On the left side of the entrance 'zawn' is a short undercut arête: quite a contrast to everything else on offer in the quarry.

Rub-a-tyre 6 metres E1 6b †   (27.6.02)
Make either a dynamic or a powerful long move up the initial leaning wall to a large sloper left of the arête. Use the arête to climb its left-hand side and finish with ease above a suspect block in the break. (Using a crash mat erases the E-grade.)

About 100 metres into the entrance 'zawn' is a good traverse on slopers, located on a low orange wall on the left. It is very useful for 'pumping out' after a day on the slabs.

The East End
Rob's Slab
This is the largest slab in the East End, identified by a diagonal stepped overlap which interrupts its right-hand side and an obvious crackline which curves to the right high up, the line of *Rob's Crack*. All the climbs here belay on a choice of stakes above the slab.

Smell the Glove   42 metres   E1 5a/b   (6.4.02)
Start below a blast-shattered alcove. Pad directly up into the alcove. Climb above the alcove towards the corner; as you near the corner veer right and step up to where you can make a delicate traverse right into *Rob's Crack*. Climb *Rob's Crack* for about 5 metres and then continue direct to the top instead of curving right past the sapling.

★★**Stepping Out**   50 metres   E3 5c   (27.4.02)
Pure in conception, complex in description, yet delightful in pursuit. A bold start leads to brilliant thin slab climbing on a rising line across the slab. Start below the blank rock between *Smell the Glove* and *Rob's Crack*. Climb the blank slab to a good handhold at four metres and continue through a steeper area to a concretion. Gain a standing position on the concretion and traverse rightwards across *Rob's Crack* before moving up on thin holds (the crux of *Four Steps to Heaven*) to a thin horizontal crack.

Follow the crack rightwards to a good horizontal break (on *Volume Eleven*), step right again, and climb the line of concretions to the top.

★★Rob's Crack   42 metres   Very Severe 4c   (1993)
A magnificent route and one of the best at this grade in the region, which climbs the crack in the slab. Start below the rib where the overlap meets the ground.
Climb the left-hand side of the rib to reach a startling crackline. Follow the crackline all the way to the top. It bends to the right past a small sapling near the top.

★★Four Steps to Heaven   42 metres   E3 5c   (13.4.02)
Brilliant climbing up the steep slab right of *Rob's Crack*.
Climb *Rob's Crack* for 6 metres and then step right to a good foothold on the arête. Climb up to a 'pancake' and then climb directly for 15 metres (thin) to a good horizontal break. Step right and continue to the top on good holds.

★★Volume Eleven   35 metres   E3 5c   (4.4.02)
Another great route. Ten metres to the right of *Rob's Crack* a thin crack can be seen in the upper slab rising from the overlap: this is the line of the route. Start on top of the blocks below the overlap. Climb diagonally leftwards across the slab to a corner. Bridge up the corner to a jug on top of a wedged block. Make demon moves leftwards, which involve a tricky hand change on a pinch grip to reach a good hold on the edge of the slab. Rock over onto the slab and follow the line of the thin crack, with continued interest, to the top.

☆Seven-mile Throb   30 metres   E5 6b †   (30.6.02)
With unusually powerful climbing for the quarry, this route tackles the stepped roof-stack beneath the right-hand side of the slab. Small cams provide vital protection on the roofs. From the top of the blocks, climb the easy slab to the roofs, where a jug precedes some great moves on slopers, pinches, and layaways. Once the roofs are conquered, step up onto the slab, and move up and immediately right to the base of a line of concretions. Follow the concretions to the top.

To the right of Rob's Slab is a large broken slab. Most of the rock on this slab is loose and unpleasant but at its left-hand end is an area of better rock with two overlaps near its base.

Demon Moves Mike   30 metres   E4 5c †   (25.6.02)
Cool climbing up the blank-looking slab. Scramble up to a hole at the left-hand side of the upper overlap. Step right and tiptoe over the overlap to gain a near-perfect nut-slot. Boldly take a line of smears and slopers above to a horizontal break after 7 metres. Follow an inclined line of footholds rightwards to join *Life in Limbo*, which leads to the top.

Life in Limbo   40 metres   Very Severe 4c †   (4.5.02)
Start below the left-hand slab. There is a crackline with a tree growing out
of it at about one-third height. Climb up below the overlaps on good rock
and step right into a shattered area. Precarious moves on shattered rock
lead to a back-and-foot position below the tree. Another move on
shattered holds leads to the welcome solidity of the tree. Follow the crack
above the tree to the top. Belay on stakes.

Who Needs Hair Anyway?   40 metres   Very Difficult †   (30.9.02)
Start 10 metres right of *Life in Limbo*. Run out at the top, and 'a tad
chossy'. Climb the long shothole with a crack in it. Move rightwards round
the roof at the top. Belay on stakes.

Left of *The Alpine Ridge*, which marks the boundary of the East End, is a
confined set of slabs with stepped overhangs on their right.

Don't Even Breathe   25 metres   XS 5a †   (30.6.02)
A reasonable line lures one to a 'God, what am I doing?' climax,
negotiating twenty tons of hanging blocks. Start from the top of a pointed
block below the stepped overhangs. Climb the right-hand of two cracks
into a left-facing corner. Take the left wall of the corner to its close; at this
point you will notice that the entire capping left-hand arête is supported by
a delicate bridge of rock which you must now pass. Pass the bridge and
escape right as fast as you can. A loose, though straightforward, slope
leads to belays.

The West End
To aid the description of this area the three prominent cave entrances are
used. These are the piles of rubble with concrete tubes housing locked gates
within them. The left-hand cave is W/L Cave, the central one is Shatter Cave,
whilst the right-hand one is Withyhill Cave.

W/L Cave Area
This area is dominated by a large brown west-facing slab and a broken
north-facing area of dark grey rock above the cave entrance. At the
left-hand side of the W/L Cave area is a small area of good quality light grey
rock (the foot of *The Alpine Ridge*).

The Alpine Ridge   100 metres PD
This is the narrow ridge which separates the East and West Ends

Short Back and Sides   10 metres   Severe 4a   (7.4.02)
Start at the very left-hand end of the good grey wall. Climb for four metres
to the bulge, traverse right to a small tree, and continue up to a larger
tree.

Odd Boots   8 metres   E1 5b   (29.6.02)
Climb the left-hand side of the good grey wall on small holds.

Back in Kansas   10 metres   Severe   4a   (7.4.02)
Start below the largest tree and a crackline. Follow the crack, climb over a
small overhang, and continue to the tree.

Back to Sandy Lane   20 metres   Very Difficult †   (7.4.02)
Start below a vertical sandy weakness to the right of the good quality grey
rock. Climb the sandy break until it is possible to step right to a tree. Climb
good quality grey rock above the tree to the top.

Little Steve's Mersey Tunnel Affair   20 metres   Hard Severe   4a   (8.4.02)
Start a metre right of *Back to Sandy Lane's* sandy break. Climb the wall to
a large undercut, and continue up the central thin crack to the top. Belay
anchor points are on the far side of the ridge.

Three metres to the right of the sandy break is a fine looking crack.

Cristel Wall   20 metres   Very Difficult   (1994)
Climb the crack and a large flake to the top.

To the right, the W/L area is characterised by brown rock and the slabs are
up to 45 metres high. Near the centre is a fine *Devil's Slide* type feature
which runs from bottom to top, the line of *Balch's Slide*. There is still some
looseness here and the routes are not well protected.

The Socialist   Hard Severe   45 metres   4a   (6.4.02)
Climb the broken groove immediately left of the fine *Devil's Slide* feature.

★**Balch's Slide**   45 metres   Hard Severe   4a   (1994)
Start where the smooth slab meets the ground, by an inconveniently
placed stake (quarryman's not climber's!). Climb the smooth slab as
directly as you can. Spaced protection, especially on the lower half.

The next route climbs the right-hand side of the *Devil's Slide* feature.

The Tory   45 metres   Very Severe   4a   (11.4.02)
Start at the cave entrance (Balch's Cave) immediately right of *Balch's Slide*.
Move up right, then back left across scree to climb a line parallel to *Balch's
Slide*; a glitzy crux is followed by some untrustworthiness.

On the left-hand side of the W/L cave entrance is another cave entrance in
the ground. It is covered with corrugated iron and boulders. It is not obvious
but this is Conning Tower Cave.

Ants in My Leg Loop   45 metres   Severe   (11.4.02)
Start below the rightmost continuous piece of rock on the brown slabs, on
the cave entrance mound. Bridge up to a tree, make some delicate moves
to gain a shallow groove just left of a hanging grassy rake, and follow this
line to the top. Poorly protected and still quite dirty.

Elephant's Back   45 metres   Severe   (7.4.02)
Climb the rounded rib feature at the right-hand end of the area of brown
slabs. Quite run out on the lower half.

The crag now swings to the right and is composed of north-facing dark grey rock.

The Conning Tower   45 metres   Severe †   (1993)
Climb the centre of the grey face via sundry cracks and ledges. Much loose rock.

At the right-hand side of the grey face is a fine grooved arête.

Back to Basics   50 metres   Very Difficult   (1993)
Climb the groove in the arête which runs the full height of the cliff on the right-hand side of the W/L Area. Clamber very carefully over stacked blocks to exit. Belay just below the top on a good thread, as cliff-top belays are a long, long way back.

Shatter Cave Area

Shatter Cave is entered by the central concrete pipe. Immediately above the cave entrance is a very smooth slab.

Backing Up   10 metres   Very Severe 4c   (24.4.02)
Start below the left-hand side of the slab on top of the cave entrance mound. Climb the slab a metre right of its left-bounding scruffy corner. At the overlap move right to the good tree and abseil off.

Back Off   10 metres   E2 5b   (27.3.02)
Start at the foot of a diagonal crack on the smoothest part of the slab. Climb straight up on smears to the first horizontal break (small runner in the break on your right). Continue straight up the apparently blank slab to join a crackline. Follow this to the overlap, where a rock-over gains the good tree. Abseil off.

Fifty metres right of the cave entrance is another smooth slab with distinctive cleaning scars. This slab, apart from a scruffy ledge at one-third height, stretches the full height of the cliff. Towards the left-hand side of this slab is a distinctive crack. The top belay anchors for the following three routes are about 25 metres back from the edge, so either pre-place it or pull up one of your ropes.

Halfway to Kansas   45 metres   Hard Severe   (6.4.02)
1 20m. 4a. Climb the poorly protected crack on the left-hand side of the slab to a tree, and make a scruffy traverse rightwards to belay on a group of trees below the upper slab.
2 25m. 4a. Climb a diagonal crack across the upper slab to a tree, and follow a borehole directly to the top. This pitch is still quite dirty.

★**Lumbar Puncture**   45 metres   E2 5c   (11.4.02)
Climb the centre of the slab past a thin diagonal crack to the scruffy ledge. Climb a shallow scoop which trends rightwards (bold). Step back left and continue up the centre of the wall to the top, with the occasional diversion right or left to put slings round trees.

Epic-dural   45 metres   E2 5c   (30.3.02)
Start towards the right-hand side of the slab.
Fine thin slab climbing with small nut protection leads directly to the scruffy
ledge. Climb the diagonal crack for four metres before taking a line up the
right-hand side of the upper wall.

Twenty metres right of *Epic-dural* is a small slab with a tree located top
centre. The following two routes head for this tree, from which an abseil
descent is recommended.

Toblerone   9 metres   E2 5b   (25.6.02)
Start below and slightly left of the tree. Amble up to an undercut. Teeter
over onto a pitted slab, and continue to a second overlap. A jug above on
the triangular slab completes a short yet entertaining route.

Truffle   9 metres   Very Severe 4b   (25.6.02)
Climb the thin central crackline to the tree.

Om Puri   45 metres   Very Severe †   (26.9.02)
Start just right of the crack of *Truffle*, below a triangular niche.
1 20m. 4c. Climb straight up the slab to the lowest point of the top
overlap and continue directly to the large tree-covered ledge. Optional
abseil descent.
2 25m. 4c. A poorly-protected pitch which should prove unpopular.
Climb the centre of the cleanest looking slab, with some friable rock at
two-thirds height. Belay below the top on a tree to the left, or pull up a
rope to reach trees 20 metres back from the edge.

The right-hand side of the slab can be climbed anywhere at Severe
standard, and with a little more cleaning would provide good entertainment
for lower-grade climbers.

Withyhill Cave Area

The right-hand (westernmost) concrete pipe is the entrance to Withyhill
Cave. Three distinct climbing areas are close by. The full-height wall of
Moving Target, just to the right of the cave entrance, is identified by a high
hanging crack with a brown streak at its base, and is guarded by smooth
slabs. To the right is the *Withy Crack* area, with gentle slabs leading up to a
steep headwall. Further right are the smooth slabs of The Glacis.

The first climb starts on top of the Withyhill Cave entrance mound.

Standing on the Shoulders of Moles   20 metres   Very Difficult   (6.8.02)
Above the cave entrance is a slab divided by a rib. Climb the right-hand
side of the rib to some flakes. Continue to the rubble-strewn ledge and
tree belays. Abseil descent.

The *Moving Target* wall has a recess at its base with broken rock on either
side. Its left-hand side is delineated by a strong corner line.

Harman's Tree   45 metres   Severe 4a †   (1993)
Climb the left-hand corner; beware loose rock at the top of the corner.
Continue in the same line following a crack to the top.

★Cassini Division   45 metres   E5 6a   (7.4.02)
Start on the left-hand side of the recess below broken rock.
Climb the broken rock to three saplings. Thin moves lead up to good
cleaned breaks, where a step up right brings a chance to lace the face with
gear. Step up, then left, then straight up, boldly, to the overlap. Move
round the right-hand side of the overlap then up to a slanting crack with a
small sapling on the headwall. Climb this crack and finish directly past
black calcite pockets. Bold.

★★Moving Target   45 metres   E4 5c   (1990s)
The *Comes the Dervish* of The South, a bold and sustained lead. Start
directly below the hanging crack in the centre of the slab. Climb up and
make a tricky move past an overlap using a slanting crack, and continue
directly up the slab past good breaks to a very bold section. Thin moves
and a 'slate mantleshelf' take you to the upper wall, where the line of the
crack is followed with some intricacy.

The Darkened Room   45 metres   E3 5c †   (6.4.02)
Enter at your peril! Start below the right-hand side of the recess. Climb
clean rock to the right-hand end of the overlap and twin saplings. Step left
and climb a rightward-slanting crack to cleaned breaks. Step left and
arrange gear on *Moving Target*. Circuitous and bold moves now lead
right, up into a scoop, back left, and up to good holds below the small
overlap. Climb straight up to a sapling high on the headwall and finish
direct.
Variation E3 5c † (2002). Instead of making the circuitous moves
rightwards and then back left, go left to *Moving Target* and climb up
rightwards to gain large black calcite pockets (Friend 5). Continue above
the pockets until forced right to join the original line – if only to place some
runners!

First Up   45 metres   Severe 4a   (25.04.02)
Start towards the right-hand side of the wall. Climb loose broken ground
to the good trees. Climb diagonally right to a fine crack in the slab. Follow
this and continue above to the top.

To the right of the *Moving Target* wall is a distinctive orange overlap about 10
metres from the ground. Below the overlap is a solid slab with a loose corner
on its left.

Back in Business   45 metres   E1 5b †   (15.9.02)
Don't forget the micro-wires on this one. Climb the slab and corner to the
overlap. Pull over into a rightward-facing groove. Move up the groove and
step left onto the upper slab. Bold moves up the slab lead to a tree in a
crack (on *First Up*). Scramble over rubble-strewn ledges to the top.

The area around *Withy Crack* has gentle slabs leading to a steep headwall. The centre of the lower slabs are split by a large diagonal break with a flake crack in it. At about half height a grassy break runs across the face.

Senile Taff Corner   30 metres   E1 5a   (4.9.02)
The left-bounding corner of the *Withy Crack* area is worthwhile and mostly well protected. Start by scrambling up unpleasant ground to belay at the foot of the corner proper. Poor rock in the initial corner leads to a bulge. Work around into a solid corner above, and climb up to immediately beneath a heap of scrub on the right wall. Neatly step left onto a ledge on the arête, and follow easy thin cracks in a clean slab to rubble and a large tree at the top.

★★Withy Crack   40 metres   Hard Very Severe 5a   (1992)
This climbs the prominent crack with a tree growing from it at the left-hand side of the headwall. Start at a small tree by a loose area of rock 3 metres right of a corner. Climb straight up easy-angled slabs to the foot of the crack. The splendid crackline is then followed to the top of the wall

★Bad to the Bone   40 metres   E1 5b   (30.3.02)
A popular and delightful pitch. Start below a niche (cave entrance below) 6 metres from the left-hand side of the wall and at the base of the diagonal flake crack which splits the lower slabs. Move up and then step left across the sentry box. Climb up the gentle slab past two saplings. At the third sapling the wall steepens. Follow a thin crack and then make good moves up a series of pockets and the fine wall above. Finish by following *Withy Crack* to the top.

Boner   40 metres   E3 5c †   (7.7.02)
This route climbs the upper wall to the right of *Bad to the Bone* and to the left of the large loose orange break. Start up *Bad to the Bone* and from its third sapling, where the wall steepens, climb up to a deep break. A bold section now leads to a horizontal slot. Step right and then trend slightly leftwards up the technical face, with hard moves to gain a good small ledge up to the left. Trend leftwards to avoid hanging blocks and exit as for *Bad to the Bone*.

★Four Paw Drive   45 metres   E3   (13.4.02)
Steep technical climbing on the headwall. Start below the lower slab with a flake and black cord on its left.
1 25m. 4c. Scramble over loose ground and climb straight up the middle of the slab, pleasant but not really protected, to the overlap. Step left, go through the overlap stepping right, and move up to belay on trees on the grassy ledge.
2 20m. 6a. Climb the thin leftward-slanting crack to the large brown pockets. Finish direct.
Variation
2a The Hillwithy Connection 15m. E1 5a † (4.6.02). A serious pitch. From a point midway between the two belay trees, climb up to a

good horizontal crack. Follow positive holds above to a slanting crack high on the wall. Move slightly right to exit past a good pocket. Don't fall off!

★**Bramble Whine**   45 metres   Hard Very Severe   (10.4.02)
The first pitch of this route is a 'twig-up', the nearest thing to a sport route in Fairy Cave Quarry. Start at the right-hand side of the *Withy Crack* area, below the lowest tongue of rock. The line of the climb is delineated by a sapling then four trees, the last of which is a hawthorn. Take normal gear for pitch 2!
1 30m. 4b. Climb broken rock to a sapling, and go up a slab to the first of the trees. Follow the line of trees to just below the hawthorn. Step left to belay.
2 15m. 5a. Move up to the right and climb the leftmost of the cracks in the headwall.

☆**The Mutant**   30 metres   E4 6a †   (17.9.02)
This strange beast lurks on the overhanging retaining wall at the end of the *Withy Crack* area, overlooking The Glacis. It does not belong here! The diagonal finger-crack is painfully obvious to see and brutal to climb.
Climb a broken slab to gain the crack by swinging round a bulging arête onto the overhanging face. Fight your way up the vicious crack for 8 metres, where a comfortable hand jam provides a good shake-out. Take a vertical flake crack to a lovely slab, and belay on a small but sturdy hawthorn. Either finish easily up the blocky arête above or descend by abseil.

The Glacis is an area of superb slabs, which looks like something left behind by a glacier rather than quarrymen. It provides a number of fine, technical pitches on near perfect rock. There are two main slabs split by a grassy rake which runs diagonally up from left to right and provides a convenient, though precarious descent for several climbs.

Three routes on the left-hand side of The Glacis (*Peanuts*, *Pueblo*, and *Ash Tree Wall*) finish below the top of the crag proper. To **descend**, a sturdy ash tree in the brambles is used as an abseil point. All the other routes finish at the top of the crag, and paths are forming where they top out. Care will be required if the grass is at all wet.

Peanuts   15 metres   Hard Very Severe 5a   (2.6.02)
A short problem at the extreme left-hand end of the left-hand slab. A prominent feature of the slab is a rising diagonal crack running from left to right. Start from a solution hollow just left of its foot.
Climb straight up the smooth slab to gain a shallow curving ramp with good holds at its top. Follow easy rock up rightwards to an ash tree amongst the brambles. Abseil descent.

Pueblo   15 metres   Very Difficult   (1.6.02)
Start at the foot of the diagonal crack. Climb straight up the slab past a small ash tree to the top. Abseil descent from the large ash tree in the scrub above the slab.

Fairy Cave Quarry
The Glacis

1	Peanuts	HVS
2	Lunar Landscape	VS
3	Pueblo	VD
4	Ash Tree Wall	VS
5	Caveman	VS
6	Jiggery Pokery	VS
7	Glacial Point	E4
8	Slight of Hand	E2
9	Lorna's Lunch	S
10	Pocket Polka	S
11	Jive Talkin'	E2
12	Minute Waltz	VD
13	Strictly Ballroom	E1

★Lunar Landscape 35 metres Very Severe 4b (1.6.02)
Climb the crackline rising from left to right across the slab.

Ash Tree Wall 20 metres Very Severe 4c (14.4.02)
Lovely climbing, despite being very escapable. Start just left of the lowest
point of the left-hand slab. Climb up to join the diagonal crack of *Lunar
Landscape*. Step up left and, with your blinkers on, climb straight up
between the two small ash trees which grow on the slab. Scramble up
through brambles to a tree belay and an abseil descent.

★Caveman 25 metres Very Severe 5a (24.4.02)
Climb the thin crack just right of the lowest point of the left-hand slab to
gain a ramp leading rightwards to a sapling. Climb straight up from the
sapling to gain a rightward-trending crack and follow it to the top.

★Jiggery Pokery 25 metres Very Severe 5a (19.4.02)
Climb the gnarled slab just right of the previous route to the
rightward-trending ramp. Continue more or less straight up to gain a
flowstone runnel which is followed to the top. Scramble up through
brambles to a tree belay and an abseil descent.

★★Glacial Point 25 metres E4 5c (12.6.02/27.6.02)
A hard crux precedes a bold runout. Escapable but superbly technical; the
best of the climbs on The Glacis. Start below an obvious hairline crack, just
left of the foot of the grassy ramp.
Climb the slab just left of the crack until the crack vanishes at 8 metres.
Climb up slightly rightwards to an overlap and pull boldly up left to gain
the crack of *Caveman*. Step left into the centre of the smooth slab and
climb more or less straight up to the top.
Variation
Probably the best solution if soloing. From the overlap, take a series of
layaways slightly right to reach a good fingerslot overhead. Step up and
right to the finishing crack of *Slight of Hand*.

★Slight of Hand 25 metres E2 5c (14.4.02)
From the foot of the grassy ramp, climb up to a distinct horizontal crack.
Smear unnervingly up the vague, shallow groove above to a good but
hidden slot slightly to the left. Step up right to gain an easy crack leading
to the top.

Lorna's Lunch 25 metres Severe (27.6.02)
From the small tree at the foot of the grassy ramp, climb straight up the
slab via a series of discontinuous cracks.

★Real Men Do Eat Quiche 25 metres Hard Severe 4b (4.7.02)
Follow *Lorna's Lunch* to the small sapling. From here, make a long stride
rightwards and climb the next crack system to the top.

Pocket Polka   20 metres   Severe 4a   (24.4.02)
Start 4 metres right of the grassy ramp. Climb the flakes until pocketed
cracks lead diagonally rightwards to a shattered blast pocket. Finish
directly above. Alternatively, from the flakes, climb straight up to the small
trees above the slab (VS 4c).

★Jive Talkin'   18 metres   E2 5b   (24.4.02)
An edgy little number. Start directly below the obvious block which
overhangs the left-hand side of the right-hand slab.
Climb the thin slab to good holds where it steepens. Move up slightly
rightwards and then back leftwards to finish at tree belays.

Minute Waltz   20 metres   Very Difficult   (30.3.02)
The prominent water-worn runnel in the centre of the right-hand slab is
followed for 10 metres. Here, a move to the right gains a black flowstone
runnel, which is followed to the top.

★Strictly Ballroom   25 metres   E1 5b   (1.6.02)
From the lowest point of the right-hand slab, climb straight up past a blast
pocket. Follow the thin seam in the slab above to a good ledge with an
ash tree. Climb the shallow curving groove above the left-hand end of the
ledge for a stimulating finish.

Rocket   15 metres   Very Severe 4c   (1.2.02)
The lower of the two isolated slabs at the right end of the glacis gives a
worthwhile pitch. Climb boldly up the centre of the slab to gain a
leftward-trending crack. Follow this until a further crack leads back
rightward; take this to a short corner. Finish up the slab on the left. Tree
belay in the alcove above. Abseil descent.

All the while you were climbing you must have been casting backward
glances over your shoulder at the large east-facing cream-coloured wall to
the right of the big scree shoot. This is home to the following adventurous
number.

Pocket Piranha   25 metres   E6 6b †   (7.7.02)
Hard, but that's not the problem: make it through the 6b section and
some cautious climbing on dangerous rock awaits. Start by scrambling up
to beneath the centre of the wall.
Climb solid calcite flows onto the white wall past a diagonal break.
Finger-traverse right for a metre; then make snappy moves past a pocket
over a bulge to larger holds. Move up to a hanging diagonal crack in a
bulge. Work carefully left and then back right to a rubble tunnel
(dangerous), which leads to the top of the huge hanging angular block
near the top. A short earthy wall leads to the top – if you're lucky!

The Holcombe Quarries   OS Ref 670 478

The Holcombe quarries are two large limestone quarries whose entrances are situated a mile from the village of Stoke St Michael in the southern half of the Mendip hills.

Cooks Wood Quarry (a.k.a. Holcombe One) is well known locally as a diving location and a swimming venue, thanks to the extensive lake in its base. For climbers, the added bonus is that, although the bulk of the climbing faces north, most of the crag does not suffer seepage and dries quickly after rain.

The quarry regularly draws crowds of youths in summer who came to party, swim, and cliff jump. Its popularity, however, has also attracted car thieves, so leaving anything valuable (like windows or wheels!) has became inadvisable, so much so that the regular climbers park in the village and walk.

Access: In 2003, two people using the lake had accidents, one of which was fatal. Security was tightened up as a result. There is no formal permission to climb here; be prepared to be asked to leave.

Bector Wood Quarry (a.k.a. Holcombe Two) is quite the opposite of Cooks Wood Quarry. Dry as a bone and (apart from the odd motorbike enthusiast) hardly a soul about. The climbing area here has a westerly aspect with the sun on all the routes during the afternoon and evening – thereby permitting a fairly casual approach to your climbing day. The quarry is slow to dry during winter months.

To members of the caving community, the area is probably better known as the location of Stoke Lane Slocker, one of Mendip's more distinctive wet caves. A good path runs from near the rear of Bector Wood Quarry along the valley bottom and passes the cave entrance where a stream is met; continue along the path and one soon enters the village of Stoke St Michael via a back route; a useful short-cut to the crag.

Approach: To get there grab your roadmap and start following the A37 south from Bristol until you come to where the B3135 heads off to Cheddar. You will now be outside The Mendip Inn. Follow the A37 a mile further and take a hairpin left turn (signposted Bath A367). Half a mile down this road is the Oakhill Inn (in the village of Oakhill). Turn right at this pub and continue for two miles to reach the Knatchbull Arms (good après-crag drinking) in Stoke St Michael.

Fifty metres past the Knatchbull Arms turn left (signposted Leigh-Upon-Mendip 2m / Frome 7¾m) and then after a third of a mile turn left again (signposted Edford 1½m / Holcombe 2m). Travel this road for two-thirds of a mile to where large limestone blocks on the left guard the entrance to Bector Wood Quarry. Directly opposite, a substantial fence attempts to prevent access to Cooks Wood Quarry.

Cooks Wood Quarry
The Left-hand Side

1	Canadian Girls Kick Ass	F6a+
2	The Incredible Holcombe	F6c
3	The Fantastic Four	F6b
4	Old School Reunion	F6a+

The Back Wall

5	Standby, Standby	F6b
6	Farewell to Old Times	F5
7	Smoking Gun	F6a+

Cooks Wood Quarry

A mixture of traditional climbing and (mostly) sport climbing is found here. A good spot for some stress-free climbing at a more amenable standard than Bector Wood Quarry.

The first view upon entering the quarry is of a large expanse of fresh water, which dominates the centre of the quarry. The climbs are described as one walks clockwise around the lake.

The Left-Hand Side

The first (solid) feature encountered is a steep and dusty slab. Although not encouraging to look at, it has produced one of the more technically interesting pitches in the quarry.

Stick to Liquid   17 metres   E4 6b/c F7a+   (12.6.00)
Technical, insecure, and fingery climbing on an unusually sculptured piece of rock. Six bolts. Start at the left-hand side of the slab, high up on the sloping grassy bank.
Step up and make a difficult traverse rightwards to gain a tentative bridging position beneath the second bolt. Now scrabble hard and frantically grab whatever you can to pull up to a welcome rest. Continually absorbing climbing above only relents at the three-quarter-height ledge, whereupon easy moves finish the pitch at a twin-bolt abseil station.

Shothole City

8	Fit for the Future	F5−
9	Bomb the Base	F4+
10	Lego Man	F3+
11	Wide-eyed in Seattle	F4

The Right-hand Side

12	Haven't Got a Clue	F6c
13	Fracture Science	F6a
14	Swinging in the Breeze	F4
15	Bolting Blues	F4

Variation

Stick to the Right   17 metres   E3 6a F6c   (12.6.00)
A right-hand variant, avoiding the hard and precarious start. The
difficulties depend on how early a step left is made onto the parent route.
Start beneath twin parallel cracks in the centre of the steep slab. Ascend
the dirty cracks past a bolt until it is possible to step left and join *Stick to
Liquid* at its second bolt. The remainder of the pitch gives enjoyable
technical climbing.

Seventeen metres further along, a much broader and cleaner sweep of
slabby wall grabs your attention, and in particular its four sport routes. The
left two sport routes share a common start and a common first bolt.

The left side of the wall is bounded by a loose-looking groove. Immediately
next to this is a curving line of six bolts telling you in no uncertain terms that…

★Canadian Girls Kick Ass   17 metres   E2 5b F6a+   (1.7.01)
An absorbing and fairly sustained pitch offering some technical play
interspersed with good rests.
Intricate climbing straight up for four metres is followed by the crux, moving
diagonally left past the second bolt to big holds and a rest atop an open
groove (the original line of the route). Now continue up, with good edges
and surprising holds appearing all the way, until you reach a twin-bolt abseil
station positioned in the top left-hand corner of the slabby wall.

★The Incredible Holcombe   17 metres   E3 6a F6c   (6/7.94)
Some excellent technical climbing that attacks the compelling, central section of the slab. High in its grade. Six bolts. Start as for *Canadian Girls Kick Ass*. Climb directly up to the third bolt, step right, and layback the thin flake's edge to reach better holds. Make further hard moves straight up (crux), step right to jugs, and enjoy the relaxing finish. Twin-bolt abseil station.

The next route climbs the thin vertical crack on the right-hand side of the wall, situated just left of a much more obvious wide crack.

★★The Fantastic Four   17 metres   E2/3 5c F6b   (6/7.94)
Beautifully sustained climbing up the thin, vertical crack. Start beneath the obvious wide crackline. Six bolts.
Scramble up diagonally left and get established by the second bolt at the base of the thin crack. Launch into the opening moves and become fully absorbed until the difficulties relent and one can clip the twin-bolt abseil station. A challenging pitch!

The Thing   20 metres   Hard Very Severe 5b   (6/7.94)
This climbs the obvious wide crackline near the right arête to the top of the crag. Bolt belay in a large block above.

★Old School Reunion   17 metres   E1 5c F6a+   (3.11.99)
The right-hand arête of the slabby wall. A good pitch with some well-positioned climbing. Seven bolts.
Straightforward climbing directly up the arête is rudely interrupted at the third bolt by the insecure crux, a high rock-over move to grasp better holds. A fun, airy finish leads to a twin-bolt abseil station.

To the right of *Old School Reunion* are four closely-packed arêtes in various states of instability. The second arête from the left appears to be the best.

Not to Be Not Recommended   18 metres   E1 5a †   (3.6.01)
Starting from the right, follow the arête past two tricky moves, and finish up its left-hand side. (A good crack for wires runs most of the way up the arête.)

The Back Wall

This is the impressive-looking face situated on the left-hand side of the back wall of the quarry. When close up The Back Wall proves to be much less steep and indeed offers some very nice slab pitches. The Back Wall has three distinct sections. The left-hand section offers three narrow strips of good rock.

Water Babies   12 metres   E1 5b F6a   (4.9.96)
A short, rather odd pitch. Three bolts. Start at the foot of a dirty crack 4 metres left of a narrow left-facing corner. Keeping left of the crack, climb up and diagonally leftwards to a twin-bolt abseil station.

★Standby, Standby   15 metres   E2 5c F6b   (4.9.96)
Captivating slab climbing that forces a direct line up the blank strip immediately right of *Water Babies*. Five bolts.

Precarious initial moves soon lead to slightly better holds and the first bolt. Continue until a thoughtful crux (beneath a bush) brings a horizontal break within reach. From a standing position in the break, a final easy move reaches the twin-bolt abseil station.

★**Farewell to Old Times**   20 metres   Hard Very Severe 5a F5 (20.6.00)
An appealing route that takes the middle of the strip of slabs 4 metres to the right of *Standby, Standby*. Seven bolts.
Climb up a thin, vertical crack past the first bolt to a small footledge. Step right, make a careful second clip, and climb directly up the centre of the slab, only deviating slightly to the left at the fifth bolt. A final teasing move at the top horizontal break gains the chained twin-bolt abseil station above.

The more pronounced central section has a surfeit of unclimbed fractures, and on abseil the reason immediately becomes clear as the prospective new-router confronts the alarming gap that separates all of the front veneer from the mother lode. Good development potential here for lovers of transient climbs.

The third section of The Back Wall is the obvious, clean sheet of slab flawed by three thin cracks running up to an unstable overlap.

★**Smear No Fear**   18 metres   E2 5c   (14.7.96)
This climbs the less distinct left-hand crackline. A tough little cookie but well protected with wires and bolts. Start by scrambling a couple of metres up semi-stable material until it is possible to gain the slab proper.
Pass the initial bolt to reach a slanting nut-slot. Step up and left across the slab until it is possible to pursue a direct line past two further bolts to the half-height ledge. Progress up the finger-crack above goes surprisingly easily until the proverbial sting in the tail – in this case a wicked little mantel onto a small ledge. Step right to a twin-bolt abseil station.

The next route, the first to be climbed on The Back Wall, originally belayed on a pre-placed abseil rope; now you can opt to step left and belay as for *Smear No Fear* to avoid the loose top.

★**Flame On**   18 metres   E1/2 5b   (6/7.94)
The middle, and most conspicuous crackline on the slab proves to be amenable, enjoyable and mostly well protected – take plenty of cams. Start directly beneath the vertical central crack.
Pull onto the slab (bolt) and climb carefully up past several wire slots to reach the base of the vertical crack. Now 'plug in a unit' and away you go!

★**Smoking Gun**   18 metres   E1 5c F6a+   (14.7.96)
Choice, open slab-climbing, the trade route of the quarry. Five bolts. Start below the centre and barest part of the slab.
Scramble up leftwards (as for the previous routes) before stepping back right to a footledge and the first bolt. Move up to the slanting ledge above and reach up to clip the third bolt before having a good look at the meat

of the route above. Continue up the slab past an optional medium wire placement and two bolts to gleefully clip the twin-bolt abseil station.

★Crack Attack   18 metres   E2 5c   (14.7.96)
The third thin crackline is well worth your attention. Good natural protection throughout.
Climb *Smoking Gun* to below its first bolt and follow the short crack immediately on the right to the base of the slanting ledge-system. Step across to the base of the main crackline and fix plenty of good small wires before making a couple of technical moves to better holds above. Continue on improving holds until it is possible to stand up in a small scoop where the crack kinks right. Have a breather, step up, and trend leftwards to finish at the twin-bolt belay of *Smoking Gun*.

The last three routes on The Back Wall prove to be the least appetizing; they take the right-hand side of the slab.

Lifting   18 metres   E2 5b †   (26.4.01)
Start at the base of a leftward-rising ledge, 3 metres right of the tree growing out of the base of the slab.
Walk along the ledge (scary if wet) to a thin rightward-slanting crack. Climb the crack for 5 metres and place good small wires. Step up left above the crack, and move up to a better-defined crack. Continue to a tree below an overlap, place a sling, and abseil off.

Shifting   18 metres   E3 5b †   (26.4.01)
A very serious lead, with moving rock to boot. Requires two hand-placed knife-blade pegs for protection. Start as for *Lifting*.
Walk along the ledge for 2 metres to a line of weakness 3 metres from the right-hand arête. Step over a small overhang (peg not *in situ*) and carefully reach a fingerhold above (peg not *in situ*). Rock up, and cross a slanting crack before trending left to the tree belay of *Lifting*. Place a sling and abseil off.

Cool Pool Jump Rave   15 metres   E6 6b †   (3.6.01)
Intense footwork on micro-holds with good plummet potential.
Climb the slab a metre short of the right-hand edge until the holds run out (wire cluster, in-situ peg). Bear very slightly rightwards up a brown streak to a good fingerhold in a slanting break (in-situ peg). Mantel onto the hold and, from cleaned holds on the edge of the muddy ledge above, step up and climb carefully to a good tree above. Place a long sling and abseil off.

Shothole City

Continuing the clockwise crag tour, the next reliable area of rock one encounters is on the right-hand side of the back wall. It stretches across to the right-angled corner where the quarry wall changes direction. This wall is riddled with quarrymen's shothole cuts. These vertical boreholes provide plenty of new route action for the motivated; however, the best of the breed are probably the following six routes.

Drill and Blast, Drill and Bolt

15 metres   Very Severe   4b/c   F4+   (23.6.00)

A worthwhile addition on compact rock. Four bolts. Start at the left end of the shot-holed wall, at a point some 50 metres to the right of *Smoking Gun*. Scramble diagonally leftwards until below a left-facing groove. Climb a short slab past an orange streak to the base of a steep corner groove, which is climbed with conviction on good holds to a ledge on the right. From the next ledge above, step right to a twin-bolt abseil station.

Holebore   15 metres   Hard Very Severe   4c †   (24.4.01)

The tall borehole immediately left of *Fit for the Future* is unprotected as a lead but has become a popular top-rope exercise.

★Fit for the Future   15 metres   Very Severe   4c   F5-   (4.9.96)

An excellent, sustained, and well-protected pitch that is likely to see a lot of traffic. Start below a particularly distinctive shothole in good rock right of *Drill and Blast, Drill and Bolt*. Four bolts.

After the initial rock step, move up rightwards past the first bolt (crux) before making your way back leftwards towards the shothole. Follow its right side to a twin-bolt abseil station.

Bomb the Base   15 metres   Very Severe   4c   F4+   (8.9.00)

A good fun pitch located approximately 15 metres to the right of *Fit for the Future*. Start beneath the most prominent (scarred) groove system hereabouts. Four bolts.

Teeter up the groove and mantelshelf up onto the ledge on the right. Ignoring the groove, climb the rib to reach sloping ledges above. Continue directly up and finish at a twin-bolt abseil station in a slight bay.

★★Lego Man   15 metres   Severe   4a   F3+   (4.9.96)

Straightforward climbing, though at the top of its grade, with very good rock and stainless steel bolt protection. This, the easiest sport route in the region, will surely entice people to vacate the climbing walls and enjoy the fresh air. Start at the foot of a short wall containing a prominent shothole located approximately 7 metres to the left of the right-hand back corner of the quarry. Five bolts.

After some opening moves up the shothole, step right and continue on small ledges to gain a spacious ledge at the foot of the main slab. Follow the large shothole up the slab until it is possible to step left into a groove. Climb the groove and shothole above to a twin-bolt abseil station.

Wide-eyed in Seattle   20 metres   Hard Severe   4b   F4   (29.7.01)

Varied climbing up a broad rib on the outside (!) of a long shothole. High in its grade. A pleasant finish compensates for a touch of poor rock low down. Start at the right-hand back corner of the quarry. Six bolts.

Climb the corner to a patch of suspect rock beneath a roof (and take a look up inside the shothole). Ease up right around the roof (tricky) and climb delicately to a big ledge on the rib. With the difficulties over, romp up the wall above and enjoy the final moves to a twin-bolt abseil station.

The next two routes are in the broad gully that forms the right-hand back corner of the quarry.

Hip Joint Man   9 metres   E5 6a †   (3.6.01)
A line on the high-level slab right of *Lego Man*. A pair of tied-off garden shears was used for protection on the first ascent. Start by scrambling up the mobile scree in the back corner and belaying behind the large bush. With the aforementioned improvised protection in a borehole and a back-up wire in the corner, climb very thinly up the centre of the slab to a slot and *in-situ* peg. Continue straight up with interest and finish on 'crockery'. Fence belay behind (and a long walk back down!).

Science Friction   12 metres   E2 5c F6b   (8.9.00)
Unusually delicate and technical climbing on the smooth corner slab just right of the back corner. Five bolts.
Climb over a bulge and get established on the slab. Follow a curving leftward line involving some high steps and tricky smearing to reach better holds below the fifth bolt. Traverse left from holds above the bolt to meet a sloping foot-ledge and a twin-bolt abseil station.
Variation
Artless Pair   12 metres   E5 6a †   (27.4.01)
A bizarre headpoint solo with an awful landing.
Surmount the bulge as for *Science Friction*, traverse left along the lip, and climb straight up to the belay. Step left and scramble back down the gully.

The Right-Hand Side

To date, only one section of the right-hand flank has been climbed upon. To find it, carry on along the circular walk until you are back alongside the lake. Just over halfway along the lakeside, and 12 metres right of a chossy break in the cliff, lies a steep bed of very compact black rock (with several near vertical seams) – just the place to be if you...

★Haven't Got a Clue   12 metres   E3 6a F6c   (14.7.96)
A recommended pitch on good rock that offers some technical and interesting climbing with a blind crux. A good pitch, which is easier when chalked up! Five bolts. Start at the curving seams.
Climb fairly easily until the angle steepens at the second bolt. Move up using undercuts and side-pulls to pass the third bolt. From a good rest position above, traverse left under the small strip roof and pull back rightwards with difficulty to finish past the last bolt. Twin-bolt abseil station.

Fracture Science   12 metres   E1 5b F6a   (18.11.99)
A well frequented yet undistinguished pitch. Start 2 metres to the right of the previous route at two small drainage pipes protruding from the cliff at ground level. Five bolts.
Indifferent and brittle climbing on the slabby wall right of the pipes is only made worthwhile by a brief, technical crux to pass the fourth bolt. Twin-bolt abseil station.

To the right are two fairly prominent leftward-facing corners.

Swinging in the Breeze   20 metres   Very Severe 4b F4   (7.9.00)
Four spaced bolts. Optional small wires protect the run-out above the
ledge to the third bolt. Worth doing. Start 10 metres to the right of *Fracture
Science* at the foot of a yellow-stained corner line.
Ascend easily to the base of the corner, which is climbed with increasing
difficulty to a rightward exit onto a ledge. Step back left and pull over a
slight bulge to a twin-bolt abseil station just above.

Seven metres further to the right lies the second corner.

Bolting Blues   12 metres   Hard Severe 4b F4   (2.9.00)
Four bolts and some suspect rock. Fairly pleasant. Tackle the corner above
the starting ledge, with the crux at the top. Twin-bolt abseil station on the
large ledge above.

Thirty metres further on is a compact wall immediately to the right of a
projecting arête formed by a thin leaf of rock. The following two routes climb
the compact wall immediately right of the arête and share a chained
twin-bolt abseil station.

Jams and Cams Beat Fliers on Wires
                         12 metres   Hard Very Severe 4c (8.9.00)
Protectable, though the rock needs careful handling. Climb the shaly
crackline a metre right of the arête to the abseil station.
Variation
Don't Turn the Page   12 metres   E1 5a †   (2.5.01)
'Limestone pretending to be culm. Easy to read but hard to trust.' Starting
on the left, this climbs the widening crack formed by the leaf of rock. From
a ledge at the top, step right onto the parent route.

Policeman Watcheth   12 metres   E2 5b †   (2.5.01)
Climb the relatively solid wall 2 metres right of the arête via a thin crack to the
abseil station. Peace of mind commences with the first runner at 6 metres.

Bector Wood Quarry

This sport climbing crag offers a variety of both climbing styles and grades of
difficulty. The routes, apart from the first route and *A Family Affair*, are well
equipped, either with resined stainless steel staples or 10mm expansion
bolts. No run-outs on this crag!

From the roadside blocks, follow the main track downhill, past an old
explosives magazine on your right, to reach some large boulders blocking a
track on the left. Pass over these boulders and follow the left-hand track
around the corner to where the size of the quarry finally becomes apparent.
(Immediately visible in the distance, over to the right, is a 25-metre-high slab
– The Slab With No Name.) Walk to your left along the broad terrace until
you reach a rectangular blockhouse; the first route is behind it.

Bector Wood Quarry

1	Professor Smith's Warning	E4
2	Barefoot in the Quarry (at Night)	F4+
3	Crocker Free Zone	F5+
4	Retroactive	F5+
5	A Taste for Disorder	F6a+
6	Old Codger	F7a
7	Killer Instinct	F6c+
8	Execution	F7b+
9	Not Flocking	F6b
10	Easy and Slow	F6a

Professor Smith's Warning   8 metres   E4 6a †   (3.02)
Start next to a large brown boulder at the base of a short leaning arête. This point is 15 metres to the left of the next route. Climb the arête direct (*in-situ* thread) finishing at a sloping ledge.

A few more paces leave you standing beneath a steep buttress sporting a prominent (and sizeable) roof – this is The Ugly Buttress. Continue along the terrace to the base of an attractive arête where the terrace ends, and then tiptoe carefully across a narrow, exposed traverse to finish at a wide, rubble-strewn ledge at the base of an impressive leaning wall – The Intrinsica Walls.

The Ugly Buttress

An intimidating and steep buttress offering some power-packed climbing interspersed (unusually) with plenty of no-hands rests. The routes prove unexpectedly friendly despite their appearance. Get on it!

The following three routes climb an amorphous slabby wall to the left of the buttress.

Barefoot in the Quarry (at Night)

15 metres   Very Severe 4c F4+   (5.9.95)

A popular pitch due to its low grade but the climbing has little to recommend it (even in shoes). Start to the left of two saplings by a shothole at shoulder level. Five bolts.

Pull up on the shothole and step right onto a ledge. Surmount the slight bulge above to reach another ledge, and climb the wall above stepping out left to a twin-bolt abseil station at the top.

Crocker Free Zone   17 metres   Hard Very Severe 5b/c F5+   (5.9.95)

A straightforward though somewhat unsatisfying pitch featuring a single hard (and insecure!) move to surmount the first overlap. Start 4 metres to the left of the deep vertical cleft. Three bolts.

Climb easy rock to the roof and make a brisk pull over to better holds and a rest. Trend up rightwards to a strip roof and step over to the final slab and twin-bolt abseil station.

Retroactive 17 metres Hard Very Severe 5a/b F5+ (20.6.00)
This pitch is a bit of a filler-in yet proves surprisingly popular. Four bolts. Start beneath a distinctive leftward-facing flake situated by the base of the deep vertical cleft.
Climb the flake to a sloping ledge at 3 metres. Move up carefully and then make a difficult move over a tiny overhang to enter the short V-groove and a welcome respite at a sloping ledge up on the right. Finish diagonally left over the bulge above to reach the twin-bolt abseil station atop *Crocker Free Zone*.

The following two routes are worth particular note as they provide a useful way of putting up a top-rope in this rather tough neighbourhood. (Mind you, virtually all the routes hereabouts are fairly easily ascended 'bolt to bolt'.)

A Taste for Disorder 35 metres E2 5b F6a+ † (25.7.96)
An amenable sightseeing girdle of The Ugly Buttress, offering mostly straightforward climbing but with a single hard move. (Two ropes recommended.) Plenty of bolt runners.
Climb *Retroactive* to its fourth bolt. Step across the yawning gap to join the ramp of *Outside, It's America* (optional wires) and follow this for a few moves until it is possible to swing down rightwards to good holds. Traverse easily across to see the *Old Codger*, whereupon a somewhat disconcerting crux brings the belay ledge on *Killer Instinct* to hand. A perfect belay position, if required. Step right, move up to a break of sorts, and continue rightwards, to finish by pulling up on the final moves of *Confetti Train*.

Outside, It's America 12 metres Hard Very Severe 5c F6a (28.8.95)
A striking line following the appealing, diagonal ramp that slashes the left face of The Ugly Buttress. Sadly, the climbing is unbalanced; the initial crux roof is hard but is then followed by easy slab climbing. Entertaining nonetheless. Start 2 metres to the right of the deep vertical cleft that delineates the left side of the Buttress. Five bolts.
Pull up to the roof; then, with the comfort of close protection, make a tricky move onto the toe of the diagonal ramp. Amble pleasantly up the ramp to a twin-bolt abseil station shared with the next two routes.

The following four routes all start behind the large block just left of centre.

Take the Bull By Its Horns 20 metres E3 6a F6c (20.8.95)
The least demanding way of breaking through the line of roofs. Arm strength and a good grip are required. Five bolts.
Pull up to a small ledge and clip the first bolt (long sling advised). Step left and follow an easy groove to bucket holds and a stunted sapling beneath the big roof. Psyche up and then pull up to find blind holds; this is followed by an unexpected sit-down rest on the lip of the overhang. Finish more easily up a short wall to the communal abseil station.

★Old Codger 12 metres E4 6b F7a (3.9.95)
An uncompromising line through the largest section of roof on The Ugly Buttress. Abundant protection will undoubtedly ensure its test-piece popularity. A route where the old stagers can still show their worth! Seven bolts (plus *in-situ* sling on the fifth bolt).
Pull up to a small ledge and make a tricky move past the second bolt to a rest beneath the imposing ceiling. Swing optimistically out to the lip where a stiff pull (crux) should bring jugs and a welcome respite before the final bulge. There is a twin-bolt abseil station above that is shared with the previous two routes.

★Killer Instinct 20 metres E4 6a F6c+ (11.7.95)
Compelling climbing which proves both delicate and strenuous, technical and thuggy. Good rests and overhead protection will surely entice. Start behind the large block. Five bolts.
Pull up to a small ledge and tiptoe right to where a couple of sneaky hard moves gain a ledge and the third bolt. Mantel up rightwards into a squat rest position. Make a determined attack to surmount the intimidating roof to reach a comfy belay ledge and twin-bolt abseil station.

★Confetti Train 27 metres E3/4 6a F6c (24.7.95)
A varied and entertaining romp that takes a sweeping line across the main bulk of The Ugly Buttress. The route is strenuous, but with an ample supply of good holds. Take plenty of quickdraws and slings – eight bolts; this route has steel appeal! Two ropes recommended.
Climb *Old Codger* to the ceiling, and then traverse easily rightwards to further overhead protection in the roof of *Killer Instinct*. Follow the constricted ramp past *Closed Conspiracy* and swing across to grab buckets at the foot of the bulging crackline. Climb the crack to reach the sloping shelf above, and finish quickly rightwards to reach a twin-bolt abseil station.

★Closed Conspiracy 21 metres E5 6c F7b+ (13.7.95)
Sustained, absorbing climbing up the steepest part of the cliff, starting with a powerful opening move and culminating in a hard crux. Start 4 metres to the right of the large block at the foot of *Killer Instinct*. Six bolts.
Pull up on incuts to the first bolt, and make a body-wrenching move left to an undercut. Good holds arrive at the second bolt, permitting a quick shakeout before a sprint up the curving arête to a cramped rest beneath the roof. Reach out over the roof to poor sloping edges and make a powerful crank to better holds above. Continue easily up the short wall above to a twin-bolt abseil station on the lip of a bulge.

Execution 21 metres E6 6b F7b+ (10.96)
A powerful and vicious test-piece, 'mean and slappy', that forces a direct line up the leaning wall immediately right of *Closed Conspiracy* to join the upper section of *Confetti Train*. Six bolts. Start as for *Closed Conspiracy*. Step onto a ledge and bridge the short, bulging corner to better holds above. Pull up and commence a vigorous and precise series of moves

where the wall steepens. Dynamic efforts from a positive layaway gain jugs in the horizontal break of *Confetti Train*, where a more amenable crack leads to a sloping shelf and a twin-bolt abseil station up on the right (all as for *Confetti Train*).

Not Flocking   21 metres   E2 5b/c F6b   (25.7.95)
Cheesy but not easy! Despite its appearance and very unpleasant start the route has received (some) favorable comment. Four bolts. The right end of The Ugly Buttress is delineated by a vertical seam of gunge and rubble that also forms the left-hand side of the big arête of *Easy and Slow*. Start at the base of the seam.
Unlikely as it may seem, 'ascend' carefully but easily to a jug on the left arête (out-of-sight bolt). Swing around leftwards on more appetizing rock and enter the obvious crack. Now climb up, and continue diagonally left, until it is possible to surmount a final bulge (as for *Confetti Train*). Twin-bolt abseil station.

The Chill-Out Zone

The easier-angled middle section of the cliff sports arêtes and slabby walls; a welcome respite from the tough stuff although not sparkling in the quality department.

Easy and Slow   18 metres   E1 5b F6a   (24.7.95)
Pleasant, delicate climbing up the prominent arête to the right of The Ugly Buttress. Low in its grade. Five bolts.
Climb the initial part of the arête to easy ledges, and clip the third bolt with a long sling. Step up and left, and ascend the steep slab above, keeping on the left of the arête. Once standing upon a large foothold by the top, reach right to the twin-bolt abseil station shared with the next two routes.

Koto Globo   18 metres   E1 5b/c F6a   (22.7.95)
A worthwhile filler-in tackling the thin crack in the right-hand side of the prominent arête. Five bolts.
Some tricky starting moves (crux) gain a hand-ledge. Climb the crack (optional wires for the faint-hearted) to easy ground, and finish up the groove above, stepping up left onto the arête at its top to reach a twin-bolt abseil station shared with its neighbours.

Powder Monkey   18 metres   E2 5b F6a+   (13.7.95)
A useful addition at this grade. Start 3 metres to the right of the prominent arête. Five bolts and a long *in-situ* thread.
Somehow get off the ground (*in-situ* thread), and pull around the bulge above to good holds in the base of a crack. Continue up the slab and crack until moves over a small roof lead steeply to a big ledge. Climb the short wall above to reach the shared twin-bolt abseil station.

Hard and Fast   12 metres   Hard Very Severe 5b/c F5+   (5.9.95)
The slabby, rounded arête, a minor tit-bit for the technically inclined, has reportedly seen many failures. Three bolts.

Scramble easily up to a sloping shelf and then follow the arête above (interesting for a couple of moves) to reach a twin-bolt abseil station.

Mistress of Measurement   15 metres   E1 5c F6a+   (20.1.96)
A disconcertingly 'soft' pitch but no soft option! Requires gentle handling. Start midway between the arêtes of *Easy and Slow* and *Vicious Eyes*, in a slight bay on the right-hand side of the arête of *Hard and Fast*. Three bolts. Climb the slabby wall to a diagonal break, ease over the bulge above, and reach for bigger holds. Pull up and finish at a twin-bolt abseil station.

The Intrinsica Walls

The Intrinsica Walls comprise two leaning walls separated by a vertical cleft. The left-hand wall is heavily stratified and has a pock-marked surface. The angle proves deceptive, thereby ensuring that on most routes the crux is located near the top. The right-hand wall is the showpiece of the quarry; a seemingly bare sheet offering sustained, technical outings all topped with a glorious jug-ridden leaning headwall.

The broad terrace ends at the foot of an eye-catching arête (*Vicious Eyes*), where the ground falls away steeply to the base level of the quarry. A short, exposed, yet easy traverse beneath *On a Mission* and *Peck Deck* leads across to a broad, boulder-strewn ledge. Here meatier fare gets to grips with the quarry's main attraction.

★Vicious Eyes   15 metres   Very Severe 5a F5   (20.1.96)
A compulsive pitch up the left-hand side of the attractive arête. Three bolts, which appear to be strangely spaced.
Overhead protection permits a determined effort on the route's initial (crux) moves, after which abundant good holds lead elegantly up the arête to a big ledge and twin-bolt abseil station on the left. (A direct start has been done up to the second bolt: F6c †.)

The next three routes run closely together up the stratified wall. They start from a common twin-staple belay near the far end of the short traverse and finish at a communal twin-bolt abseil station. They feature the best quality rock on the crag.

On a Mission   15 metres   E3 6a F6c   (22.7.95)
An enjoyable route taking the vertical wall and arête just around from *Vicious Eyes*. The route gradually builds in both difficulty and interest. Six bolts.
Start to the left of the bolt belay. Move up to a bulge and pass it on the left. Follow the wall and arête up to the fourth bolt and make an awkward step right. Continue with haste up the wall to a jug on the right, where a final big pull gains finishing holds and the abseil station above.

★Peck Deck   15 metres   E4 6a F6c+   (23.7.95)
Another good pitch, escalating in difficulty and with a tricky crux. Six bolts. Start at the bolt belay at the end of the short traverse.

Take the second of the three bolt-lines (directly up above the belay) to its fourth bolt. Move up rightwards to a pocket, step back left, and commence a sustained series of powerful side-pull moves until a large jug provides gratifying security. Clip the last bolt on *On a Mission* (to the left) and make a final steep move to the shared abseil station.

★It's Got to Be Funky   18 metres   E3 6a F6c   (10.96)
The route is centred on strata that are bounded on their right by a wide vertical break that runs the full height of the cliff. A very enjoyable, if unusual pitch. Start at the bolt belay at the end of the traverse. Six bolts. Pull up immediately right of *Peck Deck* (using a jutting spike) and layback the crack, using a thin crack to the left at times, to a small hand-ledge on the right. Carry on up the steepening wall (past double pockets) to a footledge on the right, where a swing back left joins the finish of *Peck Deck*. Shared abseil station.

★Minstrel in the Gallery   12 metres   E5 6b F7a+   (16.7.95)
Technical and insecure climbing, but at the bottom of its grade. Start 3 metres to the right of the wide, vertical cleft. Four bolts.
Climb the wall, with hard moves to pass the second bolt, a trying third clip, and a finish veering left and then back right from the fourth bolt to a chained, twin-bolt abseil station at two-thirds height.
Variation
The Jester   20 metres   E6 6b F7b+ †   (11.9.96)
An extension to *Minstrel in the Gallery*. From the chained abseil station, continue with further sustained climbing up the leaning wall above to reach the twin-bolt abseil station atop *Head Intrinsica*. Eight bolt runners in total.

★★Head Intrinsica (The Awakening)   20 metres   E6 6b/c F7b+   (3.9.95)
This, the premier line on the wall, provides a technical, fingery and engrossing pitch that blasts directly up the middle of the bare face. Eight bolts.
Layback up a small rib to good holds below the first bolt. Rock up, and follow a rib tenuously to better holds just above. Move up slightly leftwards to a pair of layaways below the fourth bolt, gain composure, and commence a series of powerful and extending reaches to gain the first horizontal break. Arm up the overhanging wall to a big bucket by the last bolt, where a final awkward move leads to a twin-bolt abseil station.

★Fistful of Steel   20 metres   E6 6b F7b+   (28.8.95)
The blank-looking space to the right of *Head Intrinsica* is the scene for some intense and fingery climbing on soft rock. A good pitch that is low in its grade. Eight bolts.
Follow *Head Intrinsica* to its second bolt, and break out rightwards on small holds to grasp a thin, horizontal break. Tiring moves rightwards along the break are the prelude to a difficult rock-up onto the narrow sloping ledge above and some debilitating finger-pulling to (thankfully) gain a series of juggy breaks. Finish up the leaning headwall of *Head Intrinsica*. Twin-bolt abseil station.

★**Never Mind the Width**   24 metres   E1   5b   F6a   (16.7.95)

An excellent, enjoyable pitch that provides surprisingly straightforward climbing up the fearsome looking off-width that bounds the right edge of The Intrinsica Walls. Five bolts. Go on, have a go!

Ascend the daunting-looking off-width (much easier than its appearance suggests), and swing left to jugs. Reach further bucket holds and make an exhilarating heave (crux) to yet more jugs and a twin-bolt abseil station.

The Red Wall

Follow the base level of the quarry beneath The Intrinsica Walls to a distinctive and deceptively steep reddish wall.

★**Rustic Flux**   17 metres   E4   6a   F6c+   (20.6.00)

A super-charged pitch tackling the centre of the leaning, red wall. Six bolts. Good holds lead rapidly up the wall to the central bulge. Pull steeply up and right to grasp a small sloping ramp, and immediately rock back left over the bulge to reach a standing position beneath a slanting crackline, which is followed to a twin-bolt abseil station.

The Red Wall terminates where a narrow slab, punctured by several boreholes, projects at right angles and presents a broken arête.

Esotrinsica   15 metres   E1   5b   F6a   (16.7.95)

A useful pitch but a little snappy low down. Start 10 metres to the right of *Rustic Flux*, at the base of the narrow slab. Five bolts and a peg.

Pull up onto a small foot-ledge. Climb straight up the slab, variously using the arête and the corner, until a short traverse rightwards leads to a chained twin-bolt abseil station.

As one continues on from The Red Wall for 50 metres towards the rear of the quarry, a lone slab comes into view on the left, its base obscured by trees.

Moderately Green   17 metres   Hard Severe   4b   F4   (23.6.00)

Some suspect and brittle rock in the lower half warrants a cautious approach. Six bolts. Start at the base of the slab.

Move up slightly rightwards, to reach a ledge beneath a short, stout tree. Climb leftwards over a slight bulge to good holds in a slanting break, and finish enjoyably on some fun edges up the centre of the slab above to a twin-bolt abseil station.

A bike track loops around the back of the quarry, passing *Moderately Green*, and then returns along the far side of the quarry. At a point directly opposite The Red Wall this track passes behind a mound and curves around into a square-cut recessed area, the residence of...

The Slab with No Name

On the left side of the recessed section of the quarry lies a prominent, uniform slab that seems to offer bountiful new-routing promise. On closer inspection, however, the rock's unpleasant true nature is revealed.

A Family Affair   22 metres   E4 5c †   (23.5.99)
A serious, disheartening, and 'scabulous' affair that ascends the middle of
the large, distinctive slab that comes into view as you enter the quarry. Not
a route for your loved ones! Start in the centre of the slab.
Climb directly up to a thin ledge and bolt, continue rightwards to a crackline,
and follow it to the second (and last) bolt. Step over the apex of the curving
overlap that runs across the face, move slightly left, and finish by moving
back right and up to a ledge. Fixed abseil station of sorts above.

At right angles to the main slab a further, broken area of slabs is split by a
prominent wide, vertical cleft. Immediately to the left of the cleft one at last
finds...

Long Time Coming   15 metres   Hard Severe 4b F4   (17.9.00)
A useful introduction to the quarry. Good protection, sustained interest,
and an accessible grade have made this route a popular choice. Start 1.5
metres left of the distinctive cleft. Five bolts.
Climb directly up to the second bolt, step up left, and continue with interest
to a twin-bolt abseil station.

Curious Holes Quarry   OS Ref 682 479

This is a small, north-facing limestone quarry just north of Leigh on Mendip.
Unfortunately the interesting rock here takes quite a long time to dry out,
although on the positive side the quarry is very sheltered. Choose a period of
settled weather to make your visit worthwhile.

Approach from Holcombe village by driving south and turning left opposite
a lorry yard, along Marsh Lane. Keep right at the junction, and at the top of a
steep wooded hill you will find the quarry on your right clearly marked by
"Danger: This is not a play site" signs. There is a lay-by with parking for two
cars here and room for two more 50 metres further up the road.

All the routes are on the north-facing walls immediately opposite as you walk
into the quarry. There are three distinct walls.

Brown Wall
This is the brown left-hand wall with the strange circular depressions.
Curiously, these act as perfect litter bins for falling leaves, so bring a soft
brush.

My Crane and My Camel   10 metres   E1 5c   (1992)
Start below the centre of the brown wall. A small sapling and a crack in
the second depression marks the way. Climb up the middle of the wall,
stepping left and right between depressions as necessary.

Enema Paradise 10 metres E2 5b (1992)
Slightly bolder than the last route. Climb the right-hand line of four depressions, using the arête between the third and fourth and finishing to the right of the tree on top.

Division Wall

This is the central wall.

Division Bell 12 metres Very Difficult † ❀ (13.4.02)
Climb up to the tree and continue direct to the top.

Division Bell Right-hand 12 metres Very Severe 4c (24.4.02)
Climb the right-hand side of the wall.

Pulse Wall

This is the right-hand wall, which has a smart-looking arête on its left-hand side.

Pulse 10 metres Difficult (13.4.02)
Climb the rightward-slanting arête.

Saucer Full of Secrets 10 metres Severe (13.04.02)
Climb the slanting crack immediately right of the arête.

★**Over the Hump** 10 metres Hard Very Severe 5a (24.4.02)
Climb the right-hand side of the wall via thin cracks.

Leigh Quarry

OS Ref 693 478

Leigh Quarry is the disused limestone quarry across the road from the active Halecombe Quarry, just north of Leigh on Mendip. It is a large quarry with much crumbling rock. Housed within it, however, are solid walls and some unusual jamming cracks which are worth a visit.

Approach from Bristol by travelling south on the A37 to its junction with the A367 coming in from the left, but only turn left when you reach the junction 150 metres further on. Go east following Halecombe Quarry signs, with a single right-then-left deviation, and after 9 kilometres turn right (still signed for the quarry). Cross a junction and at a second junction turn left. Continue a few hundred metres to a small lay-by on the right, beside large boulders at the entrance to Leigh Quarry.

Follow the main track slightly rightwards, to discover a derelict building on your left. The Upper Wall can be seen over to the left, behind buddleia bushes. For the Lower Walls, continue down a narrow track and turn left.

Upper Wall

This is a long but low wall of rough rock seamed with parallel cracks. All the routes are worthwhile.

Fifty metres from the left-hand side of the Upper Wall is a shattered pedestal of rock. The first three climbs take cracklines a few metres to its right. They belay on a horizontal stake in the far side of the grassy bank at the cliff-top.

All Keyed Up   10 metres   Very Severe   4c   (10.7.02)
The wider crackline is followed to a slippery flowstone foothold and the top.

Où Sont Vos Clés?   10 metres   E1   5b   (10.7.02)
A metre to the right, climb the thinner crackline on surprisingly good fingerlocks. Safe and satisfying.

Angry Ant Bite   10 metres   E1   5b   (23.7.02)
Start a metre right of the last route, below a pocket with a spike in it. Climb past the pocket to the break at 5 metres. Take flakes slightly rightwards up the leaning grey tower with red patches, and exit without using the perched blocks that are on your right.

Twenty metres further right, away from the wall, is a convenient gearing-up spot by a flat-topped block. Beneath the leftmost of three cliff-top ash trees are four more crack-climbs.

Supercrack of the East Mendips   10 metres   E1   5b   (14.7.02)
Climb the narrow hand-crack where the path meets the wall.

Discectomy   10 metres   Hard Very Severe   5a   (14.7.02)
The flaky hand-crack a metre to the right.

A Bit Like Indian Creek   10 metres   E1   5c †   (14.7.02)
Lurking behind the buddleia which sprouts from the crag is a shattered chimney; start 2 metres to its right. Take the hand-crack to half height, where it continues, thinner and meaner, to the top.

The Spare Man   10 metres   Very Severe   4c †   (14.7.02)
Just to the right two cracks form a V. Climb the left-hand crack, which briefly forms a rightward-facing groove. Continue up to the top.

A few metres to the right, below the second ash tree, is a fine flowstone wall with a large orange niche on its right. The wall is taken by the following two climbs.

Diving Faces   10 metres   E3   6a †   (23.7.02)
Start below a short crack on the left-hand side of the wall. Climb the short crack to jugs in a break. Using holds in the flowstone step up right, before climbing flowstone direct to a flat ledge. Exit up a short corner on the right.

The Spare Tyre   10 metres   E1 5b   (14.7.02)
High in the grade. Start beneath a slanting, sloping hold. Climb flaky
cracks to a recess near the cliff-top. Take one step rightwards and continue
to the top.

Lower Walls

At the bottom level of the quarry, to the left of the descent track, is an inviting
area of good rock, with some flowstone and good cracklines. There are
three faces: Brown Slab on the left (with no routes yet); the steep east-facing
Steep Wall; and the off-vertical north-facing Festival Wall.

It may be necessary to clear the finishing holds of gravel washed down from
above before an ascent.

Steep Wall

A fine wall which provides some well-protected routes.

Move Over, Fat Captain   15 metres   E2 5c †   (26.6.03)
Start at the left end of Steep Wall. Climb to the horizontal break and follow
it rightwards with increasing difficulty. Finish up broken rock just by the
right-hand arête.

★**Wasteria**   10 metres   E2 6a   (30.7.01)
Start 3 metres right of the corner at the left-hand end of the wall.
Climb up to the overhang and a large undercut. Layback round the bulge
to good holds and the top.

★**Holiday Crack**   10 metres   E2 5c   (1.8.01)
The crack halfway along the wall; a tricky start leads to sustained
crack-climbing.

☆**Nil by Mouth**   10 metres   E3 6a †   (29.9.02)
Climb the right-hand crack.

Eye Contact   10 metres   E5 6c †   (12.8.02)
Awesomely technical, but you need blinkers! Climb the smooth grey wall
between *Nil by Mouth* and the arête without recourse to either. You are
aiming for a two-tip pocket at 4 metres; gain it with your right hand and
proceed to the break at 6 metres, where easier climbing leads to the top.

Serley's Bulge   10 metres   Very Severe 4c   (18.7.01)
At the right-hand end of the wall, climb the crack in the arête, swing left at
two-thirds height, and continue to the top.

Festival Wall

★**Festival Crack**   10 metres   Hard Very Severe 5b   (18.7.01)
Climb the impressive crack in the centre of the wall.

Sharp Stones in my Buttock   10 metres   E1 5b   (25.7.01)
Start to the right of *Festival Crack* at a marvellous quartz groove.
Climb the groove and then make thin moves into the hanging corner
above. Finish up the corner.

Grey Slab

In the far eastern corner of the quarry is a north-facing grey slab, which is
dwarfed by the crumbling walls that surround it. At the top of the slab itself is
more untrustworthy rock. Because of this, there are stakes above the slab for
pre-placed lower-off ropes.

The two slanting cracks have been climbed. The left-hand crack (**Washing
Day** 6 metres Very Severe 4c † 29.9.02) is hardly worth doing, especially as
it requires a lower-off rope. There are two top-rope problems up the slab on
the right which can use the same lower-off: F6b+ and F6b.

Back on the Nest   8 metres   E1 5c †   (29.9.02)
Climb the right-hand crack and lower off a pre-placed rope.

The wall to the right has been top-roped at F6c.

Westdown Quarry   OS Ref 717 457

This is a very large sprawling quarry with disappointingly little potential for
climbing. There is one small area of good rock, however, which could be
very useful for beginners. The People with Unusual Names Slab is east-
facing and pleasantly situated (for a quarry).

Approach: There is ample roadside parking at Dead Woman's Bottom on
the road between Leigh on Mendip and Nunney. Enter the quarry and take
the first road up to the left. Follow this round to the right until you can see
some impressive concrete triangles. Continue on the rising road/track and,
about 300 metres beyond the concrete triangles, past some short slabby
bouldering, is the People with Unusual Names Slab. There are four large
concrete cylinders opposite the climbing area.

People With Unusual Names Slab

The People with Unusual Names Slab is bordered by a scruffy corner on its
left and a low line of overhangs to the right. Near the middle of the slab is a
small ash tree.

The first route is found on the subsidiary slab to the left of the main slab.

Hogswatch Hangover   8 metres   Very Difficult †   (4.02)
Start below the centre of the slab. Climb straight up the left side of the slab
past two deep horizontal breaks.

Uberwald Express   8 metres   Very Difficult †   (4.02)
Climbs the left-hand side of the slab, just right of the scruffy corner

The Fifth Elephant   8 metres   Very Difficult †   (19.4.02)
Start two metres left of the ash tree, below a thin crack. Climb directly to
the top.

Start Men at Arms   8 metres   Difficult   (16.4.02)
Climb directly up the centre of the slab to the tree. Finish straight up
above.

Guards! Guards!   8 metres   Difficult †   (19.4.02)
Start a metre from the right-hand edge of the slab below a small rock
sticking up on top and a silver birch tree. Climb the slab direct.

Feet of Clay   8 metres   Difficult †   (16.4.02)
Start at the right-hand side of the slab. Climb the left-hand side of the
arête and finish up an earthy groove.

Sourcery   8 metres   Hard Severe †   (5.5.02)
Start below the overhang to the right of the slab. Climb up the short corner
below the overhang and pull round onto the slab. Climb directly to the top
just right of *Feet of Clay*'s earthy groove.

Greebo's Claw   8 metres   Severe †   (10.5.02)
Climb through a break at the right-hand end of the overhang and
continue on easier rock to the top.

Mells

OS Ref 734 488

About 4 kilometres west of Frome is a cluster of short, steep limestone walls
located on the banks of the Mells stream in a very picturesque valley. Solid
and of sunny disposition, the cliffs offer a good day's climbing far from the
usual haunts. Unfortunately seepage can be a problem in winter, and some
of the climbs require a fair amount of effort to protect: difficult small-wire
protection predominates.

Park in a very restricted lay-by at the entrance to the valley, a few hundred
metres to the east of the village of Mells on the Great Elm Road. Take the
footpath along the bank of the stream for about 150 metres to the crags on
the left.

The Face of Mells

The first crag encountered and the best. This is a pristine, 12-metre-square
face that offers fine climbing.

Mells Bells   12 metres   Hard Severe 4a   (1990s)
Climb the left arête of the face.

Picturesque   12 metres   E1 5c   (21.6.95)
A good pitch. Start 2 metres right of the left arête. Climb up a tricky
opening slab to a rest and some gear. Take the vague crackline above and
finish up a little wall.

★Mells Wall   12 metres   E4 6b   (1990s)
The strongest natural line on the crag lies in the centre of the wall.
Supporting an *in-situ* thread and peg, it offers some unexpectedly
awkward and difficult climbing. Finish up the obvious crack to a tree root,
or (more worryingly) slightly to the right.

★Mellon   12 metres   E4 6a   (1994)
Start in the centre-right of the face, 5 metres short of the right-hand arête.
Technical climbing up the incipient line of weakness and flake-holds above
lead to a bold, direct finish.

Mellstrom   12 metres   E4 6a   (21.6.95)
Reasonably accommodating climbing on the face just left of the right
arête. The route has some reachy and sustained moves and acceptable
protection. (Using holds on the arête itself reduces the difficulties.)

Smells   12 metres   Hard Very Severe 5a   (1994)
Climbs the right arête of the wall, starting at some obvious right-trending
cracks. Steep moves lead up and across onto the arête. Climb the arête
before moving onto the front face to finish.

Above and to the right of the face is a 15-metre slab and a rising
overhanging wall. The rock on the slab comprises excellent 'Malham-like'
pocketed limestone.

Iron Brew   15 metres   Very Severe 4c   (1993)
Start at the lowest point of the slab. Move awkwardly onto the slab and
climb directly to the top, keeping to the left of the sapling.

★Ironed Out   15 metres   Very Severe 5a   (1994)
Start 2 metres up the slope below the overhanging wall, at an obvious line
of pockets. Cams useful. Follow the deep pockets leftwards onto the slab.
Climb the crack and slab, keeping to the right of the sapling.

Pig Iron   15 metres   E2 5a   (1994)
Starting just right of *Ironed Out*, climb the leaning pink wall to reach holds
going left to the obvious small cave. Move left to finish up *Ironed Out*.

Pumping Iron   12 metres   E4 5c †   (17.4.99)
The point is the pump, not the line (or lack of it).
Climb rightwards across the leaning pink wall of *Pig Iron*, and pull up past
a rounded grey bulge to a large shallow pocket (Friend 3½/4). Swing right
to parallel cracks and fight up these to the top.

The Chimney   10 metres   Hard Severe 4b   (1994)
The steep crack leading to an off-width/chimney.

Shed Walls

Approximately 30 metres right of The Face of Mells is a series of short faces, the central and largest of which houses the following collection. Until 1995 there was a large lean-to shed here.

Watershed   12 metres   Very Severe 5a   (1995)
Start a metre from the left edge of the Shed Wall below a vague left-facing flake. Climb to the flake and follow it rightwards with difficulty to a ledge. Move left onto another flake and finish straight up a short crack.

Right Said Shed   12 metres   E2 6a   (17.4.99)
Starting 3 metres from the left edge, climb direct to a flake-ledge. With blinkers on, finish up the difficult headwall.

★**Shed No Tears**   12 metres   Hard Very Severe 5b   (1995)
An excellent route on superb rock. Start below an obvious pocket at 3 metres, in the centre of the wall.
Reach the pocket and short flake from the right. From the sloping ledge above, climb the slabby wall on finger-jugs, trending slightly right at the top.

Shed Head   12 metres   E1 5c   (1995/17.4.99)
Boulder up the vague rib immediately right of *Shed No Tears* and, using the obvious block-hold, move left onto a smooth slab, which is climbed to the arête and the top.

Shed Arête   12 metres   Very Severe 4c   (1994)
Start 2 metres left of the right edge of the wall, below a ragged water-worn crack. Climb the crack to an obvious block-hold. Follow the slabby arête on the right to the top.

Shed Wall Upper

Above and to the left of Shed Wall is a wall containing a smooth groove. It is reached by a short scramble.

☆**Shedded Weak**   9 metres   E5 6b †   (17.4.99)
Perfect commitment on perfect rock.
From the lowest point of the wall, work rightwards to the foot of the smooth, shallow groove. Make fingery moves into the groove, using the finger-jug out to the left, and finish on good holds. An *RP0* 'protects'.

★**Unknown Route**   7 metres   E3 6a   (1995)
Rib-ticklingly blind climbing up the right-hand rib of the groove. From a good horizontal slot, move left, and follow a series of spaced fingerholds up the rib and slab.

Talbot   7 metres   Very Severe   4c   (1995)
Start 2 metres from the right edge of the wall and take the obvious steps
up left onto the slab and then direct to the top. The start is much more
awkward than appearances would suggest.

Shed Wall Right

A cute 7-metre pocketed wall 10 metres right of Shed Wall. If anything, the
adornment of wild flowers enhances the climbing. It can be climbed pretty
much anywhere, but the following are obvious ticks: the left-hand side via a
very long reach to a ragged pocket (E1 6a – not a good landing); the central
eliminate on knobbles (Hard Very Severe 5a); and the runnelled line of
pockets right of centre (Very Severe 4c).

Vallis Vale   OS Ref 757 487

This is the best (a relative term) of several quarries at Vallis Vale on the outskirts
of Frome, although all are either overgrown, loose, or both. While subject to a
flurry of interest in the early 80s (and the production of a local guidebook) the
quarry is now wholeheartedly neglected by climbers. Curiosity may have it
otherwise.

The quarry described is approached from the Egford road, and is located 2
kilometres west of Frome town centre. There is a car-park on the right of the
minor road; from here, a walk of 200 metres along a footpath northwards
into the woods leads to the quarry on the right. The quarry is owned by ARC
who have actively discouraged climbing in the past.

Although there are a few worthwhile and relatively solid routes, much of the
quarry is of doubtful stability and loose rock abounds. Currently, re-cleaning,
or at least a check from a top-rope, may be a sensible precaution for any of
the climbs (but don't forget your helmet!). The quarry is still used for very
occasional group and instruction purposes. The only belays at the top are a
fence and telegraph pole 10 metres back

Note that the routes have not been checked for this Guidebook. The majority
of the descriptions are outline only and based upon the local 1982 guide.

In the main south-west facing wall of the quarry is a prominent crack-system
(*Vallis Crack*) with a smooth and fairly solid slabby wall immediately left. Left
again is a more shattered-looking area and an overhanging rib.

The first three routes start below the overhanging rib.

Styx   24 metres   Severe   ❀   (5.82)
Climb the left edge of the crag via a slab (peg), groove, and flakes.
Vegetated and loose.

Tantalus   20 metres   Severe   (4.82)
Climb to the right of *Styx* to finish either up a ragged crack in a steep wall (peg), or the black slab to its left (4a).

Thetis   20 metres   Difficult   (5.82)
A worthwhile route.
Climb right of the rib, passing a sapling, into an open slabby groove. Step right from the top of the groove, and follow an earthy corner to a ledge beneath the final steep wall (junction with *Tantalus*, peg). Move right onto a grassy ledge and follow broken rock to the top.

Cerebus   20 metres   Severe 4a   (5.82)
Exciting at this grade, with suspect rock in places. Start 9 metres right of the rib below a steep cracked arête.
Climb a slab and pass the overlap above using flakes on the right. Step left and gain a ledge. Climb a steep wall, follow a groove on the left, and finish up the edge of a slab.

Tiptoe   20 metres   E3 5b   (1981)
Completely unprotected unless a side runner in a nut-slot 5 metres up *Wasted Metal* is used. Start in the centre of the slabby wall, just right of *Cerebus*. Climb directly for 5 metres to a line of small holds that lead to difficult moves and then a good hand-ledge. Pull leftwards and continue straight up the steep slab to the top.

Wasted Metal   20 metres   Very Severe   4c   (1977)
An interesting climb. Left of the main crack-system is a short groove at 6 metres.
Climb directly to the groove and continue to an overhang at its top (peg). Stride left to a foot-ledge at the base of a second groove. Gain a higher ledge, and exit up a steep corner (bolt runner).

Telemachus (27 metres Severe 4.82) is a contrived diagonal that links the start of *Wasted Metal* to the finish of *Tantalus*.

Vallis Crack   20 metres   Very Severe   4c   (1977)
The obvious main crack-system has some exciting moments dealing with suspect blocks and crumbling holds! What more needs to be said?

Free Stonehenge   20 metres   E3 5b   (1990)
Attacks the black headwall right of the crack-system, which is spattered with the graffiti: 'stoned henge 86!'. Poor protection; cams required for the wide break near the top, which may need pre-cleaning. Start 3 metres right of the crack-system.
Climb shattered rock to a tree, and move onto the ledge above. Continue over the obvious rock scar to a horizontal break. Move left to a series of holds which lead to the right-hand side of the capping block.

The area of rock right again has provided three climbs, the first two of which start below a blunt rib 10 metres right of *Vallis Crack*.

Scylla   20 metres   Difficult   (5.82)
Climb the blunt rib, slab, and broken arête; two peg runners.

Charybdis   12 metres   Difficult   (4.82)
Climb the short groove, overlap, and scoop right of *Scylla*.

Centaur   12 metres   Severe   (5.82)
Start 5 metres right of the rib of *Scylla* and climb to a sloping terrace,
before taking a steep wall and scoop to a peg belay in a cave.

A three-pitch traverse of the entire main face has been worked out which is
based upon the obvious faultline. **Odyssey** (90 metres Severe 4a 5.82)
starts as for *Centaur* and finishes up *Styx*, belaying in the first groove of
Wasted Metal and 10 metres below the top of *Styx*.

There is a small slab to the right of *Centaur* which provides some top-roping:
Siren Slab.

Finally, the 10-metre overhanging wall of rubble facing the main wall has
potential for a good handful of steep climbs; at least a crack on the left
should swallow gear.

Ham Hill Quarry   OS Ref 480 166

An outlying oolitic limestone quarry in a beautiful area of Somerset, well worth
a visit, particularly in combination with a day out for the family. Only salient
approach information is provided here, for the following reason. Prompted by
the preceding edition of this guidebook (which incorporated a batch of routes
that were reported as first ascents), it has since been established that the
quarry had been used intensively by climbers local to Yeovil since at least the
early 80s. The resulting climbs have been documented in a guidebook
produced by, and available from, The Yeovil Mountaineering Club. This gives
definitive information, including the rationale behind a strict local ethic based
upon either top-roping (Harrisons' style) or soloing only. Visitors are recommended to acquire a copy and to respect the local climbers' policy. For a
copy, send a stamped, addressed envelope to the secretary of Yeovil
Mountaineering Club, whose address can be obtained from the BMC.The
quarry lies in Ham Hill Country Park, Somerset. From the A303 Ilchester to
Ilminster road, turn off to Montacute and follow the signposts to Stoke sub
Hamden. At the village, take the signposted road up the hill to the Park. The
first turning on the left leads to the Prince Of Wales pub; instead continue
along the road for 500 metres and park in a car-park on the left. From here,
walk westwards (in the Yeovil direction) and then in ever-decreasing circles
until the quarry is eventually encountered hidden in woodland.

The Top One Hundred

Climb	Trauma Potential	Best Style	Your Best
Fornicator Simulator E8 6c	4	R	
Train in the Distance (bolt-free) E7 6c	10	H	
Brean Topping F8b	0	R	
Edgemaster (bolt-free) E7 6b	10	H	
The Aardvark and the Ferret (no side runner) E7 6b	9	H	
The Empire Strikes Back F8a+	0	R	
Homegrown F8a+	1	O	
Level Headed E7 6c	5	R	
Bristol Weed F8a+	1	R	
Was It You? E7 6c	4	R	
Crown of Thorns E7 6c	9	H	
Partial Eclipse (bolt-free) E7 6b/c	9	H	
The Independent Route E7 6b	9	H	
Feed Your Head (Eclipsed) E7 6b	9	H	
Licking Tarmac F8a+	3	R	
The Prince F8a+/b	0	R	
Academic F8a	1	R	
A Day Called Zero F8a (dust runners)	10	R	
Star Wars: The Trilogy E7 6c	7	R	
Spiritualize E7 6b	8	R	
Heaven-Sent Direct E7 6b	8	O	
Will Stanton F8a	2	O	
Bursting the Wave F8a	3	R	
The Quiet Mind E7 6a/b	9	O	
Coup d'État E6 6b	5	B	
To Be Is Not to Bolt E7 6b	6	O	
Taming of the Lion E6 6c	3	R	
Polar Reaches E6 6c	6	R	
Right-Hand Man F8a	1	O	
Smashing of Amps F7c+	1	B	
Every Step of the Way E6 6b	4	R	
Critic's Choice (bolt-free) E7 6b	8	O	
Spacehunter E6 6b	9	R	
The Enchanted Gordon E6 6c	7	O	
Hell-Bent E6 6c	6	H	

Ian Paisley E6 6c	7	H
Bold as Love E6 6b	6	O
Draggin' Along F7c+	4	R
Sorceress E6 6b	7	O
La Tour Noire Super E6 6b	8	H
The Wrist Business F7c+	0	R
The Other Side of Paradise F7c	3	R
Exfo '92 F7c+	1	R
Storm Warning F7c+	0	R
One Scream's Enough Direct F7c+	1	R
Red Snapper and Chips F7c	1	O
El Chocco F7c	2	R
Mescalito F7c	2	R
Me No Stereotype F7c	1	R
Heaven-Sent E6 6b	6	H
Follow the Slick Red Road E6 6b	3	B
All Guns Blazing F7c	0	B
Secret Cabaret F7c+	0	O
Circus, Circus F7c	1	O
Ultra-Violence F7c	1	R
One Man, One Island E6 6b	5	R
Return of the Gunfighter F7c	1	O
The Midnight Run F7c	2	R
Pink Insane E6 6c	5	H
Tour de France (Integral) E6 6b	3	O
Psycho-Death Drummer of Brean Café E6 6b	3	R
Defining Limits E6 6c	3	R
Leader of the Pack F7c	0	R
Showbiz E6 6c	3	Y
Shock of the New (Direct) F7c	3	R
Bristol Unillustrated E6 6b	1	R
The Harder They Come F7c	4	R
Fact or Fission F7c	2	R
Quality of Sacrifice E5 6c	5	O
L'Attraction Fatale F7c	2	B
The Jimi Hendrix Experience E6 6b	5	O
The Minute Waltz E6 6c	8	H
Cove Arête E6 6b	6	O
Midnight Express E6 6a	9	O
Edge of Eternity E6 6c	4	Y

The Shockin' Pink E6 6c	3	R
Rising above Bedlam E6 6b	6	O
For Ever and Ever E6 6b	5	R
Hard Bass Religion F7c	2	R
Jazz Defector E6 6c	3	H
Bored of Pies F7c	2	R
A Profusion of Pink E6 6b	4	O
Do or Dole F7c	0	R
Everyday Lives of Ordinary People F7c	1	O
Bullworker F7c	0	R
House Burning Down E6 6b	6	R
Millimetre Wall F7c	1	R
I'm 55 E5 6c	7	O
Just Plain Bent! E5 6c (with the jump)	3	R
Caught Under Cloud Nine E6 6b	7	O
Scarred Mind F7c	2	R
Agenda 21 F7c	1	R
The Wishing Wall E6 6b	5	R
Psychopath Way E6 6b	4	O
Pride Evans Locker F7b+	2	R
The 'Oh No!' Zone E6 6b	6	O
West Route E6 6a	5	O
SkyScrape E6 6b	3	O
The Conformist E6 6b	5	O
The Enlightenment E6 6a	6	O

Trauma Potential

```
0----------------------------------5------------------------------------10
Smugly safe.           Run-outs, fear,              Death-fall
                    exposure, difficult gear,
               hospitalization, snagged tights, etc.
```

Style

O = on-sight flash (includes on-sight solo)

B = beta-flash (watching others, info from others)

R = redpoint (includes first ascent and other flashes)

H = headpoint (i.e. leading/soloing after comprehensive top-roping)

Y = yo-yo

First Ascents List

Cheddar Gorge

No first ascent details are available for **Camp Fire's Burning** or **Nameless Horror**.

1925	Climbs on tier 'above High Rock' M Guinness, M Gentry
1931	**Knight's Climb, Eden Crack, Sugarloaf, Pyramus, Thisbe Chimney, Parallel Cracks, Heart Leaf Climb, East Climb, Green Wall, East Slab, Pinnacle Route** W Keith Marples, R Bates

Knight's Climb: '...from which rises the Raven Chimney (so named because of the odious bird which buffeted the first 'Knight' in defence of a nest).' Heart Leaf Climb: 'an exceedingly difficult and delectable climb... a rope from above is advisable until the stability of the Heart Leaf has been determined.'

1946	**Narrow Buttress, Narrow Crack, Groove and Rib, Thisbe Crack, Thisbe Slab** J V Morris, G Whitacre
1950	**The Slab, Easy Way, Rocking Horse, Original Route** G J Sutton, B Dowman

The Wind Rock climbs were possibly ascended previously by members of the RNSMC.

1950	**Prospect Gully, Humerus** G J Sutton, B Dowman, D E Davis
1950	**Colt** G J Sutton (solo)
1951 April	**Marriette Route, Elizabeth Route, Original Route, Burial Route** D N J Young, L Burton

The climbers lodged with a local family who were entertaining a number of young French ladies at the time! The Slice at the Wife variant to Mariette Route was climbed by M J Crocker (lead-solo) on 7.4.99.

1953 June 2	**Sceptre** H I Banner, P Hill

A prodigious ivy growth was attacked with hammers and secateurs causing the climbers to suffer an allergic rash for a long while afterwards.

1953 June	**5b Wall, Mike's Party Piece, Crew Cut** H I Banner
1954	**Jacko** H I Banner
1954	**Jill** P Henry
1954	**Cascara Crack, Stepped Wall, Mare's Nest** G J Sutton, Ms A Clark
1959 July	**Lucifera, The Great Unwashed** (3 pts aid) G West, B Roberts, R Jones

First free ascent of the latter R A Broomhead, M Hutchinson on 18.4.73.

1959 July	**Hammer and Sickle** G West, B Roberts, F Mallard
1950s	**Nameless Horror** First ascensionists unknown
c.1950s	**Wall of Trees, Short Cut, Nameless Horror** First ascensionists unknown
1961 Jan 15	**Genesis** (10 pts aid) M Adams, P Crew, P M Hutchinson

The addition of an alternative first pitch by M Putnam in 1973 rendered the climb free. The originally aided first pitch was reclimbed free as The Burner.

1961	**Terrace Gully** First ascensionists unknown

1964 March 16 | **Sceptre Direct**   B Annette, M White
An ominous hanging block that the first ascensionists were keen to avoid finally parted company fifteen years later, resulting in an epic rescue!

1965 Jan | **Ready Steady Go** (2 pts aid)   C J S Bonington, A Greenbank
The original finish followed the indirect version of Consolation. Climbed free and as described by R A Broomhead, S Hermalin on 2.2.74.

1965 March 27 | **Palo Alto** (1 pt aid)   C Jones, L Brown
First free ascent R A Broomhead, 18.12.72.

1965 March 28 | **Sentinel** (6 pts aid)   C Jones, L Brown
Originally attempted by C J S Bonington. The aid was reduced to one point by P R Littlejohn in 1975. First free ascent R Berzins 1979. The Sentinel Direct finish was added by M J Crocker, G A Jenkin 22.9.87.

1965 April 10 | **West Route** (A2)   C Jones, R S Dearman (two-day ascent)
Named in honour of its first defiler, G West, who pegged up to an impasse at 100 feet, the route was the first to conquer the main face of High Rock. P R Littlejohn free-climbed the first three pitches whilst producing Crow in 1970. An attempt at free-climbing the headwall from the right by Littlejohn in 1977 ended with a fall onto the top bolt: 'a rest on the bolt would have left the outcome in little doubt but we preferred retreat, knowing it would go completely free sometime…' A Strapcans and S Monks (AL) solved the problem by taking a stance on the bolt, the first pitch succumbing only after four previous visits and the final pitch being added separately on 8 October 1978. The headwall was finally climbed in one pitch by D Critchley and P Smith in 1984 and flashed by M J Crocker on 24.2.85.

1965 May 8 | **Paradise Lost** (A3)   R S Dearman, C Jones
C J S Bonington had pegged up the first pitch a little earlier. The successful pair finished the route partly 'to spite Bonington'. Climbed with a leftward variation on the first pitch and just one point of aid on the top pitch by P Livesey, J Lawrence on 11.9.76. Shortly afterwards R Harrison repeated the route still with one aid point, but a different one ('I was so excited to have got up it at the time. The ring peg I used was not the aid point used previously.') M J Crocker removed the final aid point on 26.4.84 and free-climbed the original first pitch on 15.10.89. The entry pitch is now referred to as The Common Start.

1965 May | **Coronation Street**   C J S Bonington, J Cleare, A Greenbank
Much of the route had been prepared and pushed by the same party earlier in the year. '…the thought of the whole lot (The Shield) just coming away with oneself attached to this 20 tons of rock was just too frightening so I put in a piton to one side, stood in a sling and teetered around.' The route was completed before the cameras of TTW and an audience of thousands. 'Even to this day (1988) Coronation Street is perhaps the most beautiful route I've ever made a first ascent of.'

1965 May | **Temptation, Viper Crack, Jack, Slow-worm**
C J S Bonington, M Thompson
'For a glorious week the lucky few gardened, Tyrolean-traversed, tree felled, and trundled under the approving eyes of both the police and the Marquis of Bath – whose Mercedes eventually

sustained a direct hit!' Slow-worm was superseded by Quicksnake after rock removal.

1965 Oct   **Django (4 pts aid)**   G Low, F E Bennett
First free ascent R Harrison, R A Broomhead 8.76. The huge perched flake was trundled in the early 90s by the rock clearance team, and the route reclimbed by M J Crocker, G A Jenkin on 10.5.94. Stargazer variant by F Haden, B Durston on 31.10.93.

1965 Nov   **Warlord (A2)**   G Low, F E Bennett
Pitch 2 was climbed with one point of aid by R Harrison, R A Broomhead on 12.9.76; first free ascent S Monks, 26.6.78. After a considerable gardening effort, the original first pitch was reclimbed free by R Harrison and D Carter during 10.80.

1965   **Simba (2 pts aid)**   G Low, F E Bennett, D Lloyd
First free ascent E Hart, 4.2.73.

1965   **Leadbelly**   F E Bennett
A thin Fred!

1966 Feb   **Thor (A2)**   P Lennard, M Taylor
First free ascent P R Littlejohn, F E R Cannings 1969.

1966 Aug 2   **Consolation (A2)**   R S Dearman, R Toogood
Dearman and Toogood had retreated from a very wet holiday in the Dolomites: this route was their consolation. Climbed free on a direct line through the capping overhangs by C King, R A Broomhead on 27.5.75. B.A.D. variation by P Hughes, 31.8.86: ' a serious route, but nonetheless, an experience.'

1966   **Ginsberg (A2)**   I Adams, G Mason
Originally known as Tumbler but the description was lost. P R Littlejohn reduced the aid to two points on 15.6.76,and S Monks and P Newman climbed the route free on 16.4.80.

1967 April 7   **Paradise Regained (A2)**   R S Dearman, T Morris
Followed a ten-hour, bone-shaking trip from Sheffield on Morris's motorbike and sidecar. A Strapcans and G A Jenkin climbed the route with two rest-points on the top pitch on 10.6.79. Free-climbed by M J Crocker, J Bassindale, 6.6.84.

1968 Jan 21   **Geronimo**   T Taylor, C Phillips

1968 March 22   **Utopia**   T Taylor, P Leonard
A rewarding excavation.

1968 Sept 8   **The Demon Trundler (1 pt aid)**   D A Steel, I Duckworth
The aid was eliminated and the route climbed direct by C Brear, R A Broomhead on 17 October 1985.

1969 June 1   **Toss of a Coin**   N Jago, G Rowles

1969 June   **Charge**   R A Broomhead
A young and eager Broomhead makes his debut.

1969 Nov 16/17   **Gates of Eden (A3)**   R S Dearman, D W Riley
A direct finish was pegged by R S Dearman and R A Broomhead in 1972. The route was climbed with a new independent start and with four points of aid by M J Crocker, D Ardron on 19.2.84. Two of the remaining aid-points were eliminated by M J Crocker, G A Jenkin, 7.3.86 on their ascent of Edge of Eternity.

1969 Nov 22/23   **Shangri La (A2)**   P Nunn, J Morgan
Most of the original and overgrown route was incorporated into Harrison's Stone the Crows, now also overgrown. The original first pitch was free-climbed as a separate route by M J Crocker, S Monks on 23.10.85.

1969 Dec 3   **Bird of Paradise** (A3)   R S Dearman, D Lester (Two-day ascent)
After the first day's efforts, Lester jumared back up to their highpoint using his home-made ascendeurs constructed from tin. They worked all right, but when the pair got down, Dearman was able to bend and dismantle them using his fingers. One of the most spectacular aid routes in the country was converted into one of its best free climbs by M J Crocker, D Ardron on 17.10.86.

1969 Dec 3   **Burma Road** (1 pt aid)   M Boysen, A McHardy
First free ascent P R Littlejohn, R A Broomhead in 1975.

1969 Dec 13   **Brainbiter** (4 pts aid)   F E R Cannings, P R Littlejohn (AL)
Climbed with one point of aid by R Harrison on 21.6.77; this was finally eliminated by D Hall on 15 October 1988.

1970 Jan 24   **Satori** (Very Severe A2)   R S Dearman, D W Riley (AL)
When Dearman seconded the top pitch, the rope dislodged a huge pinnacle. The only way for Dearman to get out of its way was to jump off. All but one peg was eliminated by P R Littlejohn, R A Broomhead, 27.5.76. First free ascent R Harrison, J Uren, October 1980. The top pitch is now described as a separate route – Satori Chimney.

1970 Jan 24/25   **Doomwatch** (VS A2)   P Nunn, J Morgan
First free ascent P R Littlejohn, 1970 (an easy picking!).

1970 Jan 25   **Mescalito** (A2)   R S Dearman, D W Riley, R A Broomhead
Pitch 1 climbed free by R A Broomhead, D Viggers, 7.83. Pitch two climbed with one point of aid by M J Crocker, J Bassindale on 26.12.83 and without by M J Crocker on 20.4.85 – 'never had I been so airborne, for so long'.

1970 Jan 25   **Dinner Date**   C McCombie, J Teale
McCombie's date was the UBMC annual dinner at which Dearman, engaged to the right on Mescalito, was guest speaker.

1970 Feb 28   **Asina** (Hard Very Severe, A2)   R S Dearman, D W Riley
Climbed with three points of aid by E Hart, M Haffner on 18.3.73, and free with a variation in line by A Strapcans, C King on 23.3.75.

1970 Feb   **The February Risings** (1 pt aid)   P R Littlejohn, G Morton
First free ascent E Hart, 1972. The climb originally finished up Winter Chimney; the top pitch as described was added by R A Broomhead, D Carroll on 28.10.83.

1970 March 1   **Ahimsa** (A2)   R S Dearman, D W Riley
First free ascent R Harrison, R A Broomhead on 16.6.76.

1970 March 22   **Fornicator Simulator** (A3)   R S Dearman, D W Riley
Named after friend Chris Trotter's vibrating motorbike. After the ascent of Star Spangled Banner in 1986 only five metres of aid remained. Various protagonists had taken a look (in their dreams), but a free ascent had to wait for I Vickers in 10.97.

1970 March   **Mourning Glory, What a Bringdown**   R S Dearman, D W Riley
Is it coincidental that Morning Glory seeds are supposed to have hallucinogenic properties? An independent start to the latter route was added by R A Broomhead, D Viggers on 22.1.83.

1970 April 3   **April Fools**   R A Broomhead, J Cox

1970 May 1   **The Twilight of Imperialism**   P R Littlejohn, I Duckworth
'We left a 20-foot-high pile of ivy in the car-park. Ian set fire to it and the smoke was incredible – obliterating High Rock and

eventually causing the fire brigade to be called out.' The overgrown second pitch now interrupts the climb; the upper corner crack is now described as the first pitch of Danger Bird.

1970 May 27 **Avatar** (3 pts aid)   P R Littlejohn, G Morton
The climb was extended to the top by P R Littlejohn, R A Broomhead in 1974 but this section became overgrown. First free ascent R Harrison, P R Littlejohn 14.3.76. Malaise variation by A Strapcans, C King on 30.6.76.

1970 June 6 **Nirvana** (2 pts aid)   R S Dearman, D W Riley
First free ascent P R Littlejohn, G Morton in 1970.

1970 Oct 17/18 **Crow**   P R Littlejohn, M Chambers
The pair abseiled into the third stance, their high point from the previous day, but couldn't pull their ropes down! By the time the ropes were freed 'I was so frozen – which may account for why I found the fourth pitch so hard'. The route did not receive its first one-day ascent until seven years after its inception!

1970 Nov 8 **Paranoia** (1 pt aid)   A McHardy, M Boysen, R A Broomhead
Pitch 2 climbed free and as described, R A Broomhead, G Forward on 14.4.84.

1970 Nov 21 **Megalomania**   R S Dearman, P Nunn
Pitches 1 and 2 were added by R A Broomhead, P Stewart on 11.1.75.

1970 Nov 28 **Little Hopper**   R A Broomhead, D Grey

1971 March 13 **Tremorgans**   (top pitch only) R S Dearman, R A Broomhead, D Morgan
First continuous ascent as described, R A Broomhead, R Harrison (AL) on 29.9.83.

1971 March 13 **Concorde** (A2)   R Pannatier, K Vickery
The aid was reduced to a rest-point by S Findlay on 19.4.79. First free ascent P O'Donovan on 3.10.82.

1971 June 5 **Immunity Syndrome**   R A Broomhead, D Say
Broomhead's partner was not to be confused with the Cheddar Caves Manager of the same name, who stated in 1973: 'Climbers discovered on the rocks would be liable to prosecution for trespass.' Pitches 3 and 4 were climbed by P R Littlejohn, R A Broomhead, 20.4.75.

1971 Oct **Hair Cut**   R A Broomhead, D Say
1972 Jan 9 **Hepatitis**   M Putnam, D Lister
1972 Jan 9 **Piglet's Groove**   C Millford, P Hicks
1972 Sept 16 **Picador** (A2)   R A Broomhead, P Stewart
The aid was reduced to one point by S Monks, A Strapcans on 8.10.78. First free ascent K Marsden, F Thompson, 17.6.82.

1972 Oct 26 **Choss**   R A Broomhead, M Hutchinson, M Hermalin
1972 Dec 10 **Spotlight** (1 pt aid)   R A Broomhead, P Stewart
First free ascent A Strapcans, S Monks, 4.3.79.

1972 Dec 20 **The Vertical Smile**   R A Broomhead, M Hutchinson, D Hermalin

1972 Dec 21 **Yew Tree Groove**   R A Broomhead, M Hutchinson
1972 **Big Tower** (A2)   R Bennett, J Moss
First free ascent P R Littlejohn, R A Broomhead, 11.1.76.

1972 **Seventy Foot Chimney, Subsidiary Wall**   First ascensionists unknown

1973 Jan 1 **Morituri**   E Hart, M Haffner
Climbed on aid a few days previously by R A Broomhead.

1973 Jan 5	**Resolution** M Putnam, M Hutchinson
1973 Jan 6	**New Year Grooves** R A Broomhead, M Hutchinson
1973 Jan 21	**Brass Monkey** M Putnam, T Lister
1973 March 25	**Nose Climb** D Hope

Climbed previously on aid by an unknown party.

| 1973 April 1 | **Madcap Laughs**   R A Broomhead, M Haffner, P Stewart |
| 1973 April 8 | **Dig for Victory**   D Hope, R A Broomhead |

Variation finish as described, R Harrison, 1976. The Sting variation by S Monks, G A Jenkin on 11.9.78.

| 1973 April 14 | **In Memoriam**   R A Broomhead, P Stewart |

A tribute to the many local residents who were killed in a tragic air crash in Switzerland. First pitch added by B Wyvill, R A Broomhead, Ms M McPhearson 12.4.81.

1973 April 15	**Asylum** R A Broomhead
1973 Sept 30	**Mary Jane** R A Broomhead, P Stewart
1973 Oct 23	**Schizoid** (A2) M Putnam, A Strapcans

S Monks and A Strapcans left one aid point from their ascent of 26.10.78, and this was eliminated by M J Crocker on 27.3.84.

1973 Oct 23	**Boo** R A Broomhead, A Strapcans
1973 Oct 24	**Cirrus** M Putnam, A Strapcans
1973 Oct 25	**Skid Row** A Strapcans, M Putnam
1973 Nov 18	**Chrome Nun** (A2) R A Broomhead, C Waller

Climbed free by M J Crocker, R Harrison, 8.9.84.

1973 Dec 2	**Contortion** R A Broomhead, S Hermalin
1974 April 6	**Germaline** R A Broomhead, S Hermalin
1974 April	**Kay** P Stewart, R A Broomhead, M Hutchinson
1974 Nov 10	**Rear Entry** P R Littlejohn, R A Broomhead (AL)

The top pitch was formerly A Salute to the Imperialist Lackeys (3 pts aid) climbed by P Nunn, J Morgan on 3.10.70.

| 1974 Nov 16 | **Madrugada**   P R Littlejohn, R A Broomhead |

'Dick's attention was focused on a fornicating couple on the opposite side of the Gorge. Anyway I got committed beyond the peg but couldn't finish the traverse due to wilting fingers. According to Dick I fell off with a high-pitched yell which coincided with the sounds the couple were making at the height of their activities!' The final pitch was climbed a week later by Littlejohn making a back-roped solo ascent. First free ascent R Harrison, D Carter, 9.9.80 (on sight). Subsequently the route became overgrown, but the top pitch was recleaned and incorporated into Kephalonia.

| 1975 Jan 19 | **Gaul**   P R Littlejohn, R A Broomhead |

The Amphitheatre is 'discovered'.

| 1975 March 22 | **Milky Whey**   A Strapcans, C King |

Previously aided. Climbed direct by R A Broomhead, A Burnham on 23.4.78.

1975 April 19	**Shem Shak** P R Littlejohn, R A Broomhead
1975 April 20	**The Wink** P R Littlejohn, R A Broomhead
1975 April 26	**Bad Dog** (2 pts aid) P R Littlejohn, D Garner

'A signpost to the future – giving hope for the smoother looking walls.' (A Strapcans). Although the route was pre-cleaned, the pegs were placed on lead. Climbed with one aid point by S Haston, and shortly afterwards without by R Harrison, D Carter on 11.4.82. The described direct version was climbed by M J Crocker on 19.10.95. (The original line took a more devious

route to the first roof, and quitted the groove at half-height for a ledge on the left (PR now on Big Foot), before climbing direct past a loose overhang – finally detached by the landowner – to exit into the Amphitheatre.)

1975 April 28   **Chic**   P R Littlejohn
Now Cheddar's finest rock garden!

1975 May 3   **Eat a Peach**   R A Broomhead, P R Littlejohn

1975 May 5   **Hot Lanta**   P R Littlejohn

1975 Oct 9   **The Squint**   P R Littlejohn, R A Broomhead

1975 Oct 19   **The Creaking Door, The Cone**   P R Littlejohn, R A Broomhead
The Surly Tonto finish to the latter route was climbed by D Wiggan, S Findlay on 17.4.81.

1975 Oct 25   **Short Fuse**   P R Littlejohn, D Garner

1975 Oct 25   **Smooth**   R A Broomhead, D Garner

1976 Jan 10   **Pilferer**   P R Littlejohn, R A Broomhead, D Roberts
Previously aided by an unknown party.

1976 Jan 28   **Peg Leg Crack**   R A Broomhead (solo)

1976 Feb 8   **Digit Wall**   P R Littlejohn, R A Broomhead, A Strapcans
The original Digit Wall (circa late 60s) took an indistinct line left of Brass Monkey: possibly the line of Forgotten Sacrifices. Direct finish as described climbed by R A Broomhead, S Monks, on 13.1.79. A Pot of Crock variation by F Haden, M J Crocker on 12.2.95.

1976 Feb 14   **The Nod, Shrapnel**   P R Littlejohn, R A Broomhead, S Berry

1976 Feb 19   **Privy Purse**   P R Littlejohn, R A Broomhead

1976 Mar 5   **Siberia (3 pts aid)**   A Strapcans, C King
The two final pitches were added by the same pair on 28.3.76. Two of the three aid points were subsequently eliminated by R Harrison. Much of the first three pitches is overgrown; the original finish was recleaned and is now shared by A New Siberia and Don't Make Waves.

1976 March 8   **Poon, Nero**   R Harrison, R A Broomhead (AL)
The former is a defunct line right of Portal.

1976 March 8   **Psycho**   C King, J Fivesdale

1976 March 14   **Fart**   P R Littlejohn, R Harrison

1976 March 28   **Hallowed Ground**   P R Littlejohn, H Clarke

1976 April 6   **Gladiator**   P R Littlejohn, R A Broomhead

1976 April 8   **Portal, Wall End**   R A Broomhead, P Stewart

1976 April 11   **Legionnaire (1 pt aid)**   R Harrison, R A Broomhead
First free ascent C King, N Gifford, 5.6.77.

1976 April 29   **Caesar**   P R Littlejohn, R A Broomhead
'...when Livesey repeated it he said it was as good and as hard as Mortlock's Arete.' P Littlejohn.

1976 May 1   **Subsidiary Buttress**   R A Broomhead, P Stewart

1976 May 27   **Forum (1 pt aid)**   R Harrison, J Fivesdale

1976 June 7   **Shell Shock**   P R Littlejohn, R A Broomhead
The route was climbed direct (giving it independence and a crux) by M J Crocker, G A Jenkin on 11.4.95.

1976 June 21   **High Rock Girdle**   P R Littlejohn, R A Broomhead
Most of the bedding plane had been crossed previously by the 'ubiquitous Harry Smith' in 1967 – climbing in big boots of course.

1976 June 22   **The Visionary**   A Strapcans, C King
Strapcans 'preserved the sight-leading tradition' and showed what

the future could hold for 'Sunset'. The climb superseded Sunshine
Sutra *(A2), a girdle traverse by R S Dearman, R A Broomhead,
13.2.71.*

1976 June 23   **Crown of Creation**   P R Littlejohn, R Harrison
*The name belonged to R S Dearman who had previously climbed
the final two pitches mainly free, approaching them from* Sceptre.
*Tony Willmott was reported to have climbed the line, probably
largely on aid, winter 1969/70. The route was led as described in
stages by Littlejohn and Broomhead – pitches 1 and 2, 24.5.76;
pitch 4, 13.5.76.*

1976 July 7   **Danger Bird**   P R Littlejohn, R A Broomhead
*'The easiest way up High Rock!', said Pat Littlejohn. 'Worryingly
loose and strenuous' according to Nipper Harrison after one of the
resting-ledges collapsed under him.*

1976 Nov 14   **Danemark**   A Strapcans, R A Broomhead
Previously climbed, possibly by G West in the late 1950s.

1977 May 5   **Putnam's Folly**   R Harrison, S Monks, R A Broomhead
1977 May 24   **Fossil**   R Harrison, R A Broomhead
1977 June 2   **Skeleton**   R Harrison, R A Broomhead
1977 June 5   **Free Fall**   C King, N Gifford
1977 June 22   **The Muppets**   A Strapcans, Ms H Ramsey
*This line at the left-hand end of Prospect Tier was destroyed by
rock removal.*

1977 Nov 13   **Finefinger, Fool's Overture**   R A Broomhead, N Gifford
1977 Nov   **Shaved Fish**   A Strapcans, S Monks
1977   **Right Crack**   A Strapcans
1977 Nov 20   **The Horse Knows the Way** (2 pts aid)   T Penning, P Cresswell
First free ascent K Marsden, G A Jenkin 6.7.83.

1978 Jan 8   **Sense of Doubt**   R Harrison, R A Broomhead
1978 April 16   **Mars, Forced Entry**   R A Broomhead, S Monks
1978 April 22   **Caligula**   R A Broomhead, A Burnham
1978 April 23   **Eight-line Poem**   R A Broomhead, A Burnham
1978 Sept 17   **Medusa**   S Monks, G Forward
1978 Sept 28   **Positively Bunky**   S Monks, C Gore, G Forward,
R A Broomhead
1978 Sept 30   **Dirty Dick**   A Strapcans, S Marriott
1978 Oct 12   **Prospect Eliminate**   S Monks, R A Broomhead
1978 Nov 9   **Vanguard**   A Strapcans, S Monks
*Replaced the aid route Blue Cheer by R S Dearman,
R A Broomhead, D Lester, 13.12.70.*

1978 Dec 19   **Numbskull**   A Strapcans, S Monks
1979 May 4   **Harley Street**   A Strapcans, A Hall
1979 June 12   **Roadshow**   S Monks, C King
*Recleaned and reclimbed in the described one-pitch form by
M J Crocker, J Harwood, D Pickford on 5.3.00. A second (5c)
pitch, which climbed up via a triangular roof to the Acid Rock
shoulder is very overgrown.*

1979 June 27   **The Scarecrow**   S Monks, A Hall
1979 Sept 8   **Boadicea**   S Monks, A Strapcans, S Bell
Overgrown; re-cleaned in 1985; overgrown again!

1979 Sept 27   **Greenfinger**   S Monks, R A Broomhead
1979 Oct 11   **Baseline**   S Monks, N Perry
1979 Oct 17   **Stone Warrior**   S Monks, G A Jenkin
Three-quarters of the route had been climbed as Mordor (A2) by

R S Dearman and D Lester on 12.12.70. Mordor itself was rid of all aid but one resting-point by R Harrison, N Gifford during 1978.

1980 Feb 16	**Exodus** D Viggers, Ms M Borland, P Debbage
1980 April 15	**Trotter, Spare Rib, The Sow** R A Broomhead, P Newman, S Findlay
1980 April 16	**Porker's Pride** R A Broomhead (solo)
1980 April 22	**Ashman** R A Broomhead, D Carter
1980 May 5	**The Deceiver, New Friends** R A Broomhead, D Carter (AL)
1980 May 11	**Bloody Tourists** R A Broomhead, D Carter
1980 May 13	**Ripping Yarns** R A Broomhead, D Carter
1980 May 25	**Progressive Rock** R A Broomhead, D Carter
1980 Oct 4	**Turkey Trot, Blitz, Mr X** R Harrison, D Wiggan (led latter route)
1980 Oct 5	**Hadrian's Wall** R Harrison, D Wiggan
1980 Oct 5	**Scary Monsters** R A Broomhead, D Carter

The top two pitches had been climbed as an independent route by C King, G A Jenkin on 28.10.78.

1980 Oct 9	**It Must Be the Russians** R Harrison, D Carter
1980 Oct 12	**Gobbledegook** R A Broomhead, D Carter, M Hutchinson

Direct Start by M J Crocker 10.12.00.

1980 Oct 12	**Gruesome Groove** D Carter, R A Broomhead
1980 Oct 15	**Engineers** R Harrison, J Uren

The direct version was added by C Waddy in 1986.

1980 Oct 18	**The Core** R Harrison, D Wiggan, R A Broomhead
1980 Oct 18	**Canary in a Coalmine** D Wiggan, R Harrison
1980 Nov 30	**Broken Arrow** R A Broomhead, D Lambert, D Grey
1980 Dec 7	**Bent Spear** R A Broomhead, D Lambert, D Grey
1980 Dec 10	**Ten Years On** R A Broomhead, D Grey
1981 Feb 15	**Phantom Gardener** R A Broomhead, R Harrison
1981 Feb 21	**Smart Combination** R A Broomhead, D Carter

Pitch 2 had been climbed previously by P R Littlejohn, R A Broomhead on 9 October 1975 as the finish of The Squint.

1981 Feb 21	**Stone the Crows** R Harrison, D Carter

A substantial free route based upon the original line of Shangri La and which finished up the final pitch of The Scarecrow. The central pitches became extremely vegetated within a short period.

1981 April 2	**Little Gem** R Harrison, D Carter
1981 April 3	**Catalogues of Fear** D Wiggan, S Findlay, S Monks
1981 April 4	**The Hidden Towers, Grand National, One for the Road** R A Broomhead, D Carter
1981 April 5	**Cool Hand Luke** S Monks, S Findlay
1981 April 6	**Super Creeps** R A Harrison, D Carter, R A Broomhead

The top two pitches had previously been climbed as an independent route, by C King, G A Jenkin on 28.10.78.

1981 April 7	**The Perfect Game** S Findlay, S Monks
1981 April 9	**The Prow, Newton's Wal...!** R Harrison, D Carter

The latter route was pinched from Broomhead whilst he was recuperating from a 40-foot peel.

1981 April 12	**Nagging Doubts** R A Broomhead, B Wyvill, Ms M McPhearson
1981 April 15	**Dulled Sword** R A Broomhead, A Burnham
1981 April 17	**Side Line** R A Broomhead, D Wiggan, S Findlay
1981 May 1	**The Pict** R Harrison, D Carter

1981 June 25	**Sinsemilla** R A Broomhead
	The Direct Start was added by M Ward, M J Crocker 14.8.87.
1981 June 27	**The Direct Approach** R A Broomhead, S Findlay, S Briggs
1981 June 29	**Razor Buttress** R A Broomhead, S Briggs, S Bell
1981 July 25	**Brittle Nerve** R A Broomhead, S Briggs
1981 Aug 31	**Late Entry, Claire's Complexity** R A Broomhead, S Briggs (AL)
	Africa Corps variation to the second route by M J Crocker,
	F Haden on 18.3.95.
1982 April 18	**Effendi** F Thompson, M Brown
1982 Sept 8	**Conquistador** F Thompson, M Brown
1982 Sept 19	**Babylon** R A Broomhead, F Thompson
	Reclimbed on 16.2.03 by M J Crocker, J Harwood with a more
	direct central section and after significant rock removal by the
	landowners.
1982 Dec 28	**Mohican** R A Broomhead, M J Crocker
1983 April 15	**Thriller** R Harrison R A Broomhead
1983 July 12	**The Burner** R A Broomhead, D Viggers
1983 July 21	**The Clingon** R Harrison, R A Broomhead
1983 Aug 3	**Blockbuster** F Thompson, A March
1983 Aug 8	**Hidden Beauty** R Harrison, R A Broomhead
1983 Aug 13	**Wall of Bans, The Art of Graceful Stemming**
	R A Broomhead, D Viggers
1983 Aug 31	**Maker's Nameplate** R Harrison, R A Broomhead
	The final groove had been climbed previously on 22.4.79 by
	A Strapcans, A Hall as part of the now redundant Burp.
1983 Oct 7	**Vanishing Point** D Light, M J Crocker
1983 Oct 23	**Centrefold** R A Broomhead, F Thompson
1983 Oct 28	**Eddy Grundy, Dianthus** R A Broomhead, D Carroll (AL)
1983 Oct 29	**Slow Return** R A Broomhead, G Traish
1983 Nov 12	**Dead Stop** R Harrison, R A Broomhead
	Originally climbed via the ledge on First a Fence; straightened out
	by M J Crocker, N A Coe on 12.1.02.
1983 Nov 16	**The Usual Pornography** D Carroll, Mrs M Viggers
	A phrase coined by local habitués to describe the dirtier aspects of
	climbing at Cheddar!
1983 Dec 4	**Funny Bone, Greg's Little Wall of Horrors**
	R A Broomhead, G Forward (AL)
1983 Dec 4	**Spacehunter, Beverley's Wall** M J Crocker, J Bassindale
	(1 pt aid [rest-point] on the former)
	'I lay awake all night, nerve-racked by the uncertainty of it all.'
	Spacehunter *was climbed free by M J Crocker on 2.11.85.*
1983 Dec 10	**Inter-Continental Ballistic Bonzo** M J Crocker,
	R A Broomhead
1983 Dec 27	**La Tour Noire** M J Crocker, R A Broomhead
1983 Dec 31	**Gorilla Tactics** R A Broomhead, M J Crocker (AL)
	'Richard would fail seemingly with the intention of ensuring that I'd
	pull up on the loose block that he would always leave behind.
	After several mega-lobs, I wised-up.'
1984 Feb 12	**Forbidden Zones** M J Crocker, D Ardron
1984 March 11	**Kephalonia** M J Crocker, D Ardron
1984 March 29	**The Knack** M J Crocker, J Bassindale
1984 March	**Digit Arête** P Smith
1984 Aug 28	**Killing Time** D Viggers, P Sykes, G Forward, S Briggs
1984 Aug 28	**Rachel's Crack** S Briggs, G Forward

1984 Sept 16	**Every Step of the Way** (2 pts aid) R Harrison, M J Crocker (AL)

One of the two rest-points was eliminated by M J Crocker on
16.4.85. A more direct first pitch was added and the upper pitch
redpointed by M J Crocker on 22.2.86:

1984 Sept 29	**Barbarian** R Harrison, M J Crocker

Direct start (You Had No Reason) added by G Gibson, M Ward on
22.12.86, and the whole route ascended by G Gibson on
31.1.87.

1984 Oct 15	**Fountain of Arethusa, The Empire** M J Crocker, D Carroll
1984 Nov 17	**Speedfreak** M J Crocker

A well-advanced lead; the lethal to on-sight start was neutered
when Crocker returned two years later and replaced the loose,
downward-pointing peg with a bolt.

1984 Nov 17	**Dressed to Thrill** M J Crocker, J Bassindale
1984	**Matanuska** G Hornby, Ms A Worcester

Rumoured to have been climbed before.

1985 Feb 23	**Hallucinations, Oingo B,B,B...Boingo!** M J Crocker, G A Jenkin
1985 April 13	**In from the Storm** M J Crocker, G A Jenkin
1985 June 23	**Dambuster** M J Crocker, G A Jenkin

An almighty rockfall occurred!

1985 June 26	**Sorceress, Get Kimitri!, Keystone Cop-out** M J Crocker, G A Jenkin

On the first route, the second was placed at the top of a clear run
down to the road! It was flashed on sight by I Vickers in 1995.

1985 July 18	**Another Winner** J Bassindale, Ms A Jones

Supersedes One Step Beyond by D Carter, R A Broomhead,
5.6.80.

1985 July 19	**Spitting Dust** J Bassindale, Ms A Jones
1985 July 24	**Mental Revenge** J Bassindale, Ms A Jones
1985 Sept 6	**The Harder They Fall** M J Crocker, G A Jenkin, K Marsden
1985 Sept 10	**Riotsville, Heart Leaf Direct** R A Broomhead, C Brear

The Superdirect Start to the latter was added by M J Crocker (solo)
7.4.87.

1985 Sept 14	**Blurred Vision, Show Some Restraint** R A Broomhead, G A Jenkin (AL)
1985 Sept 19	**Long Shot Kick-E-Bucket**

The 'Pioneers' were M J Crocker, G A Jenkin.

1985 Sept 25	**The Night Heat** M J Crocker, R A Broomhead
1985 Oct 5	**Why Must I?, Heaven-sent** M J Crocker, M Ward

'Cheddar is the sort of place you come to for dangerous routes.'
(R A Broomhead). The top pitch of the former route was climbed as
Midsummer Blues by S Briggs, R A Broomhead on 18.7.81.
Heaven-sent Direct was added by M J Crocker on 15.3.95: 'I
started up this at 6.20 p.m. in fading light. I had only 25 minutes
before total darkness and the close season.' The direct was
flashed on sight by I Vickers in 1995 who pronounced it to be
'gnarly'.

1985 Oct 11	**Macabre** M J Crocker, S Monks

Originally finished boldly to the right. Climbed as described by
M J Crocker, G A Jenkin, M Ward on 1 October 1986.

1985 Oct 12	**Madonna** M J Crocker, G A Jenkin, M Ward
1985 Oct 12	**Don't Make Waves** M J Crocker, G A Jenkin
1985 Oct 12	**Sloe Gin, Fellatio** R A Broomhead, Ms A E Organ

1985 Oct 13	**Shadowlands, Alaska** M J Crocker, G A Jenkin
1985 Oct 13	**Black Spitfire** S Monks, K Marsden
1985 Oct 14	**White Lady, Creeping Weakness** R A Broomhead, C Brear
1985 Oct 15	**Big Deal** R A Broomhead, C Brear
1985 Oct 16	**The Wishing Wall, Desert Rat** M J Crocker, S Monks

'...on my on-sight second ascent attempt as a callow 16-year old, wet rock and lichen expelled me from above the crux. After the subsequent thirty-five footer, I had another go, only for the same thing to happen again.' Dave Pickford reflects on his encounter with The Wishing Wall.

1985 Oct 17	**Demonic Arête** R A Broomhead, C Brear
1985 Oct 18	**Misty Morning, Candy 'O'** R A Broomhead, C Brear
1985 Oct 20	**Stitchless, Solo** R A Broomhead

On the former route, a brave attempt to hold second man (Big) Mark Hopkins left Broomhead with a broken wrist!

1985 Oct 23	**Jewel in the Sun** M J Crocker, S Monks
1985 Oct 25	**Lionheart** S Monks, H Harrison

The mountain of debris at the bottom grew bigger day by day as the route was cleaned. On the third ascent I Parnell dislodged a huge razor of rock directly above the head of his second who was belayed at the first stance. Crocker, knowing Parnell's weight (and propensity for accidents) was keeping a wary eye out for trouble, saw the block coming, and dodged with only two inches to spare. The flake missiled into the earth bank below to form a symbolic gravestone.

1985 Oct 26	**Nice Crack, Kumquat, Odds against Tomorrow, Shinanikin** M J Crocker, M Ward

The first route supersedes Nice Crack, Shame About the Face climbed by A Strapcans, A Burnham, 5.79.

1985 Oct 27	**Black Night, Live Dust** C Brear, J Potokar (AL), G Meyer
1985 Oct 27	**Hell-bent** M J Crocker

The direct start, Just Plain Bent!, was added by M J Crocker on the 14 October 1989.

1985 Nov 2	**Siouxie** M J Crocker, M Ward
1985 Nov 3	**Exiled!, No Reservations** M J Crocker, G A Jenkin
1985 Nov 7	**State of Mind, The In Spire** S Monks, M J Crocker (AL)
1985 Nov 10	**Bearing Straight, A New Siberia** M J Crocker, M Ward, G A Jenkin (latter route)
1985 Nov 11	**Ginseng** S Monks
1985 Nov 17	**House Burning Down** M J Crocker, M Ward
1985 Nov 17	**Tell It like It Is** G Gibson, J Codling

Gibson invades the Gorge! The variation A Simple Tale was climbed by G Gibson, M Ward 19.12.86.

1985 Nov 23	**Try to Remember, My Bones, My Bones, My...** M J Crocker, M Ward
1985 Nov 24	**Ice Cool** R A Broomhead, C Brear
1985 Nov 27	**Pure Joy, Black Magic Woman** R A Broomhead, C Brear
1985	**West Wall Climb, Windy Crack, Central Route** R A Broomhead
1986 Jan 1	**Skullduggery, Buried Alive** M J Crocker, M Ward
1986 Jan 11	**Lion In Winter, The Snarl, Lion's Share** M J Crocker, M Ward (led latter route)
1986 Jan 12	**English Cheddar Gorgeous** M J Crocker, G A Jenkin

1986 Jan 25	**Wild Frontier, Wham Bam Thank You Ma'am, Comfortably Numb** M J Crocker, G A Jenkin, M Ward (AL)	

1986 Jan 25   **Wild Frontier, Wham Bam Thank You Ma'am, Comfortably Numb**   M J Crocker, G A Jenkin, M Ward (AL)
Wild Frontier was led bolt-free by M J Crocker on 6.2.00.

1986 Jan 26   **Taming of the Lion**   M J Crocker
'…pull, pull, pull! – ignore the pain, the searing pain burning my fat fingers – I pull all right and, what's more, I get the jug.' The 'jug' was ripped off during a repeat ascent by P Oxley in 1.89.

1986 Feb 8   **Shock of the New, The Numb Ones**   M J Crocker, M Ward
Shock of the New was straightened out (omitting the rest-loop on the right) by M J Crocker on 30.3.93.

1986 Feb 15   **No Slings Attached**   G Gibson, M Ward, M J Crocker

1986 Feb 15   **Vic Bond**   M J Crocker, G A Jenkin

1986 Feb 15   **The Fearless Four**   M J Crocker, G A Jenkin, G Gibson, M Ward

1986 Feb 22   **Crackshot, Up against the Wall!, Mud in Your Eye**
M J Crocker, M Ward (led latter route)

1986 March 1   **The Perishers**   M J Crocker, M Ward

1986 March 2   **Hold Me Tight**   M J Crocker, Miss B A Vincent

1986 March 7   **Edge of Eternity**   M J Crocker, G A Jenkin

1986 March 8   **Sunsations, Brusque, Floaters, 'Any Moment Now'**
M J Crocker, M Ward (led latter route)

1986 March 23   **Don't Let Me Down, Strangler in Paradise**   M J Crocker, M Ward

1986 June 12   **For Ever and Ever**   M J Crocker, W Rees

1986 Aug 31   **B.A.D.**   P Hughes

1986 Sept 27   **Ripe Old Age, Donner und Blitzen**   M J Crocker, M Ward

1986 Sept 27   **Airborne Attack**   R Kingston, M Ward
Only the final bulge had not been climbed before.

1986 Sept 28   **All Hands to the Pump, Small is Big**   M Ward, M J Crocker (AL)

1986 Oct 1   **Spy in St Pauls**   M J Crocker, G A Jenkin, M Ward, R Kingston

1986 Oct 4   **Heartbleed, Bombs Away, Absolutely Amazing Climb II**
M J Crocker, M Ward (led first route)

1986 Oct 4   **Smooth Operator, Off the Wall**   R Kingston, D Vousden

1986 Oct 5   **Tied in Knots**   R Kingston, M Hopkins

1986 Oct 5   **Play the White Man**   M Ward, R Kingston
Two peg runners were in place already.

1986 Oct 6   **Eastender**   T Robbins, M Adams
Previously ascended but not recorded.

1986 Oct 11   **Afterglow, Snug as a Slug on a Jug,**   M J Crocker, M Ward (AL)

1986 Oct 12   **The Insidious Green, Arni's Arête**   M J Crocker, M Ward

1986 Oct 23   **Bullsblood**   M Ward, M J Crocker

1986 Oct 26   **Star Spangled Banner, Little Wing, The Prime Slime Climb**   M J Crocker, M Ward (led latter route)

1986 Nov 2   **Make No Mistake, Bonanza**   M J Crocker, M Ward

1986 Nov 8   **Fettered Trajectory**   M J Crocker, M Ward
Climbed originally with one bolt runner, near the crux. The direct finish: Air to Air Exit was added by M J Crocker, I Parnell on 22.10.94.

1986 Nov 9   **Rufus Roughcut (2 pts aid)**   R Kingston, B Stadden

1986 Nov 15   **Berlin Wall**   T Robbins, M Adams, R Evans

1986 Nov 15   **Hounds in the Moonlight**   R Kingston, I Freeman

1986 Nov 15	**Lonely Pride, Soopa Doopa** M Ward, M J Crocker (AL)	
1986 Nov 29	**Shakin' Like a Leaf** G Gibson, M Ward, G A Jenkin, M J Crocker, J Shaw, N A Coe	

The route saw a brief flurry of popularity before some of the in-situ gear (bolt, wire, jammed nut) was anonymously chopped, apparently to make a point about ethics. The route was led bolt-free by M J Crocker on 6.2.00 (but may have been done so earlier).

1986 Nov 29	**Take the Bull by the Horns** M Ward, J Shaw

The direct start was added pinkpoint by M J Crocker, M Ward (AL) on 8.3.87.

1986 Nov 29	**Sheer Lunacy** M J Crocker, G A Jenkin, N A Coe
1986 Nov 30	**Consenting Adults** G A Jenkin, N A Coe

Craitor Traitor variation by F Haden, M J Crocker on 5.11.94.

1986 Nov 30	**Manic Depression** M J Crocker, G Gibson
1986 Dec 6	**Cryogenics** M Ward, M J Crocker

The second became a block of ice.

1986 Dec 6	**Croaking in Woking** M J Crocker

Straightened out Choking in Woking, a variation finish to The Knack by J Codling, G Gibson, 17.11.85.

1986 Dec 6	**Silent Night, Super High-intensity Micro Climb** G Gibson, M Ward, M J Crocker
1986 Dec 10	**Still Waters Run Deep** M Ward, M J Crocker, M Bellian

A threat to 'smash out' the bolts was made but not put to effect.

1986 Dec 20	**Get That Man!** G Gibson
1986 Dec 21	**Dodo, No Time to Lose** R Kingston, I Freeman, G A Jenkin

(latter route unseconded)

1986 Dec 21	**The Ghettos** M J Crocker, M Ward
1986 Dec 22	**One Foot in the Grave** M Ward, G Gibson
1986 Dec 24	**Ian Paisley, Ten Hours BC** M J Crocker, M Ward
1986 Dec 24	**As Happy as a Slug in Slime** M Ward (solo)
1986 Dec 28	**True Colours** (3 pts aid) R Kingston

Climbed free by M J Crocker, G A Jenkin, 28.4.87.

1987 Jan 11	**Caesar Direct** M J Crocker

'The temperature that day reached -5 degrees centigrade; it took one and a half hours of running about in The Amphitheatre to warm myself up and just fifteen minutes to climb the pitch.'

1987 Jan 18	**Slalom** M J Crocker, M Ward

Some of the route was plastered with snow.

1987 Jan 24	**Ecocritical** M J Crocker, M Ward
1987 Jan 25	**Backstabbers** M J Crocker, G A Jenkin

The central crack was climbed by M J Crocker, D Carroll on 1.11.84, starting and finishing as for Caesar.

1987 Jan 25	**Comfortably Numb** M Ward, R Kingston, G A Jenkin, M J Crocker
1987 Jan 31	**Off the Beaten Track** G Gibson, J Codling

'I had a lot of problems on the top roof not being able to feel the rock or my fingers. My nose dribbled but the dribble froze before reaching my mouth.'

1987 Feb 1	**The Wayward Eliminate** M J Crocker, G A Jenkin

The first pitch appeared to have been previously pegged.

1987 Feb 22	**Plastic Bullets, Farewell to the Working Classes** M Ward, M J Crocker (AL), G A Jenkin
1987 March 8	**No Mnemonics, Free Enterprise** M J Crocker, G A Jenkin

1987 May 12	**Rat, Tat, Tat** R Harrison, K Marsden
	A line geared by G Gibson.
1987 May 19	**Igor, Theatre of Hate** M J Crocker, M Ward (AL)
1987 June 9	**Cream Tease** M Ward, R Kingston
1987 June 16	**One of These Days, Cut Glass** M Ward, R Kingston (AL)
1987 July 9	**We're Civilized** M J Crocker, M Ward
1987 July 21	**The Moon Is Made of Green Cheese** M Ward, M J Crocker
1987 July 29	**Trail of the Snail** M Ward, M J Crocker
1987 Aug 4	**Jazz Defector** M J Crocker, G A Jenkin
1987 Aug 14	**Follow the Slick Red Road** M J Crocker, M Ward (AL)
	The Gdansk variation to the former route was added by P Oxley, J Williams on 12.5.88.
1987 Sept 22	**My Wife's Apple Crumble** M J Crocker, G A Jenkin
1987 Oct 4	**Les Trois Chèvres, One for the Northern Brats**
	M J Crocker, M Ward, G A Jenkin
1987 Oct 11	**Red Beretta** M J Crocker, M Ward, G A Jenkin
1987 Oct 16	**The Scented Isle** M J Crocker, G A Jenkin
1987 Oct 17	**Thermopylae** M J Crocker, G A Jenkin
1987 Oct 17	**Rape of the Sabine Women** M Ward, M J Crocker, G A Jenkin
1987 Oct 17	**Osiris** R Kingston, M Ward (pitches 1 and 2)
	Pitches 3, 4, and 5 were climbed by R Kingston, I Freeman on 4.10.87. First complete ascent K Marsden, G A Jenkin, 25.10.87.
1987 Oct 22	**'Gentleman in Red Trousers', Rigorous Self Abuse**
	M J Crocker, M Ward
	The National Trust Warden shouted up to the climber in red trousers to stop climbing and come down. The invitation to him to come up and discuss matters was not taken up.
1987 Oct 25	**Screw Archimedes, Cruising the Med** M J Crocker, M Ward
1987 Oct 25	**Wait until the Darkness Comes** G A Jenkin, K Marsden
	Get into the Groove variation by F Haden, N Burton on 1.6.94.
1987 Nov 7	**Whippersnappers** M Ward, M J Crocker
1987 Nov 8	**Brazilia** M J Crocker, M Ward
	Supersedes Back in the Chain Gang climbed by R Kingston, M Hopkins (AL) on 8.11.86.
1987 Dec 27	**Dream Cruise** R Kingston, M Ward
	Direct Finish by M J Crocker, J Harwood on 25.2.95.
1988 Jan 17	**La Del Gioconda** M Ward, M J Crocker
1988 Feb 20	**The Bloodshed Begins, Bon Voyage** G A Jenkin, M Ward (AL) M J Crocker
1988 Feb 21	**Millimetre War** M J Crocker, G A Jenkin
	The unit by which progress the previous day could be measured!
1988 Feb 23	**Ya-Boo Yorkie!** M J Crocker
1988 Feb 27	**Insatiable** M Ward, R Kingston
1988 Feb 28	**Greed, 'Real Runners', Mutant Frenzy Bug, Raw Deal** M J Crocker, M Ward (led latter route)
1988 March 25	**Like a Virgin, Ebee G Bees** M J Crocker (solo; former self-protected with long sling)
1988 March 26	**Tot-ally Wick-ed, Ritual Slaughter, Minstrelation, Islands in the City** G A Jenkin, M J Crocker (led latter three routes)

1988 March 27	**Bee Keeping in a War Zone, Crème de la Phlegm, The Golden Road to Samarkand** M Ward, G A Jenkin, M J Crocker
1988 March 27	**Grope the Slope, Kaput Four Fingers** G A Jenkin, M J Crocker (AL), M Ward
1988 March 30	**Split Rambo, Sophisticated, Psycho-babble** M J Crocker, G A Jenkin (led latter route)
1988 April 14	**Bombay Duck, Terminate a Tourist Today, Magnus Pyke** M Ward (solo)
1988 May 6	**Big Softy** M J Crocker, G A Jenkin
1988 May 9	**Beyond the Hydra Centaurus Supercluster** M J Crocker, G A Jenkin
1988 Sept 18	**Eaten Alive, All the Juicy Bits, Vanity** G A Jenkin, M Ward (led latter two routes)
1988 Oct 1	**Toxic Shock** G A Jenkin, N A Coe
1988 Oct 2	**Rameses** R Kingston, M Ward
1988 Oct 14	**Instigate Emergency Closure** M J Crocker, G A Jenkin
1988 Oct 15	**Doc Martin's, One Track Mind** M J Crocker, M Ward (AL)
1988 Dec 31	**Valley of the Blind, The Forest** P Oxley, C Appleby (AL)
	'The crowd gawked but couldn't understand.' First route flashed on sight by I Vickers, 1993.
1989 Jan 1	**Bursting the Wave** P Oxley
1989 April	**Just Like Art** B Tilley, R White
1989 Oct 7	**Nonplus One, Bored of Pies** M J Crocker
1989 Oct 8	**Manchmals, On Radio** M J Crocker, G A Jenkin (seconded former route only)
1989 Oct 8	**Tarmac Terminator** G A Jenkin, N A Coe, M J Crocker
	An enormous block bounced down onto the road with horror-struck perpetrators Jenkin and Coe in hot pursuit.
1989 Nov 5	**The Wrecking Crew** M J Crocker
	On a preceding attempt, tea and cakes were supplied by an unknown party who later dislodged a block from the top of Coronation Street onto the roof of the first ascensionist's car. An out-of-court settlement was negotiated!
1989 Nov 12	**Pirates of Lamb Leer, Mercurian Sump Dweller, Clean Hand Man** M J Crocker
	S Findlay followed the latter route – without chalk!
1989 Nov 18	**Hard Bass Religion** P Oxley
1989 Nov 19	**The Man that Never Was, The Underground Influence** M J Crocker
1989 Nov 25	**The Midnight Run** M J Crocker, R Thomas
1989 Nov 26	**Cerebral Paralysis** M J Crocker, R Thomas
1989 Dec 9	**Chukostkiy** M J Crocker, G A Jenkin
1989 Dec 26	**SkyScrape** M J Crocker
1989 Dec 31	**Northern Lights, Déjà Rue** G A Jenkin, M J Crocker
1989 Dec 31	**Captain Morgan** M J Crocker
1990 Jan 18	**Potwalloper's Wall, Speltershake, Irradiation, Heirloom** M J Crocker
	A road closure organized by The National Trust enabled a thorough gardening job to be done!
1990 Feb 18	**Only a Lad, Nasty Habits** M J Crocker
	Mrs Crocker's objections to being a 'belay slave' were heard throughout the Gorge as she was lowered over the precipice.
1990 Feb 24	**Epoxy Soak** M J Crocker, M Woodford

1990 March 3	**Bird of Prey**	M J Crocker, M Woodford
1990 May 15	**A Day Called Zero, Hell's a Hard Place**	P Oxley, M Himble (latter route)
1990 Oct 11	**Will Stanton**	M J Crocker

Named in honour of the Mendip caving pioneer noted for his ability to stabilize underground boulder ruckles with cement; similar techniques were needed to keep in place several wobbly holds! 'Comparable in intensity to Statement of Youth' according to second ascensionist Pete Oxley. Flashed by Ian Vickers in 1995.

1990 Oct 13	**Moonmilk, Bick Zoomhead**	M J Crocker
1990 Oct 14	**The Blighter**	M J Crocker
1990 Oct 28	**Bamboleo, Abdominal Cave-in**	M J Crocker
1990 Nov 4	**Playboys**	M J Crocker
1991 May	**Life's Too Short for Plucking Mushrooms, Victim of Circumstance**	R A Broomhead, J Watson, D Targett
1991 Oct 5	**Draggin' Along**	P Oxley
1991 Oct 19	**Gubia, Pitchfork Rebellion, Editorial Axe**	M J Crocker

Most of the last route had been climbed as the top pitch of Gorilla Tactics by M J Crocker and R A Broomhead on 31.12.83.

1992 July 28	**A Friend Indeed**	D Hughes, S Mooney
1992 Oct 18	**Mea Culpa**	K Marsden, A March
1992 Oct 31	**Jon Luke, Robertson's Jam, Bollocks to Broccoli**	M J Crocker, J Robertson
1992 Nov 14	**Green Man**	D Scott-Maxwell, P Robertson
1992 Dec 26	**RPs Out, Matt Ward's In**	M J Crocker
1992 Dec 30	**Stepping Back**	G A Jenkin
1993 Jan 2	**Sherryland, Bluepoint, Decimation**	M J Crocker, J Robertson
1993 Jan 16	**Jewel Of A Son**	M J Crocker, J Robertson
1993 Jan 17	**Sing a Mean Toon, Kid**	M J Crocker
1993 Jan	**Abort, Retry, Ignore**	P Robertson, M J Crocker
1993 Jan 16	**Readers' Wives**	G A Jenkin, K Wilkinson
1993 Feb 6	**Pride Evans Locker**	M J Crocker
1993 Feb 7	**Opt-out**	P Robertson, M J Crocker
1993 Feb 12	**Sunnyside Up**	P Robertson, D Scott-Maxwell
1993 Feb 14	**St. Valentine's Day Massacre**	N Burton, S Mooney
1993 Feb 20	**Consider This, Round the Bend, The Pioneers**	M J Crocker

The first route was climbed on aid by R Pannatier in 3.71.

1993 Feb 21	**Fool's Bolt, BBG, Muchos Bebe**	M J Crocker, J Robertson (AL)

The second route may well have been climbed by R A Broomhead circa early 70s.

1993 Feb 27	**Secret Cabaret**	M J Crocker
1993 Feb 28	**Tourist Distraction**	S Mooney, R Wych
1993 Feb 28	**Parallel Lines**	P Robertson, J Pokotar
1993 Feb 28	**Rave Party**	M J Crocker, J Robertson
1993 Feb	**Sport for All**	P Robertson, D Scott-Maxwell
1993 March 4	**Cleared for Take Off, A Pinch of Thought, The Best Things in Life Aren't Things, Stripped for Action**	S Mooney, N Burton
1993 March 7	**Chalk and Cheese**	P Robertson, M Ward, H Ward

1993 March 13	**12,000 Miles** S Mooney, T Rainbow
	The distance that Tom had to travel home after doing the route –
	to Australia!
1993 March 13	**Ultra-Violence** M J Crocker, P Oxley
1993 March 15	**A Day for Feet** G A Jenkin, M J Crocker
1993 March 26	**Over Easy** D Scott-Maxwell, A Donson
1993 March 27	**British Summer Time** S Mooney, N Burton
1993 March 28	**Bikini Amber** G A Jenkin, K Marsden, S Cook
1993 Sept 5	**Towser** T Rainbow, C Snell
1993 Sept 5	**It's in the Trees** S Mooney, T Rainbow
1993 Sept 5	**Motherless Child** S Mooney (solo)
1993 Oct 8	**Grockles Galore, Subsidiary Arete** F Haden (solo)
	With a hard direct finish the former became Grockles
	Super-galore, and the latter route was given a direct start on
	21.12.97, by M J Crocker, J Harwood.
1993 Oct 9	**The Unrelenting Wit of David Turnbull** P Robertson
1993 Oct 17	**Return of the Gunfighter** M J Crocker, F Haden
	Commemorated a return to action after a horrendous accident in
	May. Quickly repeated by Paul Riley who said 'it is one of the
	finest stamina pitches around'.
1993 Oct 31	**Always Tomorrow, Scarred Mind** M J Crocker, P Twomey,
	I Parnell (second route)
1993 Oct	**Arachnophilia, Just Another Sunday, Fuzzy Logic,**
	Neural Network P Robertson, D Scott-Maxwell (led last route)
1993 Nov 7	**Lest We Forget** S Mooney (solo)
1993 Nov 7	**The China Shop, Gardener's World** P Robertson, I Perry
1993 Nov 7	**Groundrush** M J Crocker, G A Jenkin
1993 Nov 12	**Microscopic** P Robertson, M Ward
1993 Nov 22	**Wiggly Park** S Mooney (solo)
1993 Nov 24	**Sun Blind** S Mooney (solo)
1993 Nov 28	**Poached Eggs** I Perry
1993 Nov	**Wild Thyme** D Scott-Maxwell, P Robertson
1993 Dec 4	**Chartbuster, Assassin!** M J Crocker, F Haden
	New Entry variation to the former by P Twomey, I Parnell,
	B Durston, M J Crocker, F Haden 7.94.
1993 Dec 21	**It's Behind Yew, Solstice** S Mooney (first route solo),
	N Burton
1994 Jan 10	**Rock Junky** F Haden, M J Crocker
1994 Jan 22	**Pussy Galore, Human Zoo** M J Crocker, F Haden, I Parnell
	(seconded second route)
1994 Jan 26	**Audience of Goats** S Mooney (solo)
1994 Jan 28	**Circus, Circus** M J Crocker, I Parnell
	A weekday lunchtime swoop.
1994 Jan 30	**ECG, Screwballed!, Still Wanton** M J Crocker, F Haden (AL)
1994 Jan 30	**Lean Burn** M J Crocker
1994 Jan 31	**A Life of Grime Left-hand** S Mooney (solo)
1994 Feb 4	**It's a Dirty Job... But..., Zugzwang** S Mooney, N Burton
1994 Feb 6	**It's a Kind of Magic** F Haden, M J Crocker
1994 Feb 9	**Everyday Lives of Ordinary People** M J Crocker
1994 Feb 13	**Partners in Crime** F Haden, B Durston
1994 Feb 13	**A Life of Grime, The Blue Brothers** S Mooney, N Burton
1994 Feb 16	**No Bolts Please, We're British!** F Haden (solo)
1994 Feb 19	**Spy in the Sky** F Haden
1994 Feb 27	**Arson – A Burning Desire** S Mooney, R Wych

1994 Feb	**Au Bout de Souffle** I Parnell, P Twomey
1994 March 9	**Does Rock Dream?** S Mooney (solo)
1994 March 20	**Cheddar Death Knell** F Haden, M J Crocker

Required considerable preparation. An unimpressed neighbour, and climber-hater, saw to it that the unofficial ban on Lion Rock was formalized and enforced.

1994 March 26	**The Other Side of Paradise** M J Crocker, F Haden
1994 March 26	**Spider Down My Vest – Cardiac Arrest!** F Haden, M J Crocker
1994 March 27	**The Unacceptable Face of Unacceptability, 9.81 The Old Enemy, Could It Be the Mild Humble Janitor?** S Mooney, N Burton
1994 March 29	**Prodigal Sun** S Mooney, N Burton
1994 March 20	**Right-hand Man** M J Crocker

Has lost a few holds – thanks to Gareth Parry ('some fat bloater'). On-sight flashed by I Vickers.

1994 March 20	**Tumbletot** M J Crocker, I Parnell
1994 March 31	**The Passion** S Mooney (solo)
1994 April 23	**Omnirock** M J Crocker, F Haden
1994 May 9	**It's All Bull, Mean, Lean, Power Machine** M J Crocker, F Haden (AL)
1994 May 16	**'Hold, Hold, Hold!'** M J Crocker, B Durston, I Parnell
1994 May	**Peace, Love, Empathy, Whose Line Is It Anyway?** F Haden (soloed second route), M J Crocker

The second route extended a classic boulder problem.

1994 May	**Heavy Metal Eurotrash, The Harder They Come** M J Crocker, F Haden (seconded first route)
1994 June 2	**Steroid Power** F Haden, M J Crocker
1994 June 7	**Another Roadside Attraction** F Haden, N Burton
1994 June 8	**It's a Hard Life (Never Mind), Bolt Action** F Haden, M J Crocker (second route only)
1994 June 10	**Don't Cry On My Hard Shoulder** F Haden (solo)
1994 June 11	**Groovy Baby!, Groovy Man!** F Haden (solo)
1994 June 22	**Teenage Riot** F Haden, M J Crocker
1994 June 28	**Sidewinder** F Haden, M J Crocker
1994 July 1	**Bolt Wars** F Haden, M J Crocker
1994 July 5	**Sidekick** G A Jenkin, M J Crocker, F Haden
1994 July 5	**Heat's On** M J Crocker, F Haden
1994 July 28	**Hung Jury** G A Jenkin, M J Crocker
1994 Aug 16	**All Guns Blazing** F Haden, Ms L Creamer
1994 Oct 3	**Me No Stereotype** M J Crocker
1994 Oct 5	**Act Of Vengeance** F Haden, M J Crocker
1994 Oct 8	**Patitucci Bass, Corea Elektrosound, Streamline** M J Crocker, F Haden (led last route)
1994 Oct 13	**Road to Paradise** F Haden, M J Crocker
1994 Oct 15	**Easy Pickings, Immaculate Conception** F Haden (first route solo), L Percival
1994 Oct 22	**No Fit State** M J Crocker, I Parnell
1994 Oct 23	**Spiritualize** M J Crocker, F Haden
1994 Oct 26	**Driller Killer, Qu'est-ce Que C'est?** F Haden
1994 Nov 5	**Your Destiny** F Haden, A March, G A Jenkin, K Marsden
1994 Nov 6	**Watching the Days Go By** F Haden, M J Crocker
1994 Nov 7	**Project X, Dope on a Slope, On Beachy Head** M J Crocker, F Haden

1994 Nov 11	**Forgotten Sacrifices** S Mooney (solo)
1994 Dec 3	**Velcro Wall** M J Crocker, F Haden
1994 Dec 4	**Another Dick on the Wall** M J Crocker, F Haden
1994 Dec 9	**By a Nose, Don't Don't, Return of the Bunfeaster** S Mooney, N Burton *Mooney takes the piss – with inimitable style.*
1994 Dec 12	**Always on My Mind** S Mooney, N Burton
1994 Dec 15	**Quarante Pourcent Matière Grasse** A March, K Marsden *The fat content of the average Cheddar Cheese is 40%.*
1994 Dec 21	**Micawberism, Cyclists Advised to Walk, The Grail** S Mooney, N Burton
1994 Dec 23	**The Great Dane and Other Tall Tales, Avalon, Sell Your Soul, Can-Can** S Mooney (solo) *'Soloing at Cheddar demands, shall we say, that extra degree of lunacy.'*
1994	**Bouncing Barry** B Durston
1995 Dec 25	**So This Is Christmas?** S Mooney *Cheddar's first Xmas Day climb.*
1995 Jan 1	**Weasel Words, Quicksnake** M J Crocker, F Haden *The latter takes the left arête of what was the groove of Slow-worm (6.65). The right arête (and the groove) has been demolished by contractors.*
1995 Jan 1	**Another Year Over** S Mooney (solo)
1995 Jan 11	**Game Over, No Purchase Necessary, The Message, Aqueous** S Mooney, N Burton
1995 Jan 12	**Under Surveillance, A Question of Sport** S Mooney (solo)
1995 Feb 4	**Kind of Hush, Fingerboard Crack** M J Crocker, S Mooney
1995 Feb 12	**Yup, Yup, and Away, One Dry Sunday…, Do or Dole** M J Crocker, S Mooney
1995 Feb 17	**Joyride** F Haden, S Mooney, N Burton
1995 Feb 25	**Backhander, Electronic Eye, Bouncing Back** M J Crocker, J Harwood
1995 March 6	**Liquid Sky** F Haden
1995 March 10	**Lost Cause, Pipped at the Post** F Haden, M J Crocker
1995 March 13	**Touching the Void** F Haden, B Durston
1995 March 14	**The Wrist Business** M J Crocker *A stone similar to the crux pinch was glued on Crocker's garage wall and used for training his left hand, seriously damaged in an accident the previous year.*
1995 March 15	**Mooney's Route** S Mooney, N Burton, M J Crocker
1995 March 18	**Loser's Choice** M J Crocker, F Haden, S Mooney
1995 March 30	**Pump Up the Volume** M J Crocker
1995 March	**The Babbler** G Wright, S Mooney
1995 April 11	**Time to Hang Up Your Boots** M J Crocker, G A Jenkin
1995 April 12	**Anything to Declare?, The Black Prince of the South-West** F Haden, G A Jenkin, M J Crocker
1995 April 12	**Far Away Thoughts** F Haden, G A Jenkin
1995 May 15	**Megaphysical** M J Crocker
1995 July 19	**Can't Help Myself** M J Crocker
1995 Oct 1	**Billy Crystal, Crystal Gale** M J Crocker, K Marsden, A March
1995 Oct 12	**Ghosts at the End of the Line, Wake Up Dead** M J Crocker (solo, trailing rope)
1995 Oct 13	**Irreverence, Judas** M J Crocker, A March
1995 Oct 19	**Bigfoot** M J Crocker

1995 Nov 19	**Prince Andrew** A March *Even in the absence of the Duke of York a march went to the top of the hill and a march came down again.*
1995 Nov 26	**Holdloss** M J Crocker, G A Jenkin *A hold snapping put paid to the expected 8a top-out.*
1996 March 11	**Rook's Climb** A March
1997 March 23	**The Empire Strikes Back** I Vickers *Geared but relinquished by L Percival. 'Believing it to be 8b+, Luc was obviously struggling on the route, so in stepped Jarvis to redpoint the route second go at 8a+.' G Parry.*
1997 March 24	**Star Wars: The Trilogy** I Vickers, G Parry
1997 March 27	**Old Bones** I Vickers, G Parry
1997 March	**Homegrown** I Vickers *Geared and donated by Paul Twomey. 'Ian didn't have a clue what he was doing as Paul had never looked at the moves up there. Up and down, puffing and panting Ian went, finally cracking the sequence by some cunningly executed Egyptian and so completing what is definitely the hardest on-sight first ascent in Britain to date.' G Parry.*
1997 March	**Bristol Weed** I Vickers *This was Vickers' response to a padlock and 'hands-off' notice; Francis Haden, who owned the key and was working on the line, was not amused.*
1997	**Sweet Tufa** I Vickers *Another donation by Paul Twomey.*
1997 Nov 23	**Mix a Quick Fix** M J Crocker, J Harwood
1997 Dec 21	**Tell-tales** M J Crocker, J Harwood
1999 March 31	**Mon Dieu, Zut Alors!, North-West Arête** M J Crocker (solo)
1999 April 7	**Dangerous Dusk, Above and Beyond the 'I'm So Pathetic' Barrier** M J Crocker (solo)
1999 April 9	**Night Vision, Hard Lime** M J Crocker (solo)
1999 April 15	**Bramblebed, Snow in April** M J Crocker (lead-solo)
1999 April 19	**The Hunt, The Hunted** M J Crocker (solo)
1999 May 5	**Torn Limb from Limb, Fox Bites Back** M J Crocker (solo, lead-solo)
1999 May 12	**Lager-spiker, Larger-biker, Rough Roader, Rough Sleeper, Phantom Bolts** M J Crocker (solo) *The bolt and bolt stub in the latter route are of unknown origin: are they yours?*
1999 May 19	**Double-mono Wall, The Peak is Full of Gritstoners Humping Their Designer Crashmats Around, Foam Roll-up, Gotoit, Hairline** M J Crocker (solo)
1999 May 24	**Crashed Matt, Will It? Won't It?, Mattus Mattus** M J Crocker (solo)
1999 June 30	**Leader of the Pack** M J Crocker, G Percival
1999 Oct 19	**In the Balance, In the Red, Shattered, Rovers' Return, Inverted-V, Right-on-sight** M J Crocker (solo)
1999 Oct 23	**Condensation Canyon** M J Crocker
1999 Oct 23	**La Tour Noire Super, Letcher** M J Crocker, J Harwood
1999 Oct 26	**Drinking in LA, Weekends of Rain, Weekdays of Sun** M J Crocker (lead-solo)

| 1999 Oct 28 | **Prickles Numb, Bread and Jam, Sunset Over Exmoor, Daylight Robbery 1999, After Work, After Dark** M J Crocker (solo) |

A complement of minor solos, some of which may well have been climbed before (in 1925!).

1999 Nov 14	**Der Hinter Zug, Doomsday Machine** M J Crocker, J Harwood
1999 Nov 21	**B 'n' B** M J Crocker, J Harwood
1999 Nov 27	**Never Forget a Face, Best of Things, Hang This – Sucker!** M J Crocker (solo)
2000 Jan 23	**Into Dark** M J Crocker, J Harwood

Yet another last-minute climb in darkness (second not well-sighted enough to follow).

| 2000 Feb 9 | **Fat Slapper** C Newton-Goverd (after top-roping) |
| 2000 Feb 13 | **The Fall, Dig This, People, I've Started...** M J Crocker, J Harwood |

The groove of the last route was previously reached from British Summer Time and a finish made up very loose ground to a holly tree, by S Mooney, R Bloxham on 7.3.93.

2000 March 5	**Dada, Hurricane** M J Crocker, D Pickford, J Harwood (latter route)
2000 March 12	**On the Right Track, Oh! To Be Young Again** M J Crocker, J Harwood, D Pickford
2000 April 10	**Solitaire, Rationale, Hugh's Who?, Pull Pit, DJ Post Mortem** M J Crocker (solo)
2000 May 10	**Pyramus Arête, Snout's Wall, Thisbe Rib, The Sixth Thisbe** M J Crocker (solo/lead-solo)

The easier of these routes may have been climbed before. The name of Snout's Wall came from the second 'first ascensionists'.

2000 Oct 8	**Subcutaneous Tissue, Little M, Roamertherapy** M J Crocker, J Harwood
2000 Nov 12	**Emily's Dog** R Chappell, E Sloots-Wyson
2000 Dec 10	**William in Chile** M J Crocker, J Harwood
2000 Dec 16	**Condensation Street** M J Crocker

Climbed in light rain on generally wet rock: second refused to follow.

| 2001 Jan 6 | **Mir, 2001** M J Crocker, J Harwood |

Space Station Mir appeared in the western sky several hours later.

2002 Jan 12	**The Dimming of the Day** N A Coe, M J Crocker
2002 Jan 12	**Poisoned Ivy** M J Crocker, N A Coe
2002 Jan 12	**First a Fence** M J Crocker
2002 April 23	**Secrets of 2002, No Gear – Oh Dear!** M J Crocker (solo)
2002 April 25	**Thin Towers** M J Crocker (solo)
2002 April 29	**Secretly Barmy** M J Crocker (solo)
2002	**Hug the Jug, Don't Fear the Bleater** C Newton-Goverd
2002 April	**Licking Tarmac** R Barraclough
2003 Feb 10	**Plaque, Return of the Upsetters, Witch's Brew** M J Crocker, J Harwood
2003 Feb 12	**The Three Bombardiers, Nameless Scoop** M J Crocker (lead-solo)
2003 Feb 12	**Old Romantics, Just My Imagination, Once Again** M J Crocker (lead-solo)
2003 Feb 16	**Ban's Off, In a Blink, The Dead Cold** M J Crocker, J Harwood

Climbed 5 days after the lifting of the 10-year climbing ban on Pinnacle Bay.

2003 Feb 22	**Planet Perfecto, Reel Empty Feeling** M J Crocker, N A Coe

Crocker took some smashing shots of Coe on the latter route for the (this!) guidebook, only to find two hours later that Coe had forgotten to load a film.

2003 Feb 23	**Hall of Fame** M J Crocker, J Harwood
2003 March 2	**Blagging Louts, Immortals** M J Crocker, J Harwood
2003 March 6	**Needs of the Many** M J Crocker (lead-solo)
2003 March 9	**Spock Philosophy, Deathwatch, Crimewatch** M J Crocker, J Harwood
2003 March 11	**Exiled!, Disenchantment** M J Crocker (lead-solo)
2003 March 13	**Tusk** M J Crocker (lead-solo)
2003 March 15	**Stoned, The Ides** M J Crocker, J Harwood

A significant crowd at the top watched the ascent, though the SkySports TV crew missed the action, after some lame filming of two stationary motorcyclists at the cliff-top the day before.

Sand Point

1987 Sept 6	**'I've Cleaned That', The Incalculable Cleft, Psycho 2, Sands of Time** M J Crocker, M Ward
1987 Sept 12	**The Soup Dragon Warbles, Mister Fuzzy-wuz, Jutland, Severn Bore, Too Big to Swallow, Then Chew on This** M J Crocker, M Ward
1987 Sept 12	**Underdogs** M Ward, M J Crocker
1987 Sept 12	**Souvenir** M J Crocker (solo)
1987 Sept 15	**Pomp, Circumstance, Stomp** M J Crocker (solo)
1993 July 11	**Jocular Banter, Weston Approaches, Buoy Racer** D Viggers, D Carroll (AL)
1993 July 18	**Seven Bridges, Leaning Difficulties, Second Severn Crossing** D Carroll, V Moisey
1993 July 18	**Broad Reach** B Watson, V Moisey
1993 July 18	**Gay Repartee, Mass Debate** D Viggers, B Watson
1996 April 25	**S'all Yours, Rugrat** M J Crocker (solo)
1996 May 8	**Drop a Clanger, Sockthing, Memento** M J Crocker
1998 July 7	**Motorboat To Mars: The Re-release** M J Crocker (on-sight deep water solo)
2003 Feb 2	**Rasp** M J Crocker (solo)
2003 Feb 8	**Elgar, Helga, Stirling Sea Moss, Where Coral Lies** M J Crocker (solo; padding was placed on the boulder for the last route)
2003 Feb 15	**Flute Elope, Pipe Music, Ain't No Sunshine, Trench Town, Suggestive, It's Over** M J Crocker (solo; last two top-roped first)
2003 March 23	**Sub-marine Stubble** M J Crocker
2003 March 23	**Peace Protest, Never to Go Back, Pedestal Overhang, Lip Slip, A Traction** M J Crocker, J Harwood (after top-roping)

Wood Lane Quarry

1989 March 12	**Wedgey Went In, Haggis Came Out** S Rosser, J James, W Gladwin (former route only)

1989 Nov 15	**Chrality** S Westgate	

The start described was climbed as Magic Roundabout by S Westgarth, G Gillam, 13.5.90

1989 Dec 14	**Teenage Mutant Snapping Turtle Head Soup** W Gladwin
1990 March 12	**Georgy Girl** S Thompson, J James
1990 March 21	**Thanks to the Nifl Hiem** W Gladwin (solo)
1990 March 21	**Watch the E7 Undergrowth** S Westgarth (solo)
1990 March 22	**Wedgey's Revenge** M Rosser, S Thompson, W Gladwin
1990 July 22	**Corporate Image** J James, W Gladwin
1990	**Return of the Wedge** M Rosser, C McCloud
1991 April 15	**Gannets Groanies** W Gladwin, R Scully
1991 May 1	**Tour de Force** S Thompson, W Gladwin

Superseded Five Minute Walk climbed by S Westgarth (solo) on 21.3.90.

1993 July 11	**Fair Game** D Carroll, D Viggers
1993 July 28	**Screaming of the Limbs, The Clean Machine** D Viggers, D Carroll (AL)
1994 July 13	**Hot Summer Nights** G A Jenkin, J Savage, C Savage, M Jewell
1994 July 13	**The Long and Short of Wit, Wibbly Wobbly Way** J Savage, M Jewell, C Savage (first route)
1994 July 22	**Men Behaving Badly** M Jewell, J Savage, C Savage
1994 July 27	**Whingeing Jimmy** C Savage, M Jewell, A Randell
1999 June 28	**Smokey Robinson, Would You?** M J Crocker (lead-solo)

The first 6 metres of the first route was climbed on the original ascent of Chrality by S Westgarth, 15.11.89.

Brean Down

c.1960	**Castro's Corner, Pinnacle Cracks, Cyclops Gatepost, Finger Crack, Curving Crack, Backstairs, Red Slab Crack, Red Slab Central, Red Slab Corner, Red Wall Crack (Right), Ochre Groove, Eavesdrop** J Hone	
1961	**Cyclops Slab** G Mason, R Perry	
1963	**Pandora's Box** G Mason, I Adams	
1964 May 31	**Great Corner (A3)** G Mason, I Adams	

Mason called it The Great Panjandrum Himself but his description was lost. First free ascent P R Littlejohn, R A Broomhead, 31.8.75. Not a Day at the Comp variation by M J Crocker, J Harwood on 17.1.98.

1960s	**Elysium** Probably J Nixon
1975 Feb	**Pretty Boy Floyd** P R Littlejohn, D Garner

The In-a-state-again? variation was climbed by M J Crocker, G A Jenkin, N A Coe on 11.2.96.

1975 May 18	**Be Bop Arête** R A Broomhead, D J Hermalin
1975 May	**Bones Chimney** P R Littlejohn, D Garner

A rock dislodged by Littlejohn during an earlier attempt put his girlfriend into hospital.

1975 Aug 31	**Pressure Drop** P R Littlejohn, R A Broomhead
1975 Nov 16	**Idiot Wind** P R Littlejohn, R A Broomhead
1976 April 7	**Haven** R A Broomhead, P R Littlejohn
1976 July 18	**Torpedo, Quicksand** P R Littlejohn, D Roberts
1978 June 24	**Zeus** S Monks, C King

Crap Wall variation by M J Crocker, J Harwood on 17.1.98.

1978 Dec 9	**Sidewinder** S Monks, A Burnham	
1983 May 17	**Crack o'Diamonds** P R Littlejohn, T Penning	
1983 June 7	**Backdoor Beauty, Godspeed** P R Littlejohn, T Penning	
1984 April 12	**Catbrain Lane** J Bassindale, M Ward (AL)	
1985 Aug 3	**The Beast Unleashed, The Brean Machine, Force Ten**	
	M J Crocker, M Ward	
	The Tempestuous variation to the latter route was added by	
	M J Crocker on 17.2.90.	
1985 Dec 18	**L'Attraction Fatale, Sail on Past, The Fog** M J Crocker,	
	M Ward	
	…a big day for Brean! P Oxley retrobolted the first route in 1991.	
1986 Dec 20	**Tricks of the Trade, An Odd Sea** M Ward, M J Crocker (AL)	
1986 Dec 21	**Brean Team Special** M J Crocker, M Ward	
	Previously, Tony Penning had made a valiant on-sight attempt on	
	the advice of his partner, Littlejohn, who remained firmly on the	
	ground!	
1986 Dec 28	**Yer Yella!** M J Crocker, M Ward	
	Led without the bolt by M J Crocker on 31.1.99.	
1987 Jan 3	**The Root of Inequity, The Slow Sand, More of the**	
	Bravado M J Crocker, M Ward (AL)	
	The right-hand (normal) start of the latter route was added by	
	M J Crocker on 2.1.89.	
1987 Jan 8	**Sea of Sand** M Ward, M Bellian	
1987 Jan 10	**Kamikaze** M J Crocker, M Ward	
	Led without the bolt by M J Crocker on 26.6.94.	
1987 Jan 31	**Sail Close to the Wind** M Ward, M J Crocker	
1987 Feb 21	**One Man, One Island** M J Crocker, M Ward	
1987 March 14	**Hands across the Ocean** M J Crocker, M Ward (AL)	
1987 Nov 1	**Going Turbo** M J Crocker, M Ward	
1987 Nov 14	**Got the Drop on Me, Eye for an Eye, Interstate 7,**	
	Spindrift M J Crocker, M Ward (AL)	
1988 Dec 10	**Coral Sea, Pearl Harbour** M Ward, M J Crocker (AL)	
	Pearl Harbour was led bolt-free by M J Crocker on 26.6.94.	
1988 Dec 17	**Achtung Torpedo!** M J Crocker	
1989 Jan 1	**Distant Voices, Bullworker** M Ward, M J Crocker (AL)	
1989 Jan 2	**Loons of Pluto** M J Crocker	
	The lower half had been climbed previously by M Ward,	
	M J Crocker on 15.2.87. Enter Uranus variation by M J Crocker	
	(lead-solo) on 17.1.99.	
1990 Feb 4	**Prisoner of Conscience** M J Crocker	
	The gales of January 25 took their toll on the great sheet of ivy.	
1990 Feb 10	**Chulilla** M J Crocker	
1990 Feb 17	**Galebird** M J Crocker	
1990 Feb 18	**War on Cocaine** M J Crocker	
1990 Feb 25	**Casino Royale** M J Crocker	
1990 Mar 3	**El Chocco** M J Crocker, M Woodford	
1990 Nov 25	**Clashing Socks, Three Snaps to Heaven, Eso Ego Wall**	
	M J Crocker	
1991 Jan 19	**Iraqi War Machine** M J Crocker	
1991 Jan 20	**Anti-missile Missile** M J Crocker	
1991 Feb 28	**Hot X Bones** M J Crocker, A Popp	
1991 Mar 17	**The Unexpected Guest** M J Crocker	
1992 Dec 19	**Chepito, Comet Strip** M J Crocker, J Robertson	

1993 Aug 31	**Brean Bunny Blues, See You Later, Renovator, Ego Trip to Mars** F Haden, M J Crocker
1993 Nov 7	**Kraken, Bikini Atoll** F Haden, I Parnell, J Hunt
	Staples arrive at Brean Down.
1993 Dec 5	**The Leveller** M J Crocker, G A Jenkin, N A Coe
1993 Dec 15	**Throwaway Society** M J Crocker
1993 Dec29	**One Day Too Soon, Back to the Planet** M J Crocker, G A Jenkin
1993 Dec 31	**Lead Me to the Real World, Put '93 Behind** M J Crocker, F Haden
1994 Jan 2	**Cove Arete, Airy and Scary** M J Crocker, F Haden (AL)
1994 April 16	**Axe Attack** F Haden
	Possibly a right-hand version of an E1 climbed by J Clayton in the mid-80s.
1994 Aug 13	**The Guilt Edge** M J Crocker, F Haden
1994 Aug	**The Irrelevant One!** F Haden (solo)
1995 March 22	**Storm Warning** F Haden
1995 April 23	**Tide Rising** F Haden, G A Jenkin, E Heslam
1995 April 23	**Brean Dream** F Haden, G A Jenkin, E Heslam, S Cook
1995 Dec 10	**Hot Aches, Have-a-Go Hero, Creak Machine, Squeaky Clean, Chill Blane, Fruit Gum Company, Everyone's Gone to the Moon, Honeycomb, Me'Shell, Save the Down from Mankind, One False Move, Birthmark, In the Soup, Gone Fishing, Well-honed, Red Wall Crack (Left)** M J Crocker.
	A busy day. R Chappell seconded the first route declaring that it was too cold to climb. The last three route were soloed on sight.
1995 Dec16	**Loneshark, Lend-a-hand, Borrowed Time, Inwardly Extrovert, LST** M J Crocker (solo)
1995 Dec 24	**Blind Man's Paradox, Travesty, Black Comedy, Theopolis, Satyre, Fun with Pyro, Overgrade, Undergrade: Wobbling Free** M J Crocker, F Haden
	On the first route a white stick found amongst flotsam was used to place a runner.
1996 Jan 7	**Bequeathed, Beholden, Bongo Workshop Bash, Ben Badoo, Pinnochio, Nosejob** M J Crocker, A Holden
1996 Jan 13	**Purge the Week Away, The Brean Bone Chamber, Cynical of Success, Bereaved** M J Crocker, J Harwood
1996 Jan 27	**Dead Man's Handshake, The Big Chill, Pint-handle Crack** M J Crocker (last two routes on-sight solo)
1996 Jan 28	**No Worries, Nightmare Alley** M J Crocker
1996 Feb 11	**The World's Worst Dressed Climber, Two Right Feet** M J Crocker, G A Jenkin, N Coe
	Jenkin is forced to climb in two right boots, having forgotten his left. The former route extended a Direct Start to Pretty Boy Floyd, added by M Ward, M J Crocker on 20.12.86.
1996 Feb 17	**Seriously Scuppered Supertanker, Run Aground, No Oil, We're Nuke, Bow-out, Look What the Tide Brought In, Turditz, Bolero Bar, Shifting Sand Sorbet, Serious but Stable** M J Crocker (solo)
1996 Feb 24	**Tootin' Ska Moon** M J Crocker
1996 Feb 24	**Adventure Route One, Adventure Route Two** M J Crocker, F Haden

1996 March 2	**Treadmill, The Giant's Fingernail, Pigeons of the Underworld** M J Crocker, J Harwood
1996 March 3	**No Room to Run, Ice: a Tonic, The Tennis Elbow Club** M J Crocker, J Harwood

The latter ascent was accompanied by serious tendonitis.

1996 April 24	**Apparition, True Identity, OK Crack, Deception** M J Crocker (solo, some on sight)
1996 June 13	**Psycho-death Drummer of Brean Café** M J Crocker
1998 June 9	**Sunset Crack** Ms P Holt (on-sight solo)
1999 Jan 17	**Scargill's Hairpiece, Span of Attention, Shattered Silence, Pinnacle Arete** M J Crocker (lead-solo)
1999 Jan 30	**Nobody's Perfect** M J Crocker (solo)
1999 Jan 31	**Police Training Route, Scarface** M J Crocker, (PC) T Cheek, (Sergeant) C Ryan
2000 May 19	**Sargasso Seamonster** D Pickford
2000 Nov 12	**Vets' Wall** M J Crocker, J Harwood
2001 April 28	**Completely Brainless and Aimless, Groove Boat, Tired of Looking at Each Other, Cycle of Despair** M J Crocker (solo)
2001 May 16	**Route 1, Route 2, Route 3, Route 4, Route 5 (yawn), Rap Stack, Nasty Piece of Work** M J Crocker (solo)
2002	**Brean Topping** S McClure

A long-standing open project solved following an invitation to one of the country's strongest climbers.

Uphill Quarry

1962 Jan	**Gorilla Groove, Ape's Ascent, Denzil (4 pts aid)** V Hanby, J Nixon, J Wooton, J Lovatt (VL)

The latter route was climbed free by R A Broomhead, D Carroll on 8.6.84.

1963	**Seven-eighths** H Bussey, M Wooding
1963	**Graveyard Gate** J Maddox, Ms B Hess
1960s	**Tombstone, Cave Chimney, Groove and Slab, Summerfield, Uphill Corner** First ascensionists unknown
1984 May 30	**Uphill Racer** D Carroll, A Stiddard
1984 June 6	**Zombies** D Carroll, R A Broomhead
1984 June 16	**Living Dead** M J Crocker, D Carroll

Carroll led to within jumping distance of the top! The independent start was added later by M J Crocker, and the first bolt later still.

1984 June 22	**Life and Times** M J Crocker, D Carroll
1984 June 25	**Premonition** M J Crocker, D Carroll

Carroll led to within spitting distance of the top!

1984 June 26	**The Haunting** D Carroll, M J Crocker (AL)
1984 June 29	**Chiming for You** M J Crocker, D Carroll
1987 Sept 5	**The Terminator, The Enlightment, Images of War** M Ward, M J Crocker (AL)
1987 Sept 10	**Turn in the Grave** M J Crocker, G A Jenkin
1987 Sept 17	**The Jimi Hendrix Experience** M J Crocker, G A Jenkin

'The route was a total freak-out; Hendrix would have appreciated it…'

1987 Sept 20	**Taking a Line for a Walk, Wot! No Meat?** G A Jenkin, N A Coe
1987 Nov 29	**A Lesser Evil** M J Crocker, M Ward

1987 Dec 5	**Crematorium** M J Crocker, G A Jenkin
1987 Dec 5	**The Discreet Charm of the Bougeoisie** M Ward, R Kingston, G A Jenkin, M J Crocker
1987 Dec 12	**Meet Thy Creator, God Bless Celery** M J Crocker, G A Jenkin, M Ward
1988 Aug 28	**Subhuman, Get It While It's Hot** M Ward, G A Jenkin (AL)
	Originally the second route traversed into what is now a conservation area in order to retreat from the abseil station of Meet Thy Creator.
1992 May 10	**Inhuman** M J Crocker, A Tallant
1994 March 19	**Boat Percussion** M J Crocker, F Haden
1995 May 27	**Suburbia, Exhumed** F Haden
1999 Jan 30	**Behind the Boatshed, Fast-track** M J Crocker (solo)

North Quarry

1964 June 2	**Entente Cordiale, Quartz Diedre** G Mason, J C Guillory, J Hone (lines up the left-hand wall; not described; all solo)
1964 Oct 18	**Nel Gwynne, Crescendo, Geoff's Slab** G Mason, I Adams
	The first route took the broken groove splitting the centre of the slabs, and the latter two routes were lines up the smaller right-hand slab; not described.
1965	**Bad Banana** G Mason, C Swain
1984 June 10	**Short Sharp Shock, Journey Man's Wall** R Harrison, G Forward
1984 June 11	**Strong Safety, By Pass** G Forward, R Harrison (AL)
	The Under Pressure variation to the first route was climbed by F Haden, M J Crocker on 21.4.94.
1984 June 14	**Free Safety, Dickie's Downfall** G Forward, R Harrison (AL)
	Frank's Finale was added to the first route by F Haden, Ms L Creamer, M J Crocker on 9.8.94.
1984 June 17	**Tight End, Head North, Split End** R Harrison, G Forward (AL)
1988 June 12	**Galapagos** J Bull (solo)
1993 Dec	**Condition Black** F Haden, B Durston
1993 Oct 3	**Resin Resurrection, Shoot to Thrill, Motorway Sheepdog** F Haden, I Parnell
1994 Aug 9	**The Never Ending Story** F Haden, Ms L Creamer, M J Crocker
1999 Feb 28	**After Benidorm** M J Crocker, J Harwood
1999 March 7	**Quarry Squatter** M J Crocker (lead-solo)

Sandford Quarry

No first ascent details are available for *Eco-line*. The line was, however, soloed past the bolts by M J Crocker, 14.5.01.

1982 July 10	**Wo's On?** R A Broomhead, S Briggs
1982 July 10	**The Ramp** R A Broomhead (solo)
1982 July 17	**Pockets** R A Broomhead (solo)
1982 July 18	**Blow Job** R A Broomhead, S Briggs
1982 July 28	**Première** S Briggs, R A Broomhead
1982 July 28	**Sensations** R A Broomhead (solo)
1982 Aug 7	**Desolation** R A Broomhead, S Briggs
1982 Aug 8	**Dust, ...to Dust** R A Broomhead (solo)
1982 Aug 14	**Dereliction, The Crush** R A Broomhead, S Briggs (AL)

1982 Aug 20   **Isolation**   R A Broomhead, A Hall

1982 Sept 2   **Softly Softly**   R A Broomhead, G Forward

1983 Aug 7   **Fellatrice**   M Ward, M Bellian

1983 Oct 23   **Brain Donor**   M Ward, M Bellian, J Wiggington

1984 Aug 5   **Dead Glove, Handbuilt for Speed, Annihilation**
J Chapman, M Bellian, M Ward (only led latter route – which
R A Broomhead had climbed before)

1984 Aug 5   **Le Poudin Noir**   A Andrews, M Ward
*Le Poudin Noir Direct was added by R Kingston, D Vousden on
16.7.96.*

1985 July 25   **Soixante-neuf, Graduates**   D Viggers, R A Broomhead (AL)

1985 July 28   **Creep**   R A Broomhead, D Viggers

1991 March 30 to May 20
   **Mucky Pup, First Offence, Captain Buddleia,
Curvaceous, Easy Route, Doinngggg, Boinngggg,
Microsoft, After Dark, Flying Toasters, Icon, Polished
Off, Semi-redundant, Brackets, A Pensionable
Question, Bonus in Retirement, A Little Peace and Quiet**
R A Broomhead, J Watson, D Targett (VL)
*'It was not until recently that the bomb was dropped! Dick
Broomhead, with assistance from John Watson and Derek Targett,
had ascended some 17 routes on the Lower Lift! This caused all
sorts of pandemonium, with ascent dates being checked and
re-checked; but due credit must go to the trio, who effectively
blitzed the place!' F Haden 1994. The second half of the original
Microsoft was absorbed into Don't Panic. Polished Off was soloed
past the bolt by M J Crocker on 14.5.01.*

1992 July 16   **Marigold**   S Mooney, H Lyons

1992 July 21   **As Limp as a Wimp On A Crimp**   S Mooney (solo)

1993 Aug 12   **The Big Bang Burger Bar**   P Sleet, S Chen

1993 Aug 15   **Don't Panic**   P Sleet, S Chen

1993 Aug   **E For Extermination, Black as the Ace of Spades and
Twice as Tricky, Designed to Kill, Living Dangerously,
Ask the Tommyknockers, Ghosts of the Past**   F Haden
(solo)

1993 Aug   **Honky Tonk Highway, Scarcity**   R Fox (solo)

1993 Aug   **A Vision of Hell, A Date with Eternity, Shot Down in
Flames**   F Haden, B Durston
The latter was soloed past the bolts by M J Crocker on 14.5.01.

1993   **Mindwarp**   F Haden (solo)

1994   **Jez Arête**   A Starr, B Pitch

1995 July 15   **Semantic Deconstruction**   D Davies, M Vogin

1999 April 28   **Hellraiser**   M J Crocker, R Chappell

1999 May 4   **Sponsored By…, Regular Boy Scout, Shit; What Have I
Got Myself Into?!**   M J Crocker (solo)

1990s   **Mystery**   An ascent in the 90s is assumed because of the bolt.
First known ascensionist: M J Crocker (solo) on 14.5.02.

2001 May 22   **Fridge Hid**   M J Crocker (solo)

2001 May 24   **Crawler, Gaping Gill**   M J Crocker (solo)

2003 Jan 12   **Emily's Six Tomorrow**   M J Crocker (solo after top-roping)

Churchill Rocks

c.1930   **Witching Waves, Dilemma Zigzag, Oak Tree Wall, Tiro's Crack, The Right-hand Slab**   F G Balcombe and friends
'…the means to progress were little more than small pieces of bird droppings and an occasional flake of shale.' (G Balcombe describing Dilemma Zig-Zag.)

c.1930   **Ahoy There!, Shipmates, Scurvy Crack**   Probably also climbed by F G Balcombe and friends

1992 Sept 12   **Captain Fishy's Fishy Fingers**   H Lyons, S Spacey

1993   **Powers that Be**   F Haden (solo)

Rock of Ages

1988 May 10   **Cleft for Me, Kingdom's Throne**   M J Crocker, G A Jenkin

Ebbor Gorge

1950s   **Merlin, Galahad, C Route, D Route, E Route, Lancelot, Gawaine, Round Table**   Bane, Lloyd
These routes are not described as climbing is not allowed by English Nature nowadays.

Split Rock Quarry

1980 May 9   **Rustic Wall, Certain Surprise**   R Harrison, R A Broomhead
The Video Kills variation to the former route was soloed by M J Crocker before camera on 27.6.90.

1982 Sept 17   **Sahara**   R A Broomhead, A Hall

1982 Sept 25   **Gary's Gift**   R A Broomhead, D Viggers

1983 May   **Tricky Dicky**   P Smith, R Cary

1983 Aug 10   **Brazen Hussy**   R Harrison, R A Broomhead

1983 Sept 6   **Chain Reaction**   R Harrison
Many notables who have suffered or failed on this invent the excuse that holds must have fallen off. Actually, it didn't have any in the first place!

1983 Nov 6   **Demolition Man**   M Ward, J Chapman

1984 March 31   **Open Invitation**   D Viggers, J P de Rohan

1984 April 25   **Dune**   D Carroll, D Viggers
A combined effort!

1984 June 26   **End Game**   R A Broomhead, R Harrison

1984 Sept 9   **Crimson Dynamo**   M J Crocker, R Harrison

1986 April 19   **Smashing of Amps**   M J Crocker

1986 May 10   **Fact or Fission**   M J Crocker, M Ward

1986 May 19   **Smarty Marty**   M J Crocker
A bolt runner was subsequently placed in the spot where a hysterical Crocker had dived for the ab' rope!

1986 May 31   **Red Rag to a Bull**   M J Crocker, M Ward

1986 June 7   **Split Rock Girdle**   M J Crocker, M Ward

1987 Polling Day   **Polling Day Blues**   P Oxley

1989 Feb 19   **A Magenta Smudge**   M J Crocker, G A Jenkin

1991 Jan 5   **Arrakis, Medium Very Rare**   M J Crocker

1991 Jan 6   **Saboteurs of the Underground**   M J Crocker

1991 Jan 12	**Red Snapper and Chips** M J Crocker
	The chips are of unknown origin.
1999 May 17	**Corsican Days** G A Jenkin, J Allum

Horrington Hill Quarry

1990	**Face Climb, Horrington Crack, Dick's Crack** J Watson, R A Broomhead (led latter route)
	The bolt runner on Face Climb was placed by a non-climbing caver. The route was climbed (lead-solo) without the bolt runner by M J Crocker on 16.5.00 with no change in grade.
1990	**Corner-climb** J Watson (solo)
2000 May 15	**'Lellow', A Pat on the Back, The Cows Ate My Baseball Cap – Honest!** M J Crocker (solo)
2000 May 16	**Intimate Behaviour** M J Crocker (lead-solo)
2000 May 19	**Sod the Rope, Bounce** M J Crocker (solo)
2000 July 25	**Faith in the System, Outside: the Herd** M J Crocker (lead-solo)
	Crocker's Soloist device is tested to the limit.

Dinder Wood

1991	**Butcombe Buttress, Big Al's Silver Jubilee, Rattle Crack, Cave Crack, Rob's Layback, Rigor Mortis** Members of the Cerberus Speleological Society, including: J Swift, A Heath, A Lindsey, T Harman, R Connaly, J Woodlouse, M Smith, and 'Choppers' Chapman.
	Other climbs were put up on the cliffs but the descriptions were lost (or used as beermats).
2000 Sept 4	**Dindergarten, Fingernail Hell, Choppers** M J Crocker (solo)
2000 Sept 6	**P45, Humble Origins, Move All Mountains** M J Crocker (solo)
2000 Sept 12	**Down in Dingley Dell, The Reaper's Embrace** M J Crocker (solo)
2000 Sept 13	**Rosethorn, Yellowstone, Elderburied** M J Crocker (solo, second route lead-solo)
2000 Sept 19	**The Plight Of the Ordinary Working Man, Ivy Falls** M J Crocker (solo)
	The plight was the torrential rain which started the second Crocker walked out of his office.
2000 Sept 20	**Forcible Retirement, Fuel Crisis** M J Crocker (solo)
2000 Sept 26	**For Cerberus, Bowl of Nettles, Tumbling Concrete Dice, Scoop of the Day** M J Crocker (solo)
2000 Sept 27	**Swift Response, Mirror Image, Jamslip** M J Crocker (solo)
2000 Oct 8	**Dripfed** M J Crocker, J Harwood
	The start of the route was bouldered out by M J Crocker on 19.9.00.
2000 Oct 12	**Cross Combe, Escape from the Lost World** M J Crocker (solo)
2001 Nov 19	**Jo Jo, Ellie, Walking with Crinoids** R A Broomhead
2001 Nov 26	**Brewery Brake, Pewter Pitcher** R A Broomhead
2001 Dec 1	**Easy Route** J Stanbury
2002 Oct 12	**Spring Haze, Slash and Burn** J Stanbury

Croscombe Valley Cliffs

2000 March 21	**The Secret Existence of a Mendip Official, The Prow, The Shelf, Jump Start, Deadpoint** M J Crocker (solo)	
2000 March 29	**Role Reversal, Coward, Spear and Watson, Angles-sur-L'Anglin, Death at Dusk** M J Crocker (solo)	
2000 April 5	**Snowdrift, The Drip** M J Crocker (solo)	
	The Mendips were hit by massive snowfall the day before.	
2000 May 3	**Yellow Peryl, One-man Audience** M J Crocker (solo)	
2000 May 5	**Lightning Crack** J Watson (solo)	
	Climbed in a thunderstorm.	
2000 May 25	**Backache, Headache** M J Crocker, J Watson	
2000 June 4	**No Mats Required, Reasons to Be Cheerful** J Watson (solo)	
2000 June 7	**Mind the Primroses, Director's Chair** M J Crocker (solo)	
2000 Oct 4	**What's On?, All Sown Up, Winter Approaches, Dead-hanging Offence** M J Crocker (solo)	
2000 Oct 6	**Slobodan, Fright of My Life** M J Crocker (lead-solo, solo)	
	On the latter route, at dusk, a wren popped out of the crack at 8 metres and almost precipitated the on-sight soloist.	
2003 Feb 1	**Scream Pudding, Bleak Pudding, Life with Nancy Camel** M J Crocker (solo after top-roping)	

Binegar Quarry

1999 June 9	**One Bullet** M J Crocker (lead-solo)	
2002 Oct 12	**Los Americas** B Sutton, G Edwards	
2002 Oct 12	**Lithium Freedom** G Edwards, B Sutton	

Ashwick Grove

1996 March 6	**Period Piece, Stretch the Truth** MJ Crocker (solo)	
1996 April 10	**Groove of Relics, The Weiring Way** M J Crocker (solo)	
	The old pegs were placed by Pete Rees and friends 'on days when people couldn't be bothered to go climbing'.	
1996 April 11	**Nasal Symphony, Paco Robanne, Tyson** M J Crocker (solo)	
	A line of old bolt stubs up the front of The Nose were placed by members of Cerberus Speleological Society as practice for their Berger cave trip 1976/77. Pete Rees climbed a hard line on this buttress (Caver's Excuse) in the mid-80s. Apparently most of it 'dropped off into the valley below taking the crux with it'.	

Fairy Cave Quarry

The Alpine Ridge must have been climbed long, long before it was named.

1992	**Withy Crack** Cerberus Speleological Society	
	Erroneously reclaimed in 2002 by M Raine as Back in Business; this is the line described.	
1993	**Rob's Crack** R Connaly, J Swift	
	Reclimbed by M Raine, P Clark March/April 2002 as Spinal Tap Crack in ignorance of the earlier ascent.	
1993	**The Conning Tower** J Swift	
1993	**Harman's Tree** T Harman, M Poland	

1993	**Back to Basics** R Connaly
	Reclimbed and named by R Nadin (on-sight solo) in ignorance of the earlier ascent.
1994	**Balch's Slide** J Swift, A Heath
1994	**Cristel Wall** Members of the Cerberus Speleological Society
	The route as described was climbed by J Hitchins and Ms A Derodra on 8.4.02 as Back Down.
Late 1990s	**Moving Target** S Franklin, D Targett (AL)
	Franklin and Targett didn't publish their ascent, which they thought was E1/2 5b. M Hammill and M Raine cleaned, reclimbed, and named the line (as described) on 30.3.02.
2002 March 27	**Back in Business** M Raine, P Clarke, R Nadin, I Butterworth
	Mike's first route after spending the winter lying down with a slipped disc.
2002 March 27	**Back Off** I Butterworth, M Raine
2002 March 30	**Minute Waltz** R A Broomhead, J Stanbury
2002 March 30	**Bad to the Bone** M Raine, M Hammill
2002 March 30	**Epic-dural** R Nadin, P Clarke, M Raine
2002 April 4	**Volume Eleven** M Raine, R Nadin
	Climbed after an attempt three days earlier which ended with a fall from the pinch grip due to wet conditions.
2002 April 6	**Smell the Glove** M Raine, M Hammill
	The first 7 metres were practised on top-rope in lieu of bouldering mats.
2002 April 6	**The Socialist** P Clarke, R Nadin
2002 April 6	**Halfway to Kansas** R Thomson, J Hitchins
	On sight on a windy day.
2002 April 6	**The Darkened Room** M Hammill, M Raine
2002 April 7	**Short Back and Sides** R Thomson, J Hitchins (on sight)
2002 April 7	**Back in Kansas** R Thomson, J Truscott (on sight)
2002 April 7	**Back to Sandy Lane** J Hitchins, Ms A Derodra (on sight)
2002 April 7	**Elephant's Back** R Thomson, J Hitchins
2002 April 7	**The Cassini Division** M Hammill, M Raine
	Climbed after two abseil cleaning sessions and a good look at the crux on a shunt.
2002 April 8	**Little Steve's Mersey Tunnel Affair** J Hitchins, R Thomson (on sight)
2002 April 10	**Bramble Whine** M Raine, P Clark
	Mike led the whole route, on sight, in one pitch in a howling gale which made pulling up the rope very hard.
2002 April 11	**Ants in my Leg Loop** M Raine, A Fewell
2002 April 11	**The Tory** P Clark, E Findlay
2002 April 11	**Lumbar Puncture** I Butterworth, R Nadin and E Findlay
2002 April 13	**Four Paw Drive** M Raine (led both pitches), R Nadin
	Pitch 1 climbed with S Tong on 12.4.02.
2002 April 13	**Four Steps to Heaven** I Butterworth, N Hillman, M Raine, R Nadin
2002 April 14	**Slight of Hand** R A Broomhead, J Stanbury
2002 April 14	**Ash Tree Wall** J Stanbury R A Broomhead
2002 April 19	**Jiggery Pokery** R A Broomhead, J Stanbury
2002 April 24	**Caveman** J Stanbury, R A Broomhead
	The Cerberus Speleological Society had previously top-roped a route somewhere on this slab.
2002 April 24	**Pocket Polka, Jive Talkin'** R A Broomhead, J Stanbury

2002 April 24	**Backing Up** I Butterworth, N Hillman
2002 April 25	**First Up** I Harryman, P Debbage (on sight)
2002 April 27	**Stepping Out** I Butterworth, P Clarke
2002 May 4	**Life in Limbo** M Raine

An earlier attempt used the abseil rope for runners, as the shattered rock was rather worrying, despite (or because) Raine had spent two hours cleaning the line.

2002 June 1	**Pueblo** J Stanbury
2002 June 1	**Lunar Landscape** J Stanbury, R A Broomhead
2002 June 1	**Strictly Ballroom, Rocket** R A Broomhead, J Stanbury
2002 June 2	**Peanuts** R A Broomhead (solo)
2002 June 12	**Glacial Point** M J Crocker (solo after top-roping)

Climbed by what is described as the variation finish.
R A Broomhead and J Stanbury added the left-hand finish on 27.6.02 and offered the name.

| 2002 June 25 | **Demon Moves Mike, Toblerone**   M J Crocker, N A Coe |

(second route on sight)

2002 June 25	**Truffle** N A Coe, M J Crocker
2002 June 27	**Lorna's Lunch** J Stanbury, R A Broomhead
2002 June 27	**Rub-a-tyre** M J Crocker (solo)
2002 June 29	**Odd Boots** M Raine (solo)
2002 June 30	**Seven-mile Throb, Don't Even Breathe** M J Crocker, J Harwood

Don't Even Breathe was climbed on sight; if it had been inspected by abseil it probably would have been left unclimbed.

2002 July 4	**Real Men Do Eat Quiche** M Raine, A Fewell
2002 July 7	**Boner, Pocket Piranha** M J Crocker, J Harwood
2002 Sept 4	**The Hillwithy Connection, Senile Taff Corner** M J Crocker (roped solo)
2002 Sept 15	**Back in Business** M Raine, C Fryer
2002 Sept 17	**The Mutant** M Raine, M J Crocker (2 rest pts)

First free ascent by M Raine, I Butterworth, 5.6.03

2002 Sept 26	**Om Puri** M Raine, R Nadin (AL)
2002 Sept 30	**Who Needs Hair Anyway?** H Harris, O Mullis
2002 Aug 6	**Standing on the Shoulders of Moles** R Thomson, H Harris

The Holcombe Quarries

| 1994 June/July | **The Incredible Holcombe, The Fantastic Four, The Thing, Flame On**   G Percival, A Percival, C Waddy |

The first two were climbed using 4 and 3 peg runners respectively; both routes were retro-bolted with the first ascensionist's approval by F Haden 8.01.

| 1995 July 11 | **Killer Instinct**   G A Jenkin, F Haden (both led) |
| 1995 July 13 | **Close Conspiracy**   F Haden, G A Jenkin. |

Line climbed direct through the top roof by F Haden in Sept 1996.

1995 July 13	**Powder Monkey** F Haden, G A Jenkin
1995 July 16	**Minstrel in the Gallery** E Heslam, F Haden (both led)
1995 July 16	**Never Mind the Width** G A Jenkin, E Heslam, F Haden (all led)
1995 July 16	**Esotrinsica** E Heslam, D Viggers (both led), F Thompson.

The route was retro-bolted and re-cleaned by F Haden 6.00.

| 1995 July 22 | **Koto Globo**   G A Jenkin, F Haden |
| 1995 July 22 | **On a Mission**   F Haden, G A Jenkin (both led) |

1995 July 23	**Peck Deck** F Haden, E Heslam (both led), G A Jenkin, K Wilkinson	
1995 July 24	**Confetti Train** G A Jenkin, F Haden (both led)	
1995 July 24	**Easy and Slow** G A Jenkin, F Haden	
1995 July 25	**Not Flocking** K Wilkinson, F Haden, G A Jenkin (all led)	
1995 Aug 20	**Take the Bull By its Horns** F Haden	
1995 Aug 28	**Outside, It's America** G A Jenkin, F Haden (both led), S Cook	
1995 Aug 28	**Fistful of Steel** F Haden, G A Jenkin	
1995 Sept 3	**Old Codger** E Heslam, G A Jenkin, F Haden (all led)	
1995 Sept 3	**Head Intrinseca (The Awakening)** F Haden, G A Jenkin	
1995 Sept 5	**Barefoot in the Quarry (at Night)** F Haden, G A Jenkin (both led), S Sayah	
1995 Sept 5	**Crocker Free Zone** F Haden, G A Jenkin	
1995 Sept 5	**Hard and Fast** G A Jenkin	
1996 Jan 20	**Mistress of Measurement** F Haden, G A Jenkin	
1996 Jan 20	**Vicious Eyes** G A Jenkin, F Haden. *Direct Start by G McDonald, B Umney Aug 1996.*	
1996 July 14	**Smear No Fear** F Haden, K Marsden, G A Jenkin (all led)	
1996 July 14	**Smoking Gun** G A Jenkin, F Haden, K Marsden (all led)	
1996 July 14	**Crack Attack** F Haden, K Marsden (both led), G A Jenkin	
1996 July 14	**Haven't Got a Clue** F Haden, K Marsden, G A Jenkin (all led)	
1996 July 25	**A Taste for Disorder** G A Jenkin, K Wilkinson	
1996 Sept 4	**Water Babies** F Haden, G A Jenkin	
1996 Sept 4	**Standby, Standby** F Haden, G A Jenkin	
1996 Sept 4	**Fit for the Future** G A Jenkin, F Haden (both led)	
1996 Sept 4	**Lego Man** F Haden, G A Jenkin (both led)	
1996 Sept 11	**The Jester** F Haden	
1996 Oct	**Execution, It's Got To Be Funky** F Haden	
1999 May 23	**A Family Affair** T Penning	
1999 Nov 3	**Old School Reunion** F Haden, K Simmons, J Lacey	
1999 Nov 18	**Fracture Science** F Haden, G A Jenkin (both led)	
2000 June 12	**Stick to Liquid** M J Crocker. *Stick to the Right variation was climbed by F Haden on the same day.*	
2000 June 20	**Retroactive** F Haden, D Pickford. *This may have been climbed as a 'trad' route in 1996 by a Bristol team; any claimants?*	
2000 June 20	**Rustic Flux** F Haden, D Pickford (both led)	
2000 June 20	**Farewell to Old Times** F Haden, M J Crocker (both led)	
2000 June 23	**Moderately Green** F Haden, R Barraclough	
2000 June 23	**Drill and Blast, Drill and Bolt** F Haden, R Barraclough	
2000 Sept 2	**Bolting Blues** D Rundle, F Haden (both led)	
2000 Sept 7	**Swinging in the Breeze** D Rundle, F Haden (both led)	
2000 Sept 8	**Bomb the Base, Science Friction** F Haden, Ms Y Jones, P Wherlock (all led)	
2000 Sept 8	**Jams and Cams Beat Fliers on Wires** P Wherlock, F Haden	
2000 Sept 17	**Long Time Coming** C Connern, R D Jenkin, D P Jenkin	
2001 April 24	**Holebore** M J Crocker (solo)	
2001 April 26	**Lifting, Shifting** M J Crocker (lead-solo)	
2001 April 26	**Artless Pair** M J Crocker (solo after practice)	
2001 May 2	**Don't Turn the Page, Policeman Watcheth** M J Crocker	
2001 June 3	**Cool Pool Jump Rave, Hip Joint Man** M J Crocker, J Harwood	

2001 June 6	**Not to Be Not Recommended** M J Crocker (lead-solo)
2001 July 1	**Canadian Girls Kick Ass** G A Jenkin, Y Jones

The route originally climbed directly up the initial rock scar. The alternative (and better) right-hand start, as described, climbed by G A Jenkin, F Haden (both led) on 29.7.01.

2001 July 29	**Wide-eyed in Seattle** G A Jenkin, F Haden (both led)

A popular summer day with nearly 350 fun loving people gathered around the lake!

2002 March	**Professor Smith's Warning** T Randall

Curious Holes Quarry

1992	**My Crane and My Camel, Enema Paradise** J Swift (solo next to hanging rope)

Rediscovered and named in 2002 by Mike Raine, Mike Hammill. The first route wins the editor's route name prize!

2002 April 13	**Division Bell, Pulse, Saucer Full of Secrets** R Thomson, J Truscott

These may have been done before by members of the Cerberus Speleological Society.

2002 April 24	**Over the Hump, Division Bell Right-hand** M Hammill (on-sight solo)

Leigh Quarry

2001 July	**Sharp Stones in my Buttock** M Raine, I Butterworth
2001 July	**Wasteria** M Raine, P Clarke, R Nadin
2001 July	**Festival Crack, Serley's Bulge** M Raine, M Serle
2001 July	**Holiday Crack** M Raine, P Clarke
2002 July 10	**All Keyed Up** N A Coe, M J Crocker
2002 July 10	**Où Sont Vos Clés?** M J Crocker, N A Coe

An hour was spent at dusk in the rain madly searching for Coe's car keys.

2002 July 14	**Supercrack of the East Mendips, Discectomy, A Bit Like Indian Creek, The Spare Man** M Raine, N A Coe
2002 July 14	**The Spare Tyre** N A Coe, M Raine
2002 July 23	**Angry Ant Bite, Diving Faces** M J Crocker (roped solo)
2002 Aug 12	**Eye Contact** M J Crocker (solo after practice)
2002 Sept 29	**Back on the Nest, Nil by Mouth** M Raine, N A Coe
2002 Sept 29	**Washing Day** N A Coe, M Raine
2003 June 26	**Move Over, Fat Captain** M Raine, B Sutton

Westdown Quarry

2002 April 16	**Feet of Clay** R Thomson (on-sight solo)
2002 April 16	**Start Men at Arms** M Raine (on-sight solo)
2002 April 19	**Guards! Guards!** R Thomson, J Truscott (on sight)
2002 April 19	**The Fifth Elephant** R Thomson, J Truscott (on sight)
2002 April 25	**Uberwald Express, Hogswatch Hangover** R Thomson (solo)
2002 May 5	**Sourcery** J Hitchens, A Derodra
2002 May 10	**Greebo's Claw** L Freeman, R Thomson.

Mells

1993	**Iron Brew** N Hillman, C Davies
1994	**Mellon, Smells, Ironed Out, Pig Iron, The Chimney** I Butterworth, N Hillman
1994	**Shed Arête** P Clarke
1995 June 21	**Picturesque, Mellstrom** G A Jenkin, M J Crocker (AL)
1995	**Watershed, Shed No Tears, Shed Head, Unknown Route, Talbot** I Butterworth, N Hillman. Shed Head *was given a direct start by M J Crocker (solo) on 17.4.99.*
1999 April 17	**Pumping Iron, Right Said Shed, Shedded Weak** M J Crocker (lead-solo)
1990s	**Mells Bells, Mells Wall** First ascents unknown

Vallis Vale

1977	**Wasted Metal, Vallis Crack** I Butterworth *Possibly climbed before.*
1981	**Tiptoe** I Butterworth, J Jordan
1982 April	**Tantalus** T Noble, R Bignall
1982 April	**Telemachus** T Noble
1982 April	**Charybdis** R Bignell
1982 May	**Styx, Scylla, Odyssey, Cerebus** T Noble, S Noble
1982 May	**Thetis** T Noble, R Bignell
1982 May	**Centaur** T Noble
1990	**Free Stonehenge** I Butterworth, N Hillman

Index

Addendum: New Climbs

Croscombe: The Puddingstone Cliff

Pud It There (6 metres E2 5a † 15.4.03 M J Crocker solo). Best as the descent for the next two climbs. From the left end of the ramp, climb the compact wall slightly rightwards to a sapling. Exit direct on suspect puddings.

Ramp Thing (6 metres E4 6a F7a † 15.4.03 M J Crocker solo). From a pocket your left hand really does want to leave, stretch for a hold high right; then crank over onto the black wall. Finish up or down *Pud It There*. Only falling will test whether you end up on the platform or on the ground 4 metres lower.

Pudding Face (8 metres E5 6b † 15.4.03 M J Crocker solo). Start at the shothole in the pit and take finger-pockets to a hard move on a sloper or pocket to a hanging pudding. Good pockets above lead to a tentative exit; or a traverse leftwards down the first route. At this grade the platform on the left is not touched (reaching the hanging pudding from the platform relegates this fiend to E4 5c).

Accident Procedure

First Aid

If spinal or head injuries are suspected, do not move the patient without skilled help, except to maintain breathing or if this is essential for further protection.

If breathing has stopped, clear the airways and start artificial respiration. Do not stop until the patient recovers or expert opinion has diagnosed death.

Summon help as quickly as is compatible with safety. Do not hesitate or delay.

Rescue

In the event of an accident where further assistance is required, dial 999 and ask for the Police. The Police are responsible for co-ordinating all rescues and will contact other services as necessary.
- State that you require cliff rescue and report the exact location (six-figure grid reference if possible) and details of the accident.
- Be prepared to give your own name and home address if asked.
- Follow any further instructions or requests issued.

Helicopter

In the event of a Helicopter evacuation, all climbers on or off the cliff should take heed. A helicopter flying close to the cliff will make verbal communication very difficult and small stones will be dislodged by the rotor downdraught. All loose equipment should be secured and climbers in precarious positions should try to make themselves safe.

The people with the injured person should try to identify their location. **No** attempt should be made to throw a rope at the helicopter, but assistance should be given to the helicopter crew if requested. Do not approach until directions are given by the crew. In particular, keep well clear of the main rotor, the tail rotor, and the engine exhaust.

Follow-up

After an accident, a report has to be compiled. Normally the details will be collated at the scene by the Police or rescue team, who will then pass the information to the Mountain Rescue Council Statistics Olfficer.

If unreasonable equipment failure is suspected then the British Mountaineering Council's technical committee may wish to investigate; contact the BMC at 177-179 Burton Road, West Didsbury, Manchester, M20 2BB. In the event of a serious accident, any equipment used by the casualty may be impounded.

Local Hospitals
Accident and Emergency Unit
Weston General Hospital, Grange Hill, Upton, Weston-super-Mare
Tel: 01934 636363

Minor Injuries Unit
Victoria Hospital, Park Road, Frome
Tel: 01373 463591

Minor Injuries Unit
Shepton Mallet Community Hospital, Old Wells Road, Shepton Mallet
Tel: 01749 342931

Emergency Department
Bath Royal United Hospital, Combe Park, Bath
Tel: 01225 428331

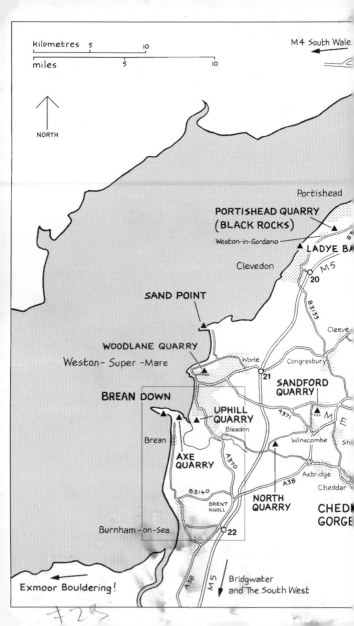